# EIGHT KINGDOMS

## Kingdom of God & Kingdom of Heaven

MICHAEL PEARL

*Eight Kingdoms*®
Copyright © 2006 by Michael and Debi Pearl
ISBN-13: 978-1-892112-62-0
ISBN-10: 1-892112-62-0
First printing: July 2006 – 20,000

Visit www.NoGreaterJoy.org for information on other products produced by No Greater Joy Ministries.

Requests for information should be addressed to:
No Greater Joy Ministries Inc. *1000 Pearl Road, Pleasantville, TN 37033  USA*

# EIGHT KINGDOMS

## And then there was ONE.

There are eight types of kingdoms spoken of in the Bible. Two of those kingdoms — the **kingdom of God** and the **kingdom of heaven** — constitute the central message of the New Testament. If all the text that speaks directly of these two kingdoms were removed from the New Testament, there wouldn't be enough left to fill up a single page in a newspaper. Yet, the kingdom message is completely unknown by a large majority of ministers and their congregations all across this land. There has never been anything spoken so much, yet understood so little. The errors of reformed theology and Armenianism alike are rooted in a misunderstanding of the kingdoms. Most cults and many of the denominational differences today can be traced to a lack of understanding of the mystery of the kingdoms. The key to understanding the entire Bible is found in knowing the differences among the eight kingdoms, but especially these two — the kingdom of God and the kingdom of heaven. When you finish reading this book, you will assuredly know the difference.

# Part One: Things different are not the same.

## It does make a difference.

The **kingdom of heaven** and the **kingdom of God** are not the same. You may ask, "*So what? What difference can it make?*"

- It is the difference between having a clear understanding of the Bible as a whole, and seeing it as an assorted collection of religious writings.

- It is the difference between believing that Israel is still God's covenant people, yet to inherit the earth, and believing that the Church has taken Israel's place in some spiritual sense.

- It is the difference between believing that Jesus gave Peter the authority to make a final offer of the Davidic kingdom to the Jews, and believing that he gave Peter the keys to control the entrance of individuals into the body of Christ during the Church age.

- It is the difference between indigenous local churches on the one hand, and Roman Catholic, Orthodox, Lutheran, Church of Christ, and Landmark Baptist churches on the other.

- It is the difference of whether it will be unbelieving children of Israel that God casts into hell at the beginning of the Millennium or Christians.

- It is the difference between believing that David will be resurrected to sit on a literal throne in Jerusalem, and believing that Christ will sit on a throne in heaven.

- It is the difference between Christians keeping the Law of Moses or not.

- It is the difference between Jewish Sabbath-keeping and New Covenant rest.

- It's the difference between the doctrine of security of the believer and that of losing your salvation.

- It is the difference between being a dispensationalist or not.

- It is the difference between pre-millennial and post-millennial eschatology.

- It is the difference between the pre-tribulation, pre-wrath, and post-tribulation and pre-wrath rapture of the church.

- It is the difference between a Bible that is confusing and one that makes perfect sense.

- It is the difference between allegorizing the Scripture and that of boldly accepting it literally.

Most of the doctrinal differences between denominations are a direct result of their failure to rightly differentiate between the eight kingdoms.

## A Kingdom Book.

The Bible is not a religious book. It is a kingdom book, first, foremost and only — authored by God. It speaks of the past, telling us of a kingdom that was lost, of the present kingdoms that vie for supremacy, and of a future kingdom that physically smashes all others and is established on a newly created earth that will endure forever. The Bible reveals God's plan of the ages, embracing history and prophecy as the unified revelation of the King building his kingdom in a manner that is entirely on schedule and successful in every way.

## Eight Kingdoms.

Most evangelical preachers, teachers, and Bible students think there is just one kingdom — a spiritual kingdom — into which all believers of all ages must enter. But the Bible speaks of eight different kingdoms. They are listed in the sequence in which they are revealed in the Bible (though not necessarily named). In due course, we will examine all (leaving none out) Scripture references to them.

1. **The kingdom of God** is the timeless spiritual rule of God over all beings, wherever they may be — in paradise, in hell, in earth, or anywhere in any of the three heavens.

2. **Satan's kingdom** is self-evident. It is the unseen evil forces and fallen angels organized into a concerted effort to thwart the purposes of God for the human race.

3. **Gentile kingdoms** are what you study when taking world history — Babylon, Persia, Greece, Rome, The Mongol Hordes, Britain, France, Germany, Spain, United States of America, etc.

4. **The Jewish kingdom (Israel)** began when the sons of Jacob left Egypt and crossed the Red Sea under Moses, and the kingdom was discontinued when Rome destroyed them in the first century A. D. It was reconstituted in 1948 and continues today in the land of Israel.

5. **The kingdom of heaven** is the kingdom that God intends for this earth. It is as physical and earthly as is any kingdom discussed in world history. And when it comes to power, it will replace *all* existing earthly kingdoms, for it will rule over and occupy every inch of their domains. As we will show from Scripture, it is not heaven ruling heaven; it is heaven ruling the earth (part of the heavens) through men.

6. **Antichrist's kingdom** appears during the seven years immediately preceding the second coming of Christ. He is Satan's counterfeit christ with a counterfeit kingdom which will be destroyed with the *brightness of Christ's coming*.

7. **Christ's kingdom** is the **kingdom of God** and the **kingdom of heaven** with Christ as the visible head. It will be revealed during his coming earthly reign. When the **kingdom of heaven** and the **kingdom of God** come together at the beginning of the Millennium, it will be called interchangeably *the kingdom of Christ, the kingdom of his dear Son, his kingdom,* and *the kingdom of our Lord and Savior Jesus Christ.*

8. **The Father's kingdom** is the all-encompassing kingdom of the Living God, in which the full unfolding and final manifestation of the mystery concerning the kingdoms is completed. The **kingdom of heaven** and the **kingdom of God** will have become *Christ's kingdom* at his coming. And when Christ turns the kingdoms over to the Father, all that remains throughout eternity and after all things have become one, is the *Father's kingdom.*

## Seven aspects of the kingdom.

The kingdoms and their differences are widely discussed in the Scriptures, but it is The New Testament that reveals the seven aspects of the kingdom. These phrases are taken directly from the Bible text.

1. Children of the kingdom

2. Gospel of the kingdom

3. Parables of the kingdom

4. Word of the kingdom

5. Mysteries of the kingdom

6. Keys of the kingdom

7. Heirs of the kingdom.

If you cannot readily differentiate between the items in the two above lists, you doubtless find many other passages in the Bible troubling and difficult to reconcile. This may have forced you to ignore all the details and to allegorize the text in order for it to make any sense at all. Be patient, for in due course, all these points will be examined in the illuminating Scriptures.

## Why there is so little understanding of the kingdoms?

The kingdom theme of the Bible is little known, owing to the fact that its objective message has been smothered by the subjective embrace of religion. God announced a coming worldwide kingdom, so Religion enthusiastically came forward with its own proposal. Judaism wanted a little kingdom between Egypt and Syria with secure borders and a return to their former glory. The Church said, "No! it must be a spiritual kingdom that ends in heavenly places." But then, through a misguided view of the kingdom and a lust for power, the Church started competing with the kingdoms of this world and became a political power. Today, the Vatican sends out ambassadors of state and dispenses salvation in its rituals. On the other end of the institutional spectrum, Independent Baptist Churches enthrone an independent pastor in an office that encourages him to assume independent control of the local congregation — all in the name of a kingdom chain of command — a form of apostolic succession similar to that of the Catholics and their popes.

As the influence of the Early Church grew, it fell prey to the lust for kingdom power. In the name of God, it pushed aside states and kings. What started out as a "kingdom within" — a kingdom of righteousness, peace and joy — soon added Clergy control, institutionalization, national recognition, special buildings of worship, liturgical worship, and, eventually, control of civil government. As our Lord warned, his little seed in the hands of men grew to be a great tree, covering the whole earth, filled with birds (devils) and leaven (false doctrine).

Just as the history of the world is the bloody chronicle of kingdoms struggling for supremacy, so the history of Christianity has been a sad and sometimes bloody chronicle of sects competing for recognition as the only legitimate heir of the Kingdom of God. The Dark Ages were kept dark with threats of excommunication, torture chambers, burnings at the stake, and murderous crusades, all done in the name of establishing God's kingdom on the earth. Evangelism was administered with the "holy" sword, under the "Christian" flag, with the blessings of the "successors" of Saint Peter, and commanded from Rome, the purported seat of "God's kingdom" upon the earth. In a few cases, the reformers didn't do much better. They, too, shed blood and coerced men into "the faith".

But, that is in the past. Today, the wary civil powers keep the denominations from killing each other, and we are all much more *civil*-ized, even if not *Christ*-ianized. Nonetheless, each of the large denominations, and many of the smaller ones, still stridently claim that their organization holds the "keys to the kingdom", that they are the true successors of the kingdom of God on the earth. In contrast, but no less accurate, the late 20th century evangelicals came to believe that the kingdom of God is just a big family of fellowship and good-will, encompassing all Christians everywhere, singing as they happily travel the road to paradise in the sky — a kingdom "up" in Heaven. The average 21st Century Christian doesn't care one way or the other as long as the local church has a lively worship leader, a good anger-management counselor, a Singles Class where divorcees can pair up again, and everyone can enjoy a "whole lot of love". In this post-doctrine age, the kingdom is something you feel, and Christianity has been re-defined as love, tolerance, and forgiveness, rather than righteousness and judgment. Truth is so little valued that the mere proclamation of it only causes more division.

## But, doesn't the Bible teach about kingdoms?

All Christians have heard of The Kingdom of God. Hardly a sermon is preached that doesn't mention it. It is in our songs, and we rightly rejoice that we are *"children of the kingdom."* We know that one *"must be born again to enter the kingdom of God."* Matthew records Jesus as saying,

*"Seek ye first the kingdom of God and his righteousness,"* and Luke writes that, *"Except ye be converted and become as little children ye will not enter the kingdom of God."* Jesus also said that, *"...the kingdom of God is within you,"* and at the Last Supper, he told his disciples, *"I will not drink of the fruit of the vine, until the kingdom of God shall come."* There are some 70 appearance in the New Testament of the term **kingdom of God** and 33 of the **kingdom of heaven,** in addition to the many undefined references to a **kingdom**.

If you were to ask the average Christian whom you know to describe the kingdom of God, he would likely identify it with the Church. When pressed further, he would say that it is a "spiritual" kingdom, organized under ministers who are ordained to administer "the holy sacraments" and to "rule" the Church of God. Many believe that this "spiritual" kingdom of God will eventually extend its "spiritual" rule to the whole world, establishing a Jewish-type theocracy, where all nations acknowledge the true God and keep his commandments — a golden age of maturity, a Christian utopia, and the triumph of the Church over evil. This belief is overflowing with confusion at best.

Premillennialists (those who believe that the Rapture and Second Coming occur before the 1000-year reign) know that no kingdom under human direction is ever going to so influence the world as to construct a heavenly kingdom upon the earth. But most Premillennial believers are primarily mistaken about the nature of the kingdom of God, in some incredible way believing that today's structured Christianity (on as small a scale as a single local church) **is** THE kingdom of God, with all the authority thereof. The church is, in fact, a small, temporary expression of the kingdom of God, but of such a nature that it is prophesized to become filled with corruption and the habitation of devils — hardly grounds for celebration.

## A kingdom study.

You are about to embark upon a study of all the kingdom passages in the Bible — several hundred of them. If you diligently follow the evidence all the way through, you will be astounded at the care the Holy Spirit has taken to always maintain a clear distinction between the **kingdom of God** and the **kingdom of heaven,** even with the variety of men He chose to record this vital information. You will see all kingdom passages placed in several different tables, parallel to their counterparts. Every similarity and difference has been noted, listed, and analyzed from various perspectives. The evidence is thorough and absolutely conclusive. It will prove beyond any doubt that the **kingdom of God** and the **kingdom of heaven** are not the same kingdom, and with that understanding you will more clearly appreciate all eight kingdoms and their relationship to each other in the great scheme of things. I promise you, with this understanding, many theological difficulties that may have been troubling you will be resolved, and you will become surprisingly comfortable with the reading of your Bible. You will feel honest and open when you teach and preach from it, and you will laugh with joy at the beauty and perfection of the Living Word of God. So vital is it to understand why God speaks so often of all these kingdoms, that you will come to an increasing love of the Word of God, and its truths will be in you like a well of water springing up into everlasting life. You will surely become a Premillennialists, and you may even declare yourself a Pretribulationist. If your first allegiance is to a denomination or a doctrinal scheme, and not the Bible only, you may want to stop reading now, for your rudimentary dogma is about to be shaken to its roots.

## What to expect.

Most busy laymen will never take the time to analyze the entire Scriptures and doggedly follow the kingdom arguments all the way through to the end. Therefore this book has been constructed in four helpful parts, each part increasingly detailing the distinctions between the kingdoms and developing their complexity. The first section is a basic introduction to the subject, purposely avoiding lengthy proofs and excess scriptural references that would unnecessarily bog down the reader before he has a clear overview. I find that I understand the details better when I know where the argument is going. I think you are that way too, so enjoy the adventure; the careful proof will come later.

Section two is chronological in nature, a Scripture panorama that follows the development of the kingdoms throughout the Old Testament, and establishes an historical and prophetic base for the New Testament kingdom doctrines introduced by Jesus and the writers of the epistles.

Section three examines in great detail all kingdom passages in the New Testament.

The last section presents all kingdom Scripture in tables and synthesized lists in a manner that provides a quick reference and comparison. The fourth section was actually created first, as this author synthesized and then analyzed all the data which eventually led to the conclusions recorded in the first two sections.

# Defining the Kingdoms.

## The Kingdom of God is. . .

The Kingdom of God, like any kingdom, is the dominion of a king over his subjects. God is the king; faithful angels, cherubim, seraphim, living creatures, unnamed spirits, and submissive humans are his willing subjects. The king is a just, yet benevolent ruler, governing by persuasion. The kingdom of God began the moment God created anything to exist outside of himself. It originated before angels and cherubim were created, before the world and universe were created, and before man was created. The kingdom of God is everything, both physical and spiritual, that is in subjection to God. The kingdom of God is not one location or one covenant or one dispensation. It is an eternal kingdom and is incapable of dissolution.

The **kingdom of God** is not an alternative to the past and present earthly kingdoms; that is, it does not seek to replace them or transform them. It has no earthly prelate or human representative, no seat of power. No one has any *"keys to this kingdom."* It is spiritual in nature, not religious, not an institution, not a nation or an ethnic group, and certainly not a church — though the true Church is presently a representative of the **kingdom of God** upon the earth.

Jesus said that the **kingdom of God** *"does not come with observation,"* that is, it is not an observable phenomenon; it will not come as spiritual renewal or righteous political rule. It is not the Church gaining ascendancy over heads of state or instituting a theocracy.

The **kingdom of God** is power and glory — the power manifested in the new birth, divine healing, casting out of devils, and other miracles.

It has no geographical, racial, or political boundaries. It is as big as God and as timeless as God is eternal, never limited by the kingdoms of men or the kingdom of Satan. It is invisible on the earth, except at an event like the transfiguration, when the three disciples saw Jesus shining in his glory.

The **kingdom of God** is preached and received individually in the message of the gospel. Those who believe the gospel enter into this invisible kingdom. It is then said to be *"within you"*, in the form of *"righteousness, peace, and joy"*. To seek the will of God is to *"seek the **kingdom of God**."* Jesus said that great sinners were *"getting into"* the **kingdom of God**, whereas great religious leaders were shut out.

He said it was a mistake to think that this kingdom would *"appear"* during his time of ministry. The **kingdom of God** will be visible at the second coming of Christ and during the Millennium based on His visible presence, at which time Jesus will again drink wine and eat with his disciples in the then-visible **kingdom of God**.

Because of its spiritual and righteous nature, *"flesh and blood cannot inherit"* the **kingdom of God**. One must be **born again to enter it**, or even to *"see"* it.

At present, the **kingdom of God** is spiritual, with no visible manifestation. Anyone who is in fellowship with God, whether on earth, in heaven, is right now in the **kingdom of God**. On this earth, at this present time, the **kingdom of God** finds its only expression in the Church. The church buildings of wood, stone, and plastics are no more the **kingdom of God** than is Hollywood. Likewise, the great ecclesiastical organizations and "church" hierarchies are no more the **kingdom of God** than is international banking.

The **kingdom of God** is near when a child of God feels the breath of heaven. When peace and the presence of God are near, when worship flows gentle and sweet, and when we hear music where no instrument plays, we know that it is come upon us. When all around is darkness and evil, yet our spirits walk in a light the body cannot see, and righteousness courses through us like a fountain, the **kingdom of God** is present indeed. The **kingdom of God** is the home for the spirit, no matter the condition of the body. It is not hindered by prison walls, stayed by ecclesiastical pronouncements, or driven out by cruel persecutions. The **kingdom of God** will lead us by an unseen hand and carry us as by an invisible Spirit until it delivers us into **The Father's Kingdom** at the beginning of the Millennium, at which time the **kingdom of heaven** will come under its complete control.

## The Kingdom of Heaven is. . .

In contrast to the **kingdom of God,** the **kingdom of heaven** is as physical as the heavens are physical. It is the earth ruled by men. The word *"heaven"* in *kingdom of heaven* speaks not only of the source of the rule, but of the location of what is ruled — the heavens, the earth being part of the heavens and the central focus of the kingdom. There is nothing spiritual or religious about this kingdom. On the day of Jesus' triumphal entry into Jerusalem, the Jews greeted their Messiah with, "Blessed be the **kingdom of our father David,** that cometh in the name of the Lord . . ." (Mark 11:10). The **kingdom of our father David** was and will be an expression of the **kingdom of heaven** just as the church is an expression, though not the whole, of the **kingdom of God.** Their greeting reveals that they well understood the nature of the **kingdom of heaven** to be physical and literal, centered in Jerusalem, and Jesus confirmed their greeting by welcoming it, even defending it to the accusing Pharisees, telling them that, if the people didn't recognize him thus, the stones would cry out. When Jesus offered the **kingdom of heaven** to Israel, he was proposing that they recognize him as supreme potentate and honor his mandate for a return of the kingdom of David to Israel.

Like its secular counterparts, the **kingdom of heaven** consists of three things: a king, a geographical district, and faithful subjects. The physical universe is the geography of the **kingdom of heaven** – the earth in particular. Adam was the first king, but he lost the throne to Lucifer. Lucifer did not become the king of the kingdom of heaven but his evil kingdom commanded the same piece of geography containing the same subjects, displacing the kingdom of heaven and reigning in its stead. Two thousand years later, Abraham was delegated to inherit the earth, beginning with one small piece in the ancient land of Canaan. God restated the promise to all of Abraham's descendents. One thousand years after Abraham, David was given a foothold on the kingdom and was promised an eternal reign. The inspired prophets declared repeatedly that the nation of Israel will play the leading role in re-establishing the kingdom. The Church has <u>nothing</u> to do with bringing about the **kingdom of heaven**.

The **kingdom of heaven,** in its righteous expression, has had its subjects appointed since God gave Adam dominion over the earth. It has had a constitution prepared since Moses came down from Mount Sinai with the Law. It has had a king appointed since Samuel anointed David. It has had a platform since Jesus delivered the Sermon on the Mount. The inauguration of its king (Jesus, son of David) and its co-regent (David) has yet to occur. It will be offered again to Israel and to the world in the Tribulation, and will commence in purity and reality at the beginning of the Millennium. Jesus qualifies to rule the kingdom of heaven by right of his earthly lineage through David.

The **kingdom of heaven** in its purest essence is all earthly kingdoms coming under the direct rule of heaven. Daniel informed king Nebuchadnezzar that he (the king) would, "know that the most High **ruleth in the kingdom of men,** and giveth it [the kingdom] to whomsoever he will… And…after thou shalt have known that **the heavens do rule**" (Dan. 4:25-26). Daniel interpreted Nebuchadnezzar's dream, telling him that there would be a succession of world kingdoms beginning with his own, Babylon, and that all the world's kingdoms would eventually be swallowed up into a kingdom ruled by the heavens. "And in the days of these kings shall the God of heaven **set up a kingdom, which shall never be destroyed:** and the kingdom shall not be left to other people, but it shall break in pieces and **consume all these kingdoms,** and it shall stand for ever" (Daniel 2:44). Daniel later said, "But the saints of the most High [the physical seed of Jacob] shall **take the kingdom,** and possess the kingdom for ever, **even for ever and ever**" (Daniel 7:18).

Even the so-called *Lord's Prayer* directs us to pray, "Thy kingdom come. Thy will be done **in earth, as** *it is* **in heaven**" (Matt. 6:10). Truly, the kingdom will come to the earth, and the will of God will be done <u>in the earth</u> just as it is in heaven. When Jesus said, "Blessed *are* the meek: for they **shall**

**inherit the earth**" (Matt. 5:5), he was speaking plainly. It is the destiny of man to inherit the earth — for-ever.

The kingdom of heaven exists at present like a King's Ship that has been seized, its flag pulled down, and is unlawfully piloted by pirates. It is a vacillating and unstable thing, fought over and died for from one generation to the next, changing human hands, but always manipulated and influenced by Satan and his devil spirits. It is present now only to the extent that it is corrupted and commandeered, but it is not present as the kingdom ruled from heaven that will eventually come at the beginning of the Millennium. It is the aspiration of all religions, including christianity (spelled with a lower case "c") and most political powers, to rise to the place of being the sole ruler of the world. All wars are kingdom wars. All soldiers die for some version of the **kingdom of heaven**. If the soldiers only knew that God has no interest in the sacrifices they make to "bring in the kingdom".

## Heaven, not heavenly.

As we have said, the **kingdom of heaven** is a kingdom in the physical heavens — the earth being a part of the heavens. But there is a great misunderstanding among Bible teachers and students regarding the word *heaven*. Religious misuse of the word in sermons and songs has created an inaccurate connotation. So great is the error that we must go to great lengths to correct it, which we have done more thoroughly in the Appendix (See HEAVEN). But, to state the issue quite simply, we can stipulate that heaven (or heavens) is the physical universe, not God's mansion.

There are three heavens spoken of in the Bible. The first one contains birds and clouds. The second contains stars and planets, and the third heaven is the space beyond the observable universe. It, too, is physical. Located somewhere in (or above/beyond) the third heaven is a mobile throne on which God is building a mobile city (the New Jerusalem) that will eventually come down through the three heavens to sit on the earth — the ultimate home of the Church.

When most people hear the word, *heaven,* they think of "divine, godly, spiritual, paradise, golden streets"— all of which are inaccurate. To define *heaven* this way has contributed to the misunderstanding of the term *kingdom of heaven*, leading most people to conjure up images of a heavenly kingdom, a godly kingdom, or a spiritual kingdom, rather than of a physical kingdom — a tangible kingdom, or a kingdom in time and place. When you read "**kingdom of heaven,**" your mind should picture the image of a kingdom located in the physical heavens (of which the earth is a part). If you continue to think of it as a "heavenly" kingdom, you will have great difficulty proceeding with the Scriptural understanding of the kingdom message.

If you can accept the definition of *heaven* as that space which is created above the earth and which is potentially accessible by space travel, then you would do well to proceed with your reading without going to the Appendix at this time. Otherwise, you will continue in confusion as you move forward in this book. Or, you may choose to do what I did 35 years ago: Take a concordance, and look up every single time the word *heaven* is used in the Bible (Using either the Authorized Version, or the Hebrew and T. R. Greek texts — you will get the same results). Read them carefully; there are over 700 references. Read the contexts, and you will be shocked at your previous misconceptions. But you will, as I did, assuredly develop a Biblical definition of *heaven,* and you will have taken the first step at letting the Bible, not denominational dogma, be your final authority in doctrine.

## The kingdoms contrasted.

The **kingdom of heaven** is linked directly to the visible or physical heavens, just as the **kingdom of God** is linked to the invisible God. The **kingdom of God** and the **kingdom of heaven** are as different as are God and the universe. The K of H is presently allotted to mankind only, whereas the K of G also contains righteous angels, cherubim, seraphim, spirits, and living creatures of many varieties. The K of G existed before the earth and the human race were created, but the K of H is concurrent with the creation of life upon the earth. The K of H is less than the K of G, by virtue of its coming into being after it and by being inside of it. The K of H can be taken by force and controlled by the kingdoms of this world, or by Satan — not so the K of G. The Jewish leaders of Jesus' day were able to shut the door to the K of H and prevent everyone from entering it. No one can shut the door of the K of G to anyone. The K of H will contain unbelievers who will be purged from it and cast into hell at the beginning of the Millennium and at various times throughout the thousand years. The K of G will never have anyone in it that is not of God. The K of G is a relationship, whereas the K of H will come as a political institution — the kind of which we are all familiar — at the beginning of the Millennium.

One man can surrender to God and enter the K of G as a single individual, but no one can enter the K of H until it is instituted in the Millennium. The K of G is personal and individual, whereas the K of H is external and corporate. All Christians and righteous angels are in the K of G right now, but no one is in the K of H (God's righteous version of it) until King Jesus returns and destroys the competing earthly kingdoms and sets up his own earthly kingdom with David on the throne in Jerusalem.

The K of G is invisible, whereas the coming of the K of H will be as visible as any government. The K of G is not tied to any location, while the K of H has already been defined as a worldwide kingdom with its capital to be located in the city of Jerusalem.

The K of G is God ruling in the hearts of men and other created beings, but the K of H is intended to be God ruling through men in the earth and the heavens — which includes all kingdoms, powers, principalities, and dominions.

## Things different are not the same.

The **kingdom of God** and the **kingdom of heaven** are similar in many ways, yet the noticeable differences found in the gospels are numerous and detailed. A careful examination of the differences — over 100 examples in all — is startling, and reveals a pattern that cannot be other than deliberate.

Most commentators have observed only the many similarities found in the gospels and quickly assumed that the kingdoms must be identical, and that the Bible is simply not clear in the matter. They learn to live with what they suspect, and sometimes say, is a lack of harmony between what they call the synoptic gospels — Matthew, Mark, and Luke. Some scholars have concocted elaborate theories that prove which of the four gospel writers is closest to the original statement and which ones copied from the others. They talk about how Matthew "preferred" the term, **kingdom of heaven** while the other writers "preferred" the term, **kingdom of God**.

With such evident differences in the gospels, differences that have been the occasion of much confusion, we are left to conclude that the Bible is either too difficult to understand and poorly written, **or**, the differences are inspired by God for the purpose of teaching us something very important. The fact is, that when every passage is considered and listed in an objective manner, as we have done here, there is no avoiding the conclusion that the two kingdoms are quite different and that the differences do dramatically affect our Bible doctrine from start to finish. To fail to distinguish between the **kingdom of God** and the **kingdom of heaven** is to fail to understand the Bible, and it is by no means an overstatement to declare that this lack of understanding is the source of most false doctrine.

## The kingdom of heaven was offered to Israel only.

John came first, offering the **kingdom of heaven** to the Jews. When Jesus came, he took up John's ministry, commanding his disciples **not to preach the kingdom message to any but Israel.** But after John was beheaded, Jesus announced that the K of H had suffered violence and that violent people had taken the kingdom by force — a reference to the violence of Rome and the Jewish leaders. Later, when it became evident that Israel was going to reject his offer of restoring the Davidic kingdom, Jesus began to speak in prophetic parables concerning the postponement of the K of H. John and Jesus had presented the K of H as a coming political institution, but Jesus later began offering the K of G on an individual basis as the means of attaining moral and spiritual strength to meet the conditions of the K of H. The nation of Israel refused both kingdoms, so Jesus prophesied in 12 different kingdom-of-heaven parables, of the postponement of the Jewish expression of K of H, holding it in abeyance until the Church dispensation would be concluded. Jesus predicted that he would take the K of G away from the Jews and give it to the predominately Gentile Church.

Peter and the apostles had the opportunity to make a final offer of the K of H to Israel, but the Jews continued to reject it. At some point, the disciples withdrew the offer of the K of H and preached only the K of G to all nations, as we continue to do in our day. The K of H will again be preached during the tribulation. Many people from all nations have been "born again" into the K of G, but the K of H awaits the return of Christ and the salvation of all Israel.

During this present hour, the **kingdom of God** remains invisible, and the only door into it is faith in Jesus Christ. The present-hour **kingdom of heaven** is and always has been corrupted and usurped by all the past and present earthly kingdoms. It has no earthly expression that is representative of God's will. It awaits the coming of King Jesus, when he will take the kingdoms by force, destroy their armies in a final world war, resurrect King David to sit on the throne in Jerusalem, convert Israel to faith in their Messiah, and gather the cooperative Gentile nations into a paradise-like kingdom. There will be no more kingdom of Satan or kingdom of darkness — only **Christ's kingdom**. The K of H will have come into conformity with the K of G; the two will coexist at the same time and in the same place. When Jesus will have accomplished all these things, **his kingdom** will be delivered up to the Father, and all that remains will be called the **Father's kingdom**.

## Why kingdoms?

Just as most people misunderstand the word *heaven*, for many Bible students there is a disconnect with the word *kingdom*. It has been commonly assumed that the **kingdom of God** and the **kingdom of heaven** are not kingdoms at all, just relationships or spiritual institutions. To our western thinking, a kingdom is either a nostalgic time of knights and castles, or it is a primitive form of oppressive government, common in a time when men were less enlightened and too weak to rule themselves. To our western culture, a kingdom is repugnant because it was based on the assumption that God had granted a divine right for one man and his descendents to exercise unchallenged authority over the souls of other men. The king had supreme powers. He owned all property, and all people were his subjects, greatly hindering creativity and spontaneity among the people. Many of the freedoms that we in a republic enjoy were vigorously suppressed under the old kingdoms.

Why does the Bible speak of kingdoms? Is the word *kingdom* necessary to accurately communicate the nature of God's program, or should we think of it, as most scholars assume, in a figurative and allegorical sense? Did God merely adopt a term that was familiar to the ancient people to whom he spoke, or did he wisely choose a timeless designation? If the apostles were communicating this same message to modern man, instead of calling it *kingdom*, would they call it something modern, like "spiritual renewal" or "the family of God" or "the community of believers", something other than that "archaic" form of government that has virtually passed away?

Democracies and republics are slow and cumbersome forms of governance. It takes time to correct an evil or a legislative mistake. Our U. S. republic is constructed with checks and balances based on the correct assumption that no single man is to be trusted with unbridled power. Yet, selfish interests in a republic find a way to circumvent justice. There is no guarantee of justice. The majority, even an active minority, can advance their agenda over others. Laws can be passed that protect evil rather than punish it. Human rights can supplant established common law and constitutional law, effectively granting people the right to their "favorite" sin with impunity. Freedom in a democracy is also freedom to be evil and to do evil to others, under the protection of law.

If the human race could produce a man who was wise, benevolent, strong, just, moral, and incorruptible, and if the people could be guaranteed that his descendants would always have those attributes, then a kingdom would be the best, most economical, and sought-after form of government. But it has never been so. Even King David, chosen and anointed by God, used his power to commit adultery and murder. Someone has rightly noted that "Absolute power corrupts absolutely."

But, what if God were to personally rule his people? Would he carry it out through a democracy, a republic, or a parliament in tandem with a monarchy? Where would he find judges to rightly interpret the constitution? Not on this earth. No, the logical form of government would be a kingdom, with God as the king — or one whom he ordained and groomed, and over whom he maintained righteous oversight.

When the Bible speaks of the **kingdom of heaven**, it means exactly that — a kingdom. The corrupt, finite human race will always need ruling. We were created with natures that need to be ruled from without as well as from within. We are insufficient unto ourselves. It is our nature to be under authority, and we reach our highest potential as we become willing subjects of a divine kingdom. No such kingdom will ever exist on this earth until King Jesus comes to reign, and then it will be the **kingdom of heaven** under the **kingdom of God,** in a combination called **Christ's kingdom.**

## Authors of confusion?

When I was in Bible college, I was told that the synoptic gospels (the first three—Matthew, Mark, and Luke) were the result of three different penmen writing on the same subject with their various style differences, two of them copying from the first and expanding each time. My professors, and the books we were assigned to read, speculated as to which gospel record was written first and which were partial copies of the others. There were discussions as to why the term **kingdom of God** was popular with Mark and Luke while Matthew "preferred" the term **kingdom of heaven**. No one ever suggested that the Holy Spirit might have been in absolute control of every word and that the differences might be a deliberate and predetermined act of divine inspiration **with the express purpose of differentiating between two different kingdoms.**

The college I attended was one of the ultimate fundamental, conscrvative institutions of the sixties. They strictly taught the verbal and plenary inspiration of the Scripture "in the original languages." My school viewed liberals, with their naturalistic explanations for Scripture, equal to communists — as the enemy without. The school considered itself to be holding ground against the great tide of liberalism of that day. But in practice, the Scriptures were never treated as if they were a book we could hold in our hands, certain that it contained all the words of God and nothing but the words of God, with the right choice of words, the right number of words, none left out, none added, all in the right order, a book given by God that only needed to be rightly divided and believed. Some time after I graduated, it was this very study on the kingdoms, done 35 years ago, that convinced me otherwise. I came to see the beauty and perfection of the Bible as originally written and now preserved in the Authorized Version — all five editions of it.

## Different gospel accounts.

Confusion comes from the fact that the book of Matthew, since it is written to the Jews, is the only one that uses the term **kingdom of heaven,** although Matthew does use the term **kingdom of God** five times. In addition, he chooses to use the word **kingdom** seven times, without once designating it as pertaining to either kingdom. He speaks five times of either **His kingdom, the Father's kingdom,** or **Thy kingdom.** Furthermore, five times Matthew writes on the same subject as the other gospels without designating his statements to any kingdom.

Further confusion results when it is observed that Mark and Luke often record a version of the very same parable or teaching found in the book of Matthew, but they stipulate that it speaks of the K of G, while Matthew calls it the K of H. In some instances, those parallel accounts are virtually identical, whereas in other cases there are very obvious differences.

These three gospels often record a similar parable, sermon, or event in the life of Christ with variations in the narrative. Sometimes, the order of events is different; the words spoken are different; one writer fails to mention one detail, while another includes a particular one that completely reverses the meaning. Some commentators see this as a difficulty, maybe even an embarrassment. Others seek to harmonize the differences as if the gospels' narratives should have concurred exactly. Only a few writers have assumed that the differences are intentional, designed by the Holy Spirit to convey contrasting realities. This author is joyously convinced that the gospel accounts, as recorded in the Greek Textus Receptus and preserved in the King James Bible, are the result of careful and deliberate planning by the Holy Spirit, to the end that additional revelation is made available to the reader when he considers the purposes behind the differences. In due course, we will examine in detail every similarity and difference.

## Theological predisposition.

To further add to the general lack of knowledge about the kingdoms, there is at this present time a growing theological predisposition to view the kingdoms as one. It is easily seen in the jealousy of "Christendom" to apply all kingdom passages to themselves, cutting Israel out altogether. The very word *Christendom* is totally inappropriate to describe the Body of Christ throughout the world, but it clearly expresses the erroneous postulations of the Catholic church and even most of the Protestant churches. The word *Christ-en-dom*, as in *king-dom*, implies something about the Church that is not true. Use of the term is an admission on the part of the visible church that it believes itself to be the recipient of the kingdom of heaven — a foolish and even dangerous error.

Since most of the Protestant and Evangelical churches today inherited their understanding of the last days from the teachings of Roman, Orthodox, and Lutheran church theologies, they readily accept the erroneous notion that the Church is the modern heir apparent of God's ancient promises to Israel and David. By displacing Israel, the Church becomes the only contender for the kingdom. But then the Church faces the impossible task of interpreting Jewish kingdom passages literally and still making them apply to the Church, which is why they resort to the allegorical interpretation to maintain the appearance of a Scriptural foundation. By allegorizing the text they are not limited to the original intent of the writers. The allegorical method is license to invent. It erases the trail of accountability as it drifts with the whims of the interpreter. It produces as many views as there are interpreters, resulting in vain debates.

Under this method, the literal dimensions of prophecy are spiritualized and reduced to ethical teachings. The literal kingdom becomes a powerful Church, and the earthly reign of Israel becomes the Gentile ascendancy of ecclesiastical powers over political ones — thus the power of Roman Catholicism which produced the Dark Ages under doctrines that gave the church authority over the state. This has produced what appears as a shadowy obstinacy that refuses to acknowledge the differences in the two kingdoms for fear of the implications it would have on the political powers of their churches — Protestant and Roman alike.

Today, the seminaries and churches are ignorant of the Scriptures, and for many generations have unthinkingly passed along teachings that they have received from those who promote the sanctity of tradition, no matter how unproven or unscriptural it may be. No one seems to question the dogma they are given by their denominations. Everyone is happy with the traditional views; why examine the Bible so closely at this late hour?

In reality, we live at a time when evangelical churches no longer promote doctrinal positions or defend the truth. The modern, sensitized man is offended at the promotion of absolute truth. It is labeled *hate speech* and branded as *divisive*. Unity and a sentimental, non-discriminating inclusiveness is the popular pursuit. American and European religion have acquired the final virtue of a decadent society — tolerance. But tolerance without truth is like a compassionate doctor with no labels on his medicines and no regard for the effect they may have upon his patients. The Devil's most frequently offered vices are tolerance and inclusiveness — lack of discrimination.

## Jesus did not mislead the disciples.

Bible teachers and writers ignore the literal meaning of prophecies concerning the Jewish kingdom on earth and then forcefully tell us that the Jews misunderstood Jesus. They assert that he was offering nothing more than a figurative kingdom — a spiritual kingdom — the church as we have it today, or maybe the church in a more triumphant state when, supposedly, it spreads its moral influence to all the nations of the earth and sets up religious rule. I remind you, Jesus repeatedly taught the disciples the nature of and differences between the two kingdoms for three and one half years, and promised them that they would personally sit on thrones judging the 12 tribes of Israel. He told them they would *"inherit the earth,"* and *"sit down with Abraham, Isaac, and Jacob in the kingdom"*. And then, at the end of his ministry of teaching them, two of Jesus' disciples asked that he grant them the right to sit by his side when he sets up his kingdom throne on the earth. He did not correct their implied concept of the kingdom (an earthly throne from which a king rules the world); he simply told them that the Father had already determined who would assume those coveted positions (Matt. 20:21), thus affirming the supposition of their request.

After his resurrection, and after spending 40 days reinforcing all he had taught, as Jesus was preparing to ascend into heaven, his well-taught disciples asked him one more time, *"Lord, wilt thou at this time* **restore again the kingdom to Israel**?*"* Jesus said unto them, *"It is not for you to know the times or the seasons, which the Father hath put in his own power"* (Acts 1:6-8). Clearly, the disciples understood that Jesus was going to restore again the kingdom to Israel, just as so many other Bible prophecies and covenants have predicted. They just wanted to know the time. If they were mistaken about the **kingdom of heaven** being literal, Jesus would have corrected their view, as was his manner anytime they misspoke. Instead, he granted their assumption by telling them that they were not permitted to know the time when the Jewish kingdom would be restored.

Can one honestly believe that Jesus misled his disciples, implying a literal fulfillment of Jewish prophecies, but knowing that the prophecies were nothing more than types of spiritual reality? With their repeated questions and his repeated answers, we must conclude that Jesus was speaking frankly with them. He never failed to say things to them that were against convention or that were difficult to believe. He spoke the truth clearly and boldly. If the disciples' assumptions were incorrect and were left uncorrected by Jesus, then he would have been the worst teacher who ever lived. But if he was actually being completely candid with them, then, indeed, we can be assured that the **kingdom of heaven** and the **kingdom of God** are not the same and the differences have great significance.

# Part 2: History of the Kingdoms

## The kingdom is at hand.

You have just read a brief synopsis of the kingdoms. Although we have not yet proven anything, the foundation we have laid should now provide you a workable overview of the subject as it will be presented, enabling you to understand where each detail fits into the bigger picture.

This brings us to a chronological examination of Old Testament Scripture concerning kings and kingdoms. Further along we will present a comprehensive study of the **kingdom of heaven** and **kingdom of God** passages in the gospels. But, as we now concentrate on the Old Testament, we will discover how well it provides us with the essential background in the history of God's promises and his development of the kingdom. If you start in the book of Matthew with the first time the word *kingdom* appears in the New Testament, you will read, *"Repent ye: for the **kingdom of heaven** is at hand."* John the Baptist did not need to explain to his audience what he meant by "**kingdom**," or "**at hand.**" All Jews, even the children and the untutored knew perfectly well what John was announcing and offering them. They were all weaned on the expectancy and constant hope for the coming kingdom. When Jesus told them to pray, *"Thy kingdom come…**on earth** as it is in heaven"*, this was not a new subject being introduced; he was just confirming their historical expectations and directing them to pray accordingly.

But the modern reader has no idea, or a rudimentary one at best, what is meant by, *"the **kingdom of heaven** is at hand."* The average Christian's lack of understanding is further diminished by ministers and books that promote the unfounded assertion that the Jews were mistaken about God's real intentions for the kingdom. This section will bring you up to date with the Jewish perspective that **was** understood and believed throughout over 4000 years of prophecy. When we eventually progress through the Old Testament and arrive at Matthew, to read that first mention, *"**repent ye: for the kingdom of heaven is at hand,**"* you will then fully and unquestionably understand what it means.

## First contender for the kingdom.

The kingdom in the heavens did not begin with Adam. It began with a cherub named Lucifer sometime before Adam was created (Job 38:4), and before the six days of creation recorded in Genesis. God first created angels, cherubim, and other living creatures. He anointed Lucifer and promoted him to rule over this planet, with his headquarters in Eden — the same location Adam would later inhabit (Ezekiel 28:13).

Adam's sin was not the original sin. Lucifer sinned before Adam and Eve were created (Isa. 14:12-17). You will recall that Lucifer was already a disembodied spirit immediately after the six days of creation, for when he would speak to Eve, he found it necessary to commandeer the body of a beast. When you consider the things the Bible says about Lucifer, events that occurred between his creation and his fall, there is no way those things could have occurred after the sixth day (when God created the mammals and man) and before he shows up in the garden to tempt Eve. Lucifer and the angels who accompanied him into rebellion had to have sinned sometime before Adam was created in order to set the stage for a fallen and disembodied Lucifer to be in the garden tempting Eve immediately afterward. Furthermore, the account of creation recorded in Genesis says nothing of the creation of angels or cherubim. It assumes they already existed — created sometime earlier.

Cain was not the first murderer or liar. The Devil was a murderer from the beginning and the father of lies (John 8:44). That verse attributes the original sin to Lucifer (the Devil), not Adam. So Lucifer must have lied before Eve sinned.

But the most conclusive proof that the angels predate the earth is that they were present when it was created. God asked Job a question designed to humble him: *"Where wast thou when I laid the foundations of the earth? … When the morning stars sang together, and all the sons of God shouted for joy?"* (Job 38:4, 7). The *"sons of God"* are angels (Job 1:6; 2:1). If you try to interpret *sons of God* as humans, then you have humans present before Adam and Eve were created — a ridiculous impossibility. According to this passage, the angels were present, shouting for joy, when God created the earth. So we can readily conclude that the angels do predate the earth, which is why there is no record of their creation or fall in Genesis. They already existed, divided into the obedient and the rebellious.

## The Anointed Cherub.

When Lucifer shows up in the garden, he is already the Devil, a fallen creature, but the Bible reveals that there was a time when he had been in Eden in a perfect state, without sin, in a position of very high honor (Ezekiel 28:13-15). Also, Ezekiel 28:14 indicates that God had created him with those express honors in mind, as one **anointed** for the purpose of **covering,** just like the anointings administered to kings and priests preparatory to their office. Lucifer was at the top of the authority chain before he sinned. He was engaged in the music department (Ezek. 28:13; Isa. 14:11), perhaps a worship leader.

His original home before he sinned was a placed called "Eden, the garden of God" (Ezek. 28:13). Later, "…the LORD God planted a garden **eastward in Eden**; and there he put the man whom he had formed (Gen. 2:8). That tells us that Lucifer was stationed on the earth, in a place called Eden. That explains why the sin of Lucifer was said to be an act of "**…ascending** above the heights of the **clouds**" (Isa. 14:15). To further strengthen the evidence that Lucifer was on the earth when he sinned, God's response was to tell him that he would be "brought **down** to hell, to the sides of the pit" (Isa. 14:15). Hell is in the heart of the earth (Ezek. 31:17; Isa. 14:9; Prov. 15:24) accessed by a lockable bottomless pit (Isa. 14:15; Ezek. 31:16; Rev. 9:1, 2, 11; 11:17; 20:1, 3). If Satan was **in Eden**, and then **ascended above the clouds**, but was brought back **down to hell**, we must conclude that his rebellion started and ended on the earth (formerly Eden). In his leadership capacity he was able to draw one-third of the angels into rebellion with him (Rev 12:4). The Scripture is clear; Lucifer's creation, anointing, reign in Eden, and his fall occurred before the six days of recreation.

## The Garden in Eden.

Prior to Lucifer's sin, he had been "upon the holy mountain of God" (Ezek. 28:14-16), and in "Eden, the garden of God". After Adam's creation, God planted a garden in the eastern part of the place called Eden (Genesis 2:8). We know from the description in Genesis 2:10-15 that Adam's garden was in the general area of what is now modern Iraq, an extremely fertile valley throughout history. So since the garden was in the eastern part of Eden, in the west of Eden is Israel, which means that the original Eden from which Lucifer ruled was the same landmass that God gave to the children of Israel to inherit forever. Eden is most likely identical to the land given to Israel. Could the mountain of God from which Lucifer ruled be the same mountain from which David ruled — Moriah or Jerusalem or its counterpart in the old world? If that is so, it would place that original mount and the throne of God right where it will eventually sit — in Jerusalem! God has not abandoned his original plan nor the ground on which it is to be executed. He will end where he started. The colony he planted in Eden will endure forever.

## Fallen conquerors.

Lucifer's rebellion against God was motivated by his desire to possess the highest seat of power. He coveted the position of God — supreme potentate. He said, "I will exalt my throne above the stars of God" (Isa. 14:13). He wanted to ascend higher than his designated position and "be like the most high" (Isa. 14:14). God responded as a responsible king should when his kingdom is threatened from within; he cast out the rebels and destroyed the planet on which they dwelt. They abode in darkness (Jude 13), outside the good graces of the benevolent king. Their existence was without conquest, challenge, or meaning. In their disembodied state they seek to dwell in warm, lustful flesh (Matt. 8:31). It is their only avenue to indulge.

We will examine the entire passage on Lucifer's sin: The prophet Ezekiel, in speaking of the judgment that would come on the heathen city of Tyre, compared their sin to that of the cherub Lucifer, later called *Satan* or the *Devil*. It gives us a little glimpse into the history of the original sinner.

> "Thou **hast been in Eden the garden of God**; [The earth, or at least a portion of it, was called Eden when angels inhabited it.] every precious stone was thy covering, the sardius, topaz, and the diamond, the beryl, the onyx, and the jasper, the sapphire, the emerald, and the carbuncle, and gold: the workmanship of thy tabrets and of thy pipes was prepared in thee in the day that thou wast created. **Thou art the anointed** [as kings are anointed] **cherub that covereth** [Cherubim are described in Ezekiel 1-10. Satan was a Cherub.]; and I have set thee so: [placed in a responsible oversight position] thou wast upon the holy mountain of God [Mount Moriah—Jerusalem?]; thou hast walked up and down in the midst of the stones of fire. Thou wast **perfect in thy ways** [this could not be said of any human] from the day that thou wast created, till iniquity was found in thee [Satan's sin occurred when he was in Eden — later called earth]. By the multitude of thy merchandise [Satan was involved in merchandising before he sinned — and he is still.] they have filled the midst of thee with violence, and thou hast sinned: therefore I will cast thee as profane out of the **mountain of God** (Dan. 9:20) [God's throne is always pictured as on a mount (Ps. 48:2; Is. 48:13): and I will destroy thee, O **covering cherub**, [The temple and the mercy seat, which were replicas of the real thing in heaven, were heavily adorned with shadowing cherubim (Ex. 25:19; 37:8; 1 Kings 6:27] from the midst of the stones of fire. Thine heart was lifted up because of thy beauty, thou hast corrupted thy wisdom by reason of thy brightness [brightness is always associated with a reigning potentate in the Authorized Version — without exception]: I will cast thee to the ground, I will lay thee before kings, that they may behold thee (Isaiah 14:9-18). Thou hast defiled thy sanctuaries by the multitude of thine iniquities, by the iniquity of thy traffick; therefore will I bring forth a fire from the midst of thee, it shall devour thee, and I will bring thee to ashes upon the earth in the sight of all them that behold thee" (Ezek. 28:13-18).

## Before the six days.

Everything God created, as recorded in Genesis chapter one, was announced with the words, "And God said …." All six of the 24-hour days of creation ended with, "and the evening and the morning were the first day…second day…third day…fourth day…etc. So, it is obvious that each day's creation was bracketed with **"And God said…."** on the opening side, and **"the evening and the morning were the…."** at the closing side of its creation. Inside those six brackets (six days) are recorded the entirety of the six days of creation.

The text is overly clear. On the first day, after the first "And God said…", what did God create? What was the first act of the six-day creation? "And God said, Let there be light…" (Gen. 1:3). Light was the first thing God spoke into existence during the six days. But there are two verses before the commencement of the first day, before light. "In the **beginning** God created the heaven and the earth, and the earth was without form, and void; and darkness *was* upon the face of the deep. And the Spirit of God moved upon the face of the waters" (Genesis 1:1-2). All this occurred before the six days — **in the beginning,** when the **foundations of the earth** were laid (Job 38:4). Observe the things that already existed before the commencement of the six days.

- ◆ God created the heaven and the earth. Stars, in proximity to the earth, were created later, on the fourth day.

- ◆ The earth pre-existed in a formless and void state.

- ◆ The earth was covered with darkness.

- ◆ The earth was covered with a deep — water.

♦ The Spirit of God moved upon the face of the darkened watery waste, no doubt in anticipation of the work of creation that was to come.

The text says the earth was **without form and void**. The Authorized Version is plain enough. We need not resort to the Hebrew text. But for those who place more faith in it, they will find it supporting this position. The Hebrew verb for **without form and void** "tohu vabohu" is found in the Hebrew Bible 20 times. It implies a previous catastrophe, a coming to confusion, as a drought causes a wilderness, or a war leaves a wasted land. In Isaiah 24:10 it is used in reference to a city **of confusion** that is broken down from God's judgment. Read Isaiah 24:1-10 noting that the same Hebrew words "tohu vabohu" are used to describe the wasted condition that results.

Isaiah provides us with another most appropriate cross reference for both the English text and the Hebrew word "tohu vabohu."

> *Isaiah 45:17* But Israel shall be saved in the LORD with an everlasting salvation: ye shall not be ashamed nor confounded world without end.
> 18 For thus saith the LORD that created the heavens; God himself that formed the earth and made it; he hath established it, **he created it not in vain** *(tohu vabohu),* he formed it to be inhabited: I am the LORD; and there is none else.

In the above passage, God is assuring Israel that they will be saved in the context of a world that will never end. To support his assertion, God calls to mind the facts of the past. He did not create the earth in **vain** ("tohu vabohu", same Hebrew word found in Genesis 1:2). If God did not create it in vain — formless and void, in a state of confusion and decay — then how did it get that way before the six days? We know the answer. It fell under the curse of sin when Lucifer was cast back down to the place from which he conceived sin (Isa. 14:15).

So the first crown holder was disqualified and damned, and God cursed the earth with darkness and destruction by water — as we find it in Genesis 1:2. It became without form and void of life. All plants and animals would have perished suddenly under the watery grave (2 Peter 3:4-7), similar to how the world was destroyed in the days of Noah.

## The Gap Fact.

Modern secular scientists believe that the earth and universe are **millions** of years old. We who know and believe the Bible reject that claim outright. In the late nineteenth century and early to mid-twentieth century, many professing Christians were made to doubt their own Bibles concerning a six-day creation. They sought to harmonize the creation miracle with what they thought was proven science — organic evolution over eons of time. These compromising Christians imagined that the six days in Genesis were vast ages that would allow enough time for God to employ a process of evolution, slowly bringing about advances in the complexity and variety of life. They called this clumsy hybrid *"Theistic Evolution"*. The Roman Pope, John Paul, affirmed his belief that life began through the process of organic evolution.

Throughout those years of unholy marriage of belief with unbelief, faithful Bible believers never wavered. We knew the Bible to be clear, that the creation events of Genesis chapter one were completed in six twenty-four-hour days. If we were to have had any doubts at all, it would have been to question how God could take as long as six days (144 hours) to do his work of creation, when he so easily could have done it with one word or thought. But we resolved any doubt by supposing that God slowed the process down to six twenty four hour days so he could give us an example of a workweek. No doubt each day's work of creation didn't even take a full second. God spent the rest of the day looking over what he had spoken into existence and saying to the angels, "Behold! (Look at it!) It is very good."

But, as already pointed out, the earth did indeed exist prior to the beginning of the six days of creation recorded in Genesis 1:3 and following. Furthermore, well before Darwin came along, and before backslidden Christians sought to make time for evolution, Bible believers knew and proclaimed that the earth existed before the six days of Genesis. One example will suffice.

Everyone is familiar with 5th century Augustine. He wrote in his Confessions that which was commonly believed in his day.

> **Chapter VIII—Heaven and Earth were made "In the beginning;" afterwards the world, during six days, from shapeless matter.**
>
> For very wonderful is this corporeal heaven; of which firmament between water and water, the second day, after the creation of light, Thou saidst, Let it be made, and it was made. Which firmament Thou calledst heaven; the heaven, that is, to this earth and sea, which Thou madest the third day, by giving a visible figure to the formless matter, which Thou madest before all days. For already hadst Thou made both an heaven, before all days; but that was the heaven of this heaven; because In the beginning Thou hadst made heaven and earth. But this same earth which Thou madest was formless matter, because it was invisible and without form, and darkness was upon the deep…"

The Jews of old recognized this obvious truth that the earth was created sometime before Genesis 1:3. They had no reason to be biased one way or the other. They just believed the Hebrew text as it read and believed in a "gap". When evolution became popular, those Christians who wanted to adopt evolution into their Biblical world-view found a convenient place for it in the time between original creation and the six-day creation. When Christian scientists got serious about defending special creation, they found many "Christian" theistic evolutionists entrenched in what they called the "gap theory". The Christian scientists sought to sweep away that argument by attacking the Biblical doctrine of the gap itself. Possibly they were not aware that it has been a well established doctrine throughout Biblical history. They do speak as if they think it is a concept invented by the theistic evolutionists.

Many things in the Bible are exotic and sometimes "embarrassing" to those who believe it as it is written. Nearly every publication on special creation, whether of magazines, pamphlets, or books, will take a swipe at "The Gap Theory." This author greatly appreciates the many works published by these Christian scientists. They have done a wonderful job of challenging the evolutionists and providing the doubting Christians with scientific proof of special creation. Our thanks go out to them. But in their zeal to rid the theistic evolutionists of their "biblical" foundation, in this one instance they have trashed the Scripture with their "science."

Let me be clear. By believing that the earth and the angels existed before the six days of recreation, we are not suggesting that the earth is millions of years old or that God needed a great deal of time to bring about creation. The earth may be just ten years older than the six days of recreation. It could be a thousand or ten thousand years older. It is probably no more than 100,000 years old, but then that is only a "scientific" guess by one who is not a scientist. The Bible doesn't suggest that the earth is old. It just states that it existed prior to the six days of recreation. With the Bible speaking clearly, we don't need science to support it, and we will not allow scientist — Christian or otherwise — to tell us differently. The evolutionists didn't sway us by pointing to "science" and neither will we be swayed by the "science" of well-meaning but wrong Christian scientists. The old book will weather all the fads.

## Re-creation.

With Lucifer leading one-third (Rev. 12:4) of the angels into rebellion against the kingdom of God, the kingdom of heaven, over which the formerly righteous Lucifer had ruled (2 Cor. 4:4), came under the curse of God and plunged into darkness. The earth that was created to be inhabited forever had become without a trace of life on its frozen deep (Gen. 1:2; Job 38:30). But God had not lost interest in the planet, for the Spirit of God contemplatively moved upon the face of the dark frozen waters.

It must have been a great mystery to the righteous angels as to why the Eternal One would place his concern upon that cursed, formless planet (1 Peter 1:12). Eden seemed to be a lost cause. The kingdom of God was untouched by Lucifer's rebellion, but the kingdom in the heavens seemed to be a failed experiment. The old planet was then formless and void. Why did the Spirit return there?

Suddenly, out of the darkness came a voice, "Let there be light!" And there was light (Gen. 1:3). "By the word of the LORD were the heavens made; and all the host of them by the breath of his mouth. For he spake, and it was *done*; he commanded, and it stood fast" (Psalm 33:6, 9). The angels observed the proceedings and could not contain themselves. At seeing their Master engaged in creation once again, they were moved to the depths of their angelic souls. Their wonder turned to joy, and their joy to shouting (Job 38:7).

The King of all spirits was laying the groundwork for a kingdom in the heavens (Matt. 25:34). So sure was he of its success that he wrote in a book the names of those who would be heirs of that kingdom (Eph. 1:3-6; Rev. 17:8). Moreover, the Father determined that all who would be his would be conformed to the very image of his Son (Eph. 1:5), that he might be the firstborn among many brethren (Romans 8:29). There was a mystery here (1 Cor. 2:7) that the angels sensed but did not understand (1 Peter 1:12).

On the sixth day, God created magnificent animals in great varieties. This must have dazzled the angels, like children getting their first puppy. No doubt they shouted for joy even more. But then, their Creator did something different from any of his former acts of creation: Instead of speaking his creation into existence, he formed a figure from the dust of the ground. When he finished his sculpture, it was in the image and likeness of God himself, yet less than the glory of the angels themselves, and smaller in statue (2 Peter 2:11; Psalm 8:4-5). There was no life in the still, earthy form. Then, there must have been a hush fall over the crowd gathered to watch the creation event as the Artist bent over and exhaled his own breath into the lifeless…No! It is alive! Man became a living soul.

As the first man stood to his feet, God crowned him with glory and honor (Ps. 8:6) and gave him authority over all of creation (Heb. 2:8). The **kingdom of God** had just instituted the new **kingdom of heaven**. The eternal spiritual kingdom of God had created a temporal kingdom in the heavens.

Adam was different from the angels, and different from the animal kingdom. There were many angels, and the animals had their own kind with which to mingle, but Adam, like God, was unique, one of a kind. He was alone. When Adam became aware of his singleness in a world of pairs, God put him to sleep and cloned a female from one of his ribs. God made her to be a suitable helper for Adam, that she might aid him in the discharge of his responsibilities as governor of the kingdom.

He told them to be fruitful and multiply, have children, and **replenish the earth** (Gen. 1:28). This word *replenish* means to fully restore life as it previously existed. It is the exact same commandment God gave Noah when he got off the ark to face a planet where all air breathing creatures had recently perished — replenish the earth with animals and humans. No one questions that God was telling Noah to *refill* the earth that had once been filled. Should we then second-guess God when he tells Adam and Eve the same thing? The earth, once populated with animals and a former race of angelic beings was in need of replenishing. Adam and Eve were to do the job by giving birth to children. The earthly kingdom would once again have subjects.

They were king and queen — living in harmony with the animals and their surroundings. Their life was meant to be simple: eat, drink, make love, rear children, and keep the garden. Then at the end of each day, they enjoyed a visit from their Creator.

## Adam given dominion.

God pronounced his blessings on the new couple and, in addition to telling them to multiply and replenish the earth, he commanded them to "**subdue it**: and **have dominion** over the fish of the sea, and over the fowl of the air, and over every living thing that moveth upon the earth" (Gen. 1:28). The words **subdue** and **dominion** are significant. The Hebrew word translated, *dominion,* is also translated in the Authorized Version as, *reign* and *rule.* The Hebrew word for **subdue,** is also translated, *to bring into subjection, bring into bondage,* and *force*. Adam was given dominion over the earth and every creature in it (Psalm 8:6).

The context in which God placed Adam clearly constituted a kingdom. Adam was the head of what was to become a great race of people, an empire inhabiting the whole earth — possibly even the stars. They were meant to become a community, a society, a kingdom of righteous subjects, living in harmony with God and enjoying the pleasures of body and soul. God himself would be King of kings, and no fairy tale would ever rival the glory and beauty of the kingdom their Creator had planned for them from before the world was created. "Come, ye blessed of my Father, inherit the kingdom prepared for you **from the foundation of the world**" (Matthew 25:34). "…for it is your Father's good pleasure to **give you the kingdom**" (Luke 12:32).

The Psalmist also says of man, "For thou hast made him a little lower than the angels, and hast **crowned** him with **glory and honour**. Thou **madest him to have dominion** over the works of thy hands; thou hast **put all things under his feet**" (Psalm 8:4-6).

The author of Hebrews, in referring to Psalm 8, adds something to it, telling us that God intends for man to rule the coming world. "For unto the angels hath he not put in **subjection the world to come,** whereof we speak. But one in a certain place testified, saying, What is man, that thou art mindful of him? or the son of man, that thou visitest him? Thou madest him a little lower than the angels [He was made lower, but he will reign higher.]; thou **crownedst** [Adam was crowned as is any king] him with glory and honour [making him fit to be a king], and didst **set him over the works of thy hands**: [Adam was appointed to be the ruler of all creation] Thou hast put **all things** in subjection under his feet. For in that he put all in subjection under him, he **left nothing** [His dominion was universal and entire] that is not put under him" (Hebrews 2:6-8). That is a very thorough pronouncement. All things were put under subjection to Adam, and, by implication, under subjection to his descendents as well. Remember, if Adam had not sinned, he would never have died. He would have worn the crown of glory and honor and continued to rule over all creation.

Adam was residing in two kingdoms. He was the leading member of the earthly branch of the kingdom of God, and he was the sole crownholder of the kingdom of heaven. It was his participation in the universal **kingdom of God** that gave him moral authority to rule the physical **kingdom of heaven.**

## Kingdom conquest.

Lucifer and the angels who sinned are wanderers in the universe (Jude 12:13). They travel from earth to heaven (Job 1:6-7), live among the stars so as to be identified with them (Daniel 8:10; Rev. 9:1; 12:4), and for that reason are called **the host of heaven** (2 Chron. 18:18; Neh. 9:6; Dan. 8:10; Zeph. 1:5; Acts 7:42). If you do a concordance search on the phrase, *host of heaven,* you will find that it applies equally to stars and angels — almost as if they were synonymous. Probably, angels are identified with the stars because they so completely inhabit the stars. Humans are identified by the places where they live — North Americans, South Americans, Africans, etc. Angels are not Englishmen or Scotsmen; they are Starmen.

When Lucifer saw his old kingdom placed under the dominion of a mere mortal, it must have infuriated him. He certainly went on the offensive. Here was the kingdom that once belonged to him now in the hands of a lesser being who didn't even know the difference between good and evil. This fallen potentate still felt that he was the rightful crownholder, and was determined to thwart God's purpose for the new Eden. He felt he must stop this new mortal from producing millions of righteous children to populate the earth and eventually the stars. But he had a problem. Since the time of his sin and the curse God placed upon him, he was without any earthly form by which he could communicate with these humans. He needed a medium through which to speak his mind, so he chose the most subtle (crafty) beast in the field.

The serpent stood tall on his hind legs, his long scaled neck held up with pride. He moved through the fields like a gentle breeze, sliding in and out of objects with grace and poise (Job 41:1-34; Rev.

20:2; Isa. 27:1). Since his fall, Lucifer was without a body, so he entered the body of this beast and commandeered its faculties for his own purposes. Once in command of the beast, he went toward the center of the garden and waited for the woman to walk by. When she drew near, the serpent/beast spoke carefully. He did not rush in with denunciations. He asked Eve a simple question designed to cause her to question God. "Yea, hath God said, Ye shall not eat of every tree of the garden?" (Gen. 3:1). As the conversation ensued, the serpent, in effect, told the woman that God had commanded them not to eat because he was holding them back from expanding their knowledge of good and evil and becoming like the gods — like the angels that they must have seen visiting the garden with God.

Eve, the queen of the kingdom, mother of all living, was caused to doubt her creator. She believed the half-truth of the serpent and ate of the forbidden tree. Then she shared the fruit with her husband, and now the whole world shares the consequences. Eden was once again in rebellion against God. Satan had retaken his old throne. He "saved" the earth from righteousness and peace. Sin entered. Death reigned. Not only was paradise lost, but a kingdom as well. God withdrew the righteous **kingdom of God** from the earth, and, with Adam in a sinful condition, the **kingdom of heaven** was headless — except for the unlawful usurper.

## Fallen man.

God found Adam and Eve hiding in their shame — the first of many shameful experiences to occur on this planet. He cursed the physical earth, including all plants and animals. And he cursed Eve with frequent conceptions. He cursed Adam with a life of toil. The curse of death fell upon mankind and also, as peripheral damage, upon the animal and vegetable kingdoms as well. But the greatest curse of all is when God turned and walked away, taking the kingdom of God with him, leaving the couple to fend for their selves, banished from his presence and daily provision. He drove them out of the garden where they soon saw their second-born son lying in a pool of blood, and their first-born fleeing for his life with an additional curse he would carry to the grave. The wages of sin is death — always has been, always will be.

In Hebrews 2:8, God, after telling us that he has placed all of creation under man's authority (quoting Ps. 115:16), explains further: "**But now we see not yet all things put under him.**" When Adam willfully disobeyed God, he broke fellowship with the **kingdom of God** and lost his **crown of glory and honor.** He no longer possessed the moral authority to exercise dominion over the **kingdom of heaven.** God placed a curse upon the earth itself, and with no one suitable to wear the crown of glory and honor (Romans 3:23), the earth lay ungoverned, and the kingdom that God had established in the heavens (the earth being a part of the heavens) fell to the prince of darkness (Eph. 2:2; 6:12). Therefore, Adam's descendents do not exercise their original dominion as intended by God. Rather, they themselves are under the dominion of the forces of darkness.

Thus, the Bible begins with a lost Paradise and a lost kingdom. From the third chapter of Genesis to the twentieth chapter of Revelation, we read about a struggle to regain a kingdom, a crown, and the glory and honor that go with them. The Bible is the drama of a kingdom that is given to Adam, lost to Satan, promised to Abraham, given to Israel, lost to Babylon, temporarily regained, offered by John and Christ, rejected by Israel, postponed while God saved Gentiles, promised again, coming, and, in the books of 1Corinthians and Revelation, we read the fulfillment, "**when he shall have put down all rule and all authority and power and the kingdoms of this world become the kingdoms of our God and his Christ…and he shall reign for ever and ever**" (1 Cor. 15:24; Rev. 11:15).

## The kingdom struggle.

Adam was the only legitimate head of the earthly branch of the **kingdom of heaven**, but when his sin disqualified him to be God's vice regent upon the earth, the kingdom was thrown into chaos, leaving a power vacuum. The throne lay idle, but not for long. Lucifer stepped in to take over, organizing his own kingdom and religion. The kingdom question became the apex, the totality of future developing history. And so it remains today. The study of history is the chronicling of struggles between competing kingdoms. Daily world news is little more than the reporting of the tragedy of kingdoms and would-be kings vying for dominion. So shall it be until "The kingdoms of this world are become *the kingdoms* of our Lord, and of his Christ" (Rev. 11:15), which occurs at the beginning of the Millennium. But, if you don't believe in a literal reign of Christ upon the earth, then the Bible is not going to make sense to you. You will have to stick with the convenient practice of allegorizing everything and using the Bible as nothing more than a book of inspiration and moral law.

## Satan takes the kingdom.

God is the creator and sustainer of the earth, and the rightful ruler over all. "The earth is the LORD'S, and the fulness thereof; the world, and they that dwell therein" (Ps. 24:1). Although God delegated all authority to man, when the first man Adam lost his moral authority, by default the corrupted kingdom came under the jurisdiction of Satanic authority, for God rules over light, not darkness. Satan could never have righteous jurisdiction over this planet, but he can fill the vacuum and rule that which Adam lost. The Bible calls him **the god of this world** (2 Cor. 4:3-4). Jesus spoke of **Satan's kingdom** (Luke 11:18), and called him **the prince of this world** (John 14:30). The angel told Daniel of his conflict with an evil spirit known as the **Prince of Persia** (Dan. 10:20). Paul spoke of **the rulers of the darkness of this world** (Eph. 6:12). And when Satan offered Jesus the **kingdoms of this world**, he reminded Jesus that it was within his power to give them to **whomsoever** he would.

> *Luke 4:5-6* "And the devil, taking him up into an high mountain, shewed unto him all the **kingdoms of the world** in a moment of time.
> 6 And the devil said unto him, All this power will I give thee, and the **glory** of them: **for that is delivered unto me; and to whomsoever I will I give it.**

Someone might argue that Satan was lying when he said the kingdoms of the world were his to give, but remember, Satan was taking his best shot at tempting the Son of God. He would know better than to make a nonsense offer to the Eternal One who created him. Satan obviously had control of the world's kingdoms. He had many years to devise the most effective temptations conceivable. He would have been foolish to offer Jesus something that would not touch upon some human and spiritual passion or desire. Satan succeeded with both Adam and Eve, why not with this starved and lonely "Second" man? (1 Cor. 5:47). Satan knew that Jesus came to be king, to set up a kingdom, to take the heathen for his inheritance as the Psalmist predicted (Ps. 2). John the Baptist had already been announcing the kingdom for six months before Jesus was tempted. So, Satan offered Jesus a shortcut to his divine desire. "You can have it all right now; I will relinquish my hold on the kingdoms of the world if you will just worship me." The Bible says that Jesus was **tempted of the devil**. That implies that he was not indifferent to the offer. Satan did indeed have some kind of leverage that could tempt Christ. It was his position as chief potentate of planet earth and his control over the kingdom of heaven that gave him the appearance of leverage.

The man Jesus refused Satan's offer for the very reason that it was "a temptation." He wanted the kingdoms, of course, but he wanted them in righteousness and in the Father's timing. The one thing the Devil couldn't understand was Jesus' motive for wanting the kingdoms. Satan reveals his motive when he shows Jesus the kingdoms **and the glory of them**." Satan wants glory — on any terms. In contrast, Jesus wants to *impart* glory that is pure and enduring.

How did Satan attain to the position of being able to offer the kingdoms of this world to Jesus Christ? Two things are readily apparent. Since Satan lived on this planet when he was yet perfect in all his ways (Ezek. 28:15), and was **anointed** to hold a position of dominion, and since it is revealed that he had enough influence to gain a following of one-third of the angels, and he dwelt in Eden, it is likely that he was the original ruler of this planet. Remember what Ezekiel 28 says of Lucifer, "Thou art the anointed cherub **that covereth, and I have set thee so.**" Kings are anointed. God set the anointed Lucifer in a position of covering (oversight), as a king covers — guards, protects, legislates — his domain. That would explain why Satan developed a lust for more power and why he had a hope of conquering. At one time, while on the old world, before Adam was created, Lucifer was anointed and installed ("set") by God to be the "god of this world" (2 Cor. 4:4; Ps. 82:1, 6; 138:1). But he wanted more of the same — to be worshiped. When Adam was given dominion over Lucifer's original domain, Lucifer sought to regain his lost dominion. Could it be that when Satan told Jesus that the kingdoms of this world were "delivered unto" him, and that he could give them to "whomsoever he will," that he was referring to his original land grant — that just as Adam was made heir of the world, Lucifer was the first heir? See 2 Cor. 4:4. Job says of Satan, "he *is* a **king** over all the children of pride" (Job 41:34).

In addition to Scripture, simple observation would lead one to the conclusion that Satan is in charge of world affairs, but from time to time God steps in and brings his choice of a man or a nation into power. God has the power to intervene any time he chooses, but he does not always choose to direct the affairs of nations. In most cases God withdraws and leaves men and nations to their own devices, for to do otherwise would be like taking the steering wheel away from someone whom you are teaching to drive. When God permits, Satan is eager and ready to fill the vacuum and to put his man in place.

The dominion God gave to Adam is still ceded to the sons of men, even though none are qualified to rule. Satan rules unlawfully, by right of conquest, by moral default, and has the right to continue doing so until there arises a man, the second man, the last Adam (1 Cor. 15:45) who is worthy to wear the crown of glory and honor. Such a man could rightfully ascend to the throne and be king and judge of the world. Nature would submit to him and the curse would be lifted. Jesus is that son of **man** who will take the kingdoms by force and make them **the kingdoms of our God and his Christ**.

In the mean time, "We wrestle not against flesh and blood, but against principalities, against powers, against the **rulers of the darkness of this world**, against spiritual wickedness in high *places*" (Ephesians 6:12). Satan now has organized resistance to the **kingdom of God** and the **kingdom of heaven**. In the end, Satan will fully corrupt the visible church and place his own christ in office.

## God's original purpose remains his eternal purpose.

Most people think of the carnal earth as a bad idea to begin with — no doubt due to living under the curse God placed on nature. Christians sing of the "sweet by and by" and "when we get over yonder." They dream of "going to heaven." The saved *will* go to heaven (1Thes. 4:17), but soon return to the new earth (Rev. 21:1-4, 24, 27; 22:1-6), which at the time will be a paradise (Isa. 65:25), to dwell in the New Jerusalem — capitol city of the **world without end** (Isa. 45:17).

God's original plan was to populate the earth with faithful children (Gen. 1:28). When Adam disobeyed and populated the earth with rebels instead, God didn't discard his first purpose. It will not be set aside for something more realistic or less risky. He will not change his program. God set out to populate the earth with loyal subjects. He will do what he started to do. He will complete his mission.

The earth was created for man. "The heaven, even the heavens, are the LORD'S: but the **earth hath he given to the children of men**" (Ps. 115:16). And so, be certain of one think, man will inhabit the earth forever. "Forever" is as long as God lives.

> "But Israel shall be saved in the LORD with an everlasting salvation: ye shall not be ashamed nor confounded **world without end**. For thus saith the LORD that created the heavens; God himself that formed the earth and made it; he hath established it, he **created it not in vain, he formed it to be inhabited**: I am the LORD; and there is none else" (Isa. 45:17-18).

If God were to forsake his goal of populating the earth with loyal subjects, then it could be said that he did in fact create it **in vain**. But God formed this planet to be inhabited, therefore it will be inhabited forever. When this present "heavens and earth" has served its purpose, God will destroy it and create a new one to take its place as the domain of his kingdom. "For, behold, I **create new heavens and a new earth**: and the former shall not be remembered, nor come into mind" (Isa. 65:17). "For as **the new heavens and the new earth**, which I will make, **shall remain before me**, saith the LORD, so shall your seed and your name remain" (Isa. 66:22). This truth of an everlasting earth is reiterated in the New Testament.

> "Looking for and hasting unto the coming of the day of God, wherein the heavens being on fire shall be dissolved, and the elements shall melt with fervent heat? Nevertheless we, according to his promise, look for **new heavens and a new earth**, wherein dwelleth righteousness" (2 Pet. 3:12-13).

God's ultimate intention is revealed in his original undertaking — the creation of man upon a perfect earth. He did not withhold his best and do the next best thing first, as if he were experimenting and working his way up to the grand scheme. There is nothing secondary about the original creation. When God finished creation on the sixth day, he said, "Behold, it is **very good**" (Gen. 1:31). Things will end where they started: in Paradise, walking with God beside the river, under fruit trees, eating and drinking, in fellowship with God and each other.

The reality of an everlasting world is confirmed by the reality that the future state of the saved will include new moons and Sabbaths. A new moon necessitates a lunar cycle, which means the earth will exist in a solar system, much as it does now. "For as the **new heavens and the new earth, which I will make, shall remain before me,** saith the LORD, **so** shall your seed and your name remain. And it shall come to pass, that **from one new moon to another**, and from one sabbath to another, shall all flesh come to worship before me, saith the LORD" (Isa. 66:22-23). New moons and Sabbaths will require a sun and a moon — a natural but incorruptible world. There will be a time when the earth again becomes a paradise as it was in the garden planted in the east of Eden.

> "And it shall come to pass, that before they call, I will answer; and while they are yet speaking, I will hear. **The wolf and the lamb shall feed together,** and the lion shall eat straw like the bullock: and dust shall be the serpent's meat. **They shall not hurt nor destroy in all my holy mountain,** saith the LORD" (Isa. 65:24-25).

God set out to create a kingdom on this earth, and he will surely do so. "Fear not, little flock; for it is your **Father's good pleasure to give you the kingdom**" (Luke 12:32). "Thy kingdom come. Thy will be done **in earth**, as *it is* in heaven" (Matt. 6:10).

## Flesh corrupted its way upon the earth.

After Adam lost his dominion, and as earth's population increased, sin increased. God had not yet established any laws to govern the conduct of men. That first 1656 years after the creation of Adam spawned a lawless (Rom. 3:9-18; 5:13-14), degenerate society (Gen. 6:5). There was no kingdom, and no man was worthy to execute heaven's rule over the sons of men.

To make matters worse, Satan, in his attempt to subvert the kingdom, led the sons of God to copulate with the daughters of men (Gen. 6:1-4), resulting in all flesh becoming corrupted (Gen. 6:12). Their offspring were giants up to ten feet tall (1 Sam. 17:4), of superior strength and intellect, and who became men of renown. After the flood, when the sons of God again copulated with the daughters of men (Gen. 6:4), more giants were produced, also men of renown. They were genetically different, not only in their height, but they had physical differences as well (2 Sam. 21:20; Num. 13:33; Deut. 3:9-11; 1 Chron. 20:5).

> "And GOD saw that the wickedness of man *was* great in the earth, and that every imagination of the thoughts of his heart *was* **only evil continually**. And it repented the LORD that he had made man on the earth, and it grieved him at his heart. And the LORD said, I will destroy man whom I have created from the face of the earth; both man, and beast, and the creeping thing, and the fowls of the air; for it repenteth me that I have made them. But Noah found **grace** in the eyes of the LORD" (Gen. 6:5-8).

Fifteen hundred years later, in obedience to God, Israel eliminated all of them (1 Chron. 20:8; Deut. 2:20). Such was the nature of this strange flesh union, that If the sons of God were to copulate with the daughters of men today, it would still produce giants (Jude 6-7; II Pet. 2:4-5). But that is another subject for another time.

As to God's response to the sinfulness and corruption of the human race, he saw the sinfulness of the human race and the corrupted flesh and decided to destroy them all (Gen. 6:13). Not only were none worthy to rule, none were worthy to live. God was about to abandon his attempt to retake the earth (Eden), but for one thing — grace. This is the first mention of grace in the Bible. It was not Noah's righteousness that saved him. It was pure, unmerited, undeserved grace. Four men and their wives, pure descendents of Adam, not sharing any of the mixed genetics of the sons of God, went into the ark, escaping damnation, and four men and their wives came out to start the new world.

## A new start.

When Noah emerged from the ark, he was the head of the human race, just as Adam had been. All people on the face of the earth are descendents of Noah. God gave Father Noah an opportunity to recapture the kingdom. You will remember that when God gave Adam dominion over the earth, he said, "Be fruitful, and multiply, and replenish the earth, and subdue it: and have dominion over the fish of the sea, and over the fowl of the air, and over every living thing that moveth upon the earth" (Gen. 1:28). See also Ps. 8:4-6; Heb. 2:6-8. Notice the similarity in what God says to Noah.

> "And God blessed Noah and his sons, and said unto them, **Be fruitful, and multiply, and replenish the earth**. And the **fear of you and the dread of you shall be upon every beast of the earth**, and upon every fowl of the air, upon all that moveth upon the earth, and upon all the fishes of the sea; **into your hand are they delivered**" (Gen. 9:1-2).

The dominion of both men was marked by their authority over even the wildest of beasts. By Divine decree, crocodiles and lions feared Adam, and now Noah. The Bible is not accidental in the point it makes of this, for you will remember that Daniel had power over animals (Dan. 6:12-27). And Jesus came representing the kingdom of God with power over wild beasts (Mark 1:13). And we are told that the Kingdom of God during the Millennium will be marked by power over the animals. "The wolf and the lamb shall feed together, and the lion shall eat straw like the bullock: and dust *shall be* the serpent's meat. They shall not hurt nor destroy in all my holy mountain, saith the LORD (Isa. 65:25). In the Millennium, when the kingdom is completely restored, even a child will have power over all beasts (Isa. 11:8). See also Luke 10:19 and Acts 28:3-6).

The throne was Noah's. He was now the Father of all living, and his wife, like Eve, was now the mother of all living. The future of the world was in his hands. Like Adam, he was commissioned to repopulate the earth (Gen. 9:1). Adam had named all the animals; Noah now watched them file off the ark. Adam received promise of a coming deliverer; Noah received promise that the world would never again be destroyed by water, as had already occurred twice. Then, like Adam, Noah received a prophecy of the coming deliverer; he would be a descendent of Shem (Gen. 9:27).

But like Adam, Noah sinned. Adam was naked when he sinned, so was Noah. Adam's sin was eating forbidden fruit. Noah's sin was drinking it. Three sons of Adam are named. Three sons of Noah are named. Each one of them had one son who was cursed by God. Each fell and took his posterity with him. But the human race now had two covenants from God. A woman will compass a man (Jer. 31:22) and produce a child of her own body, who will destroy the devil (Gen. 3:15), and God will never again destroy all flesh upon the earth by water (Gen. 9:11). The kingdom of heaven, in a usurped form, was still in the hands of Satan.

## The beginning of his kingdom was Babel (Gen. 10:10).

After the flood, men multiplied on the earth for several hundred years. It was then that a mighty man named Nimrod, a great hunter and no doubt skilled in the use of weapons, established the first kingdom since the fall of Adam. The first city in his kingdom was Babel (Gen. 10), which would later be called Babylon, located 50 miles south of what is now Baghdad in modern Iraq. From there other cities were established, from Nineveh to the Jebusite and Amorite cities of Canaan. Babylon went on to produce the first and most influential religion of all time — a Satanic mystery religion that survives to this day, blended into many religions, including Roman Catholicism, all of liturgical Christianity, and Protestant denominations to a lesser degree.

The word Babylon appears in the Bible 294 times. And in these last days before the commencing of the Millennium and the dawn of the promised kingdom, the land of Babylon, represented by several Muslim nations, is still the leading enemy of Jacob's seed, attempting to overthrow the kingdom that God would build in Jerusalem and replace it with the remnants of the first kingdom the Devil ever established upon the earth.

The book of Revelation reveals that the Babylonian religion will remain prominent until the second coming of Christ (Rev. 14:8; 16:19; 17:5 18:2, 10, 21). The Babylonian mystery religion is most influential in Western cultures, accounting for most of the believing martyrs killed down through the ages. It is not related to modern Iraq, and the ancient city of Babylon no longer exists except in a mystery form (Rev. 17:5). From this point forward (Gen. 10), Satan has the seeds of his kingdom established. It will compete with God's kingdom right up to the end of the Millennium (Rev. 20:3, 8).

## God gives Abraham the kingdom.

The promise of a deliverer seemed far away. God's original purpose for Adam was to establish an expanding kingdom of holy people. Adam and Noah's failures did not change God's intentions. He was still seeking to establish a kingdom on this earth, so he started over with one man — Abraham. Within the kingdom of what would become known as Babylon — the same landmass that was once the Garden of Eden — God spoke to Abraham and told him to leave his family and country and to travel to a land that God would show him. God promised that he would multiply Abraham's seed (children) to become as many as the sand on the seashore, and that he would be the father of a great nation (Gen. 22:17; 32:12). He called Abraham to leave his home and seek **a city** which had foundations, **whose builder and maker is God** (Heb. 11:10). Note well, Abraham was not looking for personal salvation. He was not looking forward to Christ. He was looking for a promised <u>city</u>, the capital city of a kingdom from heaven, set up on the earth. He was not wrong to look for this city <u>on the earth</u>, for that is exactly where God promised it would be. God gave Abraham a piece of real estate. We must say it again: Abraham was not called out to build a religion; he was called to seek a city built by God.

> *Genesis 12:1* Now the LORD had said unto Abram, Get thee out of thy country, and from thy kindred, and from thy father's house, **unto a land** that I will shew thee:
> 2 And I will make of thee a **great nation**, and I will bless thee, and make thy name great; and thou shalt be a blessing:
> 3 And I will bless them that bless thee, and curse him that curseth thee: and in thee shall all families of the earth be blessed.
> 4 So Abram departed, as the LORD had spoken unto him; and Lot went with him: and Abram was seventy and five years old when he departed out of Haran.

The book of Hebrews goes on to tell us that Abraham did not receive the fulfillment of the promise — that is, he did not find that city (Heb. 11:39). There was no such city at the time, only the ground on which it would be established — Jerusalem. On that same piece of real estate, Abraham was commanded to offer his son Isaac as a sacrifice to God. Later, God would offer the blood of his own son on that same ground on which the city would later be re-established. Psalm 2:6-9 is a clear prophecy of Christ assuming dominion from a throne upon that very hill. Hebrews 1:5 confirms that the passage in Psalm 2 is indeed a prophecy of Jesus Christ. If, someday Jesus should not return to that hill and set up a city over which he would rule and into which Abraham will enter, then God will be a liar, and your Bible will be worthless.

Hebrews gives a list of the early patriarchs of the faith and states that "they desire a better country, that is, an heavenly, wherefore God is not ashamed to be called their God: for he hath **prepared for them a city**" (Heb. 11:16). It will truly be an heavenly city, for "John saw the holy city, new Jerusalem, coming down from God **out of heaven**, prepared as a bride adorned for her husband" (Rev. 21:2). It comes down to the earth to take the place of natural Jerusalem, sitting directly over the piece of land God gave Abraham. And as to the foundations, the Bible says, "And the foundations of the wall of the city were garnished with all manner of precious stones. The first foundation *was* jasper; the second, sapphire; the third, a chalcedony; the fourth, an emerald…" (Rev. 21:19). God made the foundations of the city Abraham sought.

The city has already been made by Jesus in the heavens (John 14:2), but it won't be ready for occupation until at the end of the Millennium, at which time it will come to the earth (Rev. 21:2). Then, Abraham will physically see it and find it to be all that he had desired; for he had already seen it by faith. Again note, Abraham left his earthly home (Ur of the Chaldees) seeking a city, a kingdom built by God. Abraham didn't know it, but he was seeking the **kingdom of heaven** under the direction of the **kingdom of God**.

We know that Abraham was made heir of the kingdom by the statement of the prophet Isaiah.

> *Isaiah 41:2* Who raised up the righteous man from the east, called him to his foot, **gave the nations before him, and made him rule over kings**? he gave them as the dust to his sword, and as driven stubble to his bow. [verses 8-9 attribute this to Abraham]

Abraham remained faithful to God and to his covenant throughout his life. God passed on the covenant of inheriting the land to Isaac, Abraham's son.

## Ishmael

God had made it clear to Abraham that he and Sarah would have a male child who would be heir of the promise. But when God delayed Sarah's conception, she devised a carnal means (natural, but not by faith, Gal. 4:22-31) of providing an heir for the kingdom. She encouraged Abraham to take her Egyptian servant, Hagar, and produce a child through her. There were two things wrong with this: God said it would be Sarah, not Hagar, and Noah had prophesied that the promised deliverer would be a descendent of Shem, not Ham or Japheth (Gen. 9:25-27). Egyptians were descendents of Ham. It was not that one racial line was superior to another; it is just that God had provided the particulars of prophecy and there was not other option that would conform to the prophecy.

It is most refreshing how the Old Testament type remains true to form — as always. *The thing that has been, and is recorded In Scripture, is the thing that shall be.* Just as Abraham and Sarah were not content to wait for God to fulfill his promise through Abraham, so today the churches are not content to allow God to do the supernatural and fulfill his promise through Israel (Abraham's seed through his grandson Jacob). Sarah tried to superimpose Ishmael into the special position of the chosen seed, and likewise today, the church tries to insert itself into Israel's position of being the "spiritual" seed of Abraham — to take the special position promised to Israel (Jacob's descendents). The church thinks it is helping God by discarding the promise of a seed through the bloodline of Jacob and substituting the New Testament Church it its place. Those who do so will prove themselves as wrong as Saran and Hagar when they tried to fulfill God's promises with a substitute.

It is further interesting that the seed which God had designated was pure Shemite, while the seed Sarah offered God was part Hamite. God had made it explicitly clear with Noah; the promised seed will not be from Japheth or Ham; *it will be from Shem.* Modern churches today are primarily made up of the descendents of Ham and Japheth, whereas the natural seed of Jacob is Shemite only.

Abraham and Sarah, who were to bring forth the promised seed, were barren — could not produce life, just as Israel (Jacob's natural seed) is barren of spiritual life today. It will require a supernatural healing for them to bring forth the promised seed. Today, the seed of Jacob awaits that supernatural healing when the barren shall bring forth and **all Israel shall be saved**.

When Ishmael was born, and until he was fourteen years old, he was the assumed heir of the promise. But God had been clear; the heir must be of Abraham and Sarah. So, God healed Sarah and gave her strength to conceive seed. She bore the promised seed, Isaac. The kingdom would remain in the tents of Shem (Gen. 9:27), but Abraham had fathered the biggest headache his descendents would ever have. The descendents of Ishmael, half brother to Isaac, cousins to the Jews, have remained enemies of Israel up to the very present. They are in perpetual competition for the kingdom land and the kingdom title. At this very moment, Ishmael's descendents throughout the Middle East are at war, claiming that they are the true heirs of Abraham through Ishmael, not the Jews through Isaac. They want the kingdom. They demand Jerusalem — the city of the great King. They stalk and kill Jewish children, women, and old men. Their lives and religion are defined by their struggle against Israel and any descendent of Jacob. The curriculum in their kindergartens and grade schools is filled with defamation of the Jews and a call to wage "holy" war against them. The Islamic states dream of an end to Israel and the conquest of Islam over all kingdoms. It is plain for anyone to see. It is all about kingdoms, not religion. Religion is just used to justify the killing that is involved in kingdom building. The pursuit of a kingdom of heaven is so ingrained in human nature that it is the most driving force in history.

## Melchizedek

While Abraham was journeying through the Promised Land, looking "for a city which hath foundations, whose builder and maker *is* God" (Heb. 11:10), his nephew Lot was taken captive along with the entire city of Sodom. Abraham and his servants pursued the fleeing enemy and killed them in battle, rescuing Lot, his family, and all the people and goods of the city. As Abraham was returning from the battle, a mystery king, who was also a priest of the very God whom Abraham worshiped, came out to meet him with refreshments and a blessing. A prophecy in Psalms, and nine verses in the New Testament, make it abundantly clear that this mystery priest, Melchizedek, is, at the very least, a type of Christ. Many commentators believe that he was actually Christ making a pre-incarnation appearance to Abraham his friend, especially because the bread and wine he served Abraham is a prophetic picture of Jesus our high priest serving communion to his friends, the apostles.

> *Genesis 14:18* And Melchizedek **king of Salem** brought forth bread and wine: and he was the **priest of the most high God**.
> 19 And he blessed him, and said, Blessed *be* Abram of the most high God, **possessor of heaven and earth:**
> 20 And blessed be the most high God, which hath delivered thine enemies into thy hand. And he gave him tithes of all.

It is most significant that this important mystery figure chose this occasion to make his appearance. It was not after a deep spiritual experience, such as after circumcision, after the birth of Isaac, or at the sacrifice of his only son. No, Abraham has just pursued his enemies and wiped them out to the last man, rescued his own family, and taken spoil of the enemy. He is met by a king who is a priest, who, in prophesizing, blesses Abraham consistent with the covenant God had already made with him (Gen. 12:3; 22:17-18).

There are many names and descriptions of God in the Bible, any of which could be used to express his majesty, but Melchizedek chose a description that was appropriate to the occasion. Addressing Abraham, this king-priest-prophet spoke of the Most High as **possessor of heaven and earth**, which points to the kingdom of heaven covenant God made with Abraham, "...and thy seed shall possess the gate of his enemies" (Gen. 22:17-18). In other words, Abraham's God can deliver on his promise to multiply his seed, bless him and his seed, through his seed bless the whole world, and he will conquer his enemies, since his Most High God possesses heaven and earth.

This is the only time that Melchizedek ever made an appearance — just this single occasion described here in only three verses. He comes out of nowhere — "Without father, without mother, without descent, having neither beginning of days, nor end of life; but made like unto the Son of God; abideth a priest continually" (Heb. 6:3). That is quite a resume for someone who cannot be traced to any lineage, revelation or covenant. He is not Jewish, and is not necessarily even Semitic (descendent of Shem, Noah's first son). He is not under the law, and is not a Levitical priest. Nonetheless, so great was this man (Heb. 7:4) that he establishes the order from which Jesus is to be ordained to the priesthood. Jesus is described as being a **priest forever after the order of Melchizedek**. In other words, Jesus received his right to be a priest, our great high priest, not through the order of Judaism and the Levitical priesthood, but through the order of (the same authority as) Melchizedek, the king of Salem.

Psalm 104:4 also predicts that Christ will be a priest after the same order as Melchizedek, and again in the New Testament book of Hebrews, Melchizedek is commented on at length in chapters 5, 6 and 7.

> *Hebrews 7:2* To whom also Abraham gave a tenth part of all; first being by interpretation **King of righteousness,** and after that also **King of Salem**, which is, **King of peace**.

Hebrews 7:2 calls Melchizedek, **King of righteousness, King of Salem,** and **King of Peace**. These titlees correspond to the Godhead. The King of righteousness points to Christ, King of Salem to God, and King of Peace to the Holy Spirit.

> *Hebrews 7:15* And it is yet far more evident: for that after the **similitude of Melchisedec** there ariseth another priest,
> 16 Who is made, not after the law of a carnal commandment, but after **the power of an endless life**.
> 17 For he testifieth, Thou art a **priest for ever** after the order of Melchisedec.

The city Salem, of which Melchizedek was king/priest, is identified with Jerusalem – JeruSalem – or "founded safe or at peace." Here is a man who is not part of any known covenant or work of God, said to be king of a city that will eventually be the throne of David, the place in which Christ will be crucified, the place in which the Church will be baptized with the Holy Spirit, and Jesus will return to that city and rule the earth with king David for 1000 years. And the city that Jesus is preparing in the heavens, the one Abraham was looking for, which had foundations built by God, is called **The New Jerusalem**, and it will descend to the earth out of heaven and sit on the very spot where Melchizedek was then king.

Melchizedek was a three-throned king, with legitimate title to three thrones. He was the actual king of an earthly city called Salem — a natural, earthly kingdom. He was the King of righteousness, which would be identified with the kingdom of God (Heb.1:8; Rom. 14:17; Matt. 6:33). And, he was King of Peace, which would be identified with the kingdom of heaven (Isa. 9:7; Luke 2:14). Melchizedek is the first man since Adam to be a crown-holder of both the kingdom of God and the kingdom of heaven.

## The promise is reaffirmed to Isaac.

God reaffirmed his promises to Isaac, Abraham's promised son. "…and unto thy seed, I will give all these countries, and I will perform the oath which I sware unto Abraham thy father; And I will make thy seed to multiply as the stars of heaven, and will **give unto thy seed all these countries**; and in thy seed shall all the **nations of the earth be blessed**; Because that Abraham obeyed my voice, and kept my charge, my commandments, my statutes, and my laws" (Gen. 26:3-5). Note that, the promise is not about religion; it is about inheriting countries and nations.

## God reaffirms the kingdom promise to Jacob.

Abraham's grandson, Jacob, received the same assurance from God concerning the land: "And God said unto him, Thy name is Jacob: thy name shall not be called any more Jacob, but Israel shall be thy name: and he called his name Israel. And God said unto him, I am God Almighty: be fruitful and multiply; **a nation and a company of nations** [*These are detailed in Numbers 1 through 26 and from 1 Samuel to 2 Chronicles, therefore they cannot be spiritualized.*] shall be of thee, and **kings** shall come out of thy loins; And **the land** which I gave Abraham and Isaac, to thee I will give it, and **to thy seed after thee will I give the land**" (Gen. 35:10-15). God was very precise: the descendents of Abraham, Isaac, and Jacob, now called Israel, will inherit a piece of land. At this point, it has nothing to do with personal salvation; it is about land being given to the natural descendents of Abraham – through his grandson Jacob.

The kingdom promise has been affirmed by God to pass from Abraham to Isaac to Jacob, and now Jacob has twelve sons who became the fathers of the twelve tribes of Israel. But **only one** can be heir to the throne. When Jacob was dying, he prophesied about each of his sons, and specified that Judah would inherit the scepter of the king.

> *Genesis 49:8* **Judah, thou** *art he* **whom thy brethren shall praise**: thy hand *shall be* in the neck of thine enemies; thy father's children shall bow down before thee.
> 10 The **sceptre shall not depart from Judah**, nor a **lawgiver** from between his feet, until Shiloh come; and unto him shall the gathering of the people be.

So, it is the tribe of Judah from which king David and Jesus come as lawgivers and kings and rulers of righteousness. The historical books are primarily chronicles of the descendents of Judah leading up to the birth of Christ. The passage above prophesies of an uninterrupted lineage until Shiloh (Jesus) shows up to take the king's scepter. It also establishes that the seed of the woman (Gen. 3:15), who will bruise the serpent's head, will be of the lineage of Judah. And so it was.

## Joseph believed that God would honor his promise.

During a famine in the Promised Land, God directed Jacob, the grandson of Abraham, to take his entire family to Egypt. When Jacob's son, Joseph, was old and about to die, "Joseph said unto his brethren, I die: and God will surely visit you, **and bring you out of this land unto the land** which he sware to Abraham, to Isaac, and to Jacob. And Joseph took an oath of the children of Israel, saying, God will surely visit you, and ye shall carry up my bones from hence" (Gen. 50:24-25). This is further confirmation that the Abrahamic covenant was about inheriting land — about establishing a kingdom made up of Jacob's descendents. It has nothing at all to do with the Church or the **kingdom of God**. But it has everything to do with a kingdom in the physical heavens ruled by the heavens — the **kingdom of heaven**.

## The Nation of Israel.

More than 500 years after Abraham received God's promise of innumerable seed and a kingdom, his descendents had increased to two or three million and were slaves in Egypt. It looked as if the kingdoms of the world had swallowed up God's attempt at a kingdom. But God remembered his promise to Abraham, Isaac, and Jacob and sent Moses to lead them out of bondage and back to the land of Eden (Gen. 2:8-14; 4:16). After escaping Pharaoh, while they were camped before Mt. Sinai, God told Moses to tell the people, "…if ye will obey my voice indeed, and keep my covenant, then ye shall be a peculiar treasure unto me above all people: for all the earth is mine: And ye shall be unto me a **kingdom of priests, and an holy nation**" (Ex. 19:5-6). God was seeking to establish a kingdom upon the earth on that same piece of ground that had been his focus from the beginning — even since before Lucifer inhabited Eden (Ezek. 28:13).

But the land was occupied by descendents of Ham's son, Canaan, whom God had cursed (Gen. 10:10, 15-20; 15:18-21; Ex. 3:8). They had come from the city of Babylon and had brought their Satanic religion with them. They practiced human sacrifice, including their children, and they were filled with homosexuality and even bestiality. God commanded Israel to commit genocide against the inhabitants of the land. On two previous occasions God had acted in such a drastic manner. Both the flood and Sodom and Gomorrah were complete destructions of all souls including women and children and even the animals. This judgment is similar. The people of the land had become wicked beyond repentance and redemption. They were not worthy of living. God wanted to destroy them lest their sin spread. Just like the earth of Noah's day, these Canaanites — descended from Ham's son, Canaan — must be killed to the last child, lest they should give birth to another lost soul.

Another reason for such severe judgment is the same as that which prompted the flood of Noah's day. The flesh of the Canaanites had become corrupted with interbreeding between the sons of God and the daughters of men (Gen. 6:4; Num. 13:33). Note, that the children of Israel did not come as missionaries with a message; they came to be the hand of God in total judgment. It was righteous ethnic cleansing, pure and ugly. God was seeking to establish a kingdom of humans, pure descendents of Adam. It would not do for them to inner breed with the sons of God. The goal was to possess the land and establish "a kingdom of priests, and an holy nation." This was the **kingdom of heaven** emerging in a hostile world.

It sounds crude and barbaric, for many think that the Bible is a book of "peace on earth, good will toward men," but it is not. It is a kingdom book, from start to finish, and until you recognize that fact, it will be a poor book of inspiration that must be selectively handled. When preachers preach from the Old Testament, they pick their stories and treat them as inspirational fables on bravery, faith, courage, honesty, and reaping what you sow. But every time they do so, they are ignoring the context and detail and are only skimming the surface. That is why the modern Christian thinks there is just one spiritual kingdom that is something like a joyful church family all loving each other. They neither read nor believe the book. They use it in selected spots to create a Western religion, sanitized to be made acceptable to modern sensibilities.

So, through brutal military conquest, the nation of Israel becomes heir to that physical kingdom of heaven. The historical books of the Old Testament record the struggle between God's kingdom of heaven and the Devil's earthly kingdoms.

## Joshua conquers.

After Moses died, Joshua led the children of Israel into the land God promised Abraham, including the same land that was once called Eden, the place where Melchizedek was king of Salem over 500 years earlier. The land was then occupied by the descendants of Canaan, son of Ham (Gen. 9:22; 10:6; 11:31, who was the son of Noah. The 400 years that followed the conquest of the Promised Land was a time without any king but God. He ruled the people through Judges who sought the Lord as to his mind. It was a theocracy. The tabernacle continued to be prominent; it was a kingdom of priests — the **kingdom of heaven** in its infancy. The books of Joshua, Judges, and Ruth cover that time period.

## The people choose a king.

For 450 years after Israel left Egypt, they continued as a theocracy. But there came a time when the people were dissatisfied with being ruled from heaven. They wanted an earthly ruler like all other nations around them. They wanted a king to judge them and to go out and fight their battles for them (1 Sam. 8:5-6), so they went to the prophet Samuel and demanded that he seek God in choosing a king. When Samuel took their demands to God, "…the LORD said unto Samuel, Hearken unto the voice of the people in all that they say unto thee: for they have not rejected thee, but **they have rejected me, that I should not reign over them"** (1 Sam. 8:7). So after 450 years of attempting to be "a kingdom of priests, and an holy nation" (Ex. 19:6), they became like all the nations of the world.

God directed Samuel to choose Saul to be their king. He was a delight to all the people, everything they wanted in a king. But they had rejected God as their king, and the **kingdom of heaven** was usurped. Democracy turned a theocracy into a monarchy.

In giving them a king, God warned them that their king would so abuse them that they would cry out to God for relief (1 Sam. 8:11-19). Satan had the kingdom right were he wanted it — not ruled by heaven but ruled by a single earthly potentate. Saul followed his lust and was possessed with devils (1 Sam. 16:14), and in time, he turned to witches for his spiritual guidance (1 Sam. 28:7). There came a day when Israel could no longer defend itself against its enemies. They stood on a plain and suffered verbal abuse from a giant Philistine named Goliath. He was the product of the sons of

God copulating with the daughters of men (Gen. 6:4). He was Satan's answer to the kingdom of heaven. God had destroyed the entire earth to rid it of these creatures, and now the kingdom of heaven was stopped in its tracks by one of these twelve fingered, twelve toed, mixed-species men of renown.

## God chooses his king—David.

Enter David, God's choice for a king. By faith, this young strapling of a shepherd boy accepted the giant's challenge with righteous indignation:

*1 Sam. 17:42* Then said David to the Philistine, Thou comest to me with a sword, and with a spear, and with a shield: but **I come to thee in the name of the LORD of hosts, the God of the armies of Israel,** whom thou hast defied.

46 This day will the LORD deliver thee into mine hand; and I will smite thee, and take thine head from thee; and I will give the carcases of the host of the Philistines this day unto the fowls of the air, and to the wild beasts of the earth; **that all the earth may know that there is a God in Israel.**

47 And all this assembly shall know that **the LORD saveth not with sword and spear: for the battle *is* the LORD'S,** and he will give you into our hands.

About 1000 years after Abraham, God made David king. He sought to know the heart of God and to allow God to rule his people. Under David and his son Solomon the kingdom reached its zenith. God swore that David's throne would endure forever. "I have **made a covenant** with my chosen, I have sworn unto **David** my servant, (v. 4) Thy seed will I establish **for ever**, and build up thy throne to all generations…. (v. 20) I have found David my servant; with my holy oil have I anointed him…. (v. 27) Also I will make him my firstborn, **higher than the kings of the earth**. (v. 29) **His seed also will I make to endure for ever**, and **his throne as the days of heaven**" (Ps. 89:3-29).

But some will say that the promise to David was conditioned upon Israel's obedience. And they will tell us that Christ has taken David's place. But the Scripture goes on to tell us what will happen to the promise if Israel is disobedient. "**If his children forsake my law**, and walk not in my judgments; If they break my statutes, and keep not my commandments; Then will I visit their transgression with the rod, and their iniquity with stripes" (Ps. 89:30-32). Some will say, "See, there. He said he would visit them with stripes. That is why the Jews are suffering and the Church has taken Israel's place." Keep reading. "Nevertheless my lovingkindness will I not utterly take from him, nor suffer my faithfulness to fail. **My covenant will I not break**, nor alter the thing that is gone out of my lips. Once have I sworn by my holiness that I will **not lie unto David. His seed shall endure for ever, and his throne as the sun before me.** It shall be established **for ever** as the moon, and as a faithful witness in heaven" (Ps. 89:33-37). Unless "**forever**" ended in 70 AD, David will be resurrected to sit on the throne in Jerusalem. The kingdom will be established on the earth. Read all of Psalm 89 and get God's perspective on the promised earthly kingdom. And don't tell yourself that Christ is the seed of David and that it is in Christ's spiritual seed that the Davidic promises are fulfilled. You are getting the seed of Abraham and the seed of David mixed up. Romans 4:16 and Galatians 3:16 speak of Abraham's seed, not David's.

David conquered Jerusalem (JeruSalem), the Jebusite city occupied by descendents of Ham and Canaan, and ruled by Melchizedek about 1000 years earlier (Gen. 14:18; 2 Sam. 5:6-10). This was the location where God had chosen to place his name (1 Kings 9:3). This hill became "the hill of the LORD" (Ps. 24:3), "the mount Zion which he loved" (Ps. 78:68; 132:13). It is the place where Jesus was crucified and resurrected, and the place where he will return to the earth in judgment. It will be the location of the capital city of the world throughout eternity. See Ezekiel 34:23-25.

While David and his son Solomon reigned, the **righteous kingdom of heaven** was on the earth in at least one quadrant.

## King Solomon.

When David was old and ready to die, God spoke to him concerning his son Solomon who would take his place as king. "And when thy days be fulfilled, and thou shalt sleep with thy fathers, I will set up thy seed after thee, which shall proceed out of thy bowels, and I will **establish his kingdom**. He shall build an house for my name, and I will **stablish the throne of his kingdom <u>for ever</u>**. I will be his father, and he shall be my son. If he commit iniquity, I will chasten him with the rod of men, and with the stripes of the children of men: **But my mercy shall not depart away from him**, as I took it from Saul, whom I put away before thee. And thine house and thy **kingdom shall be established <u>for ever</u> before thee: thy throne shall be established <u>for ever</u>**" (2 Sam. 7:12-16). God said, *"kingdom forever, kingdom forever,"* and *"throne forever"*. How many times does God have to say *"forever"* for one to believe there **will be** a physical, Davidic kingdom in Jerusalem, forever? Any other view is devoid of simple faith in the Word of God and is an affront to God's integrity. For those of you who seek to dismiss the Davidic prophecies as pertaining to the natural seed of Solomon, note that the above verse also says that the throne of David will endure forever. There is no way to connect David's throne to the Church. The Church is a body, the body of Christ. It is a building, a holy temple of the Lord to be inhabited by God through the Holy Spirit. It is a bride, the Bride of Christ, pure and holy.

The promise God gave to Abraham, to multiply his seed as the sand on the seashore, and to live securely in the land, was well on its way to fulfillment at the end of Solomon's reign.

> *1 Kings 4:20* Judah and Israel were many, as the sand which is by the sea in multitude, eating and drinking, and making merry.

Again we have said already, while David and his son Solomon were reigning over Israel, the kingdom of heaven was in place on the earth in at least one place.

## The Kingdom splits.

The kingdom was especially glorious under Solomon, but when he died, his son Rehoboam took over the throne. He raised taxes and threatened the people with cruel burdens (2 Chron. 10:14). The ten northern tribes broke away from the two southern tribes of Judah and Benjamin, and, with Jeroboam as their king, established their own religion around the gods of the Canaanites. The kingdom was split in about 931 B. C., and the crown of David remained with the two southern tribes, which were jointly called Judah. For the next 209 years, the two factions were in nearly constant warfare. In their first big battle, the northern tribes (called Israel) lost 500,000 of their best men in one battle (2 Chron. 13:1-18).

In 722 B.C., Israel (the ten northern tribes) was defeated by Assyria and carried away to be slaves in that foreign land. Judah continued to struggle along until 586 B. C. when they too were defeated by Babylon and carried into captivity. Notwithstanding, God gave strong assurance that the kingdom still belonged to David (1 Kings 15:4-6). The prophets had predicted this captivity, and Jeremiah said that it would last 70 years (Jer. 25:11-12). While Judah was in captivity, the people said, "The **crown is fallen from our head:** woe unto us, that we have sinned!" (Lamentations 5:16). Hosea had also predicted, "For the children of Israel shall **abide many days without a king**, and without a prince, and without a sacrifice, and without an image, and without an ephod, and without teraphim" (Hosea 3:4).

The entire issue is one of the crown, of the kingdom. It should be clear. The message was not one of personal salvation, as is preached in the gospel of the kingdom of God. It is about a nation, a king, and a piece of land.

## Israel would be scattered among the nations.

The Scriptures had long predicted that if Israel did not obey God, they would be thrown out of the land. In Deuteronomy 31:16, God informed Moses that after his death there would come a time when the children of Israel would "go a whoring after the gods of the strangers of the land, whither they go to be among them, and will forsake me, and break my covenant which I have made with them." Moses relayed God's words to the people, "For I know thy rebellion, and thy stiff neck: behold, while I am yet alive with you this day, ye have been rebellious against the LORD; and how much more after my death? Gather unto me all the elders of your tribes, and your officers, that I may speak these words in their ears, and call heaven and earth to record against them. For I know that after my death ye will utterly corrupt *yourselves*, and turn aside from the way which I have commanded you; and evil will befall you in the latter days; because ye will do evil in the sight of the LORD, to provoke him to anger through the work of your hands" (Deut. 31:27-29). Then God predicts his response to their prophesied rebellion: "I said, I would **scatter them into corners,** I would make the remembrance of them to cease from among men" (Deut. 32:26).

Furthermore, God had later warned King Solomon:

> *1 Kings 9:6-9* But if ye shall at all turn from following me, ye or your children, and will not keep my commandments and my statutes which I have set before you, but go and serve other gods, and worship them:
>
> 7 **Then will I cut off Israel out of the land which I have given them**; and this house, which I have hallowed for my name, will I cast out of my sight; and Israel shall be a proverb and a byword among all people:
>
> 8 And at this house, which is high, every one that passeth by it shall be astonished, and shall hiss; and they shall say, Why hath the LORD done thus unto this land, and to this house?
>
> 9 And they shall answer, Because they forsook the LORD their God, who brought forth their fathers out of the land of Egypt, and have taken hold upon other gods, and have worshipped them, and served them: therefore hath the LORD brought upon them all this evil.

It is passages like the above, prophesying of Israel's being cast off if they forsake God, which fuel the common view today that, because of Jewish unbelief, God is through with them as a nation — forever!

## Israel will be gathered.

But the prophecies **don't** end with Israel remaining in exile and disfavor. The prophet Ezekiel also foretold that Israel would be removed from their land for a time, but would also be restored in the last days, with David himself resurrected to sit as king over Jerusalem.

Ezekiel is writing of David over 400 years after David's death.

> *Ezekiel 37:21* And say unto them, Thus saith the Lord GOD; Behold, I will take the **children of Israel** [*That is not the Church*] from among the heathen, whither they be gone, and will gather them on every side, and bring them **into their own land** [*That land is Israel*];
>
> 22 And I will make them one nation in the land upon the mountains of Israel; and **one king shall be king to them all**: and they shall be no more two nations [*Israel and Judah*], neither shall they be divided into two kingdoms any more at all:
>
> 23 Neither shall they defile themselves any more with their idols, nor with their detestable things, nor with any of their transgressions: but I will save them out of all their dwellingplaces, wherein they have sinned, and will cleanse them: so shall they be my people, and I will be their God.
>
> 24 And **David my servant shall be king over them**; and they all shall have one shepherd: they shall also walk in my judgments, and observe my statutes, and do them.
>
> 25 And they shall **dwell in the land that I have given unto Jacob my servant,** wherein your fathers have dwelt; and they shall dwell therein, even they, and their children, and their children's children **for ever: and my servant David shall be their prince for ever**.

Remember, David had long since been dead (more than 400 years) when Ezekiel made this prophecy. The Bible is not a "crystal ball" that only pretends to predict the future. King David (not Jesus) **will be** resurrected to sit on the throne in Jerusalem (not heaven) and reign over both halves of what was then a divided kingdom (Ezek. 37:19-28).

Observe carefully, verse 25 states plainly that Israel will return to their homeland and "**dwell in the land I have given unto Jacob…wherein your fathers dwelt** [*That can't be other than on the* *earth*.], and it will last **for ever,** and **David will be a prince for ever**." Could God say it any plainer? If his plans were to gather Israel from the nations and place them back on the same piece of dirt that he gave to Jacob, and resurrect David to sit on a throne in Jerusalem, and it would be a kingdom that would last for all eternity, how else could he possibly say it so you would believe it? Where are the little children whom Jesus said would believe and enter in?

Isaiah adds his witness to the prophecies of Israel's future restoration. "But Israel shall be saved in the LORD with an **everlasting salvation**: ye shall not be ashamed nor confounded **world without end**" (Isa. 45:17). Israel, not the Church, will be saved as a nation in a **world without end**.

## God is concerned with earthly kingdoms.

Many Bible commentators have taken it upon themselves to decide that an earthly kingdom is much too carnal to be God's goal. Their concept of God's program is fluffy and ethereal — heavenly and aesthetic. But the Bible says it so plainly: "For the **kingdom** is the LORD'S: and he is the **governor among the nations**" (Ps. 22:28). Though his throne is in the heavens, God rules over the affairs of men. Notice above, God's kingdom is expressed by his governing on the earth **among the nations.** "The LORD hath prepared his throne in the heavens; and **his kingdom ruleth over all**" (Ps. 103:19). "How great are his signs! and how mighty are his wonders! his **kingdom is an everlasting kingdom, and his dominion is from generation to generation**" (Daniel 4:3). In the passage, God's *everlasting kingdom* is measured by dominion from **generation to generation** (consecutive life spans), which unquestionably identifies his kingdom with natural life on the earth. It is crystal clear: God is concerned with the kingdoms of men. God is not heaven minded; He is **earth** minded, and has been since he first instituted a kingdom in the heavens (on the earth — the earth being a part of the heavens) composed of the sons of men.

## God gives the kingdom to a heathen nation.

We left off with Israel being scattered among the nations — Babylon and Assyria. We will now look at what happened to the **kingdom of heaven** during that time.

Though Satan is the **god of this world** (2 Cor. 4:4), and he does attempt to control and direct the affairs of men (Eph. 2:2), it was God, not Satan, who made Nebuchadnezzar king over Babylon and then humbled him with a dream in which angels declared that "the most High ruleth in the **kingdom of men**, and **giveth it to whomsoever he will**, and setteth up over it the basest of men" (Dan. 4:17; Rom.13:1).

Jeremiah also wrote concerning this Nebuchadnezzar, king of Babylon, saying that God had appointed this heathen king to rule over all the kingdoms of men. As an act of judgment on the sons of Jacob, God arranged for the kingdom to be ruled by a base and proud man who did not know God. "And now have I **given all these lands into the hand of Nebuchadnezzar** the king of Babylon, my servant; and the **beasts of the field have I given him also to serve him**" (Jeremiah 27:6). *Notice the last phrase about God giving Nebuchadnezzar authority over the animal kingdom.* This is revealing in the extreme! Remember, God gave the very first man, Adam, dominion over the earth and the animals (Gen. 1:26-28), and now God conveys that identical dominion to Nebuchadnezzar, a wicked ruler. It is a clear statement that this heathen king was given full earthly dominion. God handed over the natural dominion of the kingdom of heaven to this heathen idol worshipper.

When God assigned rulership over this earthly kingdom, it was with his complete commitment and support. God said he would go so far as to punish any nation that did not submit to Nebuchadnezzar. That would be like God supporting Hitler or Saddam Hussein to accomplish his purposes in today's world of nations. God had a purpose to execute in the nations of Jeremiah's and Daniel's day, and he used this heathen kingdom to fulfill it. Sometimes his purpose is judgment, the judgment of God against both sides by means of war. God maintains a balance of power between just and unjust nations and punishes evil in anticipation of the day when he will take the kingdoms by force and set up his own theocracy — after his Son's second coming (Rev. 11:15).

## Daniel predicted four world kingdoms.

After Nebuchadnezzar was fully established in his kingdom, God gave him a dream and interpreted it for him through his servant Daniel. Beginning with Babylon, there would be four world kingdoms to arise, each one after the other, yet established on the previous. Next would be Medo-Persia, followed by Greece and then Rome. Each kingdom came to power by subduing the former kingdom and ended up possessing basically the same landmass, with minimal expansion each time. In another vision and divine interpretation we find that the fourth kingdom is different from the former three in that it mutates from a single kingdom into an incompatible mixture, divided ten ways. This and subsequent prophecies end by telling Nebuchadnezzar that the God of heaven will ultimately **set up** a kingdom by force of violence against all four kingdoms embodied in the final ten-division kingdom. The "rock" kingdom (the K of H) will then **stand for ever**.

We know from this prophecy that the **kingdom of heaven** will be **set up** as Christ violently conquers the nations that were once comprised of the old Babylonian, Medo-Persian, Grecian, and Roman empires.

> *Daniel 2:36* This is the dream; and we will tell the interpretation thereof before the king.
> 37 Thou, O king, art a king of kings: for the God of heaven hath **given thee a kingdom**, power, and strength, and glory.
> 38 And wheresoever the children of men dwell, the **beasts of the field and the fowls of the heaven hath he given into thine hand**, and hath made thee **ruler over them all**. Thou art this head of gold.
> 39 And after thee shall arise another **kingdom** inferior to thee, and another **third kingdom** of brass, which shall bear rule over all the earth.
> 40 And the **fourth kingdom** shall be strong as iron: forasmuch as iron breaketh in pieces and subdueth all things: and as iron that breaketh all these, shall it break in pieces and bruise.
> 41 And whereas thou sawest the feet and toes, part of potters' clay, and part of iron, the **kingdom** shall be divided; but there shall be in it of the strength of the iron, forasmuch as thou sawest the iron mixed with miry clay.
> 42 And as the toes of the feet were part of iron, and part of clay, so the **kingdom** shall be partly strong, and partly broken.
> 43 And whereas thou sawest iron mixed with miry clay, they shall mingle themselves with the seed of men: but they shall not cleave one to another, even as iron is not mixed with clay.
> 44 And in the days of these kings shall the **God of heaven set up a kingdom, which shall never be destroyed: and the kingdom shall not be left to other people, but it shall <u>break in pieces and consume all these kingdoms</u>, and it shall stand <u>for ever</u>**.

Later, Daniel interprets another dream for Nebuchadnezzar. The king had become proud and boastful, thinking that it was by his might alone that he was able to become chief potentate of the world. The dream reveals that God will cause him to become insane for seven years until he admits that "the **heavens do rule** and that **the most High giveth it** [*the kingdom*] **to whomsoever he will**."

> *Daniel 4:26* And whereas they commanded to leave the stump of the tree roots; **thy kingdom** shall be sure unto thee, after that thou shalt have known that the **heavens do rule**.
> 27 Wherefore, O king, let my counsel be acceptable unto thee, and break off thy sins by righteousness, and thine iniquities by shewing mercy to the poor; if it may be a lengthening of thy tranquillity. All this came upon the king Nebuchadnezzar.
> 29 At the end of twelve months he walked in the palace of the **kingdom of Babylon**.
> 30 The king spake, and said, Is not this great Babylon, that I have built for the house of the **kingdom by the might of my power**, and for the honour of my majesty?
> 31 While the word was in the king's mouth, there fell a voice from heaven, saying, O king Nebuchadnezzar, to thee it is spoken; **The kingdom is departed from thee**.
> 32 And they shall drive thee from men, and thy dwelling shall be with the beasts of the field: they shall make thee to eat grass as oxen, and seven times shall pass over thee, until thou

know that the **most High ruleth in the kingdom of men, and giveth it to whomsoever he will.**

33 The same hour was the thing fulfilled upon Nebuchadnezzar: and he was driven from men, and did eat grass as oxen, and his body was wet with the dew of heaven, till his hairs were grown like eagles' feathers, and his nails like birds' claws.

## Daniel's vision.

*Daniel 7:1* In the first year of Belshazzar king of Babylon Daniel had a dream and visions of his head upon his bed: then he wrote the dream, and told the sum of the matters.

13 I saw in the night visions, and, behold, **one like the Son of man came with the clouds of heaven,** and came to the Ancient of days, and they brought him near before him.

14 And there was **given him dominion, and glory, and a kingdom**, that all people, nations, and languages, should serve him: **his dominion is an everlasting dominion**, which shall not pass away, **and his kingdom that which shall not be destroyed.**

Then the angel gave Daniel the interpretation of his vision.

17 These great beasts, **which are four, are four kings**, which shall arise out of the earth.

18 But the saints of the most High shall **take the kingdom, and possess the kingdom <u>for ever, even for ever and ever.</u>**

Daniel asked the angel about the ten divisions of the fourth world kingdom — the one that will exist just prior to when the kingdom from heaven is set up.

23 Thus he said, The fourth beast shall be the **fourth kingdom upon earth**, which shall be diverse from all kingdoms, and shall devour the whole earth, and shall tread it down, and break it in pieces.

24 And the **ten horns out of this kingdom are ten kings** that shall arise: and another shall rise after them; and he shall be diverse from the first, and he shall subdue three kings.

25 And he shall speak great words against the most High, and shall wear out the saints of the most High, and think to change times and laws: and they shall be given into his hand until a time and times and the dividing of time.

26 But the judgment shall sit, and they shall **take away his dominion**, to consume and to destroy it unto the end.

27 And the **kingdom and dominion, and the greatness of the kingdom under the whole heaven**, shall be given to the people of the saints of the most High, whose **kingdom is an everlasting kingdom,** and **all dominions shall serve and obey him**.

If the Bible is written to convey intelligent concepts, it must be admitted that the above passage teaches that all earthly kingdoms will be given to the saints (Israel) who will possess the kingdom forever. There is nothing spiritual about this. It is political and earthy. It is the **kingdom of heaven** ruled by the people of the **kingdom of God**.

## God gives the kingdom to Persia.

Daniel was still in Babylon when the second kingdom, Medo-Persia, conquered Babylon. The God who sets into power whom he will over kingdoms, removed Nebuchadnezzar as Babylon fell to Persia. After the heathen king, Cyrus of Persia, took the throne, he read the prophecies (written 200 years earlier) of his involvement in the rebuilding of the temple and responded accordingly.

*2 Chronicles 36:22-23* Now in the first year of Cyrus king of Persia, that the word of the LORD spoken by the mouth of Jeremiah might be accomplished, the LORD stirred up the spirit of Cyrus king of Persia, that he made a proclamation throughout all his kingdom, and put it also in writing, saying,

*23* Thus saith Cyrus king of Persia, **All the kingdoms of the earth hath the LORD God of heaven given me**; and he hath charged me to build him an house in Jerusalem, which is in Judah.

King Darius learned his lesson early and made a decree to his entire kingdom, declaring that the God of Daniel was king of all the earth, with a dominion that would never be destroyed.

*Daniel 6:25-26* Then king Darius wrote unto all people, nations, and languages, that dwell in all the earth; Peace be multiplied unto you.

26 I make a decree, That in every dominion of my kingdom men tremble and fear before the God of Daniel: for he is the living God, and stedfast for ever, and **his kingdom that which shall not be destroyed, and his dominion shall be even unto the end**.

## The last heathen king—Antichrist.

Much later, Daniel received additional revelation concerning the kingdom in the last days. One whom we later identify as the Antichrist will obtain the kingdom by flatteries.

*Daniel 11:21* And in his estate shall stand up a vile person, to whom they shall not give the **honour of the kingdom**: but he shall come in peaceably, and **obtain the kingdom** by flatteries.

Daniel asked the angel when the end would come. The angel indicated it would be much later. Many wicked and righteous persons would come and go. The wicked would fail to understand the revelations he had recorded, but the wise would understand about the kingdoms. The book of Daniel is about world kingdoms, as readily seen by a simple reading. In the book of Daniel, the word *kingdom* is found 59 times. Twelve of those fifty-nine are references to God's physical kingdom (the **kingdom of heaven**) taking the place of, or ruling in, the kingdoms of men.

*Daniel 12:8* And I heard, but I understood not: then said I, O my Lord, what shall be the end of these things?

9 And he said, Go thy way, Daniel: for the **words are closed up and sealed till the time of the end**.

10 Many shall be purified, and made white, and tried; but the wicked shall do wickedly: and **none of the wicked shall understand; but the wise shall understand**.

13 But go thou thy way till the end be: for thou shalt rest, and stand in thy lot at the end of the days. .

The prophet Zephaniah revealed God's **determination to gather all nations** into a war of judgment, where he will destroy their armies and set up his kingdom in their place.

*Zephaniah 3:8* Therefore wait ye upon me, saith the LORD, until the day that I rise up to the prey: for my determination is to **gather the nations, that I may assemble the kingdoms**, to pour upon them mine indignation, even all my fierce anger: for all the earth shall be devoured with the fire of my jealousy.

9 For then will I turn to the people a pure language, that they may all call upon the name of the LORD, to serve him with one consent.

Haggai confirms the other prophets and records the passage that will be quoted in the book of Hebrews. It is clear that the contention is for the kingdom of men. God has determined that the kingdoms of this earth will be run from heaven.

*Haggai 2:21* Speak to Zerubbabel, governor of Judah, saying, I will shake the **heavens** and the earth;

22 And I will **overthrow the throne of kingdoms**, and I will **destroy the strength of the kingdoms** of the heathen;

*Hebrews 12:26* Whose voice then shook the earth: but now he hath promised, saying, Yet once more I shake not the earth only, but also heaven.

27 And this *word*, Yet once more, signifieth the removing of those things that are shaken, as of things that are made, that those things which cannot be shaken may remain.

28 Wherefore we **receiving a kingdom which cannot be moved,** let us have grace, whereby we may serve God acceptably with reverence and godly fear:

Isaiah prophesized of the **child** Jesus who would be born for the purpose of establishing an everlasting kingdom; and, to be specific, he tells us that it will **not** be in heaven but **upon the earthly throne of his "father" David.**

*Isaiah 9:6* For unto us a child is born, unto us a son is given: and the **government** shall be upon his shoulder: and his name shall be called Wonderful, Counsellor, The mighty God, The everlasting Father, The Prince of Peace.

7 Of the **increase of his government** and peace there shall be no end, **upon the throne of David, and upon his kingdom,** to order it, and to establish it with judgment and with justice **from henceforth even for ever**. The zeal of the LORD of hosts will perform this.

Luke records the words of the angel making his announcement to Mary that her child will sit on the **throne of David** and reign over, not the Church, but the **house of Jacob**. God has taken very great pains to make it so crystal clear that not even a theologian or doctor of divinity could miss it. He adds that this kingdom will last **for ever**, and for the real dummies, he adds again: **there shall be no end**.

*Luke 1:31* And, behold, thou shalt conceive in thy womb, and bring forth a son, and shalt call his name JESUS.

32 He shall be great, and shall be called the Son of the Highest: and the Lord God shall give unto him the **throne of his father David**:

33 And he shall **reign over the house of Jacob for ever**; and of **his kingdom there shall be no end**.

# New Testament Kingdom Passages

You have just reviewed a sampling of kingdom passages from the Old Testament. Now you should know what the Bible means when it speaks of a *kingdom*.

## First mention of *kingdom* in the New Testament.

The people of Israel had been weaned on the milk of these prophecies for 1500 years. Even the coming of John the Baptist was well prophesied (Isa. 40:3-6; Mal. 3:1). He was expected, and his message of a coming kingdom was expected. As you read this first mention of *kingdom* in the New Testament, ask, "What did the Jews understand when John said, **the kingdom of heaven is at hand?**" According to the Word of God, what SHOULD they have understood him to be saying? If you still think he was simply offering a refreshing spiritual experience, you **must go back and read the Word again!** Now, read the first mention of the word *kingdom* in the New Testament.

> *Matthew 3:1-2* In those days came John the Baptist, preaching in the wilderness of Judæa,
> And saying, Repent ye: for the **kingdom of heaven** is at hand.

If you were to take a concordance and, starting in Genesis, read all 236 occurrences in the Old Testament of the word *kingdom* and then continue through the first three times it appears in the New Testament, you would readily understand what John the Baptist meant by, "the kingdom of heaven is at hand." It was a simple announcement that the *long-awaited Jewish kingdom,* first promised to Abraham, confirmed to Isaac, Jacob, David, and to all Israel, was about to be instituted in the nation of Israel and at Jerusalem, the capital city.

## Second mention of the word kingdom.

The second time *kingdom* is mentioned in the New Testament, Satan offers the kingdoms of the world to Christ.

> *Matthew 4:8-9* Again, the devil taketh him up into an exceeding high mountain, and sheweth him all the **kingdoms of the world,** and the glory of them; And saith unto him, **All these things will I give thee**, if thou wilt fall down and worship me.

Satan is not stupid. He can read the Bible better than we can. He was there when it was spoken and written. He had four thousand years to prepare for the temptation of this "last Adam" — the second man, Jesus Christ. Remember, he had successfully tempted Adam, Noah, Abraham, Moses, Saul, David, and millions of others. He now had the opportunity to tempt the Promised Seed, the one who was predicted to bruise his head. The temptations he would place before Christ would have to be tailored to Christ's perspective and vulnerabilities. It would have been foolish to offer something to Jesus that he did not want. There would be no temptation in it, and the Bible **does** state emphatically that Jesus was "driven" into the wilderness by the Holy Spirit "to be tempted of the devil."

Satan took Jesus up to a high vantage point and showed him **the kingdoms of the world and the glory of them**. Why would Jesus be tempted to fall down and worship Satan in exchange for the **kingdoms of the world** if heaven is all that matters? If Jesus had come to set up only a spiritual kingdom (**kingdom of God**), Satan's offer would have been meaningless — laughable. There would be nothing to give. But Jesus was tempted because Satan offered him something he wanted — the earthly throne.

Satan could offer the kingdoms because, at that time, the world's kingdoms were directed and controlled by Satan. They both wanted the same thing. Satan wanted the kingdoms because he wanted all the glory. Jesus wanted the kingdoms because he wanted to restore heaven's glory upon man. Satan wanted the kingdoms so he could take something from them; Jesus wanted the kingdoms so he could give something to them.

> *Luke 4:5* And the devil, taking him up into an high mountain, shewed unto him all the kingdoms of the world in a moment of time.

6 And the devil said unto him, All this power will I give thee, and the glory of them: for that is **delivered unto me**; and to whomsoever I will I give it.

Jesus rejected Satan's offer, not because he did not value the kingdoms, but rather because he was not willing to pay the price of disobedience. Furthermore, Jesus had two messages — two kingdoms, and he knew that the way to the **kingdom of heaven** was through the **kingdom of God**. Jesus would come away from the temptation to first publicly preach in Galilee, "Repent, for the kingdom of heaven is at hand" (Matt. 4:17). But he also instructed them, "But seek ye **first** the **kingdom of God**, and his righteousness; and **all these things shall be added** unto you" (Matt. 6:33). He had lived what he preached.

## The third mention of the word kingdom.

Matthew quotes the leading part of a very well-known prophecy from Isaiah 9:1-7.

*Matt. 4:14* That it might be fulfilled which was spoken by Esaias the prophet [*Isa. 9:1-2*], saying,

15 The land of Zabulon, and the land of Nephthalim, *by* the way of the sea, beyond Jordan, Galilee of the Gentiles;

16 The people which sat in darkness saw great light; and to them which sat in the region and shadow of death light is sprung up.

17 From that time Jesus began to preach, and to say, Repent: for **the kingdom of heaven is at hand**.

As was their manner in both speaking and writing, Matthew quoted only that portion of the prophecy by which the whole was remembered. His Jewish hearers were so familiar with the text that all he need do was make reference to the first lines, and they would remember the content of the passage in its entirety. Matthew quotes only Isaiah 9:1-2, but, the prophecy continues through verse 7, where it reads:

*Isaiah 9:6* For unto us a child is born, unto us a son is given: and the government shall be upon his shoulder: and his name shall be called Wonderful, Counsellor, The mighty God, The everlasting Father, The Prince of Peace.

7 Of the increase of *his* **government** and peace *there shall be* no end, **upon the throne of David**, and **upon his kingdom,** to order it, and to establish it with judgment and with justice from henceforth even for ever. The zeal of the LORD of hosts will perform this.

So, in this third mention of the word *kingdom* in the New Testament, Matthew records that Jesus, who has just turned down the Devil's offer of the kingdoms of the world, has come to remind the Jews of the prophecy of Messiah coming as a **child born** and as a **son given,** whose name is **The mighty God,** who will increase his **government, upon the throne of David, and upon <u>his</u> kingdom, forever.** And we are assured that it will indeed come to pass because **the LORD of hosts will perform** it. Therefore, Jesus says to the Jews, Repent, for **the kingdom of heaven is at hand.** In other words, get right with God, for the time of the fulfillment of this prophecy has come, for the **kingdom of heaven**, the kingdom of our father David, the government of God, is about to come to the earth.

Reviewing the first three mentions of the word *kingdom* in the New Testament, we are astounded at the beauty and perfection of the Word of God. John comes preaching some six months before Jesus and says, Repent (get your life right), for the long-awaited kingdom is at hand. After Jesus' public baptism by John, the Holy Spirit drives Jesus into the wilderness to be tempted of the Devil forty days. The Devil, knowing Jesus has come to set up the kingdom on this earth, offers him an immediate transfer of headship over the kingdoms. Jesus rejects the offer and goes down to the masses to make his own announcement that the prophecy is fulfilled. Messiah, the mighty God, is come to establish the throne of David and his kingdom forever. And he, too, tells them to repent, for the **kingdom of heaven** is at hand. What a marvelously complete picture of the **kingdom of heaven** we are given in just these first three passages!

# Thy kingdom come.

Many people have prayed what is called "The Lord's Prayer" and had no idea what they were actually praying. Jesus was just commencing his ministry when he taught them how to pray the will of God. **Thy kingdom come...in earth.** This kingdom was to be **in the earth**.

> *Matthew 6:10* Thy kingdom come. Thy will be done in earth, as it is in heaven.

The **kingdom of heaven** is a natural, earthly kingdom as seen by the fact that at present, it can be taken by violence. John came with the declaration that if Israel would repent, the kingdom would be set up. Rome and the Jews had conspired to prevent the earth from being ruled by heaven. They used violence to suppress the rule of God through the nation of Israel. John lost his head to **the violent** men in authority who were **taking the kingdom by force**. Jesus, the king, eventually died by an act of calculated violence perpetrated by two kingdoms — Rome and Israel. With the king of the kingdom of heaven dead, there could be no kingdom from heaven to replace the earthly kingdoms.

> *Matthew 11:12* And from the days of John the Baptist until now the **kingdom of heaven suffereth violence**, and the violent take it by force.

If the disciples held a misconception as to the nature of the **kingdom of heaven**, after three years under the daily teaching of Jesus, you would expect them to be clear on the matter. What they believed was manifested when the mother of two of the disciples came to Jesus with a request that her two sons be given the position to sit with him on the throne in his coming kingdom. Jesus did not tell her that her concept of the kingdom was flawed. He told her that the privilege of sitting on his right hand and his left would be given to the ones for whom it was prepared. His answer demonstrated that he accepted her suppositions about the literal nature of the coming earthly kingdom. Someone would sit on his right and his left when he sat on the throne ruling the earth, but he could not guarantee that it would be her sons.

> *Matthew 20:21* And he said unto her, What wilt thou? She saith unto him, Grant that these my two sons may **sit, the one on thy right hand, and the other on the left, in thy kingdom**.
> 22 But Jesus answered and said, Ye know not what ye ask. Are ye able to drink of the cup that I shall drink of, and to be baptized with the baptism that I am baptized with? They say unto him, We are able.
> 23 And he saith unto them, Ye shall drink indeed of my cup, and be baptized with the baptism that I am baptized with: but to sit on my right hand, and on my left, **is not mine to give, but it shall be given to them for whom it is prepared of my Father.**

When Jesus was at the very end of his ministry, a few days before he would be crucified, he presented himself to Jerusalem in the manner that was predicted by the prophets. The people recognized the Messianic elements of his actions and responded appropriately, hailing him as Messiah coming to sit on David's throne in Jerusalem.

> *Mark 11:9* And they that went before, and they that followed, cried, saying, Hosanna; Blessed is he that cometh in the name of the Lord.
> **10 Blessed be the kingdom of our father David**, that cometh in the name of the Lord: Hosanna in the highest.

After his resurrection, Jesus spent forty days teaching the disciples about the **kingdom of God**. If they still held misconceptions about the nature of the kingdoms, surely the resurrected Christ would have corrected their views during that forty-day seminar on the **kingdom of God**. Right before his ascension back to heaven, the disciples asked him if he was going to immediately restore the kingdom in Israel. His answer granted their assumption that there will indeed be a literal kingdom established in Jerusalem at some point in the future.

> *Acts 1:3* To whom also he shewed himself alive after his passion by many infallible proofs, being seen of them forty days, and **speaking of the things pertaining to the kingdom of God**:
> 6 When they therefore were come together, they asked of him, saying, Lord, wilt thou at this time **restore again the kingdom to Israel**?

7 And he said unto them, It is not for you to know the times or the seasons, which the Father hath put in his own power.

## No King but Caesar.

Pilate asked Jesus, "Art thou the **King** of the Jews? And Jesus said unto him, Thou sayest" (Matt. 27:11). Jesus' answer was, in effect, "I am as you say, the **king** of the Jews."

When Jesus was crucified, the inscription over him was, "THIS IS JESUS **THE KING OF THE JEWS**" (Matt. 27:37).

When Pilate placed Jesus before the people to give them a chance to determine his fate, "…they cried out, Away with him, away with him, crucify him. Pilate saith unto them, Shall I crucify your **King?** The chief priests answered, **We have no king but Caesar**" (John 19:15). With their answer, they shut the door to the kingdom of heaven. They had rejected God's king and chosen an idolatrous heathen in his place.

We will say it again. The Bible is a kingdom book from start to finish. To miss that fact, or to allegorize the kingdoms into personal, spiritual experience, is to miss the most basic message God ever gave to man.

# Answering the critics

The many Old Testament texts that we have just covered in the previous pages are powerful and irrefutable. If you are not learned in Scripture and Bible doctrines, you may be amazed that something so plain could be so little understood. But unbelief and pride have found a way for "educated" believers to dismiss all that evidence in one bold move. It has been done so often that they can do it with straight faces, quoting a hundred "Bible Scholars", many of them famous and influential. That method of emasculation is called the *allegorical interpretation of Scripture*. It is an approach to literature that none would dare use on any other book. Only "religious scholars" could get away with something so foreign to normal literary practice, and only religious people, living in an ozone atmosphere of high, gullible faith, would have allowed themselves to be duped to the degree that they could accept the allegorical method of interpretation, which can only result in the enfeeblement of God's message to them.

The proponents of the allegorical method like to characterize any other approach to interpretation as "literal", and then proceed to prove that the Bible has figures of speech that cannot be taken literally without indulging in the ridiculous. But this is obviously a "straw man," based on the fact that it is easy to show that one cannot take every word of any piece of literature in a completely literal sense. All writings abound with metaphors and similes, including Scripture. The evening newscaster says without blinking, "The Senate floor was left bloody today." Certainly, it is figurative language to say that Jesus is the *Lamb of God*, the *door*, and that he is *bread from heaven* that must be eaten for one to have eternal life. But admitting the use of figures of speech, does not thereby grant a license to turn any portion of Scripture that conflicts with one's unbelief into the shadowy world of allegory.

We are not limited to either the allegorical or the strictly literal methods. The correct method of reading and interpreting any writing, including the Bible, is called the *normal grammatical approach*. We allow every word its normal meaning, every phrase its obvious and common interpretation, and every paragraph the respect of historical authenticity. In other words, we treat the text with the same respect that we would any historical writing, assuming that it has some purpose higher than a collection of inspiring religious platitudes.

So thoroughly has the allegorical method obscured the obvious truth of Scripture that less than one percent of all preachers and Bible teachers are even aware of the differences in the kingdoms (Ezek. 20:49; Prov. 26:7; Matt. 13:13-15). *Understanding the difference between these two kingdoms is the key to understanding the entire Bible.* Until you see this truth, the Bible will seem to be a mysterious and difficult collection of allegories. When the layman comes to a full knowledge of the eight kingdoms, especially these two most critical kingdoms, his understanding of the Bible immediately exceeds that of many pastors and college professors who read both Hebrew and Greek and hold a doctorate in Biblical Studies.

## God is not through with Israel.

There are many teachers who feel comfortable with the assumption that, for 4,000 years, God would make promises in such clear language, which were understood by all to be literal, and then suddenly drop the entire prophetic program with all its glorious promises and miraculous prophecies. It is one thing for God to speak in mysteries so as to conceal the truth from unbelievers (and he even says so when he does), but for God to speak so as to deceive those who believe in him would be dark and cruel indeed.

The barrier that keeps most expositors over on the allegorical side is their firm commitment to disallow national Israel (ethnic Jews) a continuing place in God's program; but God is not through with Israel. In the following passages, God makes a point of committing himself to the geographical location of the kingdom. How could the God of Abraham, Isaac, and Jacob, and the God of David and Solomon renege on what he has promised — to return the Jews to their land and restore the kingdom promised to Abraham, Isaac, Jacob, and David?

*Genesis 15:13* And he said unto Abram, Know of a surety that thy seed shall be a stranger in a land that is not theirs, and shall serve them; and they shall afflict them four hundred years;

14 And also that nation, whom they shall serve, will I judge: and afterward shall they come out with great substance. [*This was literally fulfilled*]

15 And thou shalt go to thy fathers in peace; thou shalt be buried in a good old age.

16 But in the fourth generation they shall come hither again: for the iniquity of the Amorites is not yet full. [*Again, literally fulfilled*]

17 And it came to pass, that, when the sun went down, and it was dark, behold a smoking furnace, and a burning lamp that passed between those pieces.

18 In the same day the LORD made a covenant with Abram, saying, **Unto thy seed have I given this land, from the river of Egypt unto the great river, the river Euphrates:**

*Genesis 28:13* And, behold, the LORD stood above it, and said, I am the LORD God of Abraham thy father, and the God of Isaac: **the land whereon thou liest, to thee will I give it, and to thy seed;**

In the following passage, God swears that his covenant with Israel to inherit the land is <u>unconditional</u> and as sure as his promise to never again destroy the earth with water. God's logic is that, if you can trust me to literally keep my word to Noah, then you can trust me to literally keep my word to Israel. Imagine a scenario where it again rains for thirty-eight days and thirty-eight nights, and three men are left clinging to the last Himalayan peak. God appears and says, "You've got just thirty-six more hours before you go under water." One of the men is a seminary graduate, and he says, "But God, you promised you would never again destroy the world with water. You lied to us!" And God says, "You know that my prophecies are not literal. They are just given to communicate spiritual truth. What I meant was that I give eternal life to all who come to me, and they will never come under condemnation. After all, you took my promises to Israel figuratively; why not my promises to Noah? By the way, about this thing called *eternal life* that you guys have taken so literally…" That is not the God revealed in the Bible.

*Isaiah 54:5* For thy Maker is thine husband; the LORD of hosts is his name; and thy Redeemer the Holy One of Israel; The God of the whole earth shall he be called.

6 For the LORD hath called thee as a woman forsaken and grieved in spirit, and a wife of youth, when thou wast refused, saith thy God.

7 **For a small moment have I forsaken thee; but with great mercies will I gather thee.**

8 In a little wrath I hid my face from thee for a moment; but with **everlasting kindness** will I have mercy on thee, saith the LORD thy Redeemer.

9 For this is as the waters of Noah unto me: **for as I have sworn that the waters of Noah should no more go over the earth; so have I sworn that I would not be wroth with thee, nor rebuke thee.**

10 For the mountains shall depart, and the hills be removed; **but my kindness shall not depart from thee, neither shall the covenant of my peace be removed**, saith the LORD that hath mercy on thee.

Every Bible teacher of any persuasion will point to the above passage for assurance that the world will never again be destroyed by a great flood, but when the same assurances are given concerning the kingdom of Israel, suddenly God is speaking figuratively of the Church. By what right or by what Biblical example do they make such an unfounded claim? *There is none!*

The following passage is an awesome commitment on God's part. It contains prophecies that have yet to be fulfilled. Israel will be gathered back to the original land grant, and the land will again be married — a permanent union. Jerusalem (not the Church) will be a praise <u>in the earth forever</u> (not in heaven).

*Isaiah 62:1* For Zion's sake will I not hold my peace, and for Jerusalem's sake I will not rest, until the righteousness thereof go forth as brightness, and the salvation thereof as a lamp that burneth.

2 And the **Gentiles shall see thy righteousness,** [This passage assumes a Jew-Gentile distinction.] and all kings thy glory: and thou shalt be called by a new name, which the mouth of the LORD shall name.

3 Thou shalt also be a crown of glory in the hand of the LORD, and a royal diadem in the hand of thy God.

4 **Thou shalt no more be termed Forsaken; neither shall thy land any more be termed Desolate:** but thou shalt be called Hephzibah, and thy land Beulah: for the LORD delighteth in thee, and **thy land shall be married.**

7 And give him no rest, till he establish, and till he **make Jerusalem a praise in the earth.**

11 Behold, the LORD hath proclaimed unto the end of the world, Say ye to the daughter of Zion, Behold, thy salvation cometh; behold, his reward is with him, and his work before him.

12 And they shall call them, The holy people, The redeemed of the LORD: **and thou shalt be called, Sought out, A city not forsaken.**

At a time in the future when physical nature is changed, when Jerusalem is under a constant light from God's presence, Israel will be righteous, and they will inherit the land for ever. This clearly puts Israel in the land in the future when Christ is reigning in the New Jerusalem (Rev. 21:23).

*Isaiah 60:20* Thy sun shall no more go down; neither shall thy moon withdraw itself: for the LORD shall be thine everlasting light, and the days of thy mourning shall be ended.

21 Thy **people also shall be all righteous: they shall inherit the land for ever**, the branch of my planting, the work of my hands, that I may be glorified.

22 A little one shall become a thousand, and a small one a strong nation: I the LORD will hasten it in his time.

*Psalm 105:9* Which covenant he made with Abraham, and his oath unto Isaac;

10 And confirmed the same unto Jacob for a law, and to Israel for an **everlasting covenant**:

11 Saying, Unto thee will I give the land of Canaan, the lot of your inheritance:

In the passage above, if everlasting life is everlasting life, why is it that an everlasting covenant is not everlasting? When does everlasting mean everlasting and when does it not?

Ezekiel 36-37 gives details of Israel's restoration.

## Christ's kingdom is not of this world.

Remember John 18:36 where Jesus said, "**If my kingdom were of this world,** then would my servants fight."? It is argued that the disciples never did understand that the kingdom was only spiritual — not of this world. But notice the text carefully. Jesus' enemies were charging him with being a threat to the Roman Empire. "Jesus answered, **My kingdom** is not of this world: if my kingdom were of this world, then would my servants fight, that I should not be delivered to the Jews: but **now** is my kingdom not from hence" (John 18:36). He said, "**but now is my kingdom not from hence**", which makes it a matter of timing. Many verses speak of a future kingdom that is of this world, but first Jesus was going to win the hearts of men before he set up an earthly kingdom. Certainly the Church at present is not associated with the earthly **kingdom of heaven**. It would still be proper to say of the church (the kingdom of God), "My kingdom is not of this world". As Jesus was standing before his accusers just hours before his crucifixion, it was clear that Israel had rejected the king of the **kingdom of heaven**. The **kingdom of heaven** would not come now, as John had predicted. It would be postponed. Only the **kingdom of God** remained, since it is not subject to the control of men or Satan, and because of its spiritual nature, the **kingdom of God** would never rival the kingdoms of men. Furthermore, Jesus did not say that the **kingdom of heaven** is not of this world. He said, **my** kingdom is not of this world.

The New Testament speaks of "**my kingdom,**" with a reference to Christ's kingdom, three times. Twice in John 18:36 and one more time in Luke 22:30: "That ye may eat and drink at my table in **my kingdom**, and sit on thrones judging the twelve tribes of Israel." "My kingdom" is the same as *the kingdom of Christ, the kingdom of his dear Son, his kingdom, kingdom of our Lord and Savior Jesus Christ.*

When Christ returns to the earth, he will destroy the kingdoms of this world and replace them with his *(my)* kingdom, and reign over the earth for ever.

> *1 Corinthians 15:24-28* Then *cometh* the end, when he shall have delivered up the kingdom to God, even the Father; when he shall have put down all rule and all authority and power.
>
> 25 For he must reign, till he hath put all enemies under his feet.

> *Revelation 11:15* And the seventh angel sounded; and there were great voices in heaven, saying, **The kingdoms of this world are become the kingdoms of our Lord, and of his Christ; and he shall reign for ever and ever.**

Many people interpret Jesus' words — "if my kingdom were of this world, then would my servants fight" — as a statement of pacifism, but we read of him later:

> *Rev. 19:11* …in righteousness he doeth judge and make war.

The book of Revelation describes a war that is a campaign against the kingdoms of this world. It ends in their utter destruction and the institution of an earthly kingdom that requires the nations to submit or be judged (Zech. 14:17; Rev. 11:6; Rev. 2:27; 12:5; 19:15).

Furthermore, the coming **kingdom of heaven** is so clearly earthly that the Bible says of overcomers: "And he that overcometh, and keepeth my works unto the end, to him will I give power over the **nations**" (Rev. 2:26). And he told the disciples that in the after-life they would, "**sit on thrones** judging the twelve tribes of Israel" (Luke 22:30). How more earthly can you get? Overcomers will be seated on thrones and granted power over particular nations. There is nothing spiritual about that.

It turned out that **His kingdom** was not of this world the first time he came, but it will be when he returns (2 Thess. 1:8). Jesus said, "Fear not, little flock; for it is your **Father's good pleasure to give you the kingdom**" (Luke 12:32).

## Debunking the myth of "spiritual Israel".

The Bible never speaks of "spiritual Israel." Not once! It is a concept fabricated by traditionally "educated" religious men who envy the unique role of Israel in God's program. They want the church to be the heir of the promises to Jacob's seed, thus ruling out natural Israel.

The Roman Catholic Church believes that **it** is "THE" Church of Jesus Christ, to the exclusion of all others, as do many Protestants, cults, and independent denominations like the Church of Christ, and Landmark Baptist. The Romanists first created support for this position by claiming that they, as the representative of Christ upon the earth, are the "spiritual Israel", the benefactor of all prophecies to national Israel. For over 1,000 years the Roman church controlled kings and nations with their claim to be sole heir of the kingdom. By force of arms and threats of excommunication, the Roman church maintained its hold over the known civilized world until a segment of the Roman Catholic Church experienced a partial reformation under Martin Luther, who founded the Lutheran church. The movement was later supported by the theology of John Calvin, which is the basis of most Protestant church denominations around the world. There is a revival of the Reformed Movement going on today. It is the **re-formed** Catholic Church instead of the Roman Catholic Church, though it is still Roman and Babylonish in most of its doctrines, while trying to look and sound as "Protestant" as possible.

Most of Christianity believes that the following passages prove that the Church has taken Israel's place. They speak of "spiritual Israel" (meaning Gentiles who have taken the place of Jacob's seed), even though neither the term nor the concept ever appears in the Bible.

## Romans 9:6-13

The Reformed church, in the tradition of Roman Catholicism, offers this passage as one of the proofs for a non-Jewish Israel — a so-called "spiritual Israel". "For **they are not all Israel, which are of Israel: Neither, because they are the seed of Abraham, are they all children.**" As bizarre as it sounds to those not steeped in traditional beliefs, advocates of this belief proffer that the passage is saying something to the effect, "Just because one is a natural descendent of Abraham and his heir Israel that does not necessarily make him a true spiritual Israelite. That is, one who is a natural seed but doesn't believe in Christ will not be counted as such since he does not have faith." They then assume that if a Gentile has faith, he takes the place of the natural seed and becomes the spiritual seed, heir of the promise. You may think I am making this up, but there are many otherwise intelligent people who truly believe the passage teaches this. The verses that follow dispel any such fabrication.

> ***Romans 9:7*** "…but, In Isaac shall thy seed be called.
> 8 That is, They which are **the children of the flesh, these are not the children of God**: but the **children of the promise are counted for the seed**.
> 9 For this is the word of promise, At this time will I come, and Sara shall have a son.
> 10 And not only this; but when Rebecca also had conceived by one, even by our father Isaac;
> 11 (For *the children* being not yet born, neither having done any good or evil, that the purpose of God according to election might stand, not of works, but of him that calleth;)
> 12 It was said unto her, The elder shall serve the younger.
> 13 As it is written, Jacob have I loved, but Esau have I hated.

It looks and sounds a bit different in its context, doesn't it? It is not a discussion of natural seed (Jews) versus so-called spiritual seed (Gentile believers); it is a statement that God does not count Esau and his descendents (children of the flesh) as heirs just because he is the firstborn son of Isaac, but rather God counts only Jacob (Israel – children of the promise) and his descendents. In other words, one must be a natural descendent of Jacob (renamed Israel by God) through his son Isaac, not a natural descendent of Jacob through his son Esau. This passage has no more to do with a "spiritual Israel" or a non-Jewish Israel than it has to do with spiritual Canaanites.

If one wants to make an analogy of the passage, he would find a parallel in that segment of natural Israel who believe, and are therefore recipients of the faith of Abraham, and that segment of Israel that does not believe, and would therefore not be counted as children of the promise of salvation by faith. The passage is not contrasting the Church to Israel. It is contrasting unbelief to belief, whether of Jew or Gentile. Read all of chapters 9 -11 as if you had never seen the texts before, and ask yourself what it actually says. It is amazing how simple and direct it is when not viewed through Protestant and Roman Catholic glasses.

## Romans 2:28-29

Another passage used to support the spiritual Israel heresy is Romans 2:28-29 – "For **he is not a Jew, which is one outwardly;** neither is that circumcision, which is outward in the flesh: But he *is* a Jew, which is one inwardly; and circumcision *is that* of the heart, in the spirit, *and* not in the letter; whose praise *is* not of men, but of God."

This passage occurs in the context of Paul proving that Jews are sinners in need of redemption if they want to enter the kingdom of God. He simply points out that it is not enough to be a Jew by natural descent; Jews must also have a conversion of heart. This passage teaches the obvious, that a Jew may disqualify himself from the benefits of being a Jew by failing to have a change of heart. **It certainly does not teach that a Gentile who does have a change of heart is thereby a Jew.** The passage is designed to make sinners of Jews, not make Jews of Gentiles. But it has certainly made liars of Gentiles who say they are Jews (Rev. 3:9).

## Romans 4:11-16

The most prominent passage offered to support the "spiritual Israel" error is Romans 4:11-16. Read the entire fourth chapter, and carefully consider the context. Paul is appealing to Jews who have already rejected the kingdom of heaven offered by Jesus. His appeal now is that in order for them to enter the kingdom of God, they must enter by means of the same faith that Abraham exercised, and which God counted as righteousness. In verse 3, it tells us that "Abraham believed God, and it was counted unto him for righteousness." Then it comes to the punch line. Was it before or after Abraham was circumcised that righteousness was imputed to him? The answer: Before circumcision! Another question: Was it before the law or after the law that Abraham was counted righteous? Answer: Before the law, of course. Therefore, he concludes: "For **the promise, that he should be the heir of the world**, was not to Abraham, or to his seed, through the law, but through the righteousness of faith." His conclusion is: "Now it was not written for his sake alone, that it was imputed to him; But for us also, to whom it shall be imputed, if we believe on him that raised up Jesus our Lord from the dead." He is telling us that anyone who believes can have righteousness imputed to him just as Abraham (not a Jew) did. Since Abraham was before the law, and yet he was counted righteous by faith, and since it was before his circumcision, then the law and Jewish circumcision are not essential for one to become an heir of righteousness. Therefore, those who approach God by faith, whether they be circumcised or not, under the law or not, are in the great tradition of Abraham, "**that he might be the father of all them that believe**, though they be not circumcised; that righteousness might be imputed unto them also."

Having established Abraham's credentials as one who experienced the righteousness of faith without the law and before circumcision, he says that Abraham is the father of all who believe as he did. He was a Gentile 600 years before there were any Jews, therefore he is not only the father of Israel, he is the father of all who approach God by faith. It is the unimpeachable quality of Abraham's faith that God holds in such high honor as "the" model for all, Jew and Gentile, to emulate. This has absolutely nothing to do with Gentiles becoming Jews; it is about how both Jews and Gentiles can become faith descendents of a man who predated circumcision, the law, and the entire concept of Judaism. There is no "spiritual Israel" today, and there won't be until "all Israel shall be saved" (Rom. 11:26). That's it! There is no Scriptural support for the Church to replace Israel as the recipient of all of God's physical and spiritual promises to them.

## Two immutable things.

There is a critical phrase in the book of Hebrews that is universally overlooked. This author has yet to find it correctly expounded in any commentary. It answers the question of how Abraham can "**be the father of all them that believe**, though they be not circumcised", yet not have the Church displace or replace Israel in God's prophetic plan. Read the following passage carefully. It is most enlightening. The overlooked point, which we will discuss, is the **two** promises defined as **two immutable things** that God **said**.

> *Hebrews 6:12* That ye be not slothful, but followers of them who through faith and patience inherit the **promises** [*plural*].
>
> 13 For when God made promise to Abraham, because he could swear by no greater, he sware by himself,
>
> 14 **Saying,** Surely **blessing I will bless thee** [*one promise*], and **multiplying I will multiply thee** [*second promise*].
>
> 15 And so, after he had patiently endured, he obtained the promise [*singular—he obtained only one of the promises*].
>
> 16 For men verily swear by the greater: and an oath for confirmation is to them an end of all strife.
>
> 17 Wherein God, willing more abundantly to shew unto the heirs of **promise** [*singular*] the immutability of his counsel, confirmed it by an oath:
>
> 18 That by **two immutable things,** in which it was **impossible for God to lie,** [*two promises*] we might have a strong consolation, who have fled for refuge to lay hold upon the hope set before us:
>
> 19 Which hope we have as an anchor of the soul, both sure and stedfast, and which entereth into that within the veil;
>
> 20 Whither the forerunner is for us entered, even Jesus, made an high priest for ever after the order of Melchisedec.

Verse 12 (above) tells the Church saints that they should be followers of those (Jews) who **inherit the promises** (plural) given to Abraham. Again, verse 17 speaks of the Church saints as **heirs of the promise** (singular). There are **promises** and there is **a promise**. God gave **promises** (more than one) to Abraham, but the Church inherits the **promise** (just one — not both promises made to Abraham).

We will discuss the significance of this in a moment, but for those of you who think that observing the "number" (whether they are singular or plural) of words is excessive hair splitting, I call to your remembrance the grammatical argument Paul made based on the "number" of a single noun (Gal. 3:16-19). And Jesus built a doctrinal argument on the preciseness of the use of one word in Matthew 22:42-45. If every word is given by inspiration of God and is profitable (2 Tim. 3:16) for doctrine, then we will pay attention to exactly what the text says, and not feel forthright doing otherwise. Every day of the year, courts decide cases involving millions of dollars based on one single word in a contract.

What is greatly overlooked is that God made two promises to Abraham: One fulfilled in Israel, his natural descendents, and the other fulfilled in the Church, his faith descendents, which is made up of believing Jews and Gentiles. A believing Jew saw the fulfillment of both promises.

Look at this pivotal text again; it says, "**…by two immutable things, in which it was impossible for God to lie….**" God made two, not one, immutable [*not capable or susceptible to change*] promises to Abraham, "**saying, surely blessing I will bless thee** [*first promise*], **and multiplying I will multiply thee** [*second promise*]. In Genesis he clearly defines the first promise on two different occasions — "**in thy seed shall all the nations of the earth be blessed** (Gen. 22:18; 26:4)." God promised to bless and **multiply** his natural seed to become as many as the sand on the sea shore in number, and the second promise is that God will **bless** all the nations through Abraham's seed, which seed is Christ (Gal. 3:16).The Jews will be blessed with multiplication of their number and inheriting the land, and the Gentiles and believing Jews will be blessed with salvation by faith.

Verse 15 says that Abraham **received the promise** (singular). He did not receive both promises, but he did receive one. The promise he received was the multiplying of his seed in the birth of Isaac — *the promised child*. Abraham did not receive the promise of blessing the nations through his seed, for that did not happen until Christ, and it is fulfilled in the Church, not national Israel. Thus, we have the two immutable promises (Rom. 9:9; Gal. 3:17-28). One, Israel will inherit the land. And two, Abraham's seed, which is Christ, will bless the nations with salvation by faith. Two promises to two different people groups — two kingdoms with two kings; David over Israel (the K of H), and Jesus over the Church (the K of G).

This interpretation is supported by three occasions in the book of Genesis where the two promises are repeated.

> *Genesis 22:17* That in **blessing** I will bless thee, and in **multiplying** I will multiply thy seed as the stars of the heaven, and as the sand which is upon the sea shore; and **thy seed** [*natural seed—Jews*] shall possess the gate of his enemies;
> 18 And in **thy seed** [*This seed is Christ—Gal. 3:16*] shall all the nations of the earth be blessed; because thou hast obeyed my voice.

In the above passage, we see the twofold promise — **multiplying** Israel, and **blessing** all the nations [*the church*].

In the verses below, God restates his promises to Abraham's son, Isaac, and adds a little more clarity.

> *Genesis 26:3* Sojourn in this land, and I will be with thee, and will bless thee; [*first promise*] for unto thee, and unto thy seed, **I will give all these countries,** and I will perform the oath which I sware unto Abraham thy father;
> 4 And I will make thy seed to multiply as the stars of heaven, and will give unto thy seed all these countries; [*second promise*] and in thy seed shall **all the nations of the earth be blessed;**

Notice above, the multiplied seed is identified with those who inherit the countries comprising the old land of Canaan — which could only be natural Israel. The last phrase adds a second promise: "…in thy seed shall all the nations of the earth be blessed." The nations of the earth could only be nations other than Israel, which would be the Gentile nations and the Church, as we discover in Gal. 3:16.

In the passage below, God restates his two promises to Jacob, the grandson of Abraham, and again he adds one more degree of clarity. He is now quite specific. The land on which Jacob was lying, even as God spoke to him, is to be given to Jacob's seed (natural Israel). That seed is to be multiplied as the dust of the earth and to spread out to fill the land. Only the last phrase (the part that is underlined, below) is the second promise that speaks of blessing all the families (nations) of the earth, which includes the Church comprised largely of Gentiles. The Gentiles and the Church do not inherit the land; but they are blessed through Abraham's seed, whose seed we see as the final fulfillment of the blessings in Christ (Gal. 3:16).

> *Genesis 28:13-14* And, behold, the LORD stood above it, and said, I am the LORD God of Abraham thy father, and the God of Isaac: **the land whereon thou liest, to thee will I give it, and to thy seed;** [*to the natural seed — Israel*]
> 14 And thy **seed shall be as the dust of the earth,** and thou shalt spread abroad to the west, and to the east, and to the north, and to the south: **<u>and in thee and in thy seed shall all the families of the earth be blessed.</u>** [*to the faith seed — the Church*]

# Mysteries and Keys

## Why haven't I heard of this before?

You may ask, "If this concept is so vital, how is it that I have never heard of it before? Why haven't the great teachers and theologians taught this?" Some have, men such as Darby, Scofield, Ryrie, Gaebelein, Chafer, Ironside, Larkin, and others (truly great writers whose works are worthy of consideration), but denominational boundaries have prevented many from becoming aware of this truth. Furthermore, when you read the works of those who have recognized the differences in the kingdoms, you find very little attempt to prove the point. They mostly assume the differences without going to great lengths to show the reader the evidence. Yet, in addition to the Bible, there has always been sufficient material in print for inquiring minds if one were to actually read it. It is one of the intentions of this book to remedy that deficiency. This author, recognizing that he is not as gifted or credentialed as those who write enduring works, hopes that men of greater abilities and public esteem will be stirred by this work to go to their keyboards and produce books on the kingdoms that will be thorough and definitive and gain wide acceptance with today's needy Church.

## The key of knowledge.

But the main reason for ignorance on this subject is that many noted church leaders and writers have forfeited the key that unlocks one's understanding of the kingdom message. With the key of knowledge, even an uneducated and weak man can understand that which confounds the wise and prudent. It sounds exclusionary and even cultic to declare that there is a _key_ to the disclosure of this Divine knowledge. Even by writing about it, it seems to imply that this author is part of that small, elite group that has discovered the key. Not so. But we do not let that deter us from observing what _Jesus said_ about the **key of knowledge**, one that will unlock **mysteries** about the kingdoms. By presenting this issue, the author does not believe himself to be wiser, more learned, or more spiritual than others — only inquisitive and trusting where the Word of God is concerned. Furthermore, those who do not have absolute confidence in every word in their Bible are handicapped from discovering the truth. A pure Bible in hand produces pure doctrine in heart. He who switches translations to his liking can switch doctrines for his convenience. By believing the Authorized Version to be the **words** of God, the key of knowledge comes readily to hand. This is not just a pitch for the King James Bible; it is an explanation as to how a country bumpkin can gain such accurate knowledge of matters so overlooked by men far more intelligent and learned.

Now read what Jesus said about the key of knowledge.

> _Luke 11:52_ Woe unto you, lawyers! for ye have **taken away the key of knowledge**: ye entered not in yourselves, and them that were entering in ye hindered.

> _Matthew 23:13_ But woe unto you, scribes and Pharisees, hypocrites! for ye **shut up the kingdom of heaven** against men: for ye neither go in yourselves, neither suffer ye them that are entering to go in.

When John the Baptist and Jesus offered the kingdom of heaven to Israel, and the religious leaders refused it, Jesus warned that _in rejecting the kingdom message, they were **taking away the key of knowledge**_ and shutting the door to the kingdom of heaven on behalf of the whole nation. In their capacity as leaders of Israel, they were in a position to officially recognize the Messiah and his kingdom or reject the message and the man, thereby discarding the key of knowledge for everyone.

> _Mark 4:11_ And he said unto them [_the disciples_], Unto you it is given to know the **mystery** of the **kingdom of God**: but unto them that are without, all these things are done in parables:
> 12 That seeing they may **see, and not perceive**; and hearing they may hear, and **not understand**….

## Understanding the mystery of the kingdom is the key of knowledge!

> _Matthew 13:11_ He answered and said unto them [_the disciples_], Because it is given unto you to know the **mysteries** of the **kingdom of heaven**, **but to them it is not given.**

Notice in the passages recorded above: There is a key to knowing the truth of God! And the key has to do with knowledge of the kingdoms! Because the religious leaders did not understand the truth about the kingdoms, they had **shut** the door not only for themselves, but also for the nation whom they represented. That door is still shut today. The **kingdom of heaven**, under God's rule, has not come to the earth and will not come until the divinely imposed blindness is removed from the nation of Israel (Rom. 11:25). Furthermore, most modern Christians are equally blind, having never known that there is a key to understanding the divine **mysteries.**

## The key of the house of David.

Let us go back to about 800 years before Christ to the first mention of the keys to the kingdom. God foretold that the coming Messiah would be given the key to fulfilling the promises of the Davidic kingdom. He could either open the door or shut the door. The following verse is a prophecy of the ministry of Jesus Christ in his capacity as 'keeper of the keys to the kingdom'.

> *Isaiah 22:22* And the **key** of the **house of David** will I lay upon his shoulder; so he shall **open**, and none shall shut; and he shall **shut**, and none shall open.

Here God is revealing that Jesus will be given the responsibility to either unlock the door to the kingdom or shut the door, as he will. The common Jews of Jesus' day rightly understood his mission as Messiah. After hearing him teach for three and one-half years, they hailed him as the one to establish the kingdom of David in Israel.

> *Mark 11:10* Blessed be the **kingdom of our father David**, that cometh in the name of the Lord: Hosanna in the highest.

In Luke 19:38-40, when the Pharisees heard the people recognizing Jesus as coming to bring the Davidic kingdom, they told Jesus to rebuke them for their false understanding. Rather than rebuke them, Jesus affirmed their belief by saying that if they did not praise him, then the rocks would have to cry forth the same truth the people were proclaiming.

## Keys to the kingdom.

When Israel rejected the kingdom under Jesus, and Jesus began to announce that their rejection would lead to his crucifixion, he handed the keys to his disciples (or to Peter alone, if you would have it so; it makes no difference) and told them that they now had the responsibility to bind or loose (to open or shut the door to the kingdom), and that their decision would be honored in heaven.

> *Matthew 16:19* And I will give **unto thee** the **keys of the kingdom of heaven**: and whatsoever thou shalt bind on earth shall be bound in heaven: and whatsoever thou shalt loose on earth shall be loosed in heaven.

The reason Jesus could delegate the responsibility of opening or shutting the kingdom to these sons of Adam, these fallible mortals, is that originally God had given the earth to the sons of men. Remember Heb. 2:7-8, speaking of God's creating of man, "…and didst set him over the works of thy hands." The K of H is the birthright of the sons of men, for good or ill. He did not put **the world to come** in the hands of angels (Heb. 2:5). God **left nothing** that is not put under man (Heb. 2:8). God once entrusted the entire kingdom to one man, Adam, so it was quite appropriate that he should once again entrust it to Adam's descendents.

However, with the apostles' best efforts, the nation of Israel continued to reject the **kingdom of heaven,** even after the commencement of the Church, so, at some point, either at Christ's crucifixion, or early in the book of Acts, the Holy Spirit moved the disciples to turn their preaching and ministry from the Jews and shut the door on the K of H (Acts 13:46; 18:6; 28:28), and Paul opened another door to allow Gentiles into the kingdom of God. Now at the end of this present, predominately Gentile dispensation, the man, Jesus, once again has **the key of the house of David** (the key to the K of H) and is about to shut the door on the Gentiles and reopen it for Israel.

*Revelation 3:7* And to the angel of the church in Philadelphia write; These things saith he that is holy, he that is true, he that hath the **key of David**, he that **openeth**, and no man shutteth; and **shutteth**, and no man openeth;

At this present time, the key is still hidden from nearly all Jews and from most professing Christians. God offered the key of knowledge in the 12 kingdom of heaven parables, but so little regarded is the Word of God that few care to even consider the matter. In time, we will examine all the kingdom of heaven and kingdom of God parables, after which you will possess the key of knowledge.

## Mysteries of the kingdom.

The word *mystery/mysteries* appears 27 times in the Bible, all in the New Testament, and **all** occurrences have to do with the kingdoms. The word **mystery** is defined as: knowledge partly known and partly hidden, the hidden part inspiring a sense of awe, stimulating the imagination, suggesting greater satisfaction is to be had by gaining more knowledge and solving the questions raised by the facts we do know. Declaring a thing a mystery may also imply that someone has partly hidden and partly revealed valuable information for a purpose.

When the disciples asked Jesus why he spoke in parables, his answer was quite different from what we learned in Sunday school. There we were taught that parables are little stories to help us understand some spiritual principle. Conversely, Jesus spoke in parables to conceal the mystery of the kingdom truth!

*Matthew 13:10* And the disciples came, and said unto him, **Why speakest thou unto them in parables?**
11 He answered and said unto them, Because it is given unto you to know the mysteries of the kingdom of heaven, but **to them it is not given**.

*Luke 8:10* And he said, Unto you it is given to know the mysteries of the kingdom of God: but to others in parables; that seeing they might not see, and **hearing they might not understand**.

*Mark 4:11* And he said unto them, Unto you it is given to know the mystery of the kingdom of God: but unto them that are without, all these things are done in parables:
12 That seeing they may see, and **not perceive**; and hearing they may hear, **and not understand**; lest at any time they should be converted, and their sins should be forgiven them.

Jesus rejoiced that the God of heaven and earth had hidden the kingdom messages from the wise and prudent leaders and revealed them to the untutored.

*Matthew 11:25* At that time Jesus answered and said, I thank thee, O Father, Lord of heaven and earth, because thou hast **hid these things from the wise and prudent**, and hast revealed them unto babes.
26 Even so, Father: for so it seemed good in thy sight.

The prophet Isaiah predicted that God would respond to Israel's rejection by shutting their eyes so they could not understand the truth. Knowledge of doctrine is not primary with God; a pure heart is. If a man's motives are not right, God does not want to satisfy his intellect with details of his Divine program, for he does not care to reveal his plans to his enemies. Note in the following passage the characteristic of a blinded person. He claims that God's Word cannot be understood. How true this is of today's professing Christians.

*Isaiah 29:10* For the **LORD hath poured out upon you the spirit of deep sleep**, and hath closed your eyes: the prophets and your rulers, the seers hath he covered.
11 And the vision of all is become unto you as the **words of a book that is sealed,** which men deliver to one that is learned, saying, Read this, I pray thee: and he saith, I cannot; for it is sealed:
12 And the book is delivered to him that is not learned, saying, Read this, I pray thee: and he saith, **I am not learned.**

Matthew 13 records several kingdom of heaven parables and then interrupts the narrative with a quote from the Psalms, which foretold that Jesus would reveal **secret** things about the kingdom through the method of **parables**.

> *Matthew 13:34* All these things spake Jesus unto the multitude in **parables**; and without a parable spake he not unto them:
>
> 35 That it might be fulfilled which was spoken by the prophet, saying, I will open my mouth in **parables**; I will utter things which have been <u>**kept secret**</u> **from the foundation of the world**.

> *Psalm 78:2* I will open my mouth in a parable: I will utter dark sayings of old:
>
> 3 Which we have heard and known, and our fathers have told us.
>
> 4 **We will not hide them from their children**, shewing to the generation to come the praises of the LORD, and his strength, and his wonderful works that he hath done.

In verse 4 above, we see that the same parable that conceals kingdom truth to the unbelieving, reveals truth to those who believe.

In light of God's great effort to conceal the kingdom message, you might ask, "Is it wise to reveal the master plan to the enemy, as we are doing in this book?" It takes more than an intellectual effort to understand the kingdoms. It takes a spiritual mind. It has always been the case that religious leaders are spiritually blinded by candlelight, stained-glass windows, vestments, altars, cathedrals, holy water, bank accounts, titles, and power. If they had the opportunity, and they don't, they would still shut the door to the K of H. By divine design, the message of the kingdoms remains the most obscure truth of the Bible.

# Twelve kingdom mysteries in 27 verses

In the following verses, you will read of **mysteries** (plural) of the kingdom. There are 12 mysteries, just as there are 12 kingdom of heaven parables, 12 tribes of Israel, and 12 apostles. There are 12 gates to The New Jerusalem, and the city is 12,000 furlongs cubed. There are 12 precious stones in the foundation of the city, and the tree of life will bear 12 manner of fruits. Although the mysteries are spoken of in the plural, in a larger sense, they are **one**. Each is a different part of a single prophetic plan of God. That is, they are all related and relevant, and are to be understood as a unit. And, in particular, the kingdom of God is a mystery in regard to its similarities to and difference from the kingdom of heaven.

It is amazing that the 12 kingdom mysteries embody the plan of God chronologically throughout the ages, a continual revelation of his program among men. What makes these truths a mystery is that they were planned before the world began, known only to God, hidden to men and angels, revealed in increments to the prophets, finally made manifest in the kingdom parables, and then were completely revealed to the Church by the Holy Spirit in the New Testament Scriptures through the apostles Paul and John. They are most significant to Israel, who expected something very different.

## 1. Mystery of the kingdom of God

> *Luke 8:10* And he said, Unto you it is given to know the **mysteries of the kingdom of God**: but to others in parables; that seeing they might not see, and hearing they might not understand.
>
> *Mark 4:11* …Unto you it is given to know the **mystery** of the **kingdom of God**: but unto them that are without, all these things are done in parables:
> 12 That seeing they may see, and not perceive; and hearing they may hear, and not understand….

God's secret program for Israel and the Church was devised before he created the world, embodied in a mystery, and was kept hidden from former ages.

> *Romans 16:25* Now to him that is of power to stablish you according to my gospel, and the preaching of Jesus Christ, according to the revelation of the **mystery, which was kept secret since the world began.**
>
> *Colossians 1:26* Even the mystery which hath been **hid from ages** and from generations, but now is made manifest to his saints:
>
> *Ephesians 3:5* Which in other **ages was not made known** unto the sons of men, as it is now revealed unto his holy apostles and prophets by the Spirit;

Paul said that God had revealed the mysteries (plural) to him (2 Cor. 12:1-5; Gal. 1:11-12), and that he and the apostles were responsible to make the mysteries known to the Church.

> *Ephesians 3:3* How that by revelation he **made known unto me the mystery**; (as I wrote afore in few words,
> 4 Whereby, when ye read, ye may understand my knowledge in the **mystery** of Christ)
> 5 Which in other **ages was not made known** unto the sons of men, as it is now revealed unto his holy apostles and prophets by the Spirit;
>
> *Corinthians 4:1* Let a man so account of us, as of the ministers of Christ, and stewards of the **mysteries of God.**
>
> *Colossians 1:26* Even the **mystery** which hath been hid from ages and from generations, **but now is made manifest to his saints:**
> 27 To whom God would make known what is the riches of the glory of this **mystery** among the Gentiles; which is **Christ in you**, the hope of glory:

## 2. Mystery of the kingdom of heaven

Note, that the kingdom of heaven involves mysteries (plural), as does the kingdom of God.

*Matthew 13:11* He answered and said unto them, Because it is given unto you to know the **mysteries** of the **kingdom of heaven**, but to them it is not given.

13 Therefore speak I to them in parables: because they seeing see not; and hearing they hear not, neither do they understand.

The Jews expected a Davidic kingdom, as they should, but the mystery was that it would not come except they repent and enter the kingdom of God. Neither were they accepting of the fact that it would include Gentiles as well.

## 3. The Mystery of God becoming a man of flesh

A big part of the mystery kept hidden from Israel was that God himself would become a baby in a mother's arms, nursed, changed, instructed, and taught to speak. After the Word was made flesh, the mystery culminated in his being preached to Gentiles, seen by angels, declared to be justified by the Spirit of God, believed on in the world, and then received back into God's eternal glory. The man Jesus was very different from the Messiah they expected. Even though the Old Testament spoke of God's **son**, none expected a literal fulfillment of those prophecies.

*1 Timothy 3:16* And without controversy great is the **mystery of godliness: God was manifest in the flesh,** justified in the Spirit, seen of angels, preached unto the Gentiles, believed on in the world, received up into glory.

## 4. The Mystery of salvation by faith

The whole concept of being justified by faith was a mystery to the Jews. Abraham was justified by faith, but after the coming of the Law, Israel got bogged down in their own zealous efforts and missed the entire concept of being related to God personally by faith.

*Eph. 6:19* And for me, that utterance may be given unto me, that I may open my mouth boldly, to make known the **mystery of the gospel**,

*Rom. 16:25* Now to him that is of power to stablish you according to my gospel, and the preaching of Jesus Christ, according to the **revelation of the mystery**, which was kept secret since the world began,

26 But now is made manifest, and by the scriptures of the prophets, according to the commandment of the everlasting God, made known to all nations for the obedience of faith:

*1 Timothy 3:9* Holding the **mystery of the faith** in a pure conscience.

## 5. The mystery of the eventual oneness of all created beings

This mystery includes the revelation of a future dispensation called *the fullness of times,* wherein God will gather into one body (one kingdom) both Jews and Gentiles, as well as the angels and other created beings, whether they are already in heaven or on the earth. This will occur when, as John says, the mysteries are **finished** in the Millennium and when the **kingdom of God** and the **kingdom of heaven** merge and become **HIS kingdom** (the kingdom of Christ); and, upon the removal of all sinners, all kingdoms and powers will be submitted to the Father and become the **kingdom of our Father**.

*Ephesians 1:9* Having made known unto us the mystery of his will, according to his good pleasure which he hath purposed in himself:

10 That in the dispensation of the fulness of times he **might gather together in one all things in Christ**, both which are in heaven, and which are on earth; even in him:

## 6. The Mystery of Gentiles in the same body

This mystery reveals that God is available to all nations (not just Israel) by faith. This was truly a mystery to Israel. It would still be today. They cannot accept that the Church also comes to know God by the same means of faith as did Abraham.

> *Romans 16:25* … according to the revelation of the **mystery,** which was kept secret since the world began,
>
> 26 But now is made manifest, and by the scriptures of the prophets, according to the commandment of the everlasting God, made known **to all nations** for the obedience of faith:
>
> *Ephesians 3:3* How that by revelation he made known unto me the **mystery**…
>
> 6 That the **Gentiles should be fellowheirs,** and of the **same body,** and partakers of his **promise** in Christ by the gospel:

## 7. The Mystery of Christ and his bride

That Christ should have a Church made up of all peoples and nations, and that the Church should be one with him, was certainly a mystery to Israel.

> *Ephesians 5:30* For we are **members of his body, of his flesh, and of his bones.** [*as the bride*]
>
> 31 For this cause shall a man leave his father and mother, and shall be joined unto his wife, and they two shall be one flesh.
>
> 32 This is a great **mystery**: but I speak concerning **Christ and the church**.
>
> [*You couldn't explain this one, even if you stayed up all night.*]
>
> *Ephesians 2:6* And raised us up together and made us sit together in heavenly places in Christ Jesus.
>
> *1 Corinthians 6:17* "But he that is joined unto the Lord [*matrimony*] is one spirit [*as a man and his wife are one flesh*] (Col. 1:26, 27; 2:2; 4:3).

## 8. The Mystery of the rapture

The mystery included a revelation of the resurrection and transformation of the human body at the rapture and second coming of Christ.

> *1 Corinthians 15:51* Behold, I shew you a **mystery**; We shall not all sleep, but we shall all be changed,
>
> 52 In a moment, in the twinkling of an eye, at the last trump: for the trumpet shall sound, and the dead shall be raised incorruptible, and we shall be changed.

## 9. The Mystery of iniquity

It is part of God's end-times program that a false Christ will come and deceive the world into worshiping him. This, too, is a mystery kept secret from Israel.

The **mystery of iniquity** is the Devil's counterfeit answer to the kingdom message. The Antichrist offers a substitute kingdom with a substitute christ. He comes to set up a kingdom through the kings of the earth. Satan's man will have a message of the kingdom that will be believed, but he will not overthrow God's kingdom; instead, it will result in the damnation of those who believe Satan's man when Jesus comes back to set up **his kingdom.**

> *2 Thessalonians 2:6* And now ye know what withholdeth that he might be revealed in his time.
>
> 7 For the **mystery of iniquity** doth already work: only he who now letteth will let, until he be taken out of the way.
>
> 8 And then shall that Wicked be revealed, whom the Lord shall consume with the spirit of his mouth, and shall destroy with the brightness of his coming:
>
> 9 Even him, whose coming is after the working of Satan with all power and signs and lying wonders,

10 And with all deceivableness of unrighteousness in them that perish; because they received not the love of the truth, that they might be saved.

11 And for this cause **God shall send them strong delusion, that they should believe a lie**:

12 That they all might be damned who believed not the truth, but had pleasure in unrighteousness.

Note above, in verse 11, that God will still be in the mystery business after the Rapture of the Church and before the second coming. Those who rejected the truth in this dispensation and were left behind will be ready to believe when they see that they missed Christ, so they will be the first to acknowledge their "error" and turn to this wonder-working christ who is setting up a world kingdom. But the christ they willingly believe on is antichirst, a deceiver. God will deceive them into following the false christ.

## 10. Mystery of the seven churches

When John is carried away in the spirit, he sees a Jewish candlestick in the hand of Christ. The angel identifies the seven golden candlesticks and the seven stars with the mystery. At first, it does not seem to be related to the mystery of the kingdoms, but when the angel later identifies the seven candlesticks (Jewish in design) as seven Gentile churches and the seven stars as seven angels or messengers to those Gentile churches (which are representative of the entire Church), the connection then becomes clear. The mystery kept secret was that the Gentiles would have an inheritance in the **kingdom of God**. Here you have a Jewish, seven-pronged candlestick representing seven churches of the Gentiles. Preposterous! That is a mystery no Jew was willing to believe — Gentiles taking the place of the seed of Jacob! But, remember the light set on a hill that was not to be put under a bushel? The mystery of the kingdoms included the concealed truth that the Gentiles, for a time, would take Israel's place as the light set on the hill.

*Revelation 1:20* The **mystery** of the seven stars which thou sawest in my right hand, and the seven golden candlesticks. The seven stars are the angels of the seven churches: and the seven candlesticks which thou sawest are the seven churches.

## 11. The Mystery that Israel will be blinded for a while and then restored

The mystery included a period of time in which God would set aside the nation of Israel, leave them in a state of blindness and turn to the Gentiles to fill up his Bride and complete the Church.

*Romans 11:25* For I would not, brethren, that ye should be ignorant of this **mystery**, lest ye should be wise in your own conceits; that **blindness in part is happened to Israel**, until the **fulness of the Gentiles be come in**.

However, Paul revealed that Israel's blindness was foreseen by God and is only temporary, lasting until the **fullness of the Gentiles be come in,** that is, until the last Gentile has been added to the Church and this present dispensation has come to an end. In verse 26, he goes on to say that there will come a time when all Israel will be saved.

*Romans 11:26* And so **all Israel shall be saved**: as it is written, There shall come out of Sion the Deliverer, and shall turn away ungodliness from Jacob:

## 12. Mystery Babylon — the counterfeit kingdom

This is the final appearance of the word, *mystery*. The first appearance of the word *kingdom* in the Bible is found in Genesis 10:10. "And the beginning of his kingdom was Babel...." Babel, later called Babylon, is the place where the first mystery religion was created by Nimrod. It was the seat of Satan's attempt to control the kingdoms through religion and the sword. For a detailed history on Babylon, read Alexander Hyslop's *The Two Babylons*. Just as ancient Israel had a great enemy named Babylon who taught them idolatry and carried them off to captivity, so in the last days Israel will have an enemy, Mystery Babylon, who will kill and plague them the way ancient Babylon did. Antichrist is the antithesis of Christ, just as MYSTERY BABYLON is the antithesis of the mystery of the **kingdom of heaven**. In the same way the *tree of the knowledge of good and evil* imparted understanding of both good and evil, so the mystery kept secret from the foundation of the world involves both God's kingdom and Satan's counterfeit kingdom.

The following text is rather extensive, and a moderate commentary on it would be too lengthy for our present purposes. Such a commentary is warranted because of its relevancy to a study of eschatology, which we may do at another time. In the book, *Revelation Painted,* by this author, you will find a short commentary on Revelation 17. It is sufficient to our kingdom study to note the political nature of the text. Mystery Babylon is a religious system with political power capable of controlling the kings of the earth. "She" is called **whore,** because she is a false bride of Christ.

> *Revelation 17:1* And there came one of the seven angels which had the seven vials, and talked with me, saying unto me, Come hither; I will shew unto thee the judgment of the great whore that sitteth upon many waters: **2** With whom the **kings of the earth** have committed fornication, and the inhabitants of the earth have been made drunk with the wine of her fornication. **3** So he carried me away in the spirit into the wilderness: and I saw a woman sit upon a scarlet coloured beast, full of names of blasphemy, having seven heads and ten horns. **4** And the woman was arrayed in purple and scarlet colour, and decked with gold and precious stones and pearls, having a golden cup in her hand full of abominations and filthiness of her fornication: **5** And upon her forehead was a name written, **MYSTERY**, BABYLON THE GREAT, THE MOTHER OF HARLOTS AND ABOMINATIONS OF THE EARTH. **6** And I saw the woman drunken with the blood of the saints, and with the blood of the martyrs of Jesus: and when I saw her, I wondered with great admiration. **7** And the angel said unto me, Wherefore didst thou marvel? **I will tell thee the mystery** of the woman, and of the beast that carrieth her, which hath the seven heads and ten horns. **8** The beast that thou sawest was, and is not; and shall ascend out of the bottomless pit, and go into perdition: and they that dwell on the earth shall wonder, whose names were not written in the book of life from the foundation of the world, when they behold the beast that was, and is not, and yet is. **9** And here is the mind which hath wisdom. The seven heads are seven mountains, on which the woman sitteth. **10** And there are **seven kings**: five are fallen, and one is, and the other is not yet come; and when he cometh, he must continue a short space. **11** And the beast that was, and is not, even he is the **eighth** [*king*], and is of the seven, and goeth into perdition. **12** And the ten horns which thou sawest are **ten kings,** which have received no **kingdom** as yet; but receive power as kings one hour with the beast. **13** These have one mind, and shall give their power [*of their kingdoms*] and strength unto the beast. **14** These shall make war with the Lamb, and the Lamb shall overcome them: for he is Lord of lords, and **King of kings:** and they that are with him are called, and chosen, and faithful. **15** And he saith unto me, The waters which thou sawest, where the whore sitteth, are peoples, and multitudes, and nations, and tongues. **16** And the ten horns which thou sawest upon the beast, these shall hate the whore, and shall make her desolate and naked, and shall eat her flesh, and burn her with fire. **17** For God hath put in their hearts to fulfil his will, and to agree, and give their **kingdom unto the beast**, until the words of God shall be fulfilled. **18** And the woman which thou sawest is that great city, which **reigneth over the kings of the earth**. [*Here is a kingdom attempting to supplant the* **kingdom of heaven**.]

## The mystery will be finished

The trumpets heralded the final judgments upon the kingdoms of this earth, and particularly upon the kingdom of antichrist. The angel tells us that this great judgment, which destroys the kingdoms of men, is preparatory to finishing the mystery. And, as we have seen, the mystery was revealed in the kingdom message.

> *Revelation 10:7* But in the days of the voice of the seventh angel, when he shall begin to sound, the **mystery of God should be finished, as he hath declared to his servants the prophets**.

The mystery is finished during the Great Tribulation. The first step in the culmination of the mystery is the opening of the book of judgments. The rest of chapter 10 and on through chapter 12 reveals the basic events. John saw the rebuilt Jewish temple being measured for destruction (11:1). That temple is yet to be built as seen by the fact that John was writing this prophecy 25 years after the temple was destroyed in 70 A.D. by Rome, and there has not been a temple standing since.

*Revelation 11:1* And there was given me a reed like unto a rod: and the angel stood, saying, Rise, and measure the temple of God, and the altar, and them that worship therein.

Part of the temple yard will not be destroyed, for it will be occupied by Gentiles for 42 months (3 ½ years).

*Revelation 11:2* But the court which is without the temple leave out, and measure it not; for it is given unto the Gentiles: and the holy city shall they tread under foot forty and two months.

After receiving further details on that time of judgment, he comes to the conclusion of the mystery, and it is back to the subject of kingdoms.

*Revelation 11:15* And the seventh angel sounded; and there were great voices in heaven, saying, **The kingdoms of this world are become the kingdoms of our Lord, and of his Christ; and he shall reign for ever and ever.**
  16 And the four and twenty elders, which sat before God on their seats, fell upon their faces, and worshipped God,
  17 Saying, We give thee thanks, O Lord God Almighty, which art, and wast, and art to come; **because thou hast taken to thee thy great power, and hast reigned**.

So, the **mystery is complete** when Christ takes the kingdoms by force and reigns in power and glory over all the earth.

## Sum of the 12 mysteries.

Now let's condense the content of all the mystery verses we have just read so you can see the picture as a whole.

Before the foundation of the world, God developed a kingdom plan. He kept it secret from past ages, but spoke of it in a mystery form "to his servants the prophets" during the Old Testament dispensations. The mystery was about the **kingdom of God** and the **kingdom of heaven**. Jesus spoke of the kingdom mysteries in 12 parables, but he said the Jewish leaders would not understand it because their ears were closed. Although he spoke of and taught about the kingdom mysteries, Jesus did not reveal them until he took Paul up to the third heaven and charged him with the responsibility of making the message known to the Church and to the other apostles.

The mystery began with a revelation that all nations were going to be included in the family of God, all in the same body, and partakers together of the promise of the gospel. The big stumbling block in the mystery was that God would become a man of flesh, actually be seen of angels, preached to Gentiles (of all people), believed on by the world, as well as by the Jews, and then he would not stay to set up a Jewish kingdom, but be received up into glory. The mystery included the amazing revelation that God could be known by faith, and that he would be **one** with his Church, which is composed of Jews **and** Gentiles.

The mystery included the fact that Israel would not believe or receive their Messiah, and would be blinded to the truth. Not until the Church is filled up with Gentiles (the fullness of the Gentiles) will Israel understand the mystery, and then all Israel will be saved. In the last dispensation, all things — Jews, Gentiles, angels and everything in heaven, and all in earth — will be united in Christ.

Climaxing the mystery is the joyous rapture of the saints, both dead and alive, whose corruptible bodies will be transformed at Christ's coming into glorious, incorruptible ones like his. In a moment, in the twinkling of an eye, they will all be changed *to be like him*, for they shall see him as he is, and so shall they ever be with the Lord. There will also be a mystery person, called the Wicked One, who will come to the earth with false signs and wonders, claiming to be Christ. This Antichrist will be destroyed when Jesus comes back to the earth in power and glory. The Wicked One will deceive many with his claim to be Messiah, and God will assist him in deceiving them because they had refused to believe the truth when they had the chance. This false Messianic movement will be enforced by a religious institution called Mystery Babylon, which will be responsible for the martyrdom of many saints.

In those last days, the temple will be rebuilt and then destroyed. There will be three and one-half years of God's end-times judgment. Finally, the mystery will be fully revealed and its purpose disclosed when the kingdoms of this world come under **Christ's kingdom**. Christ will then reign over the earth forever and ever — world without end.

Isn't it amazing (almost mysterious) that God's entire agenda and calendar of events are revealed in these 27 mystery passages?

# The Book of Matthew.

## Jewishness of Matthew.

Matthew is the first book of the New Testament, and when you begin reading it, you get an immediate sense of its Jewishness. Not so with the other three gospels. Mark and Luke record the same events written by Matthew and interpret them more from the post-Pentecost perspective. That is, the events and teachings of Christ are told more in light of the gospel of grace and faith. Matthew is rooted deep in the law and prophets, and is as much a part of the last book in the Old Testament as it is the first book of the New Testament. It is a transitional book, written for the benefit of the Jews, being the only book that records Jesus telling his disciples not to preach to the Gentiles.

> *Matthew 10:5* These twelve Jesus sent forth, and commanded them, saying, **Go not into the way of the Gentiles**, and into any city of the Samaritans enter ye not:
> 6 But go rather to the lost sheep of the house of Israel.
> 7 And as ye go, preach, saying, The **kingdom of heaven** is at hand.

When a Gentile woman asked Jesus to heal her daughter, Jesus responded:

> *Matthew 15:24* I am not sent **but unto the lost sheep of the house of Israel**.
> 26 It is not meet to take the children's bread, and to cast it to dogs.

Certainly his response demonstrates that Matthew is entirely Jewish in perspective.

## The Parables have a common base and a common message.

We hear preachers say that Jesus spoke in parables to make his message easier to understand. The very opposite is true. In Theological Studies, they told us that parables are not to be understood in all their detail. Rather, we are just supposed to derive basic allegorical principles and truth from a parable and not pay attention to the particulars. Who is it that came to these conclusions? Those who had put away the key of knowledge and, therefore, did not and could not understand the mysteries of the kingdoms.

Most parables are based on a man who is in authority — the man always typifying God or Christ. There is no parable where the man in authority is anyone other than Deity.

He is:

- The man with the ax laid at the root of the tree
- The land owner
- The king
- The husband
- The father
- The head of a kingdom
- The physician
- The bridegroom
- The Lord of the harvest
- The master of the house
- The Lord of the Sabbath
- The Sower of seeds
- The Man sowing good seed

- The Man finding treasure
- The Man finding a pearl of great price
- The Man seeking lost sheep
- A king taking account of his servants
- The Man who is a householder with a vineyard
- The Goodman of the house
- The Man hiring laborers
- A man with two sons sent into the vineyard
- A man placing his vineyard under servants while he takes a trip into a far country
- A king who prepared a marriage banquet for his son
- The Lord of the servant coming in an hour when he does not look for him
- The bridegroom who tarries and then shuts out five foolish virgins
- A man traveling into a far country and giving talents to his servants
- A shepherd dividing sheep from goats
- A creditor who had two debtors
- The Lord of the servant coming in an hour when he thinks not
- A man with a fig tree planted in his vineyard
- A man inviting many to his supper, who all make excuses
- The Man seeking one lost sheep
- The Father of a prodigal son
- A nobleman went into a far country to receive for himself a kingdom.

In a contrasting parable, an anti kingdom parable, the actor is a woman sowing leaven or false doctrine.

# 12 kingdom of heaven parables

The **mysteries of the kingdom of heaven** are recorded in 12 **kingdom of heaven** parables found in Matthew, starting in chapter thirteen and continuing through chapter 25. By looking at all these parables together and identifying their common theme, we can gain an excellent understanding of the mystery of the **kingdom of heaven**.

It is revealing that Jesus interprets the first two kingdom parables, defining all their symbols, and thus, provides us with a glossary to interpret all twelve parables. We have listed the parables in the order they are recorded in the book of Matthew because their position has been ordered by the Holy Spirit, not by random choice. On a side note, it is significant that there are twelve kingdom of heaven parables, for twelve is the number for Jewish government.

## 1. The Kingdom message is like the seed sown by the sower. Some bears fruit, and some doesn't.

*Matthew 13:3* And he spake many things unto them in parables, saying, Behold, a sower went forth to sow;

4 And when he sowed, some seeds fell by the way side, and the fowls came and devoured them up:

5 Some fell upon stony places, where they had not much earth: and forthwith they sprung up, because they had no deepness of earth:

6 And when the sun was up, they were scorched; and because they had no root, they withered away.

7 And some fell among thorns; and the thorns sprung up, and choked them:

8 But other fell into good ground, and brought forth fruit, some an hundredfold, some sixtyfold, some thirtyfold.

9 Who hath ears to hear, let him hear.

### Jesus' Interpretation

The disciples asked Jesus for an explanation, so he gave them an official, detailed interpretation as follows:

*Matthew 13:18* Hear ye therefore the parable of the sower.

19 When any one heareth the **word of the kingdom**, and understandeth it not, then cometh the **wicked one**, and catcheth away that which was sown in his heart. This is he which received seed by the **way side**.

20 But he that received the seed into **stony places**, the same is he that heareth the word, and anon with joy receiveth it;

21 Yet hath he not root in himself, but dureth for a while: for when tribulation or persecution ariseth because of the word, by and by he is offended.

22 He also that received seed among the **thorns** is he that heareth the word; and the care of this world, and the deceitfulness of riches, **choke the word**, and he becometh unfruitful.

23 But he that received seed into the **good ground** is he that heareth the word, and understandeth it; which also beareth fruit, and bringeth forth, some an hundredfold, some sixty, some thirty.

### Jesus' Glossary of terms

- **Sower:** anyone bringing the message (in this case, Jesus), as interpreted in the next parable

- **Seed:** the message itself — the word of the kingdom

- **Fowls:** devils who take the word out of the heart

- **Way side:** message received into the heart but not understood

- **Stony places:** persecution or tribulation — shallow root

- ◆ **Thorns:** deceitfulness of riches and the cares of the world

- ◆ **Good ground:** hearts prepared to hear the word and to receive it

- ◆ **Fruit:** Natural, expected result of seed sown in good, prepared soil, more of the same that was sown — more word of the kingdom. He becomes a preacher of the message.

So what does the above parable tell us about the nature of the kingdom of heaven? As the first kingdom of heaven parable, it is a warning to the Jews that they have a responsibility to rightly respond to the kingdom message. They have several things working against them, but especially sinister is the Devil, who does not want the kingdom message to take root. He has his own kingdom, which he senses is being invaded by the kingdom of heaven. Secondly, persecution and tribulation are likely to turn many away from the message. And thirdly, the love of the world itself will prevent many from caring about the kingdom of heaven. But, there will be a few who will understand the kingdom message and receive it, and in time, they will bear fruit. It is obvious how appropriate this is as a first kingdom of heaven parable. It predicts the effect Jesus' ministry will have on Israel – some will believe and some won't.

## 2. Children of the Kingdom are seed sown, and there are counterfeits.

*Matthew 13:24* Another parable put he forth unto them, saying, **The kingdom of heaven** is likened unto **a man** which sowed good **seed** in **his field**:

25 But while men slept, his **enemy came** and sowed **tares among the wheat**, and went his way.

26 But when the blade was sprung up, and brought forth fruit, then appeared the tares also.

27 So the **servants** of the **householder** came and said unto him, Sir, didst not thou sow good seed in thy field? from whence then hath it tares?

28 He said unto them, An **enemy** hath done this. The servants said unto him, Wilt thou then that we go and gather them up?

29 But he said, Nay; lest while ye gather up the tares, ye root up also the wheat with them.

30 Let both **grow together** until the harvest: and in the time of **harvest** I will say to the reapers, Gather ye together first the tares, and bind them in bundles **to burn** them: but **gather the wheat** into my barn.

### Jesus' interpretation

Again, after Jesus spoke his second K of H parable, the disciples asked for an explanation, and Jesus provided further definition of terms.

*Matthew 13:36* Then Jesus sent the multitude away, and went into the house: and his disciples came unto him, saying, Declare unto us the parable of the tares of the field.

37 He answered and said unto them, He that soweth the good seed is the **Son of man;**

38 The **field is the world**; the **good seed** are the **children of the kingdom**; but the **tares are** the children of the wicked one;

39 The **enemy that sowed them is the devil**; the **harvest is the end of the world**; and the **reapers are the angels**.

40 As therefore the **tares are gathered and burned in the fire;** so shall it be in the **end of this world.**

41 The **Son of man** shall send forth his angels, and they shall **gather out of his kingdom** all things that offend, and them which do iniquity;

42 And shall cast them into a furnace of fire: there shall be wailing and gnashing of teeth

43 Then shall the righteous shine forth as the sun in the **kingdom of their Father**. Who hath ears to hear, let him hear.

### Jesus' Glossary of terms

- ◆ Man sowing good seed: Son of man — Jesus

- ◆ Field into which the children of the kingdom are sown: world

- ◆ Good seed: children of the kingdom

- ◆ Tares: children of the wicked one

- ◆ The Enemy who sowed the tares: the Devil

- ◆ Harvest: end of the world

- ◆ Reapers: angels

- ◆ Grow together: sinners in the kingdom along with saints

- ◆ Burning of tares: Devil's children taken out of the kingdom and cast into hell

- ◆ Wheat into barns: children of the kingdom entering into the Father's kingdom.

Symbols that are not interpreted by Jesus in these first two parables are interpreted elsewhere in the Scripture, so we need never guess at the meaning of the parables.

**Putting it together.**

This second parable takes the message of the first one a little further. It warns the Jews that the Devil is going to commission his own emissaries to infiltrate the kingdom of heaven. It will be difficult to distinguish the true from the false, so the counterfeit converts will remain as part of the K of H right up until the day when the angels come and personally remove them. The tares will be removed first, leaving the wheat (true children of the kingdom) to be harvested.

Jumping ahead of our proof, we point out that this event will transpire after the rapture, after the tribulation, and at the beginning of the Millennium. Jews who are in the kingdom but not true converts will be removed from the earth before the K of H merges with the K of G to become *The Father's kingdom*.

# 3. Infiltrated with devils.

> *Matthew 13:31* Another parable put he forth unto them, saying, **The kingdom of heaven** is like to a grain of mustard **seed**, which a **man** took, and sowed in his **field:**
> 32 Which indeed is the least of all seeds: but when it is **grown**, it is the greatest among herbs, and becometh a tree, so that the **birds of the air** come and lodge in the branches thereof.

This third kingdom of heaven parable is not interpreted for us, as were the first two, because all the symbols were previously defined. We now apply the definitions Jesus gave us. The man, Jesus, sows the seed of the word of the kingdom — a small, seemingly insignificant seed indeed — into the world. That was his ministry. After it matures, it becomes the largest kingdom, and as such it provides a place for many devils to congregate.

Again, this third parable adds a deeper dimension to our understanding of the kingdom of heaven. The first parable warned that many would not receive the message, and many who did receive it would not endure. The second parable warned that Satan would place false converts in the kingdom. Now this third parable warns that the devils themselves will find refuge in the extensive nature of the kingdom.

This seems to be a dismal picture Jesus is painting: converts who don't endure, false converts filling up the kingdom, and devils finding it comfortable to rest in the shadows of the kingdom. This is not at all what the Jews expected from their Messiah.

# 4. Corrupted with false doctrine.

> *Matthew 13:33* Another parable spake he unto them; **The kingdom of heaven** is like unto leaven, which a **woman took**, and hid in three measures of **meal**, till the **whole was leavened**.

This is a parable that has consistently been interpreted incorrectly. Jesus does not explain the meaning of leaven following this parable because he does so elsewhere (Matt. 16:11-12; Mark 8:15; 1Cor. 5:6-8; Gal. 5:9). Without exception, leaven is always used in the Bible to represent corruption. Leaven is a bacterium that causes deterioration in meal. The rotting causes the meal to bloat, which gives the bread a light texture. In all Scripture types, a **woman** is never the Church. It is a "woman" in Revelation 17-19 that comprises the last mystery of the kingdom, and she is the enemy of the saints of God. This parable says that the K of H is going to be like false doctrine and hypocrisy that completely corrupts the potential bread. This interpretation is consistent with the theme of all 12 parables, whereas an interpretation that sees this as a statement that the Church is going to influence the world to good until it spreads righteousness to all the nations is contradictory to the other 11 parables.

The picture gets even more dismal: converts who don't endure, false converts filling up the kingdom, devils finding it comfortable to rest in the shadows of the kingdom, and now false doctrine preached by a woman spreading through the entire kingdom, corrupting it completely. Four parables so far, all pointing to a failed kingdom of heaven.

## 5. The field itself is purchased for the treasure that is in it.

> *Matthew 13:44* Again, the **kingdom of heaven** is like unto **treasure hid** in a **field**; the which when a **man** hath found, he hideth, and for joy thereof goeth and **selleth** all that he hath, and **buyeth that field.**

Again, the Holy Scriptures interpret the symbols for us. Israel is God's peculiar treasure (Ex. 19:5; Ps. 135:4). Many Old Testament passages record God's intention to **hide** Israel among the nations — to cast them out of the land and scatter them in strange lands. It is critical to the interpretation of this parable to be consistent with Jesus' definition of the man in his parables. The man — the king, the householder — is always Jesus or God. So the K of H is the nation of Israel hidden among the nations of the world. After the fullness of the Gentiles is come into the K of G, all Israel will be saved when Christ takes control of the world (field) so as to control his peculiar treasure — Israel.

This parable and the one following are very similar, which is why their meaning must be found in their differences. In both parables, there is an object greatly valued by the man. In both parables the man sells all that he has to secure the valuable object. In the above parable, the thing that is unique is that the treasure is hid, found, hidden again, and then the field in which the treasure is hidden is purchased, not the treasure itself. The assumption is that the one who owns the field will own the treasure. In the parable below there is no field and nothing is hidden. The pearl of great price is valued and must be purchased to be owned.

Putting the first five parables together: Converts fail to endure, false converts fill up the kingdom, devils lodge in its shadows, false doctrine permeates the entire kingdom, and now we are told that Israel, for whom the kingdom was prepared, will be cast off and hidden in the world, making it necessary for God to come back and purchase the world (not redemption) unto himself in order to gather his peculiar treasure of Israel unto himself. This is the first parable that offers some hope, although it is in the distant future. These parables are examined in more detail, with supporting scripture, later. The next parable tells us that more than the field is in need of purchase; so does the treasure — Israel itself.

## 6. The kingdom is valued as a pearl and purchased.

> *Matthew 13:45* Again, the **kingdom of heaven** is like unto a merchant **man**, **seeking** goodly pearls:
>   46 Who, when he had found **one pearl of great price**, went and **sold all that he had**, and **bought it**.

Just like the previous parables, the man is Jesus. As we saw above, Israel is God's treasure. Jesus pays the great price (1 Pet. 1:18-19) and purchases Israel. This is perfectly in order chronologically.

Starting with the first parable, Jesus sowed the word of the kingdom. The message was largely rejected. Jesus sowed the children of the kingdom. The Devil sowed his fakes. The otherwise righteous kingdom fills up with devils and is corrupted with false doctrine. Israel is scattered among the nations, found, hidden again, and a price of redemption paid. This present parable emphasizes God's seeking of Israel and paying the price of redemption, but alas, in the next parable we discover that the kingdom will have a mixture of true and false believers right up until the judgment.

## 7. Corrupted with wicked people.

*Matthew 13:47* Again, the **kingdom of heaven** is like unto a **net**, that was cast into the sea, and gathered of **every kind**:

48 Which, **when it was full**, they drew to shore, and sat down, and **gathered the good** into vessels, but **cast the bad away**.

49 So shall it be at the **end of the world**: the **angels** shall come forth, and **sever the wicked** from among the just,

50 And shall cast them into the **furnace of fire**: there shall be wailing and gnashing of teeth.

The kingdom itself will gather unto itself both the good and the bad — the true children of the kingdom and the false. At the end of the world, the angels separate the bad from the good and cast them into hell. It is noteworthy that in this kingdom judgment parable, it is not the righteous who are removed but the evil, as will be the case at the beginning of the Millennium, when the wicked are removed from the kingdom — removed from the earth.

Looking on the surface, this parable may seem to be redundant. The second parable represented the Devil sowing false converts into the kingdom — tares among the wheat. This parable also tells us that the wicked will be present with the righteous in the day of harvest. But the second parable makes a point of the fact that the Devil would sow his false converts. This parable takes us further and points out that, even apart from the Devil, the momentum of the kingdom itself will attract wicked people who later will need to be separated out of the kingdom. Just because one is not planted by the Devil doesn't make him an acceptable part of the kingdom. He must be righteous as well. The former parable was about the children of God or the children of the Devil. This parable is about being righteous or being wicked — good or bad fish found in the one net.

The parables have progressed chronologically. They have taken us forward to the day of judgment (end of the Tribulation — beginning of the Millennium). The following parable expands upon this one and discusses what it means to be righteous — like the good fish that were kept.

## 8. A King requires one to forgive personal debts.

*Matthew 18:23* Therefore is the **kingdom of heaven** likened unto a **certain king**, which would **take account** of his **servants**.

24 And when he had begun to reckon, one was brought unto him, which owed him ten thousand talents.

25 But forasmuch as he had not to pay, his lord commanded him to be sold, and his wife, and children, and all that he had, and payment to be made.

26 The servant therefore fell down, and worshipped him, saying, Lord, have patience with me, and I will pay thee all.

27 Then the lord of that servant was moved with compassion, and loosed him, and forgave him the debt.

28 But the same servant went out, and found one of his fellowservants, which owed him an hundred pence: and he laid hands on him, and took him by the throat, saying, Pay me that thou owest.

29 And his fellowservant fell down at his feet, and besought him, saying, Have patience with me, and I will pay thee all.

30 And he would not: but went and cast him into prison, till he should pay the debt.

31 So when his fellowservants saw what was done, they were very sorry, and came and told unto their lord all that was done.

32 Then his lord, after that he had called him, said unto him, O thou wicked servant, I forgave thee all that debt, because thou desiredst me:

33 **Shouldest not thou also have had compassion on thy fellowservant, even as I had pity on thee?**

34 And his lord was wroth, and **delivered him to the tormentors**, till he should pay all that was due unto him.

35 So likewise shall my heavenly Father do also unto you, **if ye from your hearts forgive not every one his brother their trespasses.**

This parable clarifies the previous one, telling us something about the criteria for separating the good from the bad in judgment at the beginning of the Millennium. King Jesus will demand of his servants (Jews) an accounting as to how they have shown mercy to others. The Jews had contented themselves with maintaining a personal relationship to the dead law. Righteousness is not an abstract state of mind. It is the act of loving your neighbor with your substance and your time.

## 9. Latecomers will be rewarded equal to the first.

*Matthew 20:1* For the **kingdom of heaven** is like unto a **man that is an householder,** which went out early in the morning to hire **labourers** into **his vineyard.**

2 And when he had agreed with the labourers for a penny a day, he sent them into his **vineyard.**

3 And he went out about the third hour, and saw others standing idle in the marketplace,

4 And said unto them; Go ye also into the vineyard, and whatsoever is right I will give you. And they went their way.

5 Again he went out about the sixth and ninth hour, and did likewise.

6 And about the eleventh hour he went out, and found others standing idle, and saith unto them, Why stand ye here all the day idle?

7 They say unto him, Because no man hath hired us. He saith unto them, Go ye also into the vineyard; and whatsoever is right, that shall ye receive.

8 So when even was come, the **lord of the vineyard** saith unto his **steward,** Call the labourers, and **give them their hire,** beginning from the last unto the first.

9 And when they came that were hired about the eleventh hour, they received every man a penny.

10 But when the first came, they supposed that they should have received more; and they likewise received every man a penny.

11 And when they had received it, they murmured against the goodman of the house,

12 Saying, These last have wrought but one hour, and thou hast made them equal unto us, which have borne the burden and heat of the day.

13 But he answered one of them, and said, Friend, I do thee no wrong: didst not thou agree with me for a penny?

14 Take that thine is, and go thy way: **I will give unto this last, even as unto thee.**

15 Is it not lawful for me to do what I will with mine own? Is thine eye evil, because I am good?

16 So the last shall be first, and the first last: for many be called, but few chosen.

This parable would indeed be strange if it were not for its K of H context. Israel is God's vineyard (Isa. 5:3-7; Jer. 12:10). The laborers are hired to work in the vineyard (kingdom). At various times throughout the day, additional workers are called to work in the kingdom. At the end of the day, the ones who worked only a short time are paid the same wages as those who worked all day. It is offensive to the early workers that they did not receive more pay relative to those who worked fewer hours. The message is that the kingdom will have early volunteers and late volunteers, and the latecomers may be rewarded first and with just as much pay. This was offensive to the earlycomers, just as it will be to the Jews when they find out that, those who join the kingdom late in the Tribulation may receive a reward just as great as the early Apostles who bore the heat of persecution. Righteousness is rejoicing in your neighbor's prosperity.

## 10. Those called don't come and are replaced.

*Matthew 22:1* And Jesus answered and spake unto them again by parables, and said,

2 The **kingdom of heaven** is like unto a certain **king,** which made a **marriage** for his **son,**

3 And sent forth his **servants** to call them that were bidden to the wedding: and they **would not come.**

4 Again, he sent forth other servants, saying, Tell them which are bidden, Behold, I have prepared my dinner: my oxen and my fatlings are killed, and all things are ready: come unto the marriage.

5 But they made light of it, and went their ways, one to his farm, another to his merchandise:

6 And the remnant took his servants, and entreated them spitefully, and **slew them.**

**7** But when the king heard thereof, he was wroth: and he **sent forth his armies,** and destroyed those murderers, and **burned up their city.**

8 Then saith he to his servants, The wedding is ready, but **they which were bidden were not worthy.**

9 Go ye therefore into the **highways,** and as many as ye shall find, bid to the marriage.

10 So those servants went out into the highways, and gathered together all as many as they found, **both bad and good:** and the wedding was furnished with guests.

11 And when the king came in to see the guests, he saw there a man which had not on a wedding garment:

12 And he saith unto him, Friend, how camest thou in hither not having a wedding garment? And he was speechless.

13 Then said the king **to the servants,** Bind him hand and foot, and take him away, and **cast him into outer darkness;** there shall be weeping and gnashing of teeth.

14 For **many are called,** but few are chosen.

This parable is marvelous with its detailed prophecy. It brings us right down to the end, giving some detail about false converts and bad fish that must first be weeded out of the kingdom. Obviously, the king is God and the son is Jesus. The marriage is of Christ to his Church. The servants' guests at the wedding are Jews. We know that to be so because the Church could not be the bride and the guests at the same time.

Clearly, it is prophecy with dual application. It had application to those who heard it and still has, right up until the beginning of the Millennium. In both cases, it is a warning to those who will not receive the **kingdom of heaven.**

Looking at it as contemporary with Jesus, the Jews, as potential members of the kingdom of heaven, are invited to come and be part of the Church — the Bride. They will not come, for they did not believe Jesus and so continued on in their traditions and daily affairs. The servants (including John and all those who went out preaching the gospel of the kingdom of heaven) invite them, but John is killed. The king, God, responds by sending his Roman armies to destroy the city of Jerusalem in 70 AD. The Father of the bridegroom again sent out **his servants (Church age missionaries)** into the highways to bid as many as they could find to the wedding. They go out into the highways, a place where one might encounter Gentiles, and invite those previously not invited. And, amazingly, the invitation is extended to the **bad** as well as the **good.** Sinners are invited to the wedding. But someone had the audacity to attend the wedding in his own garment rather than the one provided for him. That man rejected the gift of righteousness and came dressed in his own good works. He was cast into hell. And the concluding statement is a summary of the facts surrounding this parable: many Jews are called to come into the kingdom, but only a few are chosen to actually sit down at the wedding supper.

In the chronological order of prophetic events, this occasion is perfectly placed as the tenth parable. It is the beginning of the Millennium, or after the Second Coming and immediately before the commencement of the Millennium, depending on whether or not there is a bracket of time between them. In its final fulfillment, the Tribulation is over, and those left on earth must be judged. In the land of Israel there are surviving Jews, some who are believers and some who are not. They have not taken the mark of the beast, but neither have they received the gift of righteousness. They are still in natural bodies when they are invited to be guests at the wedding supper of Jesus Christ. A Jew expects to be accepted in the marriage feast dressed in his own religious perspective. He does not accept by faith the gift of righteousness. He is accordingly thrown out of the supper and into hell.

## 11. Watchfulness required, some turned away.

> *Matthew 25:* **Then** shall the **kingdom of heaven** be likened unto **ten virgins**, which took their lamps, and went forth to **meet the bridegroom**.
>
> 2 And five of them were wise, and five were foolish.
>
> 3 They that were foolish took their lamps, and took no oil with them:
>
> 4 But the **wise took oil** in their vessels with their lamps.
>
> 5 While the **bridegroom tarried,** they all slumbered and slept.
>
> 6 And at midnight there was a cry made, Behold, the **bridegroom cometh**; go ye out to meet him.
>
> 7 Then all those virgins arose, and trimmed their lamps.
>
> 8 And the foolish said unto the wise, Give us of your oil; for our lamps are gone out.
>
> 9 But the wise answered, saying, Not so; lest there be not enough for us and you: but go ye rather to them that sell, and buy for yourselves.
>
> 10 And while they went to buy, the **bridegroom came**; and they that were ready **went in with him to the marriage**: and the **door was shut**.
>
> 11 Afterward came also the other virgins, saying, Lord, Lord, open to us.
>
> 12 But he answered and said, Verily I say unto you, I know you not.
>
> 13 **Watch therefore,** for ye know neither the day nor the hour wherein the **Son of man cometh.**

He again turns to marriage as the basis for this parable, because it is the marriage of Jesus to his Bride that is the occasion. You will notice in this parable and the parable above, the status of the bride is never an issue. The marriage is certain, planned, and a date set. In both parables, it is the guests who are undecided. In the former parable it was the general guest that made light of the wedding. In this parable it is the bridesmaids who must remain prepared.

It is obvious that the 10 virgins waiting on the bridegroom are not his brides. No Jew ever married 10 women at the same time, unless it may have been Solomon. Christ has just one bride. The bridesmaids are defined in Psalm 45 (a prophecy of Jesus) as virgins who attend to the bride.

> *Psalm 45:6* Thy throne, O God, is for ever and ever: the sceptre of thy kingdom is a right sceptre.
>
> 7 Thou lovest righteousness, and hatest wickedness: therefore God, thy God, hath anointed thee with the oil of gladness above thy fellows.
>
> 13 The king's daughter is all glorious within: her clothing is of wrought gold.
>
> 14 She shall be brought unto the king in raiment of needlework: the virgins her companions that follow her shall be brought unto thee.
>
> 15 With gladness and rejoicing shall they be brought: they shall enter into the king's palace.

Clearly, this is a parable informing the Jews that Jesus will come back to attend his own wedding and that the guests must remain always in a prepared state, for he will tarry much longer than they might expect. And when he comes, some Jews who were to attend the wedding will not be ready and will not get in. Remember, this is what the kingdom of heaven is like, meaning that when Jesus comes back to set up the kingdom, it will begin with a wedding to the predominately Gentile Church and result in five out of ten Jews not being allowed to attend. Beautiful in all its details! Is it not?

So, the message is that, those of you Jews who are still waiting for Messiah must have oil (Holy Spirit) in your lamp (since the Jews are the light of the world, a city set on a hill to give light unto the world) when Jesus returns, for it will then be too late to acquire the oil. Watch therefore, for you do not know the day that Jesus will return to set up his kingdom.

## 12. Ruling in the kingdom depends on stewardship.

This last kingdom of heaven parable is the most direct and revealing. It is based on all the other parables, and sums them up.

*Matthew 25:14* For the **kingdom of heaven** is as a **man traveling into a far country,** who called his own **servants,** and **delivered unto them** his goods.

15 And unto one he gave five talents, to another two, and to another one; **to every man according to his several ability;** and straightway **took his journey.**

16 Then he that had received the five talents went and traded with the same, and made them other five talents.

17 And likewise he that had received two, he also gained other two.

18 But he that had received one went and **digged in the earth, and hid his lord's money.**

19 **After a long time** the lord of those servants **cometh, and reckoneth** with them.

20 And so he that had received five talents came and brought other five talents, saying, Lord, thou deliveredst unto me five talents: behold, I have gained beside them five talents more.

21 His lord said unto him, Well done, thou good and faithful servant: thou hast been faithful over a few things, **I will make thee ruler over many things:** enter thou into the joy of thy lord.

22 He also that had received two talents came and said, Lord, thou deliveredst unto me two talents: behold, I have gained two other talents beside them.

23 His lord said unto him, Well done, good and faithful servant; thou hast been faithful over a few things, I will make thee **ruler over many things**: enter thou into the joy of thy lord.

24 Then he which had received the one talent came and said, Lord, I knew thee **that thou art an hard man**, reaping where thou hast not sown, and gathering where thou hast not strawed:

25 And I was afraid, and went and hid thy talent in the earth: lo, there thou hast that is thine.

26 His lord answered and said unto him, Thou wicked and slothful servant, thou knewest that I reap where I sowed not, and gather where I have not strawed:

27 Thou oughtest therefore to have put my money to the exchangers, and then at my coming I should have received mine own with usury.

28 Take therefore the talent from him, and give it unto him which hath ten talents.

29 **For unto every one that hath shall be given, and he shall have abundance: but from him that hath not shall be taken away even that which he hath.**

30 And cast ye the unprofitable servant into **outer darkness**: there shall be weeping and gnashing of teeth.

The contents of this parable make it perfect as the last kingdom of heaven parable. This is a warning and a prophecy. The man, Christ Jesus, is going to travel into a far country (heaven). Before he goes, he will entrust money and responsibility to his servants — each according to his ability. He immediately and suddenly takes his journey — as Jesus commissioned the disciples and then ascended into heaven. Two of the servants applied themselves and their resources and gathered a return. One man was fearful and hid his Lord's money so he wouldn't lose it. After a long time (he emphasizes that it will be a long time before Jesus returns), the Lord returned to reckon with his servants. The two who were faithful to multiply their seed money were rewarded with ruling over cities — as Jesus told the disciples they would do in his coming kingdom. The man who was fearful and kept his money buried returned the principal to his master without any gain. He pleaded fear as his motive for not investing, and was rebuked, and the money was taken from him and given to the man who already had much more. Then the reticent, fearful investor was cast into hell because of his fear and unbelief.

Without an inspired interpretation, this parable would be strange in some of its points. For example, what has money got to do with the kingdom? Why would a man be cast into hell for not investing his money? The fearful, unbelieving servant buried it so he would not lose it and would be able to return what was not his. He did not waste the money on foolish living. He was frugal, self-disciplined and cautious. Why such severe punishment for what appears to be a small offense at worst?

But the sermon does not stop there. Jesus continues and makes practical application of the parable. We will continue with the very next verse. Notice that the first word is *When* — dating the events of the parable. Remember, this chapter began with, "Then shall the **kingdom of heaven** be likened unto…." The *then* reflected back on the previous chapter, which described the Tribulation and the Second Coming of Christ. The next verse before us, 25:31, updates our memories as to when this particular parable will be applicable, "When the Son of man shall come in his glory…" To interpret this parable accurately, it is absolutely essential to accept the dating Jesus gives it. Then it makes perfect sense in every detail.

The following portion follows the parable above, but is not a parable. It is Jesus' interpretation of the parable. The events of the parable and the explanation below will occur at the beginning of the Millennium.

> *Matthew 25:31* **When** the Son of man shall come in his glory, and all the holy angels with him, then shall he sit upon the throne of his glory:
> 32 And before him shall be gathered all nations: and he shall separate them one from another, as a shepherd divideth his sheep from the goats:
> 33 And he shall set the sheep on his right hand, but the goats on the left.
> 34 **Then** shall the King say unto them on his right hand, Come, ye blessed of my Father, inherit the kingdom prepared for you from the foundation of the world:

**When** (25:31) Jesus comes to the earth to sit on the throne of the world's kingdoms, the people of the earth are brought before earth's king (Jesus) by their nations. As in the parable above, the man who traveled to a far country has now returned and called his servants before him to give an accounting of how they handled their "goods" — tangible assets. And, as in the parable above, those who had been faithful were rewarded with positions in the kingdom.

The big question created by the above parable is, why were they rewarded for the way they handled money? Why was the fearful man cast into hell for failing to invest the money? Because "**I was an hungred, and ye gave me no meat: I was thirsty….**" (verse 42, below).

> 41 Then shall he say also unto them on the left hand, Depart from me, ye cursed, into everlasting fire, prepared for the devil and his angels:
> 42 For I was an hungred, and ye gave me no meat: I was thirsty, and ye gave me no drink:
> 43 I was a stranger, and ye took me not in: naked, and ye clothed me not: sick, and in prison, and ye visited me not.
> 44 Then shall they also answer him, saying, Lord, when saw we thee an hungred, or athirst, or a stranger, or naked, or sick, or in prison, and did not minister unto thee?
> 45 Then shall he answer them, saying, Verily I say unto you, Inasmuch as ye did it not to one of the least of these, ye did it not to me.
> 46 And these shall go away into everlasting punishment: but the righteous into life eternal.

Remember, in the parable above, the man had given his servants money to invest, expecting to receive a return. They were only entrusted with the money and commanded to invest it for profit. The text immediately above, v. 41-46, reveals what kind of a return God wants for the money he gave to his servants (Jews and Gentiles of the Tribulation era). The Jews and some Gentiles who refused the mark of the beast and were not allowed to buy or sell had to run for their lives during the reign of Antichrist. They were hungry, thirsty (when there was nothing but blood to drink), naked, sick, and in prison. The nations will have to give an account for how they responded to the needs of God's people during this time of tribulation. Did you use your money to clothe and feed my people? Did you visit them with care packages and a drink of water when they were in prison? Did you provide them with a place to stay when they were fleeing for their lives? If you were (as in the parable above) afraid to invest your goods in that manner, everything will be taken from you, and you will be cast into hell. If you did invest your goods in the lives of those in need, then, according to the text, you served Christ himself. You multiplied your investment, and God received the return as though you had actually fed him.

Those who were faithful will then (as in the parable above) be granted positions in the kingdom, ruling over cities.

This will be a confusing and contradictory parable if you do not accept the prophetic context in which it is found. But when we understand it in its chronology, it is beautiful in every detail. As the last parable, it brings us to the commencement of the kingdom upon this earth.

## Basic theme of each kingdom parable in the order they were recorded:

1. 13:3 The message is seed. Some bears fruit, and some doesn't.
2. 13:24 Children of the Kingdom are seed-sown, and there are counterfeits.
3. 13:31 The Kingdom corrupted with devils.
4. 13:33 The Kingdom is corrupted with false doctrine.
5. 13:44 The world is purchased for the treasure that is in it.
6. 13:45 The kingdom itself is valued like a very precious pearl and is purchased.
7. 13:47 It is corrupted with wicked people who will be removed from among the just.
8. 18:23-35 The King requires people to forgive others in matters of debt.
9. 20:1-16 The last to come into the kingdom may be the first to be rewarded.
10. 22:1-14 Those who are called and don't come are replaced by those who come.
11. 25:1-13 Watchfulness is required, and some are turned away.
12. 25:14 Ruling in the kingdom depends on proper stewardship.

## The Man in all parables is Jesus.

*Ten of the parables have a man as the primary actor. In all of them, Jesus is the man.*

1. He is the man sowing the seed of the word — the kingdom message.
2. He is the man sowing the good seed — children of the kingdom — in the kingdom.
3. Jesus is the man sowing the grain of mustard seed. The seed becomes the kingdom.

In the first three parables, Jesus has sown the word of the kingdom, the children of the kingdom, and then the kingdom itself.

4. This fourth parable does not have a man sowing, and well it shouldn't, for the leaven that is sown produces nothing but corruption. It is a woman (perhaps a Marian apparition) sowing false doctrine in the kingdom.
5. Jesus is the man who finds the treasure (Israel) hidden in the field (world).
6. Jesus is the seeker of goodly pearls and pays a great price to buy one.
7. This is the second parable where Jesus is not the initiator. The angels are the fishermen who cast a net into the kingdom and bring out good and bad fish.
8. Jesus is the king taking account of his servants.
9. Jesus is the householder hiring laborers and paying them as he sees fit.
10. Jesus is the king making a marriage for his son.
11. Jesus is the bridegroom coming to his wedding, prepared to shut the door on any who are not ready.
12. Jesus is the man going away and placing his goods in the hands of servants, who, when he returns, rewards faithful stewardship with positions of ruling over cities (Luke 19:17-19).

## Summing up the kingdom parables.

We will sum up the 12 kingdom parables in the order they are given, drawing the basic inference from each. Jesus is the one who sows seed that produces good children for a kingdom that becomes large and eventually full of devils. The devil sows fake children in the kingdom, along with the real, and Jesus allows both the good and the bad to grow together until the end. We are then told that a woman is going to sow false doctrine in the kingdom as well. The kingdom is going to be hidden in the world, but Jesus will take possession of the world so he can claim the treasure of the kingdom that is in it. Jesus is seeking Israel, the goodly pearl, and will pay the supreme price to purchase her. There is a warning that at the end, angels will separate out of the kingdom the true converts from the false. Jesus will bring all his servants into judgment. The king requires each one to forgive debts as he has been forgiven of his sins. Those who get involved in the work of the kingdom at a later hour may receive the same reward as those involved from the very beginning. Those who are called, but don't come, will be replaced with willing strangers from the highways and byways. Watch, for the kingdom will commence with a wedding, and if you are not ready, you will be left out. After he returns, those who have been faithful will be granted prominent positions of ruling over cities in the coming kingdom.

This is marvelous indeed! It is like finding hidden treasure, like discovering sub-atomic particles or the genome sequence. Jesus gives 12 **kingdom of heaven** parables to his 12 apostles concerning the 12 tribes of Israel — 12 being the number of Jewish government throughout the Bible. The parables which most people think are just random in their message and sequence, are, in fact, carefully crafted by the Holy Spirit and ordered in the Bible so as to tell us the entire story of the **kingdom of heaven** chronologically. What are the chances of that occurring apart from divine design? Most Bible scholars have had too little respect for the Word of God. It is almost too late to treat it with the respect it deserves. Wonderful things have been hidden, and few have even suspected they were there. There is much more hidden in the Word of God, just waiting for some believing soul to believe it when he reads it.

# 7 Kingdom of God parables.

There are seven **kingdom of God** parables, as one who is familiar with the meaning of biblical numbers might expect, whereas there were 12 **kingdom of heaven** parables. Seven is the number of completion, as in seven days makes a week; seven colors are a complete pallet, and there are seven notes in a music scale. There are seven churches in the book of Revelation representing the entire church. Christ is in the midst of seven golden candlesticks, seven stars in his right hand, and there are seven angels. There are seven spirits of God around the throne and seven lamps burning. Jewish history and feast days are full of seven days, seven weeks, seven months, seven years, 49 (7 X 7), and finally, Israel's history is divided into seven 490-(7 X 70) year periods. The Jews were delivered into captivity for 70 years. Daniel's seventieth week will last seven years. There will be seven seals, seven trumpets, seven thunders, seven vials. The sun will be seven times hotter. Jesus told the disciples that they were to forgive a repentant brother 7 X 70 times — and much, much more. Seven is the number of completeness. Its repeated presence in matters that are Divinely ordered and prophesied are the certified fingerprints of God on his book.

In examining the seven Kingdom of God parables, we are now going to add a new dimension to this study. You will see the K of G parables alongside their K of H counterparts, enabling us to contrast the two. Underlined portions indicate differences in the two kingdoms.

Mark records three K of G parables, and they match in order and basic content the first three K of H parables found in Matthew. The parable of the sower (below) is the first parable recorded by Matthew, Mark, and Luke. Luke records four K of G parables, and he, too, records the parable of the sower first, as do Matthew and Mark. Jesus' interpretation is recorded in all three accounts. And, Mark declared this first parable to be the foundation of understanding all parables (Mark 4:13).

Mark adds a most interesting sidenote to it. "And he said to his disciples, Know ye not this parable? and how then will ye know all parables?" (Mark 4:13). His remark indicates that **this parable of the sower** (the first of only three that Jesus interpreted; one of only two parables that all three gospels record) **is the key to understanding all other parables**. As we saw when we reviewed the K of H parables, in his interpretation of those first two parables Jesus provided us with a glossary of parable terminology, erasing all doubt as to their meanings.

We have been told to never base our doctrine on parables. Notice that in chapter 4:2, Mark calls Jesus' parables, **doctrine**. Parables are more than moral stories. They are absolute, detailed truth about the eight kingdoms — **doctrine** taught by Jesus Christ and explained all the way down to the nitty-gritty detail.

## Parables 1 & 2. Kingdom of God parable of the sower.

| Kingdom of God | Kingdom of God | Kingdom of heaven |
|---|---|---|
| *Mark 4:2* And he taught them many things by parables, and said unto them in his doctrine, <br> 3 Hearken; Behold, there went out a sower to sow: <br> 4 And it came to pass, as he sowed, some fell by the way side, and the fowls of the air came and devoured it up. <br> 5 And some fell on stony ground, where it had not much earth; and immediately it sprang up, because it had no depth of earth: | *Luke 8:1* And it came to pass afterward, that he went throughout every city and village, preaching and shewing the glad tidings of the **kingdom of God**: <br> 4 And when much people were gathered together, and were come to him out of every city, he spake by a parable: <br> 5 A sower went out to sow his seed: and as he sowed, some fell by the way side; | *Matthew 13:3* And he spake many things unto them in parables, saying, Behold, a sower went forth to sow; <br> 4 And when he sowed, some seeds fell by the way side, and the fowls came and devoured them up: <br> 5 Some fell upon stony places, where they had not much earth: and forthwith they sprung up, because they had no deepness of earth: <br> 6 And when the sun was up, they were scorched; and because they had no root, they withered away. <br> 7 And some fell among thorns; and the thorns sprung up, and choked them: |

6 But when the sun was up, it was scorched; and because it had no root, it withered away.

7 And some fell among thorns, and the thorns grew up, and choked it, and it yielded no fruit.

8 And other fell on good ground, and did yield fruit that sprang up and increased; and brought forth, some thirty, and some sixty, and some an hundred.

9 And he said unto them, He that hath ears to hear, let him hear.

10 And when he was alone, they that were about him with the twelve asked of him the parable.

11 And he said unto them, Unto you it is given to know the **mystery of the kingdom of God:** but unto them that are without, all these things are done in parables:

12 That seeing they may see, and not perceive; and hearing they may hear, and not understand; lest at any time they should be converted, and their sins should be forgiven them.

13 And he said unto them, Know ye not this parable? and how then will ye know all parables?

14 The sower soweth the word.

15 And these are they by the way side, where the word is sown; but when they have heard, Satan cometh immediately, and taketh away the word that was sown in their hearts.

16 And these are they likewise which are sown on stony ground; who, when they have heard the word, immediately receive it with gladness;

17 And have no root in themselves, and so endure but for a time: afterward, when affliction or persecution ariseth for the word's sake, immediately they are offended.

18 And these are they which are sown among thorns; such as hear the word,

19 And the cares of this world, and the deceitfulness of riches, and the lusts of other things entering in, choke the word, and it becometh unfruitful.

20 And these are they which are sown on good ground; such as hear the word, and receive it, and bring forth fruit, some thirtyfold, some sixty, and some an hundred.

and it was trodden down, and the fowls of the air devoured it.

6 And some fell upon a rock; and as soon as it was sprung up, it withered away, because it lacked moisture.

7 And some fell among thorns; and the thorns sprang up with it, and choked it.

8 And other fell on good ground, and sprang up, and bare fruit an hundredfold. And when he had said these things, he cried, He that hath ears to hear, let him hear.

9 And his disciples asked him, saying, What might this parable be?

10 And he said, Unto you it is given to know the **mysteries of the kingdom of God**: but to others in parables; that seeing they might not see, and hearing they might not understand.

11 Now the parable is this: The seed is the word of God.

12 Those by the way side are they that hear; then cometh the devil, and taketh away the word out of their hearts, lest they should believe and be saved.

13 They on the rock are they, which, when they hear, receive the word with joy; and these have no root, which for a while believe, and in time of temptation fall away.

14 And that which fell among thorns are they, which, when they have heard, go forth, and are choked with cares and riches and pleasures of this life, and bring no fruit to perfection.

15 But that on the good ground are they, which in an honest and good heart, having heard the word, keep it, and bring forth fruit with patience.

8 But other fell into good ground, and brought forth fruit, some an hundredfold, some sixtyfold, some thirtyfold.

9 Who hath ears to hear, let him hear.

10 And the disciples came, and said unto him, Why speakest thou unto them in parables?

11 He answered and said unto them, Because it is given unto you to know the **mysteries of the kingdom of heaven**, but to them it is not given.

12 For whosoever hath, to him shall be given, and he shall have more abundance: but whosoever hath not, from him shall be taken away even that he hath.

13 Therefore speak I to them in parables: because they seeing see not; and hearing they hear not, neither do they understand.

14 And in them is fulfilled the prophecy of Esaias, which saith, By hearing ye shall hear, and shall not understand; and seeing ye shall see, and shall not perceive:

15 For this people's heart is waxed gross, and their ears are dull of hearing, and their eyes they have closed; lest at any time they should see with their eyes, and hear with their ears, and should understand with their heart, and should be converted, and I should heal them.

16 But blessed are your eyes, for they see: and your ears, for they hear.

17 For verily I say unto you, That many prophets and righteous men have desired to see those things which ye see, and have not seen them; and to hear those things which ye hear, and have not heard them.

18 Hear ye therefore the parable of the sower.

19 When any one heareth the word of the kingdom, and understandeth it not, then cometh the wicked one, and catcheth away that which was sown in his heart. This is he which received seed by the way side.

20 But he that received the seed into stony places, the same is he that heareth the word, and anon with joy receiveth it;

21 Yet hath he not root in himself, but dureth for a while: for when tribulation or persecution ariseth because of the word, by and by he is offended.

22 He also that received seed among the thorns is he that heareth the word; and the care of this world, and the deceitfulness of riches, choke the word, and he becometh unfruitful.

23 But he that received seed into the good ground is he that heareth the word, and understandeth it; which also beareth fruit, and bringeth forth, some an hundredfold, some sixty, some thirty.

From all three accounts, we know that both kingdoms are alike in the way in which the **word of the kingdom** will be sown and the manner in which the seed will either fail or bring forth fruit. There are a few minor omissions in Luke's more abbreviated record, but Luke has added an element that could only be applicable to the K of G. When the devil takes away the seed, Luke adds, **lest they should believe and be saved.** No one is challenged to believe in the K of H and no one gets saved. The concept of being saved never appears in connection with the K of H.

The greatest difference is the little phrase in Mark 4:12, "…and their sins should be **forgiven** them." Matthew says, (v. 15) "…and I should **heal** them." The gospel of the K of G is first of all about forgiveness. The **word of the kingdom** of heaven is about the nation being healed and restored. The word *heal* is used many times by the prophets (not in reference to healing disease), rather, speaking of restoring the nation to repentance and blessing. The K of H message was never offered as something to believe or as an appeal for personal forgiveness. That was the very essence of the K of G gospel.

But as a whole, the K of G and the K of H are alike in that a message is preached, eliciting various responses, Satan is interfering, persecution comes, and the cares of the world are drawing men away from what they hear, while some seed takes hold and bears fruit. In these things they are identical. Under the gospel of the K of G, they receive forgiveness; under the K of H, the nation is healed and made ready for the king to set up his kingdom on the earth. The basic point of these three parables, whether kingdom of God or kingdom of heaven, is that a few will receive the seed of the word and bear fruit, but most will not.

## 3. The Kingdom of God parable of the harvest (tares).

There is a fascinating contrast in these two parables. Mark starts off his second K of G parable with terms and images that seem to match Matthew's second K of H parable, but takes a turn that creates a clear differentiation between the two kingdoms. Because they are similar in their basic symbols and in the event of a man sowing seed in his field and then sleeping while his crop comes up, **and,** because they maintain the same order (the second of three parables recorded in the same order), Mark's departure from Matthew's parable is all the more noteworthy. We have to ask why Mark took such a radical turn. The answer is obvious. The particular distinctive of Matthew's parable could in no way be associated with the K of G. The parables differ markedly as they must, since the kingdoms differ in the same manner.

| Kingdom of God | Kingdom of heaven |
|---|---|
| *Mark 4:26* And he said, So is the **kingdom of God**, as if a man should cast seed into the ground; 27 And should sleep, and rise night and day, and the seed should spring and grow up, <u>he knoweth not how.</u> 28 For the earth bringeth forth <u>fruit of herself</u>; <u>first the blade, then the ear, after that the full corn in the ear.</u> 29 But when the fruit is brought forth, <u>immediately</u> he putteth in the sickle, because the <u>harvest is come.</u> | *Matthew 13:24* Another parable put he forth unto them, saying, The **kingdom of heaven** is likened unto a man which sowed good seed in his field: 25 But while men slept, his <u>enemy came and sowed tares</u> among the wheat, and went his way. 26 But when the blade was sprung up, and brought forth fruit, then <u>appeared the tares also.</u> 27 So the servants of the householder came and said unto him, Sir, didst not thou sow good seed in thy field? from whence then hath it tares? 28 He said unto them, An enemy hath done this. The servants said unto him, Wilt thou then that we go and gather them up? 29 But he said, Nay; lest while ye gather up the tares, ye root up also the wheat with them. 30 Let <u>both grow together until the harvest</u>: and in the time of harvest I will say <u>to the reapers</u>, Gather ye together <u>first the tares</u>, and bind them in bundles to burn them: but gather the wheat into my barn. |

This K of G parable starts out just like the second K of H parable, the parable of the tares, but it quickly takes another turn. In both parables a man casts seed *(the word — the message)* into the ground and then goes to sleep, which allows for the growth of the seed. In the K of H account, the enemy *(Devil)* comes and sows tares while the man is sleeping. In the K of G version *(the Church)*, while the man is sleeping a miracle takes place. The seed wondrously springs up and progresses through three stages until it is ready for the harvest *(rapture)*. At harvest time there is no hustle or bustle taking place, no tares to be removed first, no false converts to be judged. "Immediately he putteth in the sickle." The completed Church is raptured out in the twinkling of an eye.

We have already reviewed the parable of the tares in Matthew 13, but we need to recall and review several points of contrast to Mark's parable of the harvest. *The two parables, and the two kingdoms, part ways at the tares.* The K of G is not a political institution that can contain or control the tares, whereas the K of H, by its very tangible, earthly nature, can and will rule over unsaved individuals at the beginning of the Millennium. Just as in Jesus' day, if he had set up the K of H, Judas would have been a member. He would have been a tare, sown by the devil, in the **kingdom of heaven**. But Judas never was in the K of G. He was not born again, and he never saw the K of G, other than seeing Jesus.

The main thrust of Matthew's parable of the tares is that both the real and the imposter grow together until the angelic harvest, at which time the tares are removed and burned, leaving the wheat in the kingdom. Whereas, in Mark, the K of G progresses from the blade to the full corn, at which time it is harvested — immediately. The K of G ends with *all the saved who will be saved and the bride complete,* immediately followed by a harvest (rapture) of the wheat. There are no tares involved. But the K of H has been under alien control for the past 2,000 years, filled with mostly tares, devils, corruption, false doctrine, and unbelief. During the Tribulation period, 144,000 saved Jews will bring back the K of H to where it was during the ministry of John the Baptist — **at hand**. Israel will then be a mixture of wheat and tares, believing and unbelieving. The order in Matthew is clear, "Gather ye together **first** the tares…." At the beginning of the Millennium, the tares (sinners) will be removed from the kingdom, leaving only the wheat (saved Jews and those Gentiles whom they have converted).

Notice some of the particulars in Mark's gospel concerning the K of G. He makes a point of the seed sower's lack of involvement in the wondrous growth and development of the plant. It **springs up**, and he **knoweth not how**. This is clearly a reference to the effectual working of the Word of God empowering the gospel to transform men by the new birth, which is effected by the Holy Spirit apart from human agency, but utilizing the obedient believer to deliver the message (Col. 1:6; 1Thes. 2:13). Mark's parable also makes a point of the sure, steady growth and development of the seed, describing its progress through its stages, just as a plant grows to maturity and is harvested on schedule. This is in great contrast to the K of H parables where there are all kinds of difficulty, conflict, and delay involved. The Church as part of the K of G will grow as the body of Jesus Christ, more added to the kingdom each generation, until the elect are all brought into the fold, at which time the wondrous process is complete and the harvest is come (which will be the Rapture). No tares or sinners are involved in this harvest. Isn't it wonderful how God could design two parables so alike and yet by their differences teach us so much? It is just such carefully crafted internal structure as this that proves that every word of God is inspired and preserved with complete integrity.

## 4 & 5. Kingdom of God parable of the mustard seed.

Again, both Matthew and Mark record the parable of the mustard seed as their third kingdom parable. Luke also records it. This is the second of only two kingdom parables recorded by all three so-called synoptic gospel writers.

On a side note: The similar structure of the first three gospels (same or similar parables recorded in the same order) has led many to conclude that they must have been copied one from the other. If indeed the few parables recorded in the gospels were randomly selected from what must have been hundreds of parables delivered over three and one half years, then the odds that three gospel writer would independently choose the same parable and the same order would be small. It would be more reasonable to conclude that there was some collusion between them or that two writers copied from the first. But such a position is based on unbelief — a naturalistic perspective. The similar structure that does exist is based on the fact that the particular parables and their very order represent a structure that is essential to the message itself. The Holy Spirit is the author of all the gospels and, though the emphasis is different in each, their order is essential to the integrity of the original message, as we saw in the 12 kingdom of heaven parables that are in chronological order according to the sequence in which those prophesied events have and will occur.

| Kingdom of God | Kingdom of God | Kingdom of heaven |
|---|---|---|
| *Mark 4:30* And he said, Whereunto shall we liken the **kingdom of God**? or with what comparison shall we compare it? <br> 31 It is like a grain of mustard seed, which, when it is sown in the <u>earth</u>, is less than all the seeds that be in the earth: <br> 32 But when it is sown, it groweth up, and becometh greater than all herbs, and shooteth out great branches; so that the fowls of the air may lodge under the shadow of it. | *Luke 13:18* Then said he, Unto what is the **kingdom of God** like? and whereunto shall I resemble it? <br> 19 It is like a grain of mustard seed, which a man took, and cast into <u>his garden</u>; and it grew, and waxed a great tree; and the fowls of the air lodged in the branches of it. | *Matthew 13:31* Another parable put he forth unto them, saying, The **kingdom of heaven** is like to a grain of mustard seed, which a man took, and sowed in his <u>field</u>: <br> 32 Which indeed is the least of all seeds: but when it is grown, it is the greatest among herbs, and becometh a tree, so that the birds of the air come and lodge in the branches thereof. |

These three accounts of the mustard seed parable are essentially the same. There seems to be no attempt by the writers to emphasize any distinctions. We can therefore conclude that the two kingdoms are alike in that they will grow to be large conglomerates with devils lodging under their shadows — within the confines of its orginizations. This parable of the mustard seed is different from that of the tares. The tares were men, not devils, and they were IN the kingdom. The birds are devils, and they are not IN (part of) either kingdom; but they find comfort and rest in its great structure. So it is today; Structured Christianity, in all of its vastness and corruption, provides aid and comfort to devils.

## 6. Kingdom of God parable of leaven.

| Kingdom of God | Kingdom of Heaven |
|---|---|
| *Luke 13:20* And again he said, Whereunto shall I liken the **kingdom of God**? <br> 21 It is like **leaven**, which a **woman** took and hid in three measures of **meal**, till the whole was **leavened**. | *Matthew 13:33* Another parable spake he unto them; The **kingdom of heaven** is like unto leaven, which a woman took, and hid in three measures of meal, till the whole was leavened. |

These two accounts are virtually identical. Both kingdoms will be corrupted with false doctrine. See Matthew 13:33 discussed under the *12 kingdom of heaven parables* for documentation as to the meaning of leaven.

## 7. Kingdom of God parable of receiving a kingdom.

This last K of G parable is longer and much more detailed than the other parables. Just like the last K of H parable, this final K of G parable is advanced in its revelation of the nature of the kingdom. In the second column of the chart below is the last K of H parable that Matthew recorded. It has many similarities to Luke's account, but its striking differences tell us much about the differences in the two kingdoms. Both parables are based on similar circumstances. A man of means, before traveling into a far country, entrusts his servants with his money. After a long time, the man returns and demands an accounting from each servant. Some had invested in the kingdom, but one was afraid and hid the money entrusted to him. The nobleman rewarded those who had multiplied their money, but the man who was afraid and hid his money, was rebuked by his lord, and the money was taken from him to be given to the man who had made the most on his investment.

| Kingdom of God | Kingdom of heaven |
|---|---|
| *Luke 19:11* And as they heard these things, he added and spake a parable, because he was nigh to Jerusalem, and because they thought that the **kingdom of God** should immediately appear.<br><br>12 He said therefore, A certain nobleman went into a far country to receive for himself a kingdom, and to return.<br><br>13 And he called his ten servants, and delivered them ten pounds, and said unto them, Occupy till I come.<br><br>14 But his citizens hated him, and sent a message after him, saying, We will not have this man to reign over us.<br><br>15 And it came to pass, that when he was returned, having received the kingdom, then he commanded these servants to be called unto him, to whom he had given the money, that he might know how much every man had gained by trading.<br><br>16 Then came the first, saying, Lord, thy pound hath gained ten pounds.<br><br>17 And he said unto him, Well, thou good servant: because thou hast been faithful in a very little, have thou authority over ten cities.<br><br>18 And the second came, saying, Lord, thy pound hath gained five pounds.<br><br>19 And he said likewise to him, Be thou also over five cities.<br><br>20 And another came, saying, Lord, behold, here is thy pound, which I have kept laid up in a napkin:<br><br>21 For I feared thee, because thou art an austere man: thou takest up that thou layedst not down, and reapest that thou didst not sow.<br><br>22 And he saith unto him, Out of thine own mouth will I judge thee, thou wicked servant. Thou knewest that I was an austere man, taking up that I laid not down, and reaping that I did not sow:<br><br>23 Wherefore then gavest not thou my money into the bank, that at my coming I might have required mine own with usury?<br><br>24 And he said unto them that stood by, Take from him the pound, and give it to him that hath ten pounds.<br><br>25 (And they said unto him, Lord, he hath ten pounds.)<br><br>26 For I say unto you, That unto every one which hath shall be given; and from him that hath not, even that he hath shall be taken away from him.<br><br>27 But those mine enemies, which would not that I should reign over them, bring hither, and slay them before me. | *Matthew 25:14* For *the* **kingdom of heaven** *is* as a man travelling into a far country, *who* called his own servants, and delivered unto them his goods.<br><br>15 And unto one he gave five talents, to another two, and to another one; to every man according to his several ability; and straightway took his journey.<br><br>16 Then he that had received the five talents went and traded with the same, and made *them* other five talents.<br><br>17 And likewise he that *had received* two, he also gained other two.<br><br>18 But he that had received one went and digged in the earth, and hid his lord's money.<br><br>19 After a long time the lord of those servants cometh, and reckoneth with them.<br><br>20 And so he that had received five talents came and brought other five talents, saying, Lord, thou deliveredst unto me five talents: behold, I have gained beside them five talents more.<br><br>21 His lord said unto him, Well done, *thou* good and faithful servant: thou hast been faithful over a few things, I will make thee ruler over many things: enter thou into the joy of thy lord.<br><br>22 He also that had received two talents came and said, Lord, thou deliveredst unto me two talents: behold, I have gained two other talents beside them.<br><br>23 His lord said unto him, Well done, good and faithful servant; thou hast been faithful over a few things, I will make thee ruler over many things: enter thou into the joy of thy lord.<br><br>24 Then he which had received the one talent came and said, Lord, I knew thee that thou art an hard man, reaping where thou hast not sown, and gathering where thou hast not strawed:<br><br>25 And I was afraid, and went and hid thy talent in the earth: lo, *there* thou hast *that is* thine.<br><br>26 His lord answered and said unto him, *Thou* wicked and slothful servant, thou knewest that I reap where I sowed not, and gather where I have not strawed:<br><br>27 Thou oughtest therefore to have put my money to the exchangers, and *then* at my coming I should have received mine own with usury.<br><br>28 Take therefore the talent from him, and give *it* unto him which hath ten talents.<br><br>29 For unto every one that hath shall be given, and he shall have abundance: but from him that hath not shall be taken away even that which he hath.<br><br>30 And cast ye the unprofitable servant into outer darkness: there shall be weeping and gnashing of teeth. |

We have already discussed the passage in Matthew. Now let us examine the two together.

The last K of G parable is in Luke and is based on the same story as the last K of H parable in Matthew, but there are remarkable differences, as we have already noted. The K of H version focuses on how faithful some servants were to multiply their money so as to be able to return to their master the principal with interest. The investors are rewarded with inheriting a prominent place in the kingdom. The one who hoarded the money because he was fearful of investing is cast into hell.

In this K of G version of the parable, there is the additional point early in the parable that the nobleman (Jesus) was going into a far country (Christ's ascension into heaven) to **receive a kingdom and to return**. When he returns, he has already received the kingdom — as will be the case with the K of G at the Rapture. The nobleman gave one pound each to ten servants and told them to occupy until he comes back — as is the duty of Christians in the K of G right now. Some wisely invested and multiplied their money. When Jesus returned, the faithful investors inherited cities over which to rule based on their investments. The man who hid his pound, fearful of taking a risk, was rebuked, was divested of his money, and got no reward at all. Since he is in the K of G and not the K of H, **he was not cast into hell as was the same man in the K of H version**.

There is an additional group mentioned in the K of G parable, not found in the K of H version. The **citizens** who would not allow the nobleman to reign over them during his absence are the ones who are slain. They did not receive any money to invest. They were not servants of the nobleman, but were said to be his **enemies**. They were not under any obligation to develop their resources, but they were under obligation to submit to his rule, which they refused, and were afterward slain for their rebellion. This matches the sinners during our present dispensation who are expected to submit to the K of G, even in the absence of the king, while Christians are expected to invest their money and resources while the nobleman is away receiving the kingdom.

These two parables could in no way be exchanged one for the other, and instead, the two kingdoms maintain their distinctions and place in God's grand plan of the ages. They are powerful arguments for two different kingdoms.

We should pause here and again take the opportunity to reflect on God's method of constructing a mystery. To the novice, these two similar but different parables will seem to be a confusing tangle of detail. "Couldn't God have been clearer? Why entangle the truth in such a manner?" The answer is simple. God deliberately created a mystery. The two texts are meant to confuse and frustrate the casual reader. The Bible is like an ancient treasure map directing us to truth in a book of prophecy, first concealing and then revealing truth to believers. But, like a puzzle, when the pieces all fit together, there is no doubt that you have solved the mystery and found the hidden message.

# Proofs from their similarities

We have discussed the 12 Kingdom of Heaven parables and the seven Kingdom of God parables, but we have by no means exhausted the available evidence. There are many passages that make statements about one kingdom or the other that add new depth to our understanding of the kingdoms. We will now look at those statements that seem to indicate that the kingdoms are identical. These are the passages that cause the average reader to think that the kingdoms are the same, but upon close examination, they prove otherwise. At first consideration, it would seem to be impossible to prove that two things are different by observing their similarities, but there is Biblical precedent for this. In Romans chapter five, Paul points out the similarities between Adam and Christ as a way of showing how they differ.

By examining all those similar passages that most commentators would offer as proof that the two kingdoms are identical, we are able to observe — sometimes subtle, sometimes bold — differences between the two kingdoms. When we are following their similarities and we come to a passage that breaks with the pattern, we are constrained to ask why they are different in this one particular. The similarities are also defining by their omissions. Sometimes, Luke seems to be saying the identical thing about the **kingdom of God** that Matthew is saying about the **kingdom of heaven**, but then he changes a word or phrase. Why? It could be coincidental two or three times, but not fifty times, and certainly not when it always follows a consistent pattern.

The following references are taken in their chronological order from the *New Testament Parallel Table*. You can get a quick overview of our subject from that table. The numbers at the top left of the table are used throughout this study as a guide to locate the same passages in other tables. The numbers are assigned to New Testament kingdom verses, beginning in Matthew and progressing through the other 26 books, ending with the book of Revelation.

## Both kingdoms are similar in that they were "at hand," but only the K of G was "upon" them.

| | | | |
|---|---|---|---|
| *Matthew 3:1* In those days came John the Baptist, preaching in the wilderness of Judæa, 2 And saying, Repent ye: for the **kingdom of heaven is at hand.** | *Mark 1:14* … Jesus came into Galilee, preaching the gospel of the **kingdom of God,** 15 And saying, The time is fulfilled, and the **kingdom of God** is **at hand**: repent ye, and <u>believe the gospel</u>. | *Luke 10:9* And heal the sick that are therein, and say unto them, The **kingdom of God** is **come nigh** [*same Greek word as "at hand"*] unto you. 11 Even the very dust of your city, which cleaveth on us, we do wipe off against you: notwithstanding be ye sure of this, that the **kingdom of God is come nigh unto** you. *Luke 11:20* But if I with the finger of God cast out devils, no doubt the **kingdom of God** is **come** <u>**upon you.**</u> | *Matthew 12:28* But if I cast out devils by the Spirit of God, then the **kingdom of God** is **come** <u>**unto you.**</u> |

What does it meant to say that the kingdom is **at hand?** The Greek word (Gk: *eggizo*), which is here translated **at hand,** is used many times in the gospels and the New Testament, and is also translated **draw near** and **approaching**. Following is a sample of its use in an application other than the kingdoms.

> *Matthew 26:45* Then cometh he to his disciples, and saith unto them, Sleep on now, and take your rest: behold, the hour is **at hand**, and the Son of man is betrayed into the hands of sinners.
> 46 Rise, let us be going: behold, he is **at hand** that doth betray me.

The hour was **at hand** that Jesus should be betrayed — that is, the hour was imminent — for Judas was **at hand,** just outside the garden.

When John said the K of H was **at hand**, and Jesus said the K of G was **at hand**, they were both alerting us that the respective kingdoms were close to being instituted. If the Jews as a nation *had* *received* their Messiah, they would have individually entered into the K of G, and during his then earthly ministry, Jesus would have set up a kingdom on the earth — the K of H. Both kingdoms would have come at the same time — one personal and individual, and the other corporate and institutional.

Though both kingdoms are alike in that they were offered to the Jews as imminent, Luke, in reference to the K of G, adds a preposition (Gk; *epi*) saying it is come nigh **unto** you. In a similar manner, Luke 11:20 declares that the K of G is come **upon** you (Gk: *epi*), which is to say that it was more than imminent; it was actually *then present*. Both Matthew and Mark use the same Greek word to say that the two kingdoms were **at hand**, but, the distinguishing factor is that Matthew never uses that Greek preposition (*epi*, translated in the KJV: **unto/upon**) with regards to the K of H. Furthermore, most remarkable is the fact that in 12:28, Matthew chooses the same Greek word, *epi* — (**unto/upon**), with reference to the K of G, which indicates that the K of G, in contrast to the K of H, was not only imminent; its power was already intimately present and personal.

It can be no coincidence that Matthew declined to speak of the K of H as **unto/upon** you, but then followed Mark and Luke's use of it when referring specifically to the K of G. So, in all the similarities, we can clearly distinguish a contrast between the two. Although both kingdoms were spoken of as being imminent, the K of G was something more; it was as close as **unto** and **upon** them! That could only be so because of its spiritual and individual nature.

To better understand the meaning of the Greek preposition *epi*, we have recorded two of the many times Matthew makes use of it in a different context.

> *Matthew 11:29* Take my yoke <u>upon</u> you, and learn of me....
> *Matthew 9:2* And, behold, they brought to him a man sick of the palsy, lying <u>on</u> a bed....

**In summary:** All three gospels agree; both kingdoms are **at hand** — imminent. But they also agree that the K of G is something beyond **at hand** — it is **unto/upon** them like a sick man is on his bed or like a yoke is upon an ox. The K of H could not come **upon** anyone, since it was not personal and individual, but corporate and institutional.

**Just a note:** We made reference to the Greek text, not because the King James English text is not accurate or clear; quite to the contrary. It is perfectly accurate, but for those who place more faith in any of the 24 differing Greek Bibles, we thought it might help to defend the wording of the Authorized King James English text.

## The kingdoms are similar in that they both required repentance, but only the K of G required belief.

| | |
|---|---|
| *Matthew 3:1* In those days came John the Baptist, preaching in the wilderness of Judæa.<br> 2 And saying, **Repent** ye: for the **kingdom of heaven** is at hand. | *Mark 1:15* And saying, The time is fulfilled, and the **kingdom of God** is at hand: **repent** ye, and <u>believe the gospel</u>. |

All dispensations require repentance. God cannot fellowship with a man until he repents toward God in faith and humility. So it is expected that each kingdom would demand repentance. But, here again there is a difference. Only the K of H required a man to *repent from his sins*, with no mention of *believing the gospel*, as was the case with the K of G. To enter the K of G, one must repent *toward* God, not from his sins. See this author's book **Repentance**.

## Jesus preached concerning both kingdoms after John was cast into prison.

| *Matthew 4:12* Now when Jesus had heard that John was cast into prison, he departed into Galilee; 17 From that time Jesus began to preach, and to say, Repent: for the **kingdom of heaven** is at hand. | *Mark 1:14* Now after that John was put in prison, Jesus came into Galilee, preaching the <u>gospel</u> of the **kingdom of God**, 15 And saying, The time is fulfilled, and the **kingdom of God** is at hand: repent ye, and <u>believe the gospel.</u> | *Luke 4:43* And he said unto them, I must preach the **kingdom of God** to other cities also: for therefore am I sent. *Luke 8:1* ...he went throughout every city and village, preaching and shewing the <u>glad tidings</u> of the **kingdom of God:** |
|---|---|---|

Jesus preached concerning both kingdoms **after John was cast into prison**. The Jews had rejected John, who was sent by God to prepare the way for Messiah, so Jesus took over John's ministry of offering the kingdoms to the Jews. If they had received Christ and he had commenced his reign upon the earth, the two kingdoms would have been immediately instituted as **Christ's kingdom**, as will occur in the Millennium.

There is a difference, however, in these passages. While Jesus preached about both kingdoms, he defined the K of G as *the gospel*, but not so the K of H. Furthermore, the K of G required belief, but the K of H did not. After his resurrection, his teaching only dealt with the K of G.

## Healing is manifested in both kingdoms.

| *Matthew 4:23* And Jesus went about all Galilee, teaching in their synagogues, and preaching the **gospel of the kingdom**, and healing all manner of sickness and all manner of disease among the people. [See Matt. 9:35; 24:14] 24 And his fame went throughout all Syria: and they brought unto him all sick people that were taken with divers diseases and torments, and those which were possessed with devils, and those which were lunatick, and those that had the palsy; and he healed them. **9:35** And Jesus went about all the cities and villages, teaching in their synagogues, and preaching the gospel of the **kingdom**, and healing every sickness and every disease among the people. *Matthew 10:7* And as ye go, preach, saying, The **kingdom of heaven** is at hand. 8 <u>Heal</u> the sick, cleanse the lepers, raise the dead, cast out devils: freely ye have received, freely give. | *Luke 10:9* And heal the sick that are therein, and say unto them, The **kingdom of God** is come nigh unto you. 11 Even the very dust of your city, which cleaveth on us, we do wipe off against you: notwithstanding be ye sure of this, that the **kingdom of God** is come nigh unto you. *Luke 9:2* And he sent them to preach **the kingdom of God**, and to heal the sick. 11 And the people, when they knew it, followed him: and he received them, and spake unto them of the **kingdom of God**, and healed them that had need of healing. |
|---|---|

The preaching of both kingdoms was accompanied with manifestations of healing, but there was one difference. Widespread healing and miracles were a *sign* that God was prepared to install the K of H. But in the K of G, healing was an indication to the people that the K of G was **near** at the moment. Since the K of H is a system of government that must be established, healing could not bring it near. But the K of G is the presence of God, which presence was manifested by the miracles. So, once again even the similarities of the two kingdoms demonstrate a contrast between them.

## Both kingdoms involved righteousness.

| *Matthew 5:20* For I say unto you, That except your righteousness shall exceed the righteousness of the scribes and Pharisees, ye shall in no case enter into the **kingdom of heaven.** | *Matthew 6:33* But seek ye first the kingdom of God, and his righteousness; and all these things shall be added unto you. |
|---|---|

Notice that both passages above are in Matthew. It is fascinating to see him speak of first one kingdom and then the other concerning righteousness and to consistently express the differences that exist in the two kingdoms. Both kingdoms embrace righteousness, as would be expected in any dispensation. But righteousness is the *precondition* to entering the **kingdom of heaven**, whereas, for the **kingdom of God,** righteousness is sought in connection with the K of G as a means to receiving the daily provision and blessings of God. One gets into the K of H by his righteousness — not so the K of G. But for those who are already in the K of G, righteousness should be one's continual concern. Mark and Luke never mention righteousness in connection with any kingdom. Since Matthew provided his own contrast between the two kingdoms, there was no need for the other gospels to do so.

## Both kingdoms will eventually occur on earth.

| | | |
|---|---|---|
| *Matthew 6:10* Thy **kingdom** come. Thy will be done in <u>earth</u>, as *it is* in heaven.<br><br>*8:11* And I say unto you, That many shall come from the east and west, and shall sit down with Abraham, and Isaac, and Jacob, in the **kingdom of heaven**.<br><br>*20:21* And he said unto her, What wilt thou? She saith unto him, Grant that these my two sons may sit, the one on thy right hand, and the other on the left, in **thy kingdom.** | *Mark 11:10* Blessed be the **kingdom of our father** David, that cometh in the name of the Lord: Hosanna in the highest. | *Luke 11:2* And he said unto them, When ye pray, say, Our Father which art in heaven, Hallowed be thy name. Thy **kingdom** come. Thy will be done, as in heaven, so <u>in earth</u>.<br><br>*Luke 13:28* There shall be weeping and gnashing of teeth, when ye shall see Abraham, and Isaac, and Jacob, and all the prophets, in the **kingdom of God**, and you yourselves thrust out.<br>  29 And they shall come from the east, and from the west, and from the north, and from the south, and shall sit down in the **kingdom of God**.<br><br>*Luke 19:11* And as they heard these things, he added and spake a parable, because he was nigh to Jerusalem, and because they thought that the **kingdom of God** should immediately appear.<br><br>*Luke 22:29* And I appoint unto you a **kingdom**, as my Father hath appointed unto me;<br>  30 That ye may eat and drink at my table in **my kingdom**, and sit on thrones judging the twelve tribes of Israel. |

Matthew records Jesus as saying that the patriarchs (Fathers of the Jews) will come from the east and west to **sit down in the K of H**. Luke says the same thing about the K of G. It is parallels like this that have caused so many to conclude that the kingdoms are the same and that Matthew just preferred one term while the rest of the Bible writers preferred another. If that were the case, by what authority did the writers take such extreme liberty with Jesus' words, changing them to a term they "preferred"? Could we trust any of their records if they were that heedless of the words of our Lord?

As to the two texts before us, there is no doubt that they are both referring to the same future event. There could not be two such occasions when the Jews come from all points on the globe to gather in Jerusalem before Abraham, Isaac, and Jacob. Certainly, Christ could have spoken of that future event more than once, and it must be admitted that he could have said K of H one time and K of G another. In which case, Matthew could be reporting one public address and Luke could be reporting another, or Jesus could have referred to both kingdoms at different times during the same two- or three-hour discourse.

What then do we learn from these similar statements? Since they address the same event, one describing it as the K of H, and the other as the K of G, only two possibilities remain. Either there is just one kingdom with two names, or, as is the case, it is two kingdoms emerging onto the scene at the same time and place.

In the passages above, both Matthew and Luke speak of **thy** kingdom and **my** kingdom. As we saw from our study in the Old Testament, God has explicit, eternal plans for a kingdom on this earth. It is predictable that any kingdoms that have to do with man will eventually merge on the earth. When

Jesus taught the disciples to pray that the kingdom would indeed come to the earth, it was in full accord with God's goal to gather all things together in one body (Ephesians 1:10). At the moment the Church (recipients of the K of G) returns to the earth at the beginning of the Millennium, and Israel returns to Jerusalem in obedient faith, the Old Testament saints will be resurrected to receive the kingdom prepared for them from the foundation of the world. It is at that time that the K of H and the K of G will have merged under Christ's control, and will become **Christ's** kingdom — also called **his** kingdom or **thy** kingdom. For the Jews present, it will be the **K of H**. For the Church-age saints present, it will be the **K of G**, but by the time the new earth is established at the end of the Millennium, it will be the **Father's** kingdom.

## Abraham, Isaac, and Jacob sit down in the kingdom.

| *Matthew 8:11* And I say unto you, That many shall come from the east and west, and shall sit down with Abraham, and Isaac, and Jacob, in the **kingdom of heaven**. | *Luke 13:28* There shall be weeping and gnashing of teeth, when ye shall see Abraham, and Isaac, and Jacob, and all the prophets, in the **kingdom of God**, and you yourselves thrust out.<br>29 And they shall come from the east, and from the west, and from the north, and from the south, and shall sit down in **the kingdom of God.** |
|---|---|

Both kingdoms are alike with respect to a time when the Old Testament patriarchs will **sit down** with all saints of all ages. This is another one of those statements that have caused students of the Bible to believe that there is just one kingdom with two different names. If these were the only two passages on the subject then that position would be justified, but here we have just two pieces of a puzzle with several hundred pieces.

We called this section *Proof from their similarities*. How is it proof that the kingdoms are different when in this instance we find no differences? Because in the few times that the kingdoms are spoken of as exactly alike it is in respect to points on which they should be in agreement if in fact they are different. Rain and ice, both made of $H_2O$, will be different in many respects and should be identical in others. When a description of them is identical where it should be in respect to them both being water, we know that they are articulately defined. So it is in respect to two kingdoms. Both are kingdoms, both are God's making, both involve righteousness and redemption, and both will come to complete fruition at the same time. They must be similar in these respects. The fact that our definitions prove to be similar where they should be and different where they should be, and that there is no confusion, is confirmation that we are indeed seeing an accurate picture as was intended.

When the Jews refused to accept the K of H, God had no choice but to postpone it until such time as the nation of Israel should be saved. In the interim, God continued his work among the Gentiles by bringing them into the K of G. The Mystery kept secret from the foundation of the world was that there would eventually be one body of believers comprised of both kingdoms, containing both Jews and Gentiles. That merging of the kingdoms will occur when Israel has believed and the K of H is instituted in Jerusalem as prophesied. When Israel is **born** into the K of G, God will then set up the K of H, and both kingdoms will be present together at the same time, in the same place, and among the same people. The Gentiles who are saved will also come from the east and the west and will sit down with Abraham, Isaac, and Jacob in the kingdom at the beginning of the Millennium.

## The disciples commanded to preach about both kingdoms.

| *Matthew 10:1* And when he had called unto him his twelve disciples, he gave them power against unclean spirits, to cast them out, and to heal all manner of sickness and all manner of disease.<br>5 These <u>twelve Jesus sent forth</u>, and | *Mark 6:7* And he called unto him <u>the twelve</u>, and began to send them forth by two and two; and gave them power over unclean spirits; | *Luke 10:1* After these things the Lord appointed <u>other seventy also</u>, and sent them two and two before his face into every city and place, whither he himself would come.<br>9 And heal the sick that are therein, and say unto them, **The kingdom of God** is come nigh |
|---|---|---|

| commanded them, saying, Go not into the way of the Gentiles, and into *any* city of the Samaritans enter ye not:<br><br>6 But go rather to the lost sheep of the house of Israel.<br><br>7 And as ye go, preach, saying, The **kingdom of heaven** is at hand, | 12 And they went out, and <u>preached that men should repent.</u><br><br>13 And they cast out many devils, and anointed with oil many that were sick, and healed them. | unto you.<br><br>10 But into whatsoever city ye enter, and they receive you not, go your ways out into the streets of the same, and say,<br><br>11 Even the very dust of your city, which cleaveth on us, we do wipe off against you: notwithstanding be ye sure of this, that the **kingdom of God** is come nigh unto you. |
|---|---|---|

Jesus commanded the disciples to preach about both kingdoms, but toward the latter part of his ministry, there is no record that they preached anything but the K of G. However, there is a great and significant difference again in these parallel passages; Jesus commanded them <u>not to preach the K of H to Gentiles</u>. Notice again the difference in the proximity of the kingdoms. In Matthew, the K of H was "at hand" (about to come), whereas in Luke, the K of G was "come nigh".

Since the commission to the twelve was most likely a onetime event, Matthew and Mark (not Luke) must be recording the same event. The original commission, as recorded by Matthew, being early in Jesus' ministry, was a command to preach the K of H, with no mention of the K of G, and in Matthew's version, the disciples are told to take the message to Israel only. This distinguishes his account as being exclusively Jewish in its nature.

It is extremely significant that when Mark seeks to include the commission in his record, he is not able to call it K of G, and he does not include the exclusion of Gentiles. It is further significant that when Mark is writing from a K of G perspective while recounting a K of H event, leaving out all K of H dimensions, he still does not include the distinctive K of G statements, as does Luke, concerning believing.

If the reader has had trouble sorting all this, let us say it another way. Mathew recounts a K of H event with several exclusive characteristics of the K of H. When Mark records the same event in a K of G context, he is careful never to include any of the exclusively K of H characteristics, nor does he go beyond the original statements of Jesus and add any exclusively K of G characteristic. He is careful to be completely accurate in representing what was originally said while not speaking of the K of H — an amazing juggling act done by the Holy Spirit.

Now, to add an even further layer of complexity to the narratives, and to confuse the indifferent reader, Luke records a commission that is designated as K of G. But note that it is not the same commission! It is much later, when Jesus has added seventy men to his original twelve disciples. Apparently, by the time Jesus commissioned the seventy, he was including the K of G in his presentation.

Just think of all the many ways the details of this triangle could have been shifted or slightly altered in forms that would have destroyed the distinction between the two kingdoms! This is unquestionably the work of the Holy Spirit. Such a beautifully written and preserved piece of literature, bearing the stamp of God upon it, moves us and compels us to bow in worship and praise. We are freed from the constraining interpretations of the great human institutions erected and perpetuated by men. God speaks through his Word in much more detail and clarity than we have been led to believe.

## John the Baptist was not "in" either kingdom.
## Neither kingdom had "come" during John's lifetime.
## Both kingdoms are much greater than the old covenant John was under.

| | |
|---|---|
| *Matthew 11:11* Verily I say unto you, Among them that are born of women there hath not risen a greater than John the Baptist: notwithstanding he that is least in the **kingdom of heaven** is greater than he. | *Luke 7:28* For I say unto you, Among those that are born of women there is not a greater prophet than John the Baptist: but he that is least in the **kingdom of God** is greater than he. |

Even considering all the special distinctions and differences of the two kingdoms, they are identical in regards to John's relationship to them.

On a side note, these passages are ruinous to those who claim that there are no dispensations in which God relates differently to men and values some of them higher. God is not obligated to be politically correct. He has ordained special plans for and placed his preferred value on the various populations living in different dispensations. John was the greatest prophet and man in the entire pre-Christian era — none greater, according to Jesus; yet, the least person in either of the two coming kingdoms will be greater than John. We would be blind and volitionally ignorant to pretend that those in the Church age are not in a greater and higher dispensation.

Since John is the greatest in his dispensation, but less than the least in either of the coming kingdoms, then John was not a part of either kingdom. We therefore can say with certainty that neither kingdom had officially *come* during the time of John.

Another significant question has been raised: if John was not in the K of G, then, was he born again? John was not saved by grace and faith through the blood of Christ. If he had been, he would be in the K of G. His ministry was to prepare the Jews for their coming kingdom. He did not enter the K of G, nor did he offer it. Not until after John was killed did anyone **press into** the K of G (Luke 16:16).

On another side note, it should be obvious that anyone who is in the K of G today is not under any of the previous dispensations. However, agreeing to this difference will move you at least one step closer to being a dispensationalist of some sort. Fortunately, accepting the concept of dispensations does not necessitate that you adhere to all that is taught by dyed-in-the-wool, traditionally-known dispensationalists. But, it is also true that you cannot make an honest claim of believing the whole Bible if you deny the existence of dispensations.

## Both kingdoms were held in mysteries.

| | | | |
|---|---|---|---|
| *Matthew 13:10* And the disciples came, and said unto him, Why speakest thou unto them in parables? 11 He answered and said unto them, Because it is given unto you to know the <u>mysteries</u> of the **kingdom of heaven**, but to them it is not given. | *Mark 4:11* And he said unto them, Unto you it is given to know the <u>mystery</u> of the **kingdom of God**: but unto them that are without, all these things are done in parables: | *Luke 8:10* And he said, Unto you it is given to know the <u>mysteries</u> of the **kingdom of God**: but to others in parables; that seeing they might not see, and hearing they might not understand. | *1Corinthians 4:1* Let a man so account of us, as of the ministers of Christ, and stewards of the <u>mysteries</u> of God. |

Both kingdoms were kept secret as mysteries to be revealed to some and concealed to others. Taken as a whole with the many other passages, the similarity at this point, where it is appropriate for them to be alike, and the lack of similarity on points where they are clearly distinct one from another, confirms that the kingdoms are indeed different. In other words for the writers to preserve both the similarities and the differences time after time, and keep it all straight, lends credibility to the concept that there are many respects in which they are different. See the section on *The Twelve Mysteries*.

# Response to the "word" spoken is alike.

| *Matthew 13:18* Hear ye therefore the parable of the sower. | *Mark 4:11* And he said unto them, Unto you it is given to know the mystery of the **kingdom of God**: but unto them that are without, all these things are done in parables: | *Luke 8:1* And it came to pass afterward, that he went throughout every city and village, preaching and shewing the glad tidings of the **kingdom of God**: and the twelve were with him, |
|---|---|---|
| 19 When any one heareth the word of the kingdom, [*of heaven, verse 11*] and understandeth *it* not, then cometh the <u>wicked</u> one, <u>and catcheth away that which was sown in his heart</u>. This is he which received seed by the way side. | 14 The sower soweth <u>the word.</u> | 11 The seed is <u>the word of God.</u> |
| 20 But he that received the seed into <u>stony places</u>, the same is he that heareth the word, and anon with joy receiveth it; | 15 And these are they by the way side, where the word is sown; but when they have heard, <u>Satan cometh immediately, and taketh away the word that was sown in their hearts</u>. | 12 Those by the way side are they that hear; then cometh the <u>devil, and taketh away the word out of their hearts,</u> lest they should believe and be saved. |
| 21 Yet hath he not root in himself, but dureth for a while: for when tribulation or persecution ariseth because of the word, by and by he is offended. | 16 And these are they likewise which are sown on <u>stony ground</u>; who, when they have heard the word, immediately receive it with gladness; | 13 They <u>on the rock</u> are they, which, when they hear, receive the word with joy; and these <u>have no root</u>, which for a while believe, and in time of temptation fall away. |
| 22 He also that received seed among the <u>thorns</u> is he that heareth the word; and the care of this world, and the deceitfulness of riches, choke the word, and <u>he becometh unfruitful.</u> | 17 And <u>have no root in themselves</u>, and so endure but for a time: afterward, when affliction or persecution ariseth for the word's sake, immediately they are offended. | 14 And that which fell among <u>thorns</u> are they, which, when they have heard, go forth, and are choked with cares and riches and pleasures of this life, <u>and bring no fruit to perfection</u>. |
| 23 But he that received seed into the good ground is he that <u>heareth the word, and</u> understandeth it; which also <u>beareth fruit, and bringeth forth, some an hundredfold, some sixty, some thirty</u>. | 18 And these are they which are sown among <u>thorns</u>; such as hear the word, 19 And the cares of this world, and the deceitfulness of riches, and the lusts of other things entering in, choke the word, and it <u>becometh unfruitful.</u> 20 And these are they which are sown on good ground; such as hear the word, <u>and</u> receive it, <u>and bring forth fruit, some thirtyfold, some sixty, and some an hundred.</u> | 15 But that on the good ground are they, which in an honest and good heart, having heard the word<u>,</u> keep it, <u>and bring forth fruit with patience.</u> |

The "**word**" preached in the two kingdoms is alike in the manner in which it is delivered and received. The preaching in the kingdoms is like sowing seeds; some will bear fruit, and some will not for a variety of reasons. All three accounts have the same elements present. Three applications of the seeds fail to bear fruit for the same cause, and each bears fruit in one instance. Whether it is in the K of H or in the K of G, the Devil is ready to remove the word that is sown in a heart. Likewise, in both cases, the word falls onto stony ground and seems to take root for a while, but eventually fails under persecution or temptation. Hearers of the word of both kingdoms are also like seeds received among thorns, where the cares of the world and the deceitfulness of riches prevent the message from bearing fruit. Finally, both kingdom messages will have those who hear the word and understand it, or receive it, and bear fruit in varying proportions.

There is very little difference in the two kingdoms as revealed in these parallel accounts. But one difference stands out starkly: Luke, in writing about the K of G, adds the statement, **"lest they should believe and be saved."** The concept of **believing** and being **saved** upon receiving the word belongs exclusively to the K of G. No one was ever commanded to believe the word of the K of H, nor are we ever told that anyone did.

Another difference in Matthew's account occurs where it says, they **understood** the word of the K of H, whereas Mark states that they **received** it. Receiving the word of the K of H would never have saved anyone. It would not even have placed them in the K of H. Only in the K of G can one **believe** and **receive** the message and be **saved**. While this is a small difference in the two accounts, it is a great difference in the nature of the two kingdoms.

## Both kingdoms will become large and filled with birds (devils).

| | | |
|---|---|---|
| *Matthew 13:31* Another parable put he forth unto them, saying, The **kingdom of heaven** is like to a grain of mustard seed, which a man took, and sowed in his field: <br><br> 32 Which indeed is the least of all seeds: but when it is grown, it is the greatest among herbs, and becometh a tree, so that the birds of the air come and lodge in the branches thereof. | *Mark 4:30* And he said, Whereunto shall we liken the **kingdom of God**? or with what comparison shall we compare it? <br><br> 31 It is like a grain of mustard seed, which, when it is sown in the earth, is less than all the seeds that be in the earth: <br><br> 32 But when it is sown, it groweth up, and becometh greater than all herbs, and shooteth out great branches; so that the fowls of the air may lodge under the shadow of it. | *Luke 13:18* Then said he, Unto what is the **kingdom of God** like? and whereunto shall I resemble it? <br><br> 19 It is like a grain of mustard seed, which a man took, and cast into his garden; and it grew, and waxed a great tree; and the fowls of the air lodged in the branches of it. |

The two kingdoms are identical in the manner in which they will be beset by devils. Probably the most popular argument against Christianity is the excuse that "the Church is full of hypocrites," and these passages have been inaccurately interpreted as such. Jesus was well aware that both kingdoms would be full of fake adherents, and he addresses that subject in the parable of the tares. He speaks of false doctrine in the next parable about leaven. He addresses the subject of the lost and the saved being in the kingdoms in the parable of the good fish and bad fish, both in the same net. But this parable of the birds lodging in the branches of the great tree deals with the presence of *devils* in the kingdoms, not hypocrites. Take a concordance and look at all the symbolic references to birds. Birds represent spirits; they fly through the air unhindered. So, these parables, one about the K of H, and two about the K of G, teach that the kingdoms will become large and filled with evil spirits — with devils. All one need do is look closely at any large denomination today, and it becomes obvious that devils inhabit it. Note that they are not part of its branches or trunk; they are simply aliens nesting in its branches or under its shadow. By the time Jesus returns to the earth, the Church will be filled with devils, not as part of the tree itself, but nesting in its branches and sitting in its shade. To the outside observer, the devils will appear to be an essential part of the kingdom.

## Both kingdoms will be corrupted with leaven—false doctrine.

| | | | |
|---|---|---|---|
| *Matthew 13:33* Another parable spake he unto them; The **kingdom of heaven** is like unto leaven, which a woman took, and hid in three measures of meal, till the whole was leavened. | *Mark 8:15* And he charged them, saying, Take heed, beware of the leaven of the Pharisees, and of the leaven of Herod. | *Luke 13:20* And again he said, Whereunto shall I liken the **kingdom of God**? <br><br> 21 It is like leaven, which a woman took and hid in three measures of meal, till the whole was leavened. <br> *Luke 12:1* Beware ye of the leaven of the Pharisees, which is hypocrisy. | *1 Corinthians 5:6* Your glorying is not good. Know ye not that a little leaven leaveneth the whole lump? <br><br> 7 Purge out therefore the old leaven, that ye may be a new lump, as ye are unleavened. For even Christ our passover is sacrificed for us: <br><br> 8 Therefore let us keep the feast, not with old leaven, neither with the leaven of malice and wickedness; but with the unleavened bread of sincerity and truth. |

The kingdoms are identical in the way in which they will be corrupted with leaven. There is not a single positive use of *leaven* in the fifteen times it appears in the New Testament. It is always used to typify something corrupting and evil. Leaven is a bacterium that spreads its deterioration throughout a lump of dough. So it is obvious that this parable, like the other K of H parables, is about the corruption of the kingdom.

This parable is just one of several that Jesus gave consecutively which speak of decay and corruption rather than righteous expansion, as many believe. In a chronological order, he has told us that the kingdom will be full of tares that will grow with the wheat until the harvest, that it will be a giant tree full of evil spirits, that it is like a net cast into the sea, gathering good and bad fish, and now he tells us that the kingdom is going to be like leaven that corrupts the whole lump of dough.

Most Bible teachers, in agreement with Roman Catholic theologians, think that this parable predicts the advance of the Church in spreading its righteous influence. Matthew has gone to great lengths to establish the point that the seeds sown will mostly fail, so why would he suddenly reverse the theme he has established and contradict his entire line of reasoning? Furthermore, why would he try to convey something positive by employing a term that is always used to express the negative? So, we have these four parables taught, one after the other, each expressing a different aspect of the negative expansion of the kingdom.

The Postmillenarians believe that the Church is going to spread its "positive influence" over the world until all nations come under the righteous control of the Church. That this defies reality as well as contradicts Scripture has done little to deter its acceptance by them. Those who believe thus cannot accept the obvious fact that in Scripture, in all cases, leaven is false doctrine, hypocrisy, malice, and wickedness. The New Testament gives no other definition of leaven. If they admit that leaven is corruption, then they must admit that the kingdom is going to become corrupted along with the world, rather than to sanctify it. So, in order to maintain a positive outlook, and to protect the Post Millennial view, they claim that leaven is the righteous influence of the Church, and that this parable predicts the victory of the Church over the world.

It is clear to any reasonable Bible student. The two kingdoms will both become corrupted. The **kingdom of heaven** was already corrupted with tares even as it was offered by Jesus. It will continue to become corrupted during the Tribulation, and even during the Millennium under the rule of Christ, when the **kingdom of heaven** will again have false converts and experience false doctrine, as seen by the fact that sinners are killed during the reign of Christ, and a large number rise up at the end of the Millennium in an attempt to overthrow Christ.

The **kingdom of God** is corrupted even as I write these lines. When Jesus comes back to the earth, it is to bring judgment on the very Church he founded. His greatest enemy will be the head of the Christian Church, called antichrist.

## Both kingdoms have a similarity to little children.

| | | |
|---|---|---|
| *Matthew 18:2* And Jesus called a little child unto him, and set him in the midst of them,<br><br>3 And said, Verily I say unto you, Except ye be converted, and become as little children, ye shall not enter into the **kingdom of heaven.**<br><br>4 Whosoever therefore shall humble himself as this little child, the same is <u>greatest</u> in the **kingdom of heaven**.<br><br>*19:13* Then were there brought unto him little children, that he should put *his* hands on them, and pray: and the disciples rebuked them.<br><br>14 But Jesus said, Suffer little children, and forbid them not, to come unto me: for of such is the **kingdom of heaven.** | *Mark 10:14* But when Jesus saw it, he was much displeased, and said unto them, Suffer the little children to come unto me, and forbid them not: for of such is the **kingdom of God**.<br><br>15 Verily I say unto you, Whosoever shall not <u>receive</u> **the kingdom of God** as a little child, he shall not enter therein. | *Luke 9:46* Then there arose a reasoning among them, which of them should be greatest.<br><br>*Luke 18:16* But Jesus called them unto him, and said, Suffer little children to come unto me, and forbid them not: for of such is the **kingdom of God**.<br><br>17 Verily I say unto you, Whosoever shall not <u>receive</u> **the kingdom of God** as a little child shall in no wise enter therein. |

The kingdoms are alike with regards to little children, but note again that there is a difference. One must be converted and **become** as a little child as a prerequisite to entering the K of H, whereas one must **receive** the K of G **as** a little child. It is the distinction between a precondition of childlike humility to enter the K of H and the demand that one receive the message of the K of G with the faith of a little child. The K of H places prior demands upon those who would be a part of it. The K of G does not require a certain moral condition. It is simply *received* by faith. The K of H is never received, never a gospel, and never requires faith. The K of G is associated with all three.

## The Rich can hardly enter into either kingdom.

| | | | |
|---|---|---|---|
| *Matthew 19:23* Then said Jesus unto his disciples, Verily I say unto you, That a rich man shall hardly enter into the **kingdom of heaven.**   24 And again I say unto you, It is easier for a camel to go through the eye of a needle, than for a rich man to enter into the **kingdom of God.** | *Mark 10:23* And Jesus looked round about, and saith unto his disciples, How hardly shall they that have riches enter into **the kingdom of God!**   24 And the disciples were astonished at his words. But Jesus answereth again, and saith unto them, Children, how hard is it for them that <u>trust in riches</u> to enter into the **kingdom of God!**   25 It is easier for a camel to go through the eye of a needle, than for a rich man to enter into the **kingdom of God.** | *Luke 18:24* And when Jesus saw that he was very sorrowful, he said, How hardly shall they that have riches enter into the **kingdom of God!**   25 For it is easier for a camel to go through a needle's eye, than for a rich man to enter into the **kingdom of God.** | *1 Timothy 6:17* Charge them that are <u>rich</u> in this world, that they be not highminded, nor trust in uncertain <u>riches</u>, but in the living God, who giveth us richly all things to enjoy;   18 That they do good, that they be <u>rich</u> in good works, ready to distribute, willing to communicate;   *James 5:1* Go to now, ye <u>rich</u> men, weep and howl for your miseries that shall come upon you. |

The kingdoms are alike with regards to the rich. It is difficult for a rich man to meet the conditions of entering either kingdom. 1Timothy tells is that a rich man is inclined to be highminded and to trust in uncertain riches. In Luke 18 we read of a rich young ruler who went away sorrowful, giving up hope of salvation because he loved his riches. There are many passages warning the rich of the dangers of trusting in their wealth rather than in living a life of faith. This would be true in any dispensation, for "without faith it is impossible to please him", and wealth keeps one from having to exercise faith.

This passage in Matthew is unique. After stating that it is difficult for a rich man to enter the K of H, Matthew gives the warning again and applies it to the K of G. It is clear that Matthew did not believe that the kingdoms were synonymous, for he made a point of telling us that the warning to the rich applies to both kingdoms.

There is one difference in the two kingdoms. Mark, in speaking of the K of G, adds the phrase, "**trust** in riches." If there is any point at all to be made of this, it is that a rich man **could** enter into the K of G if he did **not trust** in his riches.

## Those who forsake all will be rewarded.

| | | |
|---|---|---|
| *Matthew 19:27* Then answered Peter and said unto him, Behold, we have forsaken all, and followed thee; what shall we have therefore?   28 And Jesus said unto them, Verily I say unto you, That ye which have followed me, in the regeneration when the Son of man shall sit in the throne of his glory, ye also shall sit upon twelve thrones, judging the twelve tribes of Israel.   29 And every one that hath forsaken houses, or brethren, or sisters, or father, or mother, or wife, or children, or lands, **for my name's sake**, shall receive an hundredfold, and **shall inherit everlasting life.**   30 But many that are first shall be last; and the last shall be first.   [According to 20:1, this is the K of H.] | *Mark 10:28* Then Peter began to say unto him, Lo, we have left all, and have followed thee.   29 And Jesus answered and said, Verily I say unto you, There is no man that hath left house, or brethren, or sisters, or father, or mother, or wife, or children, or lands, **for my sake, and the gospel's,**   30 But he shall receive an hundredfold now in this time, houses, and brethren, and sisters, and mothers, and children, and lands, with persecutions; and in the world to come **eternal life**   31 But many that are first shall be last; and the last first. | *Luke 18:29* And he said unto them, Verily I say unto you, There is no man that hath left house, or parents, or brethren, or wife, or children, for the **kingdom of God**'s sake,   30 Who shall not receive manifold more in this present time, and in the world to come **life everlasting.** |

The kingdoms are alike in that those who forsake the things of value in this life will be compensated in the next, and the compensation will be meted out in a fashion that will seem inequitable to some. Jesus taught the parable of those who labored all day for wages to which they had agreed, but when they found that those who had worked only one hour (the last) received the same wages as they who worked all day, they accused the master of not being fair.

The disciples asked what reward they would receive for the sacrifices they had made. Jesus told them that they would be compensated in this life, and in the next life they would enjoy everlasting life. But then he adds that tidbit that warned them that many of those who first followed Christ (those who walked with him and were part of the early church) could be the last with the least, whereas some of those who followed Christ at a later time could be first in rewards.

However, in their similarity we discover one very stark difference. In Matthew, where he speaks of the K of H, he promises the disciples that they will sit on twelve thrones judging the twelve tribes of Israel. This could not have occurred during their lifetime, nor could it occur at any time during the Church age. This can only be fulfilled during the Millennium when the disciples are raised from the dead and the **kingdom of heaven** is restored to the nation of Israel. Nothing like this was said regarding the K of G. If it had been, it would have completely destroyed the distinction that has been so carefully preserved in the Scriptures.

## The two kingdoms come at the Second Coming of Christ.

| | |
|---|---|
| *Matthew 25:31* When the Son of man shall **come in his glory,** and all the holy angels with him, then shall he **sit upon the throne** of his glory:<br>32 And before him shall be **gathered all nations**: and he shall separate them one from another, as a shepherd divideth his sheep from the goats:<br>33 And he shall set the sheep on his right hand, but the goats on the left.<br>34 Then shall the King say unto them on his right hand, Come, ye blessed of my Father, **inherit the kingdom prepared for you from the foundation of the world:**<br>41 Then shall he say also unto them on the left hand, Depart from me, ye cursed, into everlasting fire, prepared for the devil and his angels:<br>46 And these shall go away into everlasting punishment: but the righteous into life eternal. | *Luke 22:15* And he said unto them, With desire I have desired to eat this passover with you before I suffer:<br>16 For I say unto you, I will not any more eat thereof, until it be fulfilled **in the kingdom of God.**<br>17 And he took the cup, and gave thanks, and said, Take this, and divide it among yourselves:<br>18 For I say unto you, I will not drink of the fruit of the vine, **until the kingdom of God shall come**. |

The statement in Matthew 25:34, **inherit the kingdom prepared for you from the foundation of the world**, is spoken just after the Son of man **comes in his glory** to **sit upon the throne of his glory** (v. 31). So we can conclude from this and other passages that the kingdoms will commence as institutions right after the Second Coming of Christ. There is a significant difference however in the way the kingdoms *come*. In this passage Matthew upholds the earthy, political nature of the kingdom. As a group, all are invited into the kingdom of heaven at one time. It is a corporate event. In the kingdom of God we see no mass entering at some point in history. Each person has entered the kingdom of God one at a time, but then the kingdom of God finds full expression at the second coming of Christ and the commencement of the Millennium at the same time as the kingdom of heaven.

# Proof from their uniqueness

As we have seen in our look through Scripture, the kingdom of God and the kingdom of heaven are alike in many ways, yet there are numerous statements that clearly express their individual uniqueness. It is those passages that we now examine.

Matthew is written to the Jews and therefore focuses on the **kingdom of heaven**. Mark and Luke are written primarily from the perspective of the Church and speak only of the **kingdom of God**. As you have seen, sometimes Matthew will recount a parable or sermon from the perspective of the K of H, while Mark or Luke will discuss the same parable from the perspective of the K of G.

At other times, Matthew alone will record the words of Jesus without reference to any kingdom and the statements are of such a nature that they could never be associated with any kingdom but the K of H. You won't find Mark and Luke speaking in a manner that would apply strictly to the K of H, as they have confined their books to discussing the K of G. And just as Matthew writes primarily from the perspective of the K of H, Mark and Luke write entirely from the perspective of the K of G. It is amazing how these three gospel accounts can discuss much of the same material yet always maintain a clear distinction between the two kingdoms.

But, on five occasions Matthew did make mention of the K of G and fell in line completely with Mark and Luke.

The following verses on the K of H, drawn from Matthew, have no exact parallel in the K of G, as found in both Matthew and the other two gospels. For your examination, we have listed additional passages on the K of G that are a near parallel or that express a contrast to the K of H passages in Matthew.

There will be redundancies with reference to other lists. For the sake of thoroughness, if a passage fits in several categories, it is discussed in each with regard to its uniqueness from that particular perspective. Now, let us look at those passages the Bible text designates as K of H.

A Number has been assigned to each passage in its chronological order. This number appears through the book as a means to cross reference the passage in different tables.

## John the Baptist preached the K of H only.

| *Matthew 3:1* In those days came John the Baptist, preaching in the wilderness of Judæa, 2 And saying, Repent ye: for the **kingdom of heaven** is at hand. | *Mark 1:4* John did baptize in the wilderness, and preach the baptism of repentance for the remission of sins. |
| --- | --- |

Since Mark's purpose is to relate the gospel of Jesus Christ, and because he is not writing to the Jews concerning their K of H, he never speaks of the K of H. You see in this passage the first of an interesting pattern. Mark and Luke will attribute many sayings and parables to the K of G, but when they discuss a point that Matthew designated as the K of H, to be absolutely correct and faithful to the original statement, they do not mention any kingdom. What else could it be but Divine inspiration for the sake of distinguishing between the kingdoms?

## The K of H is for the poor in spirit.

| *Matthew 5:3* Blessed *are* the poor in spirit: for theirs is the **kingdom of heaven**.<br><br>*Matthew 11:5* The blind receive their sight, and the lame walk, the lepers are cleansed, and the deaf hear, the dead | *Luke 6:20* Blessed be ye poor: for yours is the kingdom of God.<br><br>*Luke 4:18* The Spirit of the Lord is upon me, because he hath anointed me to preach the gospel to the poor; he hath sent me to heal the brokenhearted, to preach deliverance to the | *James 2:5* …Hath not God chosen the poor of this world rich in faith, and heirs of the **kingdom** which he hath promised to them that |
| --- | --- | --- |

| | | |
|---|---|---|
| are raised up, and the <u>poor</u> have the gospel preached to them. | captives, and recovering of sight to the blind, to set at liberty them that are bruised…. | love him? |

The K of H is offered as relief from the state of being **poor in spirit.** It has been popular to interpret the condition of being **poor in spirit** as a condition of heart that one must attain in order to enter the K of H. This is inaccurate, for you will note that in the accompanying verses, those who mourn will be comforted, those who hunger after righteousness will be filled, and those who are persecuted will inherit the kingdom. Jesus is offering the K of H to those who are desperate and in need of something more. They inherit the kingdom so they won't be poor in spirit (Luke 1:80), so they won't mourn, be lacking in righteousness, or be persecuted. So Jesus is making a wonderful announcement to the needy that the kingdom is going *to bring relief from the depressing condition of being "poor in spirit".* To desire a poor spirit as a Christian trait is like desiring to mourn or be persecuted. Self-flagellation would be the next step. The quest for a poor spirit is more in keeping with Buddhism than Bible faith.

Luke speaks of a different kingdom, not for the poor in spirit, but for the **poor.** There is no similarity between **poor in spirit** and **poor.** One is an impoverished condition of the soul, the other an undesirable condition of the finances. Neither is desirable, but they are not even in the same ballpark. There is nothing shameful about being poor, but being poor in spirit, if not sin itself, is certainly a result of sin.

Why did God write two different things so similarly — **poor, poor in spirit**? It seems to open the door for confusion. It is as though God intended to **hide these things from the wise and prudent** (Matt. 11:25). Jesus later answered the question as to why he spoke in this concealing fashion: "**Because it is given unto you to know the mysteries of the kingdom of heaven, but to them it is not given**" (Matt. 13:11). The Bible is written to deceive as much as to inform. The heart of the reader determines which it will be.

The parallel passages that speak of the K of G being for the poor are in good company. God chooses the **poor** to be **rich in faith**, for it is hard for a rich man to enter the K of G.

While we are discussing the passage, notice that in Matthew 11:5 (in the table above), Matthew breaks with his usual manner and mentions the **gospel.** But, just as Mark and Luke are careful not to mention the K of H when discussing a subject that might pertain to it, so Matthew, when speaking of the gospel specifically, is careful not to call it K of H, a statement otherwise popular with him.

## The kingdom of heaven is offered to those who are persecuted.

| | | |
|---|---|---|
| *Matthew 5:10* Blessed *are* they which are <u>persecuted for righteousness' sake</u>: for theirs is the **kingdom of heaven.** | *Mark 10:29* And Jesus answered and said, Verily I say unto you, There is no man that hath left house, or brethren, or sisters, or father, or mother, or wife, or children, or lands, for <u>my sake, and the gospel's,</u><br>30 But he shall receive an hundredfold now in this time, houses, and brethren, and sisters, and mothers, and children, and lands, with <u>persecutions;</u> and in the world to come eternal life. | *Luke 6:22* Blessed are ye, when men shall hate you, and when they shall separate you from their company, and shall reproach you, and cast out your name as evil, <u>for the Son of man's sake.</u><br>23 Rejoice ye in that day, and leap for joy: for, behold, your reward is great in heaven: for in the like manner did their fathers unto the prophets. |

The **kingdom of heaven** is unique in that it is offered as relief to those who are already persecuted, whereas the result of being in the K of G is to suffer persecution, just as Jesus did. It is a question of, which comes first, the kingdom or the persecution? Since the K of H is an institution directly under the government of David and Christ in Jerusalem, those who have been persecuted during the Tribulation will look forward to the relief the K of H will bring.

No one gets into either kingdom on the condition of suffering persecution for righteousness' sake. Furthermore, the K of G never relieves anyone of persecution. On the contrary, those who are in the K of G are not promised to be delivered from persecution, but to **suffer** persecution just as their Savior did, and to do it because of their allegiance to and love for him.

Think how devastating it would be to our understanding of the gospel of Jesus Christ if Mark had said the same thing about the K of G that Matthew said about the K of H. Mark would have said, "Blessed are they which are persecuted for righteousness' sake, for theirs is the K of G." That would make personal salvation the reward of those who are persecuted. It is wonderful that Mark never made such a ridiculous statement.

## The Mosaic Law is in force during the K of H.

> *Matthew 5:19* Whosoever therefore shall **break one of these least commandments**, and shall teach men so, he shall be called the least in the **kingdom of heaven**: but whosoever shall do and teach *them*, the same shall be called great in the **kingdom of heaven.**

This statement of Jesus refers to the K of H only. Mark or Luke never come close to telling us that we must keep the commandments **as a condition** to entering the K of G. The only condition to entering the K of G is repentance and faith (one act). On the other hand, one must be morally worthy to become an abiding member of that great **kingdom of heaven** that is promised to Israel.

We are not raising the issue of whether or not one *should* keep the commandments in the K of G. The issue we are discussing is that of similarities between the two kingdoms. We see in this passage a clear distinction. The K of H could have been instituted under the dispensation of the old covenant. The K of H is a legal dispensation, maintained under strictly enforced laws.

## Some will be called the greatest and some called the least in the K of H.

> *Matthew 5:19* Whosoever therefore shall break one of these least commandments, and shall teach men so, he shall be called the least in the **kingdom of heaven:** but whosoever shall do and teach *them*, the same shall be called great in the **kingdom of heaven**.

If you are in the K of H and you break one of the least commandments that God gave to Moses, or if you teach that such commandments need not be observed for any reason, then, when the kingdom is instituted, you will be **called,** the least. That means that when people speak of you, or when they address you personally, you will be publicly identified as of less value than others who keep every single commandment.

This is amazing. If you take this for what it says, and certainly we do, there will actually be some IN the K of H who teach other people that they need not observe one or more of the smaller, more insignificant commandments that God gave to Moses — like the one that commands a man to marry the wife of his brother if he dies being childless, even if he already has one or two wives — or, the law that requires one to eat no meat except that which has been ritually slaughtered. What about the commandment that one should not demand payment of a loan after the seventh year has passed, or the commandment ordering a man not to borrow money from, or loan money to, one who is an Israelite? There are 613 such commandments. Even the cults and sects today, who claim that they keep the Law of Moses, treat many of the commandments as **least** and not worthy of note. There is no religious order at present on the face of the earth (not even in Israel) that teaches that one should keep all of the commandments of Moses.

In the K of H, in order to observe the law, you must stone a man to death for bringing firewood into his cold house on the Sabbath, and yet in the K of G if you keep the Sabbath, you are denying Christ. If you don't recognize the difference in the two kingdoms, you are forced to juggle the text and allegorize certain of those passages. You will be uncomfortable with much of the Scriptures. There is no way to believe and practice all that is said concerning both kingdoms. You cannot take all the text at face value unless you have the key of knowledge and recognize the differences in the two kingdoms.

## A high level of righteousness is demanded as a precondition to entering the K of H.

> *Matthew 5:20* For I say unto you, That **except your righteousness shall exceed** the righteousness of the scribes and Pharisees, ye shall in no case enter into the **kingdom of heaven.**

One cannot enter the K of H unless his righteousness is exceptional. In other words, the K of H is based on good works.

It is in stark contrast to the K of G, which is never defined as something one must earn by his own righteousness. The righteousness imputed because of Jesus' redemptive work will qualify one to get into the K of G. It is a gift of grace, not an earned position. But the K of H was offered to Israel if they would repent and bring forth works consistent with that repentance. They were to make straight paths for their feet and cease their sinning. They were to experience the baptism of repentance and keep the commandments. If they would prepare the way with righteousness, Messiah would come and set up the **kingdom of heaven**.

It is becoming apparent, dear reader, why this study is so critical. It makes all the difference in what you believe one must **do** to be saved. On the one hand, there are those who do actually teach that, in this "age of the Spirit and of grace", one's salvation is partly based on his works of obedience. This is true of the Roman Catholic, the Orthodox, the Church of Christ, all Pentecostal denominations, modern Methodists, Seventh-Day Adventists, and all cults without exception. Of those who don't believe that one's works of obedience have anything to contribute to one's salvation by faith and grace, like the Baptists, some Presbyterians, a few Lutherans, the Bible churches, and many non-denominational churches, most are unwilling to admit that there has ever been or ever will be a dispensation when works of obedience are required for one's salvation. This puts the latter group in the difficult and embarrassing position of trying to either explain away or altogether avoid hundreds of passages that demand obedience as a condition of salvation. Only under the Old Covenant and during the Tribulation and Millennium are works required. Following is a small list of passages that must be explained away in order to maintain the position that, believers in all dispensations are "saved" by the same means as in this present one — salvation by faith alone, the faith of Abraham: Ezek. 3:20; 18:24-26; 33:12, 18; Deut. 11:26-28; 30:19; 30:15-19; Rev. 22:14-16; Isa. 1:18-20; Matt. 19:17; Rev. 14:12. There are many more that could be considered. This next one in Matthew should be added to the list.

## Children of the kingdom will be cast into outer darkness.

| | | |
|---|---|---|
| *Matthew 8:11* And I say unto you, That many shall come from the east and west, and shall sit down with Abraham, and Isaac, and Jacob, in the **kingdom of heaven**.<br> 12 But the children of the kingdom [*of H, verse 11*] shall be **cast out into outer** | *Luke 14:15* And when one of them that sat at meat with him heard these things, he said unto him, Blessed is he that shall eat bread in the **kingdom of God**.<br> 16 Then said he unto him, A certain man made a great supper, and bade many:<br> 17 And sent his servant at supper time to say to them that were bidden, Come; for all things are now ready.<br> 18 And they all with one consent began to make excuse. The first said unto him, I have bought a piece of ground, and I must needs go and see it: I pray thee have me excused.<br> 19 And another said, I have bought five yoke of oxen, and I go to prove them: I pray thee have me excused.<br> 20 And another said, I have married a wife, and | *Luke 13:24* Strive to enter in at the strait gate: for many, I say unto you, will seek to enter in, and shall not be able.<br> 25 When once the master of the house is risen up, and hath shut to the door, and ye begin to stand without, and to knock at the door, saying, Lord, Lord, open unto us; and he shall answer and say unto you, I know you not whence ye are:<br> 26 Then shall ye begin to say, We have eaten and drunk in thy presence, and thou hast taught in our streets.<br> 27 But he shall say, I tell you, I know you not whence ye are; depart from me, all ye workers of iniquity. |

| | | |
|---|---|---|
| **darkness**: there shall be weeping and gnashing of teeth. | therefore I cannot come.<br><br>21 So that servant came, and shewed his lord these things. Then the master of the house being angry said to his servant, Go out quickly into the streets and lanes of the city, and bring in hither the poor, and the maimed, and the halt, and the blind.<br><br>22 And the servant said, Lord, it is done as thou hast commanded, and yet there is room.<br><br>23 And the lord said unto the servant, Go out into the highways and hedges, and compel them to come in, that my house may be filled.<br><br>24 For I say unto you, That none of those men which were bidden shall taste of my supper. | 28 There shall be weeping and gnashing of teeth, when ye shall see Abraham, and Isaac, and Jacob, and all the prophets, in the **kingdom of God**, and you yourselves thrust out.<br><br>29 And they shall come from the east, and from the west, and from the north, and from the south, and shall sit down in the **kingdom of God**.<br><br>30 And, behold, there are last which shall be first, and there are first which shall be last. |

It should be clear by now that the **children of the kingdom** are the Jews to whom the **kingdom of heaven** was offered. Remember, the disciples were instructed not to preach the K of H to the Gentiles. They had no part in the K of H. Notice how Luke in two different texts speaks of the same events as Matthew but is careful not to say that the children of the **kingdom of God** will be cast into outer darkness. If he did, we would have to conclude that one who is saved could come to the Millennium and then lose his salvation. It gets crazy if you don't know the mysteries revealed in the parables.

This is one of those verses that so well defines the differences between the kingdoms. The text dates this event. It is when Abraham, Isaac, and Jacob and all the prophets are resurrected to sit down in the K of H. This, of course, takes place at the beginning of the Millennium. In light of such Scriptures as these, it would be embarrassing to be an Amillenarian.

The Jews are the **children of the kingdom**, for they are the ones for whom the kingdom was prepared and to whom it was offered. Being a child of the K of H does not make one a child of the K of G. The children of the **kingdom of heaven** must be converted, or they will be thrown out of the kingdom. This passage was spoken to the Jews of Christ's day, warning them that, while they will see the patriarchs in the kingdom, they may find themselves cast into hell.

You will note that both Matthew and Luke speak of the Jews sitting down in the kingdom, Matthew calling it the K of H, and Luke calling it the K of G. Both kingdoms will therefore sit down together to eat in what will then be called the **Father's kingdom**.

## The K of H message was for Jews only.

| | | |
|---|---|---|
| *Matthew 10:1* And when he had called unto him his twelve disciples, he gave them power against unclean spirits, to cast them out, and to heal all manner of sickness and all manner of disease. *10:5* These twelve Jesus sent forth, and commanded them, saying, **Go not into the way of the Gentiles,** and into *any* city of the Samaritans enter ye not: | *Mark 6:7* And he called unto him the twelve, and began to send them forth by two and two; and gave them power over unclean spirits;<br><br>8 And commanded them that they should take nothing for their journey, save a staff only; no scrip, no bread, no money in their purse:<br><br>9 But be shod with sandals; and not put on two coats.<br><br>10 And he said unto them, In what place soever ye enter into an house, there abide till ye depart from that place.<br><br>11 And whosoever shall not receive you, nor hear you, when ye depart thence, shake off the dust under your feet for a testimony against them. Verily I say unto you, It shall be more | *Luke 10:1* After these things the Lord appointed other seventy also, and sent them two and two before his face into every city and place, whither he himself would come.<br><br>4 Carry neither purse, nor scrip, nor shoes: and salute no man by the way.<br><br>5 And into whatsoever house ye enter, first say, Peace be to this house.<br><br>6 And if the son of peace be there, your peace shall rest upon it: if not, it shall turn to you again.<br><br>7 And in the same house remain, eating and drinking such things as they give: for the labourer is worthy of his hire. Go not from house to house.<br><br>8 And into whatsoever city ye enter, and they receive you, eat such things as are set before you:<br><br>9 And heal the sick that are therein, and say unto them, **The kingdom of God** is come nigh unto you.<br><br>10 But into whatsoever city ye enter, and they |

| 6 But go rather **to the lost sheep of the house of Israel**. 7 And as ye go, preach, saying, The kingdom of heaven is at hand, | tolerable for Sodom and Gomorrha in the day of judgment, than for that city. 12 And they went out, and preached that men should repent. 13 And they cast out many devils, and anointed with oil many that were sick, and healed them. | receive you not, go your ways out into the streets of the same, and say, 11 Even the very dust of your city, which cleaveth on us, we do wipe off against you: notwithstanding be ye sure of this, that the **kingdom of God** is come nigh unto you. |
|---|---|---|

Above are three parallel accounts of Jesus sending his disciples out to minister. In Matthew, where they are sent out to preach the K of H, Jesus commanded them not to preach to Gentiles or to mixed-blood Jews. They were told to preach the K of H message to the house of Israel only. It would have been a sin for them to have invited Gentiles to prepare themselves for the coming K of H. But in Luke, where they are sent out to preach the K of G, there is no Gentile exclusion. Gentiles had nothing to do with the Davidic kingdom of heaven.

When this author was in Bible College, they explained Jesus' rather embarrassing exclusion of the Gentiles as a strategic move on Jesus' part; he just wanted to win the Jews first so they could in turn win the Gentiles. And again, some explained the difference between the gospels as an ethnocentric attitude on Matthew's part. Others will say of the differences, "So what! It is just an oversight on the part of Mark and Luke. This was the same commission, but Matthew just has a different emphasis. One accidental exclusion does not prove that the Holy Spirit was communicating that the kingdoms are not the same." And my answer is: If these differences stood alone, drawn from a great volume of otherwise similar passages, one could make a credible case that we are reading something into the text. But more than 100 such "oversights" that consistently follow the same course and point to one conclusion cannot be accidental. The Holy Spirit is smarter than that; He does not "move" upon writers of Scripture accidentally.

Can you imagine how devastating it would be if the Bible had excluded Gentiles from the message of the K of G? The unique statements concerning the two different kingdoms weave such a careful and fragile path, always on the edge of crossing over and creating confusion, but never marring the clear distinctions in a single instance. What an incredible feat of Divine inspiration!

## The K of H is subject to violent overthrow.

| *Matthew 11:12* And from the days of John the Baptist until now the **kingdom of heaven** suffereth violence, and the violent take it by force. | *Luke 16:16* The law and the prophets were until John: since that time the **kingdom of God** is preached, and every man presseth into it. |
|---|---|

Violent people (the religious establishment and the authorities) were seizing the K of H and preventing it from being instituted under God's rule. Now, here is a passage that has made hoop-jumpers and dodgers out of many expositors. If you think the kingdoms are identical, you will have to allegorize this one to make it fit your theology.

In the above passages, Jesus is responding to the news that John has been cast into prison. The authorities had taken John to prison at Herod's command, and he will soon come to a violent end. John testified that he was the one who was prophesied to come before Messiah and to prepare the people for the coming kingdom. But the authorities had rejected his message, refusing to be baptized of him. John was the "press secretary" for the Messiah, but the authorities will soon kill him. Jesus says that from the time John began his announcement, the K of H had suffered violence, and violent people had used violence to take the kingdom — prevented it from coming to fruition.

This is not a difficult passage if you let *kingdom* be *kingdom*. Was not the original kingdom of Israel taken by violence when Nebuchadnezzar sacked Jerusalem? Did not the Romans take the kingdom by violence? John came offering a restoration of that kingdom, to be ruled by Messiah himself, and again the authorities are using violence to prevent heaven from ruling the earth. The truth is beautifully simple. Theologians are not needed to interpret this, unless you want to make it say something other than what it says.

Notice how Luke carefully avoids saying that the K of G is taken by violence. One slip like that and the whole doctrine would implode. The K of G is manifested in the Church, which cannot be taken by violence. On the other hand, if you believe that the Church is only an organized institution, then, of course, it could be taken by violence. When the authorities rush into a church building and seize the preacher, they have not touched the K of G. It cannot be stopped by seizing property and killing the members of the K of G.

Notice two other subtle points. Matthew does not say, as does Luke, that from the time of John, the K of H is preached, because it was not a new message as was that of the K of G. Nor does Matthew say that **the law and the prophets were until John**, because the Law and the prophets would not end with the K of H. Nor does Matthew say that "every man **presseth into** the K of H." No one ever entered the K of H. It could not be entered on an individual basis. It was an institution that must come as a political system is installed, with the only difference being that the kingdom would be ruled by heaven. So many variations, so perfectly placed, with no slip ups at any time, what could it be but the hand of an omniscient God? This proves more than the distinct natures of the kingdoms; it proves that the Bible is indeed the product of God, perfect in every single word, without exception.

## The K of H will have tares in it that must be separated from the kingdom and burnt.

| | | |
|---|---|---|
| *Matthew 13:24* Another parable put he forth unto them, saying, The **kingdom of heaven** is likened unto a man which sowed good seed in his field: <br> 25 But while men slept, his **enemy came and sowed tares among the wheat**, and went his way. <br> 26 But when the blade was sprung up, and brought forth fruit, then appeared the tares also. <br> 27 So the servants of the householder came and said unto him, Sir, didst not thou sow good seed in thy field? from whence then hath it tares? <br> 28 He said unto them, An enemy hath done this. The servants said unto him, Wilt thou then that we go and gather them up? <br> 29 But he said, Nay; lest while ye gather up the tares, ye root up also the wheat with them. <br> 30 Let <u>both grow together until the harvest</u>: and in the time of harvest I will say to the reapers, Gather ye together <u>first the tares</u>, and bind them in bundles to burn them: but gather the wheat into my barn. | *Mark 4:26* And he said, So is the **kingdom of God**, as if a man should cast seed into the ground; <br> 27 And should sleep, and rise night and day, and the seed should spring and grow up, he knoweth not how. <br> 28 For the earth bringeth forth fruit of herself; <u>first the blade, then the ear, after that the full corn in the ear</u>. <br> 29 But when the fruit is brought forth, immediately he putteth in the sickle, because the harvest is come. | *2 Corinthians 11:13* For such are false apostles, deceitful workers, transforming themselves into the apostles of Christ. <br> 14 And no marvel; for Satan himself is transformed into an angel of light. <br> 15 Therefore it is no great thing if his ministers also be transformed as the ministers of righteousness; whose end shall be according to their works. <br> *1 Peter 1:23* Being born again, not of corruptible seed, but of incorruptible, by the word of God, which liveth and abideth for ever. |

The tares are actually **in** the kingdom of heaven, and the angels do not separate them from it until the time of the harvest, which is the day of judgment. Since the K of H is a political event, all who live on the earth will be **in** the kingdom at that time, whether they are a part of the K of G or not. The K of H will begin some time during Daniel's 70th week, possibly when the 144,000 Israelites are sealed. As they preach, many will believe and enter into the K of H, but there will be many tares who join them. When Jesus returns to the earth after the seven years, he will judge the nations, destroy the competing kingdoms and their armies, and then set up the K of H upon the earth as a heaven-run earthly power. At the very least, the K of H "comes" with the presence of the Man Christ Jesus. At that time, there will be many on the earth — in the K of H — who are not in the K of G. They will not be "believers"— just survivors of the Tribulation. They will be tares among the wheat, needing to be purged from the kingdom. This will take place at the beginning of the 1000-year reign of Christ.

The same situation existed during the life of Christ. He embodied the essence of the K of H, yet among his own disciples was a tare needing to be purged.

It is remarkable that Mark relates a similar event of sowing seeds and of reaping a harvest, designating it as being the K of G, but he is careful not to include the part about it containing tares that are burnt. If he had included the burning of tares, or if the kingdoms are the same, we would be forced to conclude that some who are now in the Church — the K of G — will suffer everlasting fire in the day of judgment, which is exactly what many have unfortunately concluded.

## The K of H is like a treasure hid in a field that must be purchased.

> *Matthew 13:44* Again, the **kingdom of heaven** is like unto treasure hid in a field; the which when a man hath found, he hideth, and for joy thereof goeth and selleth all that he hath, and buyeth that field.

This short kingdom parable is fascinating. Down through the centuries there has been little variation in its interpretation, but it has been consistently misunderstood — made to fit salvation by works. And indeed, if the K of H is the same as the K of G, and the kingdom is the Church, then the parable encourages people in this age to go out and sell all they have so they can take the proceeds and buy their way into the Church. How is that for confusion? Time to allegorize again! Spiritualizing the text allows one to shift right or left, or even to do a complete turn-around, as may suit the subjective need of the expositor.

This parable is as simple as it is short. Jesus has already identified the field as the world at large (Matt. 13:38), and the man of the parable as the Son of man (Matt. 13:37). And, we know that Israel is God's peculiar treasure (Exodus 19:5; Psalm 135:4).

Now, look carefully at exactly what the parable says. **The kingdom of heaven is the treasure**. There it is! The Scripture clearly states that Israel is God's **treasure** (Ex. 19:5; Ps. 135:4). God sent Jesus to the earth to set up a kingdom headquartered in Jerusalem. "He came unto his own, and his own received him not" (John 1:11).The kingdom was taken by force the first time, and Israel was scattered among the nations (Deut. 4:27; 28:64; 30:30; 32:26) as predicted, and buried in a field (the world — Matt. 13:38) for the past 2,000 years. Many Jews have returned to the land of Israel, but most haven't. They are still God's **treasure**, and they are **hidden** in the **field** (world). God is the one who sold "**all that he had**", **his Son**, to buy the field in which the treasure is hidden, not the treasure itself. When Christ takes the kingdoms of this world unto himself, he will bring Israel from afar and she will be God's treasure once again.

So, in a sense, the K of H is present today among the descendents of Israel, though buried and scattered in the world. It lacks a proper expression, for the mystery of the kingdom is that it would exist for over 2,000 years in a buried state, gathering tares.

It is significant that no such parable was given in regard to the K of G. The Church could not represent the concept of a treasure hidden in the world. Until the Church is redeemed, there is nothing to hide, and the Church is commanded to go out into all the world and preach the gospel — openly!. A scattered K of H is no kingdom at all; a scattered and dispersed Church is God's ideal.

## The K of H is like a man buying one pearl of great price.

> *Matthew 13:45* Again, the **kingdom of heaven** is like unto a merchant man, seeking goodly pearls:
> 46 Who, when he had found one pearl of great price, went and sold all that he had, and bought it.

This shortest of kingdom parables and the previous one are about a man buying something valuable that has to do with the K of H.  At first glance, the two parables seem to be redundant. But look again. In the former parable, the man (Jesus) is prevented from obtaining the hidden treasure (Israel) because he does not have possession of the field (the world). In this parable, however, there is no field to be purchased. It is the pearl itself (the treasure) that is purchased. The pearl is not hidden as was the treasure in the field. The first parable typifies Jesus eventually taking the kingdoms of the world, whereby he can set up the K of H and obtain his treasure, Israel. But in the parable of the pearl, it is Israel herself (pearl/treasure) that Jesus purchases unto himself. This parable is not about the land on which the kingdom will be established; it is about the people of the kingdom, the nation of Israel herself.

Most commentators say that the "pearl of great price" is referring to the K of H, which they interpret to be the Church — two mistakes in row. The passage does not say that the kingdom of heaven is like unto a pearl; it says quite clearly, **the kingdom of heaven is like a merchant man.** The K of H is like the man seeking the pearl, not like a pearl that one desires greatly to purchase. The parable is generally interpreted to be a statement that one must give up everything in order to gain Christ — sell everything you have as a way to win entrance to the kingdom. To hold such an absurd view, one would have to ignore the definitions of words and symbols that Jesus provided in the first two parables of this chapter.

The man (*Jesus or God, in all the parables*) is always the assertive one, doing the seeking and the purchasing. There is no sinner seeking a kingdom or buying a kingdom for himself. Jesus alone is the seeker and buyer of the world and the pearl. The pearl of great price here is, once again, the nation of Israel, and Jesus is the man who finds the pearl and pays the ultimate price to purchase Israel unto himself. Who is it that pays the price for sinners to come into fellowship with God? Does the sinner have anything to sacrifice? Does he have anything of value? Can the gift of God be purchased? Amazingly, some, if not, many, are saying, "Yes."

> *1 Peter 1:18* Forasmuch as ye know that ye were not redeemed with corruptible things, as silver and gold, from your vain conversation received by tradition from your fathers;
> 19 But with the precious blood of Christ, as of a lamb without blemish and without spot:

## The K of H is like a net filled with fish, both good and bad.

| | |
|---|---|
| *Matthew 13:47* Again, the **kingdom of heaven** is like unto a net, that was cast into the sea, and gathered of every kind:<br>  48 Which, when it was full, they drew to shore, and sat down, and gathered the good into vessels, but cast the bad away.<br>  49 So shall it be at the <u>end of the world</u>: the angels shall come forth, and <u>sever the wicked</u> from among the just,<br>  50 And shall cast them into the furnace of fire: there shall be wailing and gnashing of teeth. | *Matthew 13:30* Let <u>both grow together until the harvest</u>: and in the time of harvest I will say to the reapers, Gather ye together <u>first the tares,</u> and bind them in bundles to burn them: but gather the wheat into my barn. |

The parable does not say that the kingdom is like a man casting a net; it says that the K of H is like the net itself — full of good and bad fish. It is important to pay attention to exactly what the text says.

The parable stops with verse 48, and verses 49-50 give the interpretation. The time during which this occurs is clearly stated to be at the **end of the world**. This interpretation is not part of the parabolic statement. It is the clear explanation of Jesus about the parable. The ones engaged in the harvest are **angels**.  Notice carefully; we have seen it before. The angels **first** remove the wicked **from among the just** and cast them into a furnace of fire. Matthew 13:30 said, **"Gather ye together first the tares…and burn them."**

There is no way that this could ever be said of the K of G. The wicked are never IN the **kingdom of God** to begin with. If they were, then the first thing on God's calendar would be the "rapture" of the wicked. We would not be looking for the imminent return of Christ but for the imminent judgment of the wicked. This is one of those K of H parables that stands out starkly unique, defining the K of H in a way that sets it forever apart from the K of G.

# Knowledge of the K of H will be a mixture of things new and old.

> *Matthew 13:51* Jesus saith unto them, Have ye understood all these things? They say unto him, Yea, Lord.
>
> 52 Then said he unto them, Therefore **every scribe** *which is* instructed unto the **kingdom of heaven** is like unto a man *that is* an householder, which bringeth forth out of his treasure *things* **new and old**.

After revealing seven parables of the K of H to the disciples, and telling them that it was a mystery teaching, Jesus asked them if they understood his instruction. When they said they did, he then informed them that every scribe (Jewish men who were responsible to know and copy the Scriptures) who was discipled concerning the K of H would bring out of his treasure (Israel, Ps. 135:4)) things new and old. In other words, a scribe who is knowledgeable of the kingdom message will hold truth that is both old and new — the **Old** Covenant and the **New** Covenant.

This is an amazing revelation. Whereas the K of G stands alone and is not a mixture of the Old Covenant and the New, the K of H will be established on the Old Covenant with new elements added to it. During the Millennium, when the K of H is fully inaugurated in Jerusalem, the Jewish temple will be rebuilt and sacrifices will resume, but Christ will be the centerpiece of the temple, and everyone will understand that the sacrifices only typify Jesus in his atonement. They will keep the Law of Moses during the Millennium, and they will "…sing the song of Moses the servant of God, and the song of the Lamb…" (Rev. 15:3).

> *Zechariah 14:16* And it shall come to pass, that every one that is left of all the nations which came against Jerusalem shall even go up from year to year to worship the King, the LORD of hosts, and to keep the feast of tabernacles.
>
> 17 And it shall be, that whoso will not come up of all the families of the earth unto Jerusalem to worship the King, the LORD of hosts, even upon them shall be no rain.
>
> 18 And if the family of Egypt go not up, and come not, that have no rain; there shall be the plague, wherewith the LORD will smite the heathen that come not up to keep the feast of tabernacles.
>
> 19 This shall be the punishment of Egypt, and the punishment of all nations that come not up to keep the feast of tabernacles.
>
> 20 In that day shall there be upon the bells of the horses, HOLINESS UNTO THE LORD; and the pots in the LORD'S house shall be like the bowls before the altar.
>
> 21 Yea, every pot in Jerusalem and in Judah shall be holiness unto the LORD of hosts: and all they that sacrifice shall come and take of them, and seethe therein: and in that day there shall be no more the Canaanite in the house of the LORD of hosts.

> *Matthew 5:19* Whosoever therefore shall break one of these least commandments, and shall teach men so, he shall be called the least in the **kingdom of heaven:** but whosoever shall do and teach *them*, the same shall be called great in the **kingdom of heaven.**

You can see how much confusion it would cause if the same had been said of the K of G. The K of G will not be a combination of **things new and old**. Matthew 9:17 "Neither do men put new wine into old bottles: else the bottles break, and the wine runneth out, and the bottles perish: but they put new wine into new bottles, and both are preserved." Those who are born again are not in any way responsible to keep the Law of Moses. If one who is in Christ does try to blend the new with the old, he will **fall from grace** (Gal. 5:4). Instead, such a born-again person is a **new** creation; old things have passed away, and everything now is new (2 Cor. 5:17). New wine, new wineskins!

> *Romans 6:14* For sin shall not have dominion over you: for ye are not under the law, but under grace.
>
> 15 What then? shall we sin, because <u>we are not under the law</u>, but under grace? God forbid.

> *Galatians 5:18* But if ye be led of the Spirit, ye are <u>not under the law</u>.

> *Galatians 4:21* Tell me, ye that desire to be under the law, do ye not hear the law?
>
> 22 For it is written, that Abraham had two sons, the one by a bondmaid, the other by a freewoman.
>
> 23 But he who was of the bondwoman was born after the flesh; but he of the freewoman was by promise.
>
> 24 Which things are an allegory: for these <u>are the two covenants</u>; the one from the mount Sinai, which gendereth to bondage, which is Agar.

25 For this Agar is mount Sinai in Arabia, and answereth to Jerusalem which now is, and is in bondage with her children.

26 But Jerusalem which is above is free, which is the mother of us all.

27 For it is written, Rejoice, thou barren that bearest not; break forth and cry, thou that travailest not: for the desolate hath many more children than she which hath an husband.

28 Now we, brethren, as Isaac was, are the children of promise.

29 But as then he that was born after the flesh persecuted him that was born after the Spirit, even so it is now.

30 Nevertheless what saith the scripture? Cast out the bondwoman and her son: for the son of the bondwoman shall not be heir with the son of the freewoman.

31 So then, brethren, we are not children of the bondwoman, but of the free.

5:1 Stand fast therefore in the liberty wherewith Christ hath made us free, and <u>be not entangled again with the yoke of bondage</u>.

## The keys of the K of H were given to Peter and the disciples.

| *Matthew 16:19* And I will give unto thee the **keys of the kingdom of heaven**: and whatsoever thou shalt bind on earth shall be bound in heaven: and whatsoever thou shalt loose on earth shall be loosed in heaven. | *Matthew 18:17* And if he shall neglect to hear them, tell it unto the church: but if he neglect to hear the church, let him be unto thee as an heathen man and a publican. 18 Verily I say unto you, Whatsoever ye shall bind on earth shall be bound in heaven: and whatsoever ye shall loose on earth shall be loosed in heaven . 19 Again I say unto you, That if two of you shall agree on earth as touching any thing that they shall ask, it shall be done for them of my Father which is in heaven. 20 For where two or three are gathered together in my name, there am I in the midst of them. | *John 20:23* Whose soever sins ye remit, they are remitted unto them; and whose soever sins ye retain, they are retained. |

This passage in Matthew has been adopted by Catholic and Protestant churches as justification for their claim to be the sole representative of Christ on the earth. They actually think that Jesus passed on to Peter the office of head of the Church. They believe that the key (or keys) to the kingdom (which they interpret as the Church) belongs exclusively to their institution through an unbroken apostolic succession. With what we know of church history, not to mention of the Scriptures, it is an incomprehensible position, but millions have been deceived by it.

This is probably the most critical kingdom passage of all. A failure to differentiate between the two kingdoms at this point has supported more serious error in the churches than any other passage. For years, Protestants and Roman Catholics have debated their interpretations. Was Jesus speaking to Peter alone or to all of the disciples? The Roman Catholics say that Jesus was speaking to Peter, giving him sole authority over the Church, to bind and to loose as the Vicar of Christ, and to be the final authority in all matters of faith and practice. They believe that the church of Rome is the seat of that authority, residing in the "elected" Pope. Protestants and Baptists in particular believe that Jesus gave the keys of the kingdom to all of the apostles, not just one, and that final authority rests in a church that is something much less than universal.

Which interpretation is correct? Do Peter's successors have the keys to the Church, or does the Church itself have the keys? Neither. It does not matter whether Jesus gave the keys to one apostle or to twelve, for it was not the keys to the Church. It had nothing to do with the Church. It was the **keys to the kingdom of heaven**, not to the **kingdom of God**. John the Baptist came to open the door for Messiah and to prepare the hearts of the people of Israel to receive the King and the earthly kingdom. For a while, John carried the keys of the K of H, but after he was imprisoned and executed, Jesus took the keys and continued to offer the kingdom to Israel. When it was clear that the Jews were rejecting Jesus, he began telling the disciples that he would be crucified. Now, he passed the keys on to them (or to Peter, as you will) so Israel would have one last chance to accept the **kingdom of heaven**. Israel confirmed their rejection at the crucifixion of Christ and afterward when they persecuted the Christians. The K of H went into exile with the Jews in 70 AD, and has been hidden ever since. The K of H will not surface again until the 144,000 descendents of Jacob are converted and sealed (Rev. 7:4-17). Their presence indicates that once again the offer of the kingdom of heaven is open to Israel. No one on this earth today has the keys to anything, except knowledge, and the least Christian can have that key without going through any church or Pope. When the mystery of the kingdom is not understood, the result is rampant confusion and false doctrine.

In Matthew, Jesus passed on the keys to the K of H, but in John there is no mention of keys in connection with the K of G. There are no keys to the K of G. Man cannot open or shut the spiritual door to the **kingdom of God**.

The table above includes two other passages that have often been confused with the keys to the kingdom of heaven. There is no relevance whatsoever, but we have included the passages for your examination. Notice that the keys to the K of H did not include power to forgive sins. That duty belongs to all Christians (2 Cor. 2:10), and has nothing to do with the K of H or the keys to it. Any pope or priest or pastor who claims to hold a special office from which he can forgive sins does so without any Scriptural foundation.

## Some are greater in the kingdom?

| *Matthew 18:1* At the same time came the disciples unto Jesus, saying, Who is the **greatest** in the **kingdom of heaven**? | *Mark 9:34* But they held their peace: for by the way they had disputed among themselves, who should be the **greatest**. | *Luke 9:46* Then there arose a reasoning among them, which of them should be **greatest**. |
|---|---|---|

Jesus' response to the disciples' queries validated the supposition of the question — that in the K of H some would be greater than others. He told them what they must do to be recognized as greater than others. He also described what one must do to be **called** least.

Mark and Luke record the question, stopping short of mentioning any kingdom, because Jesus never said that some would be greater than others in the K of G, and they avoid the subject of the K of H since it is a Jewish message. One may ask, "Why, then, did they record the question in part?" Because they were discussing the answer Jesus gave about being converted and becoming as little children. So, they recorded the question in an abbreviated version, not mentioning the K of H, but, then gave answers that were applicable to both kingdoms.

The K of G is not, as is the K of H, an earthly kingdom in which some are exalted to greater positions of service and glory than are others. Christians will not be ranked in the K of G (The New Jerusalem) according to their greatness.

## In the K of H one must forgive or lose his forgiveness.

| *Matthew 18:21* Then came Peter to him, and said, Lord, how oft shall my brother sin against me, and I forgive him? till seven times? 22 Jesus saith unto him, I say not unto thee, Until seven times: but, Until seventy times seven. 23 Therefore is the **kingdom of heaven** likened unto a certain king, which would take account of his servants. 34 And his lord was wroth, and **delivered him to the tormentors**, till he should pay all that was due unto him. 35 So likewise shall my heavenly Father | *Mark 11:25* And when ye stand praying, forgive, if ye have ought against any: that your Father also which is in heaven may forgive you your trespasses. 26 But if ye do not forgive, neither will your Father which is in heaven forgive your trespasses. | *Luke 17:3* Take heed to yourselves: If thy brother trespass against thee, rebuke him; and if he repent, forgive him. 4 And if he trespass against thee seven times in a day, and seven times in a day turn again to thee, saying, I repent; thou shalt forgive him. *Luke 6:37* Judge not, and ye shall not be judged: condemn | *James 2:13* For he shall have judgment without mercy, that hath shewed no mercy; and mercy rejoiceth against judgment. |
|---|---|---|---|

| do also unto you, if ye from your hearts forgive not every one his brother their trespasses. | | not, and ye shall not be condemned: forgive, and ye shall be forgiven. | |
|---|---|---|---|

This would be a scary parable if it applied to us in the K of G. Most of our theology would fly out the window, never to return. It would be in contradiction to Paul's message of imputed righteousness.

This parable teaches that in the K of H, if one who has been graciously forgiven of his debt to God were to fail to forgive others who trespass against him, then God would withdraw his forgiveness and turn the unforgiving person over to the tormentors.

I have heard preachers trying to expound this as if it were written to those of us in the K of G. It is not a pretty sight. It reminds one of a child trying to explain what "because" means.

When we look at the parallel passage in Mark, we find that he does not designate it as the K of G, but he does say that if one does not forgive others, God will not forgive him. However, Mark does not say, as does Matthew, that one who is already forgiven will lose his forgiveness if he fails to forgive his brother.

It is marvelous, indeed, how the Holy Spirit has led the writers to so carefully thread the different messages of the kingdoms, and to emerge with such a strong bond. There are so many places where they could have slipped by including a phrase or word that would have destroyed the distinction that is so carefully crafted throughout the four gospels and the remainder of the New Testament. It seems almost as if the Holy Spirit is teasing us with how close the text can come to marring the distinction without actually doing so.

## Men make themselves eunuchs for the sake of the K of H.

> *Matthew 19:12* For there are some eunuchs, which were so born from *their* mother's womb: and there are some eunuchs, which were made eunuchs of men: and there be eunuchs, which have made themselves eunuchs for the **kingdom of heaven's** sake. He that is able to receive *it,* let him receive *it.*

This is Jesus' answer to the disciples who had a difficult time accepting his teaching on marriage and divorce. They suggested that in consideration of the law against putting away your wife, marriage is a bondage that should be avoided. Jesus told them that some men are born eunuchs — lacking characteristic male sexual function or interest — and some men are castrated by other men, and that some voluntarily make themselves eunuchs — castrate themselves — for purposes that have to do with the K of H.

It is noteworthy that no such statement is made regarding the K of G. Only for the sake of the K of H would one make himself a eunuch — as a way of avoiding sin. This is because the K of H is a political kingdom with laws that must be obeyed or one will suffer exile or imprisonment, as in the above verse where the unforgiving one is turned over to the tormenters and cast into debtor's prison until he pays his monetary debt. One cannot get into the K of G by a disciplined and obedient life, but one can remain in the Millennial K of H if he is obedient and faithful. Each one in the K of H will be given 1000 years in which to come into compliance, after which, if he remains a sinner, he will be executed (Isa. 65:20). If a man's "member" offends him — prevents him from obedience — in the K of H he would be wise to cut it off as a means to enter into life (Matt. 5:29-30; 18:9).

By now you should have a good understanding of Matthew's presentation of the K of H: It is very much without grace and faith. It is tough on sinners. If the kingdoms are one and the same, and Matthew is talking about the Church, there can be no hope or assurance of salvation. "Amazing grace" will have to be found somewhere other than in the K of H and the book of Matthew.

# The 12 apostles will sit on 12 thrones in the kingdom.

| | | |
|---|---|---|
| *Matthew 19:27* Then answered Peter and said unto him, Behold, we have forsaken all, and followed thee; what shall we have therefore?<br>28 And Jesus said unto them, Verily I say unto you, That ye which have followed me, in the regeneration when the Son of man shall sit in the throne of his glory, ye also shall <u>sit upon twelve thrones, judging the twelve tribes of Israel.</u><br>29 And every one that hath forsaken houses, or brethren, or sisters, or father, or mother, or wife, or children, or lands, for my name's sake, shall receive an hundredfold, and shall inherit everlasting life.<br>30 But many that are first shall be last; and the last shall be first.<br>*20:1* For the **kingdom of heaven** is like unto a man that is an householder, which went out early in the morning to hire labourers into his vineyard. | *Mark 10:28* Then Peter began to say unto him, Lo, we have left all, and have followed thee.<br>29 And Jesus answered and said, Verily I say unto you, There is no man that hath left house, or brethren, or sisters, or father, or mother, or wife, or children, or lands, for my sake, and the gospel's,<br>30 But he shall receive an hundredfold now in this time, houses, and brethren, and sisters, and mothers, and children, and lands, with persecutions; and in the world to come eternal life.<br>31 But many that are first shall be last; and the last first. | *Luke 18:29* And he said unto them, Verily I say unto you, There is no man that hath left house, or parents, or brethren, or wife, or children, for the **kingdom of God**'s sake,<br>30 Who shall not receive manifold more in this present time, and in the world to come life everlasting.<br><br>*Luke 14:26* If any man come to me, and hate not his father, and mother, and wife, and children, and brethren, and sisters, yea, and his own life also, he cannot be my disciple.<br>27 And whosoever doth not bear his cross, and come after me, cannot be my disciple. |

According to the conjunction, "For" (meaning "because, since"), in Matthew 20:1, the statements of 19:28 are in reference to the K of H. This passage is most interesting when compared to the parallel passages in Mark and Luke. What they don't say is as instructive as what Matthew does say.

In Matthew the apostles are told that they will sit on 12 thrones, judging the 12 tribes of Israel. You will never fit that statement into the Church age. Bible expositors have done end-runs around this one so often that they have left a rutted path on the expositor's playground.

If there is just one kingdom, at what point are you going to get Israel separated from the Church and the apostles resurrected to come back into Jerusalem and sit upon 12 thrones and judge the 12 tribes throughout the land of Israel? How will you identify the tribe of each Jew, return them to that portion of land allotted their particular tribe, and then get them to accept one of the Christian apostles as judge over their tribe? It's time to bring out the book on allegories; you are going to need it if you are not willing to allow the Bible to make you a dispensationalist.

The interpretation is clear and simple to those who have the key of knowledge (understanding of the kingdoms). God promised a kingdom to Abraham and confirmed it to Isaac and Jacob, and he restated the promises to David and Solomon (Psalm 89). Ezekiel declared them again in chapter 37, and many other references in the Scriptures confirm that God will yet build the kingdom in Israel, and David will sit on the throne in Jerusalem. Now, we learn from Jesus that the 12 Jewish (yet Church-age) apostles will also judge the individual tribes. This will commence at the beginning of the Millennial reign of Christ. You could only convince someone that this passage should be interpreted allegorically and applied to the K of G if they have more faith in you than they do in their ability to read the plain text of the Bible.

# The K of H is like a man who hired laborers for a penny.

| |
|---|
| *Matthew 20:1* For the **kingdom of heaven** is like unto a man *that is* an householder, which went out early in the morning to hire labourers into his vineyard.<br>2 And when he had agreed with the labourers for a penny a day, he sent them into his vineyard.<br>3 And he went out about the third hour, and saw others standing idle in the marketplace,<br>4 And said unto them; Go ye also into the vineyard, and whatsoever is right I will give you. And they went their way.<br>5 Again he went out about the sixth and ninth hour, and did likewise. |

6 And about the eleventh hour he went out, and found others standing idle, and saith unto them, Why stand ye here all the day idle?

7 They say unto him, Because no man hath hired us. He saith unto them, Go ye also into the vineyard; and whatsoever is right, *that* shall ye receive.

8 So when even was come, the lord of the vineyard saith unto his steward, Call the labourers, and give them *their* hire, beginning from the last unto the first.

9 And when they came that *were hired* about the eleventh hour, they received every man a penny.

10 But when the first came, they supposed that they should have received more; and they likewise received every man a penny.

11 And when they had received *it,* they murmured against the goodman of the house,

12 Saying, These last have wrought *but* one hour, and thou hast made them equal unto us, which have borne the burden and heat of the day.

13 But he answered one of them, and said, Friend, I do thee no wrong: didst not thou agree with me for a penny?

14 Take *that* thine *is* and go thy way: I will give unto this last, even as unto thee.

15 Is it not lawful for me to do what I will with mine own? Is thine eye evil, because I am good?

16 <u>So the last shall be first, and the first last:</u> for many be called, but few chosen.

This passage is a continuation of a discussion begun in 19:27 when the disciples said unto him, **Behold, we have forsaken all, and followed thee; what shall we have therefore?** Jesus told them that they would **sit on 12 thrones** in the coming kingdom, but then he offers a word of caution to these seekers of reward. They were the first to respond to the call to "repent, for the **kingdom of heaven** is at hand." They had been baptized by John in anticipation of the coming Christ. They had gone out into the vineyard of Israel and labored from the very first call. No one came before them. They were the first on the job, and Jesus has agreed with them as to their reward for their labor. They will sit on thrones in Jerusalem.

But then he warns them that there will be others employed to work in the vineyard. Some won't be hired until most of the work is done. They may not exert the same effort that the disciples have exerted, or be awarded the disciples' place of honor, yet they will be rewarded just as liberally, maybe more so, for the first ones hired may be last, and the last ones hired may be first. Nevertheless, he assured them that **whatsoever is right**, the master of the vineyard will pay them, for it is his to do with as he pleases.

The disciples must have felt a mixture of elation and humility. They wanted to know what they would receive, and he told them, but he also told them that others who come later would receive just as much as they.

The K of H is a literal, earthly kingdom. Some will indeed hold higher positions than others. There will be those known as and called the *greatest* or the *least*. This passage fits the K of H beautifully, but it would wreak havoc on the K of G.

This is not a difficult passage if you examine it in its context and don't treat it in a "devotional" manner. Not everything in the Bible is written *to* the Christian, but, it is all written *for* our learning and admonition (Rom. 15:4; 1 Cor. 10:11).

## Someone will sit on his right and left in the coming kingdom.

| | | |
|---|---|---|
| *Matthew 20:20* Then came to him the mother of Zebedee's children with her sons, worshipping *him*, and desiring a certain thing of him.<br><br>21 And he said unto her, What wilt thou? She saith unto him, Grant that these my two sons may sit, <u>the one on thy right hand, and the other on the left</u>, **in thy kingdom**.<br><br>22 But Jesus answered and said, Ye know not what ye ask. Are ye able to | *Mark 10:37* They said unto him, Grant unto us that we may <u>sit, one on thy right hand, and the other on thy left hand</u>, **in thy glory**.<br><br>38 But Jesus said unto them, Ye know not what ye ask: can ye drink of the cup that I drink of? and be baptized with the baptism that I am baptized with? | *Matthew 25:34* Then shall the King say unto them on his right hand, Come, ye blessed of my Father, inherit the **kingdom** prepared for you from the foundation of the world:<br><br>*Matthew 19:28* And Jesus said unto them, Verily I say unto you, That ye which have followed me, in the <u>regeneration</u> when the Son of man shall sit in the **throne of his glory**, ye |

| | | |
|---|---|---|
| drink of the cup that I shall drink of, and to be baptized with the baptism that I am baptized with? They say unto him, We are able.<br><br>23 And he saith unto them, Ye shall drink indeed of my cup, and be baptized with the baptism that I am baptized with: but to sit on my right hand, and on my left, is not mine to give, but it <u>shall be given to them for whom it is prepared of my Father.</u> | 39 And they said unto him, We can. And Jesus said unto them, Ye shall indeed drink of the cup that I drink of; and with the baptism that I am baptized withal shall ye be baptized:<br><br>40 But to sit on my right hand and on my left hand is not mine to give; **but it shall be given to them for whom it is prepared**. | also shall sit upon twelve thrones, judging the twelve tribes of Israel.<br><br>*Acts 1:6* When they therefore were come together, they asked of him, saying, Lord, wilt thou at this time <u>restore again the **kingdom to Israel**</u>?<br><br>7 And he said unto them, It is <u>not for you to know the</u> times or the seasons, which the Father hath put in his own power. |

This is a continuation of the subject raised by the question of the disciples in Matthew 19:27 as to who would be the greatest in the K of H.

The mother of these two disciples, James and John, no doubt got her understanding of the nature of the K of H from her sons, who had now been with Jesus for three and one-half years. Therefore, she rightly expects the kingdom to be literal, with a throne, having a need for co-regents. She is ambitious, wanting her sons to share the honor and power of the kingdom. She is not thinking in terms of the Christian "heaven"; she is thinking earthly, as she should be.

Jesus' answer does not repudiate her concept of the kingdom; rather, he assents to her basic assumption that the kingdom will be restored to Israel. He does not deny that there will be someone sitting on his right hand and on his left. He seems to casually tell her that it is not within his authority to grant such a request; only the Father has the authority to assign someone to those positions.

Once again, we see the Holy Spirit's delicate balance maintained in the distinctiveness of the different accounts of Matthew and Mark. The woman asks the question, but she does not say K of H or K of G, just, **"your kingdom"**. Jesus' answer to her question signifies his approval of her wording.

The Millennial kingdom will be the point at which the "mystery" is fulfilled. The K of H and the K of G will coexist as part of **Christ's kingdom**. When Christ turns **his kingdom** over to the Father, it will then be called the **Father's kingdom**.

# The K of H is like a king inviting guests to his son's marriage.

| | | |
|---|---|---|
| *Matthew 22:1* And Jesus answered and spake unto them again by parables, and said,<br><br>2 The **kingdom of heaven** is like unto a certain king, which made a <u>marriage for his son,</u><br><br>3 And sent forth his servants to call <u>them that were bidden</u> to the wedding: and they would not come.<br><br>4 Again, he sent forth other <u>servants,</u> saying, Tell them which are bidden, Behold, I have prepared my dinner: my oxen and *my* fatlings *are* killed, and all things *are* ready: come unto the marriage.<br><br>5 But they made light of *it,* and went their ways, one to his farm, another to his merchandise:<br><br>6 And the remnant took his servants, and entreated *them* spitefully, and slew *them.*<br><br>7 But when the king heard *thereof,* he was wroth: and he <u>sent forth his armies, and destroyed those murderers, and burned up their city</u>.<br><br>8 Then saith he to his servants, The wedding is ready, but <u>they which were bidden were not worthy</u>.<br><br>9 Go ye therefore into the highways, and as many as ye shall find, bid to the marriage.<br><br>10 So those servants went out into the highways, and gathered together all as many as they found, <u>both bad and good</u>: and the wedding was furnished with guests.<br><br>11 And when the king came in to see the guests, he saw there a man which had not on a wedding garment:<br><br>12 And he saith unto him, Friend, how camest thou in hither not having a wedding garment? And he was speechless.<br><br>13 Then said the king to the servants, Bind him hand and foot, and take him away, and <u>cast *him* into outer darkness; there shall be weeping and gnashing of teeth</u>.<br><br>14 For many are called, but few *are* chosen. | *Luke 14:15* And when one of them that sat at meat with him heard these things, he said unto him, Blessed is he that shall eat bread in the **kingdom of God.**<br><br>16 Then said he unto him, A certain man made a great supper, and bade many:<br><br>17 And sent his servant at supper time to say to them that were bidden, Come; for all things are now ready.<br><br>18 And they all with one consent began to make excuse. The first said unto him, I have bought a piece of ground, and I must needs go and see it: I pray thee have me excused.<br><br>19 And another said, I have bought five yoke of oxen, and I go to prove them: I pray thee have me excused.<br><br>20 And another said, I have married a wife, and therefore I cannot come.<br><br>21 So that servant came, and shewed his lord these things. Then the master of the house being angry said to his servant, <u>Go out quickly into the streets and lanes of the city, and bring in hither the poor, and the maimed, and the halt, and the blind.</u><br><br>22 And the servant said, Lord, it is done as thou hast commanded, and yet there is room.<br><br>23 And the lord said unto the servant, Go out into the highways and hedges, and compel them to come in, that my house may be filled.<br><br>24 For I say unto you, <u>That none of those men which were bidden shall taste of my supper.</u> | *John 3:29* He that hath the bride is the bridegroom: but the friend of the bridegroom, which standeth and heareth him, rejoiceth greatly because of the bridegroom's voice: this my joy therefore is fulfilled. |

This is a warning and a prophecy directed specifically to the "blinded" and unbelieving Jews, informing them that they were the intended guests at an up-coming wedding. But, since they rejected his offer and slew all the prophets (including John the Baptist), the city of Jerusalem and the temple will be destroyed, and Gentiles will take their place.

This is one of the great parables, in that it gives us the most thorough overview of **the mystery of the kingdom.** The king (God) made a marriage for his son (Jesus) to be married to a Bride (the Church). The king's servants (John the Baptist and other prophets and apostles) went out to invite guests (Jews) to the wedding. The Jews **made light** of the invitation and **killed the servants** — as they had killed John. The king responded by sending his armies (Rome — Joel 2:1-11) to burn their cities (Jerusalem in 70 AD). Then the king sends his servants (preachers) out to the highways to invite unworthy Gentiles and Jews, both bad and good, to fill up his kingdom.

When the wedding is furnished (when the Bride, the Church, is complete) and everything is set, the king goes to view the guests (after the Tribulation, at the beginning of the Millennium). He found a man who had refused the wedding garment that was provided for each guest. The man came self-willed and independent, refusing to cooperate with the wedding party. This would have its counterpart in the tares that are found in the **kingdom of heaven** at the beginning of the Millennium. The king commands his servants to cast the man into outer darkness (hell) where there will be weeping and gnashing of teeth. For many (Jews) are **called** to the wedding, but **few are chosen** to be guests at the wedding of the Son of God.

Luke gives a different parable of the K of G, with some similarities to the wedding parable. The differences are most revealing. He is careful to leave out anything that could be taken exclusively as the K of H. If Luke had given a parable of a wedding and spoken of the invited people not coming, he would have already been completely away from the facts of the K of G. Church-age saints could never be typified as *guests* at a wedding. They *are* the Bride. The story Luke recorded is not a wedding, and there is no one making light of the invitation, nor do they kill the servants who bring the message. In Matthew, the focal point was the wedding guests. In Luke's parable, the focal point is those who were invited to a dinner, the dinner being representative of the primary gospel provision — Jesus, the bread from heaven (John 6:35). The ones invited apologetically excuse themselves from the supper. The master of the house sends his servants out to gather those who know they are unworthy to come and those who cannot bring themselves — the blind and crippled. This is a beautiful picture of the gospel message going out to the poor and broken in this age. There is no mention of anyone coming into the wedding without a wedding garment. Luke closes with the statement — the main point of the parable — that those who were bidden (Israel) will not taste of his supper. This is a picture of the Jews rejecting the gospel (the K of G) and of the Gentiles coming to the feast of the gospel.

Can you see how devastating it would be to Luke's parable if he had written of a man at the supper without proper garments? It would place an unsaved man in the K of G. How preposterous! But Luke was faithful to his leading as he penned these words, and the Holy Spirit once again preserved the carefully-crafted distinction between the two kingdoms.

## The religious leaders shut up the K of H, preventing others from entering.

| | |
|---|---|
| *Matthew 23:13* But woe unto you, scribes and Pharisees, hypocrites! for ye <u>shut up</u> the **kingdom of heaven** against men: for ye neither go in *yourselves,* neither suffer ye them that are entering to go in. | *Luke 11:51* From the blood of Abel unto the blood of Zacharias, which perished between the altar and the temple: verily I say unto you, It shall be required of this generation.<br>  52 Woe unto you, lawyers! for ye have taken <u>away the key of knowledge</u>: ye entered not in yourselves, and them that were entering in ye hindered. |

The K of H is of such a nature that a few men in authority could temporarily prevent it from being established. No one can **shut up** the K of G against another's acceptance or prevent it from coming. This passage is distinctively K of H. Since the K of H is a kingdom that must be instituted among men, it requires the assent of those who hold the reins of power. When the political and religious leaders of that day rejected the kingdom, they shut the door for everyone. God does not push himself onto his people. He does not rule as a dictator. Heaven will rule earth when the children of the kingdom welcome the king. After the Jews had rejected Jesus, he said to them, **"Ye shall not see me henceforth, till ye shall say, Blessed is he that cometh in the name of the Lord"** (Matt. 23:39). So the Jews exercised their free will to shut the door of the kingdom.

No such thing is said regarding the K of G. Without designating it, Luke says that they took away the key of knowledge, but he does not say that they shut the door on the K of G. The K of G is a spiritual kingdom that men enter individually — by faith, one at a time. No one can shut the door for another by his own rejection. However, one could hinder another person from entering the K of G by depriving him of the truth, thereby taking away the key of knowledge.

How beautifully Matthew and Luke preserve the integrity of the two kingdoms in their varied accounts! Passage after passage leads us to the same conclusion: It could not be an accident! If you still think so, then you have the logic that would permit you to be a Darwinian evolutionist.

# The gospel of the kingdom will be preached during the Tribulation.

| | |
|---|---|
| *Matthew 24:9* Then shall they deliver you up to be afflicted, and shall kill you: and ye shall be hated of all nations for my name's sake.<br> 10 And then shall many be offended, and shall betray one another, and shall hate one another.<br> 11 And many false prophets shall rise, and shall deceive many.<br> 12 And because iniquity shall abound, the love of many shall wax cold.<br> 13 But he that shall endure unto the end, the same shall be saved.<br> 14 And this **gospel of the kingdom** shall be preached in all the world for a witness unto all nations; and then shall the <u>end come.</u><br> 15 When ye therefore shall see the abomination of desolation, spoken of by Daniel the prophet, stand in the holy place, (whoso readeth, let him understand:) | *Luke 21:29* And he spake to them a parable; Behold the fig tree, and all the trees;<br> 30 When they now shoot forth, ye see and know of your own selves that summer is now nigh at hand.<br> 31 So likewise ye, when ye see these things come to pass, know ye that the **kingdom of God** is nigh at hand.<br> 32 Verily I say unto you, This generation shall not pass away, till all be fulfilled. |

Verse 14 is fascinating. Heretofore, the K of H message has never been called **gospel**. Matthew is careful, even now, not to call this the "gospel of the **kingdom of heaven**." It is during the Tribulation when all hope seems to be lost that there is a gospel message preached by 144,000 Jewish males. It is not the gospel of Jesus Christ; it is too late for that gospel. It is the good news that the kingdom is at hand. It will be nearly the same message John the Baptist preached: **Repent, for the kingdom of heaven is at hand,** with the addition of the Second Coming of Messiah in power and glory to force compliance and offer forgiveness to those who stop sinning.

The gospel of the kingdom will contain things **new, and things old** (Matt. 13:51) — the **old** message of the kingdom under the law of Moses, with the **new** emphasis that Messiah has already come and offered the blood sacrifice.

These events described in Matthew 24 occur during the Tribulation, just preceding **the end**. He dates it with the reference to **the abomination of desolation** that Antichrist will erect in the holy place — in the rebuilt temple in Jerusalem. So, at a time when the temple is rebuilt and Antichrist has made his appearance and placed an image of himself in the *Holy of Holies* inside the temple, 144,000 Jewish males will go forth over the whole earth and preach the gospel of the kingdom until they are all martyred (Rev. 20:4); then the end comes with the second advent of Christ and the judgment of the nations.

Luke gives an account that is consistent with the K of G. The **fig tree** represents Israel (Jer. 24:1-9; Matt. 21:17-21; Luke 13:6-7; 21:29). **All the trees** represent the Gentile nations. So, here we are told that when we see Israel begin to bud as a nation and *all the nations* rising out of obscurity into prominence, you can take this as a sign that the K of G is close to being manifested on the earth. The generation that sees the budding of Israel and *all the nations* will live to see the Second Coming of Christ.

Notice carefully, that if Matthew had just added the word *God* to the statement about the gospel of the kingdom being preached concurrent with the *abomination of desolation*, it would have destroyed the truth of a pre-tribulation rapture of the saints by placing the Church on earth during the Tribulation.

Luke's statement regarding signs does not take us into the Tribulation as does Matthew's comments. Everything Luke says speaks of events before the Tribulation.

Marvelous indeed is the care that God took in so carefully directing these texts through the men he chose to be moved by the Holy Ghost.

# The K of H is obtained by good works.

Verses 1 and 14 make it clear that Matthew is speaking of the K of H in verse 34.

> *Matthew 25:1* Then shall the **kingdom of heaven** be likened unto…
>
> 34 Then shall the King say unto them on his right hand, Come, ye blessed of my Father, inherit the **kingdom** prepared for you from the foundation of the world:
>
> 35 For I was an hungred, and ye gave me meat: I was thirsty, and ye gave me drink: I was a stranger, and ye took me in:
>
> 36 Naked, and ye clothed me: I was sick, and ye visited me: I was in prison, and ye came unto me.
>
> 37 Then shall the righteous answer him, saying, Lord, when saw we thee an hungred, and fed *thee*? or thirsty, and gave *thee* drink?
>
> 38 When saw we thee a stranger, and took *thee* in? or naked, and clothed *thee*?
>
> 39 Or when saw we thee sick, or in prison, and came unto thee?
>
> 40 And the King shall answer and say unto them, Verily I say unto you, Inasmuch as ye have done *it* unto one of the least of these my brethren, ye have done *it* unto me.
>
> 41 Then shall he say also unto them on the left hand, Depart from me, ye cursed, into everlasting fire, prepared for the devil and his angels:
>
> 42 For I was an hungred, and ye gave me no meat: I was thirsty, and ye gave me no drink:
>
> 43 I was a stranger, and ye took me not in: naked, and ye clothed me not: sick, and in prison, and ye visited me not.
>
> 44 Then shall they also answer him, saying, Lord, when saw we thee an hungred, or athirst, or a stranger, or naked, or sick, or in prison, and did not minister unto thee?
>
> 45 Then shall he answer them, saying, Verily I say unto you, Inasmuch as ye did *it* not to one of the least of these, ye did *it* not to me.
>
> 46 And these shall go away into everlasting punishment: but the righteous into life eternal.

If you make hospital visits and go to the prisons to see the inmates, if you give your money to the poor and receive the homeless into your house, feed them, clothe them, then you will stand a chance of getting into the K of H. But if you just believe with all your heart and worship God regularly, abstain from any overt sin, raise your children to be Christians, but get too busy to go to the prisons and entertain the homeless, then you will be cast into everlasting punishment — that is, of course, if the **kingdom of God** and the **kingdom of heaven** are the same.

If the K of G and the K of H are one and the same, then this passage is applicable to us today, and salvation is obtained by good works. Preachers of grace are able to take some of the K of H passages and reconstruct them to fit Paul's message of imputed righteousness, but this passage is avoided like anthrax. There is no way to get grace out of this one and still appear forthright.

The key to accurately interpreting this passage is, of course, to differentiate between the two kingdoms, but there is another important factor that is overlooked. The first verse of the chapter sets the context and thereby dates the three parables that follow. **"Then shall the kingdom of heaven be likened unto…."** At that time, the K of H will be just as it is described. It was not like that then, and it is not like that now, but it will be that way, **then**. When is **then?** The previous Scripture told us when.

> *Matthew 24:27* For as the lightning cometh out of the east, and shineth even unto the west; so shall also the coming of the Son of man be.
>
> 29 Immediately after the tribulation of those days shall the sun be darkened, and the moon shall not give her light, and the stars shall fall from heaven, and the powers of the heavens shall be shaken:
>
> 33 So likewise ye, when ye shall see all these things, know that it is near, *even* at the doors.
>
> *Matthew 25:1* **Then** shall the **kingdom of heaven** be likened unto ten virgins, which took their lamps, and went forth to meet the bridegroom.
>
> *Matthew 25:32* And before him shall be gathered all nations: and he shall separate them one from another, as a shepherd divideth his sheep from the goats:
>
> 33 And he shall set the sheep on his right hand, but the goats on the left.
>
> 34 **Then** shall the King say unto them on his right hand, Come, ye blessed of my Father, inherit the **kingdom** prepared for you from the foundation of the world:

35 For I was an hungred, and ye gave me meat: I was thirsty, and ye gave me drink: I was a stranger, and ye took me in:

The word **"Then"** dates the events of this chapter as occurring <u>after the Tribulation</u>, <u>after the Son of Man comes with his holy angels</u>, and <u>after the nations are gathered before Jesus to be judged</u>. **Then**, at that time (not now), entrance into the **kingdom of heaven** will be like one who is admitted into the recently set up kingdom, based on how he has performed during the Tribulation. Did he feed the homeless Jews — **the least of these <u>my brethren</u>?** Did he visit Jesus' **brethren** who were imprisoned by Antichrist and sick? Did he feed Jesus' **brethren** (Jews) when they were hungry and fleeing from Antichrist?

The only Gentiles who will qualify to go into the Millennium and experience the **kingdom of heaven** will be those who earned that right through the way they treated the Jews during the Tribulation. After all, it will be the kingdom **promised to our father David**. The Church will already **be caught up together in the clouds, to meet the Lord in the air: and so shall we ever be with the Lord** (1Thess. 4:17). The Church, obviously, will not be in the judgment of the nations described in Matthew 25:32-46. That judgment will be for those who survived the great Tribulation and sought to enter the **kingdom of heaven** — which will again be "**at hand**." It will be too late to **repent, for the kingdom of heaven "is" at hand**. At that time, entering the kingdom of heaven will be by pure works. Did you keep his commandments? Were you faithful unto the end? Did you show compassion on the persecuted Jews? There will be no "new birth" or "salvation by faith and grace" available to mankind at that time.

## The K of H is like 10 virgins.

| |  |
|---|---|
| *Matthew 25:1* <u>Then</u> shall the **kingdom of heaven** be likened unto ten virgins, which took their lamps, and went forth to meet the bridegroom.<br><br>2 And five of them were wise, and five *were* foolish.<br>3 They that *were* foolish took their lamps, and took no oil with them:<br>4 But the wise took oil in their vessels with their lamps.<br>5 While the bridegroom tarried, they all slumbered and slept.<br>6 And at midnight there was a cry made, Behold, the bridegroom cometh; go ye out to meet him.<br>7 Then all those virgins arose, and trimmed their lamps.<br>8 And the foolish said unto the wise, Give us of your oil; for our lamps are gone out.<br>9 But the wise answered, saying, *Not so*; lest there be not enough for us and you: but go ye rather to them that sell, and buy for yourselves.<br>10 And while they went to buy, the bridegroom came; and they that were ready went in with him to the marriage: and the door was shut.<br>11 Afterward came also the other virgins, saying, Lord, Lord, open to us.<br>12 But he answered and said, Verily I say unto you, I know you not.<br>13 Watch therefore, for ye know neither the day nor the hour wherein <u>the Son of man cometh</u>. | *Luke 12:36* And ye yourselves like unto men that wait for their lord, when he will <u>return from the wedding</u>; that when he cometh and knocketh, they may open unto him immediately.<br><br>37 Blessed are those servants, whom the lord <u>when he cometh</u> [after his wedding] shall find watching: verily I say unto you, that he shall gird himself, and make them to sit down to meat, and will come forth and serve them.<br>38 And if he shall come in the second watch, or come in the third watch, and find them so, blessed are those servants.<br>39 And this know, that if the goodman of the house had known what hour the thief would come, he would have watched, and not have suffered his house to be broken through.<br>40 Be ye therefore ready also: for the Son of man cometh at an hour when ye think not. |

As we have seen, the most important word in this entire chapter is the first one — **Then**, at that time, and after the events described in the preceding verses of chapter 24. After the Tribulation and after the Second Coming of Christ, the K of H will be like the ten virgins.

Consider the historical event on which Jesus bases this parable. A man is due to arrive at his wedding. The bride and all the family are inside waiting for the groom. Outside are 10 virgin girls who are to attend the wedding as something like bridesmaids. They are there to furnish the light by which he makes his entrance into the wedding.

He is not going to marry them, for that would make him a polygamist with eleven wives, and all married on the same day. And what kind of wedding makes the "brides" wait outside alone for the groom? Jesus would never teach by a parable that had no grounds in popular social customs.

The parable states that the groom delays his coming, just as Messiah is delaying his coming. Everyone is waiting inside except the virgins who sit outside with their lamps burning, waiting to provide light for the bridegroom as he enters the chamber. The ten virgins represent the Jews who anticipate their Messiah. After several hours pass, five of the virgins begin to run low on oil. They did not expect to wait so long, and they did not bring enough oil. The other five virgins are wiser, for they brought enough oil to see them through the entire night, which would represent the Tribulation. When the five foolish virgins see that they are going to run out of oil and therefore will not be able to fulfill their purpose — to give light —, they request that the other five virgins share their oil. These refuse on grounds that if they do so, they too will run out of oil if the groom tarries till morning.

While the five foolish virgins are gone to buy oil, the bridegroom comes and goes in to the wedding and shuts the door. When the five foolish virgins return, the wedding is already in progress and their services are no longer needed. They were supposed to accompany the groom, but they missed him. The door was shut. It is too late.

It would take a Biblical contortionist to make this parable fit the K of G. Can you imagine the problems? I have heard preachers say that the virgins represented the Bride of Christ. You can see where that will go: half of the bride not making it to heaven, "buying" your oil (the Holy Spirit), etc. That is why they teach that parables are to be understood for their general content, not in their particulars. They cannot let it say what it says and be faithful to the text as written.

The K of G is never like this parable at any time, not during the life of Christ, not now, and not during the Tribulation or Millennium. The K of H is like this parable **"then",** and only then, at the Second Coming of Christ. The Bible is a wonderfully accurate and easy to understand book.

The following passage confirms our interpretation of the virgins as wedding companions and not brides. This Psalm is about Jesus, the bridegroom, as Hebrews 1:8 confirms. God never leaves us without a parallel passage to aid our interpretation. Only the King James Bible, of all English translations, perfectly leaves intact all of the parallel passages.

> *Psalm 45:6* Thy throne, O God, is for ever and ever: the sceptre of thy kingdom is a right sceptre.
> 7 Thou lovest righteousness, and hatest wickedness: therefore God, thy God, hath anointed thee with the oil of gladness above thy fellows.
> 13 The king's daughter is all glorious within: her clothing is of wrought gold.
> 14 She shall be brought unto the king in raiment of needlework: <u>the virgins her companions that follow her shall be brought unto thee.</u>
> 15 With gladness and rejoicing shall they be brought: <u>they shall enter into the king's palace</u>.

### Israel is God's chaste virgin.

In the above parable (Matt. 25:1-13), we can readily identify the groom as Christ, the Bride as the Church, and the wedding as the union of Christ to his Church. The 10 virgins represent Israel. Jesus is speaking these parables to the Jews, and every parable has been a warning to them. The warnings always have to do with entering the kingdom or being left out. This parable anticipates the Jewish rejection of Messiah, introduces the salvation of the Gentiles, and discloses the composition of the Bride of Christ.

The Jews and Gentiles who respond to the gospel of the kingdom during the Tribulation will be anticipating the coming of the bridegroom and the beginning of the kingdom reign. They will have to experience an unknown period of waiting for the bridegroom, who will delay his coming. Some of them will not be prepared to wait, and they will not be patient.

> *Luke 12:45* But and if that servant say in his heart, My lord delayeth his coming; and shall begin to beat the menservants and maidens, and to eat and drink, and to be drunken;

46 The lord of that servant will come in a day when he looketh not for him, and at an hour when he is not aware, and will cut him in sunder, and will appoint him his portion with the unbelievers.

Those Jews who endure unto the end of the Tribulation and have oil in their lamps, still anticipating the coming of Christ, will be allowed to enter the K of H and attend the wedding of Christ to the Church. Remember, the virgins were not part of the Bride; they were attendees at the wedding.

To further identify the role of the virgins, note that the 144,000 Jewish men who are sealed and redeemed during the Tribulation are called **virgins**.

> *Revelation 14:3* And they sung as it were a new song before the throne, and before the four beasts, and the elders: and no man could learn that song but the hundred and forty and four thousand, which were redeemed from the earth.
>
> 4 These are they which were not defiled with women; **for they are virgins**. These are they which **follow the Lamb whithersoever he goeth.** These were redeemed from among men, being the firstfruits unto God and to the Lamb.

This parable, like the ones that follow, is a warning to the Jews that if they are not prepared, they will be shut out of the kingdom.

Luke records a parable that has some of the elements found in Matthew's parable, but he does not say anything about anyone running out of oil and being shut out. Rather, we find Christ girding himself and serving his servants.

We are amazed once again at the consistency of the Word of God. Like clockwork, it keeps on delineating a clear distinction between the K of G and the K of H.

## The K of H is like a man who distributed talents to his servants.

*Matthew 25:14* For *the kingdom of heaven is* as a man travelling into a far country, *who* called his own servants, and delivered unto them his goods.

15 And unto one he gave five talents, to another two, and to another one; to every man according to his several ability; and straightway took his journey.

16 Then he that had received the five talents went and traded with the same, and made *them* other five talents.

17 And likewise he that *had received* two, he also gained other two.

18 But he that had received one went and digged in the earth, and hid his lord's money.

19 After a long time the lord of those servants cometh, and reckoneth with them.

20 And so he that had received five talents came and brought other five talents, saying, Lord, thou deliveredst unto me five talents: behold, I have gained beside them five talents more.

21 His lord said unto him, Well done, *thou* good and faithful servant: thou hast been faithful over a few things, I will make thee ruler over many things: enter thou into the joy of thy lord.

22 He also that had received two talents came and said, Lord, thou deliveredst unto me two talents: behold, I have gained two other talents beside them.

23 His lord said unto him, Well done, good and faithful servant; thou hast been faithful over a few things, I will make thee ruler over many things: enter thou into the joy of thy lord.

24 Then he which had received the one talent came and said, Lord, I knew thee that thou art an hard man, reaping where thou hast not sown, and gathering where thou hast not strawed:

25 And I was afraid, and went and hid thy talent in the earth: lo, *there* thou hast *that is* thine.

26 His lord answered and said unto him, *Thou* wicked and slothful servant, thou knewest that I reap where I sowed not, and gather where I have not strawed:

27 Thou oughtest therefore to have put my money to the exchangers, and *then* at my coming I should have received mine own with usury.

*Luke 19:11* And as they heard these things, he added and spake a parable, because he was nigh to Jerusalem, and because **they thought that the kingdom of God should immediately appear**.

12 He said therefore, A certain nobleman went into a far country to receive for himself **a kingdom**, and to return.

13 And he called his **ten servants**, and delivered them **ten pounds**, and said unto them, Occupy till I come.

14 But his citizens hated him, and sent a message after him, saying, We will not have this man to reign over us.

15 And it came to pass, that when he was returned, having received **the kingdom**, then he commanded these servants to be called unto him, to whom he had given the money, that he might know how much every man had gained by trading.

16 Then came the first, saying, Lord, thy pound hath gained ten pounds.

17 And he said unto him, Well, thou good servant: because thou hast been faithful in a very little, have thou authority over ten cities.

18 And the second came, saying,

28 Take therefore the talent from him, and give *it* unto him which hath ten talents.

29 For unto every one that hath shall be given, and he shall have abundance: but from him that hath not shall be taken away even that which he hath.

30 And cast ye the unprofitable servant into outer darkness: there shall be weeping and gnashing of teeth. [*This could not be true in the K of G.*]

31 When the Son of man shall come in his glory, and all the holy angels with him, then shall he sit upon the throne of his glory: [*This is a continuation of his answer in chapter 24 as to when these things will be.*]

32 And before him shall be gathered all nations: and he shall separate them one from another, as a shepherd divideth *his* sheep from the goats:

33 And he shall set the sheep on his right hand, but the goats on the left.

34 Then shall the King say unto them on his right hand, Come, ye blessed of my Father, inherit the kingdom prepared for you from the foundation of the world:

35 For I was an hungred, and ye gave me meat: I was thirsty, and ye gave me drink: I was a stranger, and ye took me in:

36 Naked, and ye clothed me: I was sick, and ye visited me: I was in prison, and ye came unto me.

37 Then shall the righteous answer him, saying, Lord, when saw we thee an hungred, and fed *thee*? or thirsty, and gave *thee* drink?

38 When saw we thee a stranger, and took *thee* in? or naked, and clothed *thee*?

39 Or when saw we thee sick, or in prison, and came unto thee?

40 And the King shall answer and say unto them, Verily I say unto you, Inasmuch as ye have done *it* unto one of the least of these my brethren, ye have done *it* unto me.

41 Then shall he say also unto them on the left hand, Depart from me, ye cursed, into everlasting fire, prepared for the devil and his angels:

42 For I was an hungred, and ye gave me no meat: I was thirsty, and ye gave me no drink:

43 I was a stranger, and ye took me not in: naked, and ye clothed me not: sick, and in prison, and ye visited me not.

44 Then shall they also answer him, saying, Lord, when saw we thee an hungred, or athirst, or a stranger, or naked, or sick, or in prison, and did not minister unto thee?

45 Then shall he answer them, saying, Verily I say unto you, Inasmuch as ye did it not to one of the least of these, ye did it not to me.

46 And these shall go away into everlasting punishment: but the righteous into life eternal.

Lord, thy pound hath gained five pounds.

19 And he said likewise to him, Be thou also over five cities.

20 And another came, saying, Lord, behold, here is thy pound, which I have kept laid up in a napkin:

21 For I feared thee, because thou art an austere man: thou takest up that thou layedst not down, and reapest that thou didst not sow.

22 And he saith unto him, Out of thine own mouth will I judge thee, thou wicked servant. Thou knewest that I was an austere man, taking up that I laid not down, and reaping that I did not sow:

23 Wherefore then gavest not thou my money into the bank, that at my coming I might have required mine own with usury?

24 And he said unto them that stood by, Take from him the pound, and give it to him that hath ten pounds.

25 (And they said unto him, Lord, he hath ten pounds.)

26 For I say unto you, That unto every one which hath shall be given; and from him that hath not, even that he hath shall be taken away from him.

27 But those mine enemies, which would not that I should reign over them, bring hither, and slay them before me.

[*He does not slay the man who did not develop his talent. The enemies were citizens who would not submit to his authority.*]

This parable is the longest and the most complex of all the parables, and, no doubt, the least understood. Its original meaning has been so cluttered with homespun sermonizing that it is of no use to anyone other than a preacher who wants to encourage his congregation to get more involved in church activities.

To begin with, it is purely coincidental and unfortunate that the word **talent** (an ancient unit of measurement for gold or silver coins) happens to be spelled and pronounced just like the English word we use for those special gifts and abilities each individual possesses to various degrees, such as music, art, public speaking, etc. Preachers talk about "dedicating your *talents* to God": If you are musically inclined, sing in the choir, etc. However, this parable is not an encouragement to dedicate your abilities to the church program. The subject is Tribulation survivors investing money in persecuted Jews. He told us clearly that it is a revelation of the K of H. It has nothing to do with the K of G, and even if it were applicable to the K of G, the message would have been: "Invest your money in the stock market and keep the profits in the bank in reserve for Jesus when he returns." This would work really well for some of the modern TV "evangelists." Hurry, reduce it to allegory!

Verse 31 dates these events: **When the son of man shall come in his glory… and before him shall be gathered all nations.**

The K of H is like the 32 verses following Matthew 25:14. As in all the parables, the man is God or Jesus. Before going into a far country, he gave each of his servants various amounts of money and commanded them to invest it so as to provide him with a return. When he returned, the two who had received the most had doubled their capital. But the man who had received the least was timid and fearful of losing his money in an investment, so he buried it. When asked to give an account, he returned the original gift and defended his failure to invest by saying that he was afraid because he knew that his master was a hard man who would demand more than he had given. The master acknowledged that he did indeed demand more than he gave, and on that basis rebuked the fearful and timid servant, calling him wicked and slothful. He stripped the man of the little money he had and gave it to the man who had the most and whose investment had produced the most.

Then, Jesus momentarily interrupts his parable to draw out a principle: The man who has multiplied the money that he has been given will be given more, but the man who hides his money and does not multiply it will be stripped of what he has and then cast into hell. That is a terrible price to pay for refusing to take a risk with someone else's money.

So far, this parable has been about money and how you invest it for the **kingdom of heaven**. Would we feel better adopting an interpretation that rushes to some dainty spiritual application that has no purpose higher than inspiring us to a deeper walk? If you don't look at this parable honestly, you will never understand what it is teaching about the K of H — and, you will miss the key of knowledge.

The parable does not end in verse 30. If you stop there, you will forever be in the dark. Verse 31 continues the thought with a statement as to when this will occur — **When the son of man shall come in his glory.** Verses 31 and 32 do not have the markings of a change of subject. There is no statement "the **kingdom of heaven** is like unto" as has been Jesus' pattern thus far. A cursory reading will reveal the continuity of the passage. The parable of the talents given, and the expected return, continues with an interpretation and application. The investment scenario prefigures the prophetic events revealed in the verses that follow. Remember, the theme of the parable is: Invest the money God has given you, so that when he returns you will have multiplied it.

Now, we know from many other verses that God is not at all concerned that we should get rich, and he certainly is not going to demand his share in the profits we make in the stock market. Then, why the parable on money? And what kind of monetary investment is so important that failure to invest would result in damnation?

Verse 32 begins the discussion of prophesied catastrophic events that relate to the K of H. After his second coming, Christ will gather the nations before him so they can answer for their conduct. Based on their "performance," they will be separated into two groups, the one to everlasting life and the other to everlasting punishment.

Keep in mind, the nations in this judgment are those that survived the great tribulation period. They have experienced horrible times of persecution and suffering. They have seen the Jews hunted down with worse intensity than Nazi Germany ever hunted them. They have seen people starving and sick with plagues and diseases. Many Jews and Gentiles who refused the mark of the beast were imprisoned and killed. Everyone is now judged according to whether or not he has endured unto the end (Matt. 25:13; Rev. 12:11). Has he been faithful? Is he worthy to enter into the Millennial kingdom, or will he be one of **the children of the kingdom** who will be cast into outer darkness?

Verse 35 describes the criteria on which they receive their reward or punishment. How have they invested their money, time, energy, and influence in feeding the Lord Jesus when he was hungry, naked, homeless, sick, and in prison? When the question is put to them, they will stand dumbfounded and ask, "When did we not feed you and clothe you and visit you, Lord?" And he will say, "If you didn't do it for my brethren, the Jews, you didn't do it for me." At this point some will answer, "But Lord, I didn't have much, and I was afraid, so I took my money and hid it so it wouldn't go to waste; I saved my money for you, Lord. You see, I knew that you are a hard man, expecting a return from money you have not personally invested." And the Lord will say, "You wicked and slothful servant; if you were truly afraid of me, and knew that I would demand a return on your possessions, you should have taken your money and invested it to feed my brethren who were hungry, naked, and in prison." And then he will say to the angels, "Take this wicked man's possessions and give them to the blessed man who invested his money in caring for my brethren, and cast out this man from my kingdom and into hell, for it was I that he did not feed."

If it seems too carnal to you that possessions should be of concern in the K of H during the Tribulation, read the following verses:

> *Matthew 19:28* And Jesus said unto them, Verily I say unto you, That ye which have followed me, in the regeneration when the Son of man shall sit in the throne of his glory, ye also shall sit upon twelve thrones, judging the twelve tribes of Israel.
> 29 And every one that hath forsaken houses, or brethren, or sisters, or father, or mother, or wife, or children, or lands, for my name's sake, <u>shall receive an hundredfold</u>, and shall inherit everlasting life.
> 30 But many that are first shall be last; and the last shall be first.

The parable of the talents sets before our minds the concept of our responsibility to invest our carnal things to the benefit of our Master — which means to the benefit of persecuted and needy Christians. In this parable, the master came seeking a return on their money. In the reality of the context, the master comes to collect his return in the person of his persecuted brethren — for "Inasmuch as ye have done *it* unto one of the least of these my brethren, ye have done *it* unto me."

Then the prophetic section presents a future event when this principle of investment and return will be the deciding factor on who gets to remain permanently in the K of H and who is to be thrown out. God expects you to invest your money so as to have the means to support persecuted Jews. Fear will not be a valid excuse. Claiming limited resources will not be acceptable. Dedicating what you have to God and hoarding it will earn you the condemnation of being wicked and slothful. There is, of course, also an application here for the Church age, but it is certainly not dated to the present age. This is what the K of H will be like at the judgment that follows the Tribulation.

## The Parallel Passages

You will have noticed the parallel passage recorded in Luke and designated as pertaining to the K of G. Each servant is given the same amount of money and is expected to invest it while the master is *receiving* a kingdom. This would be the K of G at this present time. When they next see their master, the work of securing the kingdom (of heaven) will already be completed, quite apart from them. They are not involved in this kingdom activity. When the master has received his kingdom and returns, which typifies the return of Christ to set up the Millennial kingdom, he calls his servants to see how much they had gained by trading. The first two have multiplied their money and received reward in proportion to their gain. Their reward was to reign over cities in the Millennial kingdom. One of the men had kept his money hidden out of fear of losing it. As in the previous K of H parable, the man had his money taken from him and given to another, but he was not cast into hell as in the K of H parable, for he is a member of the K of G — a Church-age saint.

In Luke, there is no judgment on the servants who failed to multiply their money. Their salvation is not based on their performance in regards to the use of their money. Instead, we see something that is not in Matthew: the **citizens** who would not submit to the authority of the nobleman were slain. The **citizens** who would not allow him to reign over them would be the Jews and Gentiles who did not get saved prior to this judgment — prior to the Rapture and second coming.

These two parallel passages are yet another example of the marvelous perfection of the inspiration of the Scriptures. Despite the many twists and turns, both Matthew and Mark give **similar** but **different** accounts, each consistent with all that has been revealed about the two kingdoms. The Word of God is beautiful, is it not?

# The Kingdom of God is unique.

We now turn to an examination of the many passages that demonstrate the uniqueness of the kingdom of God. Most of these are found in places other than Matthew, although Matthew does reveal some unique aspects of the K of G in his five references to it. We will revisit some of the verses we have already covered, but each section is meant to be a complete listing of all verses that fit into that category. Different aspects are emphasized each time we repeat a passage in a different category.

## Power over devils indicates the immediate presence of the K of G.

| | | |
|---|---|---|
| *Matthew 12:28* But if I cast out devils by the Spirit of God, then the **kingdom of God** is come <u>unto you.</u> | *Luke 11:20* But if I with the finger of God cast out devils, no doubt the **kingdom of God** is come <u>upon you.</u> | *1 Corinthians 4:20* For the **kingdom of God** is not in word, but in <u>power.</u><br>*Revelation 12:10* And I heard a loud voice saying in heaven, Now is come salvation, and strength, and the **kingdom of our God**, and the power of his Christ: <u>for the accuser of our brethren is cast down,</u> which accused them before our God day and night. |

This is one of the five places that Matthew departs from his normal pattern of speaking of the Kingdom of Heaven. And, for good reason, because what he said (…is come unto you) could only apply to the Kingdom of God. He could not have made the same remark about the K of H without confusing their distinctive natures. The K of G is spiritual and is associated with **power** (1 Cor. 4:20) — power to heal, to cast out devils, to regenerate, to give eternal life, and to manifest Christ in his transfiguration. It is to be observed that in Matt. 10:7-8 Jesus commissioned the twelve to go and heal and cast out devils, and, as they did so, to preach the K of H. But he did not say that the working of miracles indicated that the K of H was "come unto you", as he so said here regarding the K of G. Remember, after John, both kingdoms were being preached at the same time, but the miraculous power indicated the presence of the K of G not he K of H.

Matthew records Jesus saying, "…the **kingdom of God** is come **unto you**." Luke says, "**upon you**." When Christ is present, when there is power or healing, the K of G is **unto** and **upon you**, and it is **near** at that moment.

Since the K of G is spiritual in nature, it can be present in one's personal experience. Or, it can be manifested (seen) as at the transfiguration. But no such thing is ever said of the K of H. To have said "The **kingdom of heaven** is come **upon** you" would have contradicted all that has carefully been revealed about the nature of the two kingdoms. It is no coincidence that in over 150 references, no Bible writer ever slipped up in his wording and confused the nature of the two kingdoms.

## Sinners and publicans get into the K of G by believing.

| |
|---|
| *Matthew 21:28* But what think ye? A *certain* man had two sons; and he came to the first, and said, Son, go work to day in my vineyard.<br>29 He answered and said, I will not: but afterward he repented, and went.<br>30 And he came to the second, and said likewise. And he answered and said, I *go,* sir: and went not.<br>31 Whether of them twain did the will of *his* father? They say unto him, The first. Jesus saith unto them, Verily I say unto you, That the publicans and the harlots **go** into the **kingdom of God** before you.<br>32 For John came unto you in the way of righteousness, and ye **believed him not:** but the publicans and the harlots **believed** him: and ye, when ye had seen *it,* repented not afterward, that ye might **believe** him. |

This is the second of the five times Matthew speaks of the K of G. In Jesus' day, sinners were going **into** the K of G — that is, they were entering, becoming a part of the K of G by means of faith. They **believed** according to verse 32, something that is never said of the K of H.

It is clear why Matthew switched terms and did not follow his usual course of speaking of the K of H. The K of G is the only kingdom that could be *entered* at the time. It is also the only kingdom into which people can enter *before* another person enters. The K of H will come at the end of the Tribulation, and everyone will enter it at the same time. The condition for entering the K of G at that time (and even now) is repentance and faith. Personal faith has no bearing on the K of H. You cannot enter the K of H by faith or by any other means. It must come as an institution, whereas the K of G is personal and individual, so that a sinner can exercise faith and enter it immediately.

## The K of G will be taken from Israel and given to the Gentiles.

> *Matthew 21:33* Hear another parable: There was a certain householder, which planted a vineyard, and hedged it round about, and digged a winepress in it, and built a tower, and let it out to husbandmen, and went into a far country:
>
> 34 And when the time of the fruit drew near, he sent his servants to the husbandmen, that they might receive the fruits of it.
>
> 35 And the husbandmen took his servants, and beat one, and killed another, and stoned another.
>
> 36 Again, he sent other servants more than the first: and they did unto them likewise.
>
> 37 But last of all he sent unto them his son, saying, They will reverence my son.
>
> 38 But when the husbandmen saw the son, they said among themselves, This is the heir; come, let us kill him, and let us seize on his inheritance.
>
> 39 And they caught him, and cast *him* out of the vineyard, and slew *him*.
>
> 40 When the lord therefore of the vineyard cometh, what will he do unto those husbandmen?
>
> 41 They say unto him, He will miserably destroy those wicked men, and will let out *his* vineyard unto other husbandmen, which shall render him the fruits in their seasons.
>
> 42 Jesus saith unto them, Did ye never read in the scriptures, The stone which the builders rejected, the same is become the head of the corner: this is the Lord's doing, and it is marvellous in our eyes?
>
> 43 Therefore say I unto you, The **kingdom of God** shall be taken from you, and given to a nation bringing forth the fruits thereof.

This is the most significant of the five times Matthew departs from his trend of speaking about the K of H. If he had said that *"the kingdom of heaven shall be taken from you"* (taken from Israel) and given to another (Gentiles), you would not be reading this book. For that one statement alone would have totally destroyed the distinction that is so clearly maintained throughout the gospels. We would be forced to conclude that the Church has taken the place of Israel — that the Church is Israel, that God is through with the natural seed of Abraham, that there will be no literal Millennial kingdom with David sitting on the throne, ruling the world from Jerusalem — that is, if Matthew had said *heaven*, as he usually does, instead of *God*. What a difference one word could have made!

Like many of the parables, there is a man, in this parable, a householder, representing God, who is in authority. Several parables have the man entrusting his substance to his servants and then going away, only to return unexpectedly and demand an accounting. The parables typically have the servants, which represent Israel, failing in their duty. There is a judgment in which some are exonerated, but most are thrown out or killed. The master then rewards those who were faithful, and commences his kingdom. All the parables predict the course of the **kingdom of heaven** (Israel's earthly kingdom). If you miss this reoccurring theme, you have missed the most rudimentary truth of the gospels.

Now we will look at the individual parts of this parable. The householder (God) planted a vineyard. The kingdom in Israel was God's vineyard (Ps. 80:14-15; Isa. 5:1-7; Jer. 12:10). He let it out to husbandmen (priests, kings, prophets, scribes, and lawyers). God gave Israel his laws and established them as a nation, making them responsible for the kingdom. The man (God) goes into a far country (heaven). He then sends servants (prophets, apostles) to receive the fruit (righteousness and justice). But the caretakers (Jewish leaders) beat the servants, and some they killed (as they did John the Baptist). At the last, the man (God) sent his son (Jesus) to receive the fruit, but they recognized him as the heir, the one who would ascend to the throne, so they killed him, trying to take the kingdom by force of violence.

Thus far, this parable has exactly described the actions of the nation of Israel up until the crucifixion of Christ. Now the mystery finds its way into the parable. The landowner kills the husbandmen (Jewish caretakers — happened in 70 AD) of his vineyard (kingdom) and turns the vineyard (the K of G) over to others (the Church) who will be responsible for the vineyard (kingdom).

Verse 43 then reveals the overall intent of the parable. Israel, who rejected and killed their prophets, including the son (Christ), forfeits their privileged position to someone else. The K of G (but not the K of H) will be taken from them and given to a "nation" (the Church, 1 Peter 2:9), which **will** bring forth fruit.

Many expositors say that parables are not meant to be understood in their many particulars; we are supposed to look for the one guiding principle and discount the rest. Those who say such things reveal their ignorance and demonstrate that they have never used the key of knowledge to open the door to understand the kingdom message. The Holy Spirit is smart enough to construct a parable that is exact in every particular. Bunyan and Milton and C. S. Lewis have done so; is the Holy Spirit less capable as a writer?

This parable is a marvelous treasure of things new and old, a perfect example of the distinctiveness of the Kingdom of God from the Kingdom of Heaven.

## "To Believe" was preached in connection with the K of G only.

> *Mark 1:15* The time is fulfilled, and the **kingdom of God** is at hand: repent ye, and <u>believe</u> the gospel.

We have already made this point elsewhere, but to keep all related material together and provide the reader with a complete view, we also include it here. The K of H is never connected with teachings of the gospel, and no one is ever told to believe anything regarding it. The K of G is good news that brings regeneration upon believing it. This salvation by grace and faith is unique to the Church-age dispensation.

## The K of G has no tares in it, and is harvested immediately.

| | |
|---|---|
| *Matthew 13:24* Another parable put he forth unto them, saying, The **kingdom of heaven** is likened unto a man which sowed good seed in his field:<br>  25 But while men slept, his **enemy came and sowed tares among the wheat**, and went his way.<br>  26 But when the blade was sprung up, and brought forth fruit, then appeared the tares also.<br>  27 So the servants of the householder came and said unto him, Sir, didst not thou sow good seed in thy field? from whence then hath it tares?<br>  28 He said unto them, An enemy hath done this. The servants said unto him, Wilt thou then that we go and gather them up?<br>  29 But he said, Nay; lest while ye gather up the tares, ye root up also the wheat with them.<br>  30 Let <u>both grow together until the harvest</u>: and in the time of harvest I will say to the reapers, Gather ye together <u>first the tares</u>, and bind them in bundles to burn them   : but gather the wheat into my barn. | *Mark 4:26* And he said, So is the **kingdom of God**, as if a man should cast seed into the ground;<br>  27 And should sleep, and rise night and day, and the seed should spring and grow up, he knoweth not how.<br>  28 For the earth bringeth forth fruit of herself; <u>first the blade, then the ear, after that the full corn in the ear.</u><br>  29 But when the fruit is brought forth, immediately he putteth in the sickle, because the harvest is come. |

The distinguishing nature of the Kingdom of God is best understood by comparing it to similar passages in Matthew that are designated Kingdom of Heaven. Take note of what Mark says in regard to the K of G and of what Matthew doesn't say regarding the K of H.

The K of G is like a man (God) sowing gospel seeds. While the sower is sleeping (not contributing anything further to the seeds that now lie in the soil), the seeds mysteriously spring up. The life was in the seed; just as the Word of the gospel is effectual (1 Thess. 2:13). Then the fruit comes in a prescribed sequence, first the blade (perhaps, the Apostolic church), then the ear (perhaps, the early church), after that the full corn in the ear (perhaps, the completed Church at the time of the Rapture). The crux of Mark's account is that when the ear comes to fruition, it is immediately harvested (raptured).

There are no tares (children of the Devil) in the K of G as there are in the K of H. And the harvest does not involve a protracted process of first binding the tares into bundles and burning them. The harvest is timely; it occurs on schedule when the fruit goes through its final stage and comes to maturity. So it is with the Church. There will be no sinners gathered into bundles and removed from the Church before the saints are harvested. The Rapture will come immediately upon the last member of the body being saved.

It is obvious that when Jesus told similar parables on different occasions or even in the same discourse, attributing one to the K of H and another to the K of G, he differentiated between the kingdoms by precise variations in the parables. What better way to draw a contrast to them and still let them remain mysterious — as was his stated intent.

See Matt. 13:24 for commentary on the K of H counterpart to this parable.

## The Kingdom of God <u>comes</u> with power and glory.

| *Matthew 16:28* Verily I say unto you, There be some standing here, which shall not taste of death, till they see the Son of man coming in **his kingdom.** | *Mark 9:1* And he said unto them, Verily I say unto them, That there be some of them that stand here, which shall not taste of death, till they have seen the **kingdom of God** <u>come</u> with power. | *Luke 11:20* But if I with the finger of God cast out devils, no doubt the **kingdom of God** is <u>come</u> upon you. | *1 Thessalonians 2:12* That ye would walk worthy of God, who hath called you unto **his kingdom** and glory.<br><br>*Revelation 12:10* And I heard a loud voice saying in heaven, Now is come salvation, and strength, and the **kingdom of our God**, and the power of his Christ: for the accuser of our brethren is cast down,… |
|---|---|---|---|

The key word in Mark is **come**. The Kingdom of God *came* momentarily in the experience of three disciples, when they saw Jesus manifested on the mount of transfiguration in **power and glory**.

Many passages speak of the K of G **coming,** or **coming upon** them, **unto** them, **nigh unto them**, or, as in this case, they saw **the K of G come with power**. This expresses the spiritual and individual nature of the K of G as contrasted with the institutional nature of the K of H, which is never said to **come** unto or upon, or near to anyone.

Notice that Matthew is certainly speaking of the same event that Mark and Luke documented, for there can be but one transfiguration in the life of Christ. But since Matthew's purpose is to speak to the Jews concerning the K of H, and since the Holy Spirit is maintaining a mystery surrounding the kingdoms, Matthew just drops the words "**of God**" after the word "**kingdom.**" But this, too, reveals to us that the K of G is also called **his kingdom.**

The K of G is such that, a *temporary physical and spiritual manifestation* of Jesus in power and glory **is** a manifestation of the K of G. So it is today. When healing occurs, or when the power of God is manifested in a distinct way, the K of G is **upon** those involved. It is **come**. It is **nigh unto** them. We **see it**. Where Jesus is, the K of G is.

## The Scribe was not far from the Kingdom of God.

> *Mark 12:34* And when Jesus saw that he answered discreetly, he said unto him, Thou art not far from the **kingdom of God**. And no man after that durst ask him any question.

The Scribe had answered Jesus correctly as to what was the greatest commandment — *Love your neighbor.* So Jesus told him that his understanding had put him in such a state so as to be **near** the K of G. Several passages speak in the same or similar manner concerning the K of G. No such thing could ever be said of the K of H. No amount of faith or understanding could bring the K of H *near* to an individual. But the K of G is the present spiritual power of God acting in and upon individual lives. It is a relationship. It has a corporate expression in the Church, but, with the exception of an occasional supernatural manifestation, it remains unseen and personal.

## Jesus will not drink wine until he does so in the Kingdom.

> *Mark 14:25* Verily I say unto you, I will drink no more of the fruit of the vine, until that day that I drink it new in the **kingdom of God.**

The Kingdom of God, as expressed in Jesus' body, the Church, will come back to the earth at the beginning of the Millennium and will coexist with the K of H. When the two kingdoms merge, the physical and institutional nature of the K of H will blend its attributes with the formerly spiritual nature of the K of G. The Old Testament saints will sit down (Matt. 8:11) with Christ in his glorified body and eat and drink. The first such occasion will be at the Marriage Supper of the Lamb (Rev. 19:9).

In Mark 14:25, Jesus is speaking to his disciples who will go on to become a major part of the Church-age dispensation — its founding fathers. They will be a part of the K of G, not the K of H. At the last Passover, Jesus, knowing that he is about to be crucified, tells them that the next time he and they drink wine together, it will be when the K of G finds tangible expression in the world to come.

## The Kingdom of God is especially for the poor.

> *Luke 6:20* And he lifted up his eyes on his disciples, and said, Blessed be ye poor: for yours is the **kingdom of God**.

See Matthew 5:3.

You will remember that in Matthew 5:3, we are told that the K of H is for the **poor in spirit** — not the poor. No one would get into the K of H based on being poor. But being poor does place one in a better position to enter the K of G. Just as wealth causes one to trust in his **uncertain riches** (1Tim. 6:17), poverty causes one to turn to God in faith (James 2:5). Per capita, there will be far more poor people in the K of G than rich people. Missionaries in poor Third World countries report great harvests of souls coming to Christ. They are saved by the thousands. Little church buildings burst out of their concrete blocks and tin roofs every year. But in wealthy countries, a missionary does well to win one or two people each year. The poor are in need, and they are more willing to listen.

# The Kingdom of God is gospel (good news).

| | |
|---|---|
| *Matthew 4:23* And Jesus went about all Galilee, teaching in their synagogues, and preaching the **gospel of the kingdom, and healing** all manner of sickness and all manner of disease among the people. | *Mark 1:14* Now after that John was put in prison, Jesus came into Galilee, preaching the **gospel of the kingdom of God….** |
| *Matthew 9:35* And Jesus went about all the cities and villages, teaching in their synagogues, and preaching the **gospel of the kingdom, and healing** every sickness and every disease among the people. | *Acts 20:24* …to testify the **gospel of the grace of God.** |
| *Matthew 11:5* The blind receive their sight, and the lame walk, the lepers are cleansed, and the deaf hear, the dead are raised up, **and the poor have the gospel preached to them**. | *Romans 1:9* For God is my witness, whom I serve with my spirit in the **gospel of his Son,** |
| *Matthew 24:14* And this **gospel of the kingdom** shall be preached in all the world for a witness unto all nations; and then shall the end come. | *1:16* For I am not ashamed of the **gospel of Christ**: for it is the power of God unto salvation to every one that believeth; to the Jew first, and also to the Greek. |
| *Matthew 26:13* Verily I say unto you, Wheresoever **this gospel** shall be preached in the whole world, *there* shall also this, that this woman hath done, be told for a memorial of her. | |

Matthew uses the word **gospel** five times. Three of those times he speaks of the **gospel of the kingdom**, and the other two times he says **this** gospel and **the** gospel. Mark speaks of the **gospel of Jesus Christ** and the **gospel of the kingdom of God.** The book of Acts says, **the gospel of the grace of God.** Romans declares **the gospel of his son, the gospel of Christ,** and **the gospel of God.** The rest of the epistles repeat these terms many times.

Now, what is amazing is that Matthew never says "gospel of the **kingdom of heaven**." There is no such thing as a gospel of the **kingdom of heaven**, for it is not, as is the K of G, good news concerning one's personal salvation. The K of G is a message to be preached and believed. The K of H is a political system that must be physically instituted. Every single reference confirms this.

We might rightfully ask, "If there is no K of H gospel, why does Matthew use the word **gospel** five times, or why use it at all?" Matthew was not limited to speaking of the K of H by the Holy Spirit. It is, however, his main emphasis, and he therefore minimizes any comments he must make concerning the K of G. But, when Matthew does speak of the K of G as noted by the five times he actually uses the term, of those five times, he uses it three times associated with healing. One time he speaks prophetically of the future message being preached during the Tribulation as, **gospel of the kingdom** — which would be the good news of the coming K of G and K of H combined in Christ's kingdom. And, the last time, Matthew writes about a very personal act by a repentant woman that Jesus wanted to be included in the preaching of the gospel (which would be prophetic of the K of G) until he returns.

One could argue that the five times Matthew says **gospel of the kingdom**, he is referring to the K of H. If the testimony of the use of the word **gospel** stood alone, our argument that the K of H is not called gospel would be weak. We couldn't prove that it was not an oversight that Matthew failed to add "**of heaven**" to the **gospel of the kingdom**. You could argue that it was implied. But it must be admitted that if Matthew had said "gospel of the K of H," it would have changed the picture completely. As part of a consistent stream of carefully crafted distinctions, his additions and omissions continue to support the peculiar natures of the two kingdoms.

## Man looking back is not fit for the Kingdom of God.

| | |
|---|---|
| *Matthew 8:21* And another of his disciples said unto him, Lord, suffer me first to go and bury my | *Luke 9:57* And it came to pass, that, as they went in the way, a certain man said unto him, Lord, I will follow thee whithersoever thou goest.<br>58 And Jesus said unto him, Foxes have holes, and birds of the air have nests; but the Son of man hath not where to lay his head.<br>59 And he said unto another, Follow me. But he said, Lord, suffer me first to go and bury my father. |

| father. 22 But Jesus said unto him, Follow me; and let the dead bury their dead. | 60 Jesus said unto him, Let the dead bury their dead: but go thou and **preach the kingdom of God.**<br><br>61 And another also said, Lord, I will follow thee; but let me first go bid them farewell, which are at home at my house.<br><br>62 And Jesus said unto him, **No man, having put his hand to the plough, and looking back, is fit for the kingdom of God.** |
|---|---|

To understand exactly what is being said, observe the context carefully. A man offers to be one of Jesus' devoted disciples, but wants to take care of some family business first. His father is old and soon to die. He wants to hang around and take care of him until after the funeral. Jesus says that if a man puts his hand to the plow (becomes a minister of the gospel of the K of G) and then looks back to family matters, he is not fit to be a worker in the **kingdom of God**. This tells us that the K of G was present to the point of employing workers in its service. The same could not be said of the yet-to-be-instituted K of H.

## One should seek the Kingdom of God as the ruling factor of life.

| *Matthew 6:33* But **seek ye** first the **kingdom of God**, and his righteousness; and all these things shall be added unto you. | *Luke 12:31* But rather **seek ye** the **kingdom of God**; and all these things shall be added unto you. |
|---|---|

All those entering the kingdom of God should not be consumed with care for their food and clothes and carnal things. Their first attention and main focus should be dedicated to pursuing personal **righteousness** and advancing the K of G.

This is one of the five times Matthew uses the term K of G. Most commentators think Matthew uses the two terms interchangeably, preferring the term K of H, while Mark and Luke prefer the term K of G. If Matthew just preferred the term K of H, why then did he depart from it five times? And why are those five uses also a departure from the distinctness of the K of H?

Matthew used the term K of G in this passage because there was a vital truth in this sermon, as originally given, that he wanted to convey, and, in fact, Jesus called it the K of G rather than the K of H. Furthermore, it would be devastating to the uniqueness of the kingdoms if Matthew had attributed this statement of Jesus as referring to the K of H. Only the K of G is present in such a fashion that a man can daily and moment by moment apply himself to it — seeking the advancement of the kingdom. No one can seek the K of H moment by moment, since it is a political institution and beyond the reach of single individuals. Until it "comes" as the only government on earth, there is nothing to seek. But one who gives himself to advancing the gospel of the kingdom is seeking first the K of G, and when one does dedicate himself to serve the K of G, God promises to provide his daily food and clothes, for he is then God's employee.

## Men were entering the Kingdom of God at the moment.

| *Matthew 11:12* And from the days of John the Baptist until now the **kingdom of heaven suffereth violence**, and the violent take it by force. | *Lu ke 16:16* The law and the prophets were until John: since that time the **kingdom of God** is preached, and every man **presseth into it**. |
|---|---|

This passage in Matthew is probably the most dramatic and defining statement about the Kingdom of Heaven. Those who will challenge the translation of these two passages do so because they cannot handle it the way the Holy Spirit wrote it. The King James Bible is perfectly correct in the way these two verses are translated; the translators accurately represented the Greek language as written by Matthew and Luke.

While the K of H was subjected to the violence of the Roman government and the Jewish Sanhedrin, the K of G was always an open door to those who would enter. There is no way any human or angelic agent could take the K of G by force. Like Nicodemus, many were pressing into the K of G. What does this reveal about the uniqueness of the K of G? It was (and always is) a personal and individual experience immediately available to *whosoever will.* No one could **press into** the K of H; they had to wait for it to come.

## The Kingdom of God is personal and internal.

*Luke 17:21* Neither shall they say, Lo here! or, lo there! for, behold, the **kingdom of God** is **within you**.

The Kingdom of God is a personal experience of God. Never do we find a statement similar to this concerning the Kingdom of Heaven. The K of H is without; the K of G is within. Very defining! Don't believe anyone who points to an institution today and says, "That is God's kingdom on the earth." Many people believe that their particular church is THE **kingdom of God** on the earth. Jesus tells us not to believe them. They are wrong, for the K of G is inside the human soul, not outside in buildings and creeds. The Vatican is not the K of G on the earth. Anyone who makes such a claim is challenging the Lord Jesus. The true Church on the earth (not institutional church) is, at best, only a partial expression of the K of G, capable of having devils sitting in its shadow, but it is so spiritual in nature, that no one can confidently point to it as an establishment. The Church of Jesus Christ does not have a tax number, a charter, an address, a sign, or a property deed.

The Samaritan woman tried to engage Jesus in a discussion as to which location was the proper **place** to worship. Jesus said, "But the hour cometh, and now is, when the true worshippers shall worship the Father in spirit and in truth: for the Father seeketh such to worship him. God *is* a Spirit: and they that worship him must worship *him* in spirit and in truth" (John 4:23-24).

And that is the difference between the two kingdoms. The K of H will have a throne and a temple as its central focus. The K of G has a throne in heaven and a temple in the body of each true believer.

## People had left houses or lands for the Kingdom of God.

| | | |
|---|---|---|
| *Matthew 19:27* Then answered Peter and said unto him, Behold, we have forsaken all, and followed thee; what shall we have therefore? 28 And Jesus said unto them, Verily I say unto you, That ye which have followed me, in the regeneration when the Son of man shall sit in the throne of his glory, ye also shall sit upon twelve thrones, judging the twelve tribes of Israel. 29 And every one that hath forsaken houses, or brethren, or sisters or father, or mother, or wife, or children, or lands, for **my name's sake**, shall receive an hundredfold, and shall inherit everlasting life. 30 But many that are first shall be last; and the last shall be first. | *Mark 10:28* Then Peter began to say unto him, Lo, we have left all, and have followed thee. 29 And Jesus answered and said, Verily I say unto you, There is no man that hath left house, or brethren, or sisters, or father, or mother, or wife, or children, or lands, for **my sake**, **and the gospel's,** 30 But he shall receive an hundredfold now in this time, houses, and brethren, and sisters, and mothers, and children, and lands, with persecutions; and in the world to come eternal life. 31 But many that are first shall be last; and the last first. | *Luke 18:29* And he said unto them, Verily I say unto you, There is no man that hath left house, or parents, or brethren, or wife, or children, for the **kingdom of God**'s sake, 30 Who shall not receive manifold more in this present time, and in the world to come life everlasting. |

You will notice that Matthew and Mark begin their accounts the same way, with Peter asking what reward they will receive for having followed Jesus. Both accounts then record Jesus' statement about those forsaking houses, lands, etc., that they shall receive an hundredfold return, and in the end, eternal life. Finally, they both conclude with the statement about the first being last and the last being first. It seems obvious that both Matthew and Mark are writing about the same event. Mark quotes Jesus saying that it is for **my sake and the gospel's,** while Luke says it is for the **kingdom of God's sake,** which links his *gospel* with the K of G. Matthew avoided saying, *the gospel of the K of G,* not attributing it to any kingdom.

Someone may ask, "If they are reporting the same event, why does their wording differ?" With each account being only four verses long, it is very likely that the original discussion took much longer and contained more detail. But, each writer is reporting accurately that portion of the conversation which the Holy Spirit inspired him to record. The Author of the Holy Scriptures has masterfully maintained the mystery of the kingdom. Some will read the different accounts and be certain that the kingdoms are identical. Others will read them and see clearly that they are different. That is the nature of a mystery.

Matthew records Jesus' dating of this future event (when some would receive an hundredfold): **"when the son of man shall sit on the throne of his glory,"** which is the Millennium. And then, Matthew omits the portion that states they will receive an hundredfold in this present time. Furthermore, Matthew never speaks of forsaking all for the K of G's sake, as does Luke. Nor does Matthew say *for the gospel's sake*, as in Mark's account. Instead, he says, for **my sake**.

So, the K of G continues to be portrayed as unique and distinct in that, one who forsakes all will receive an hundredfold **now in this time**, as well as **eternal life** in the end. The text confirms that part of the reward for K of G saints is in this present age, for he identifies the kingdom as concurrent **with persecutions**. The K of H would be a relief from persecutions, whereas the blessings of this present kingdom age come with persecutions.

If, as some will contend, these several differences found in the texts are just accidental variations not intended to convey any mystery, why is it that the "accidental differences" repeatedly construct a picture of two different kingdoms? Is God so careless as to allow his Word to be so poorly written that it unintentionally teaches dispensational truth? I could accept the possibility that two parallel passages could accidentally produce five distinctions that suggest a pattern not originally intended, just like the clouds can occasionally form the shape of animals or faces — if you look long enough, and have a good imagination, and want to see something there. But if every "cloud" (150 of them), one after the other were to display 150 different forms of a variety of animals, all parading through the sky as though they were marching into Noah's ark, I would drive over the horizon and fully expect to see the ark.

## They mistakenly thought the Kingdom of God would immediately appear.

We are discussing now the parable in Luke 19:11-27, which has already been explained in our remarks about Matthew 25:14-30. We record the text here again because it is so critical to make the comparison for a second time from the perspective of the K of G as found in Luke, for this is a vital statement regarding the exact nature of the K of G.

As you read these two portions, note the similarities and differences. Matthew does not write, as does Luke, that Jesus is speaking this parable **because they thought the K of G should immediately appear**. He records this parable in Luke to dissuade them from the belief that the K of G was about to come to the earth in a **visible** expression — as was the case with the K of H. Notice how the parable conveys the idea of a long lapse of time, and places the coming of the kingdom after the Second Coming of Christ — which would be true of both kingdoms. Observe also that the later events of Luke's record occur at a time when Jesus is placing the apostles in positions of ruling over the 12 tribes of Israel, which will occur during the Millennium.

It is very significant that Matthew did not say the same thing about the K of H. What if he had said, "The disciples **thought** the K of H should immediately appear"? This author would then be foolish in trying to prove his point, for Jesus' actual statement and the answer would have implied that they were mistaken in what they thought. We know that the entire content of the K of H passages clearly offer the K of H as "a possible present event." If Jesus had answered that the K of H could not come presently, it would have been a contradiction of all that has already been said. Marvelous indeed is Divine inspiration of the Scriptures!

*Matthew 25:14* For *the kingdom of heaven is* as a man travelling into a far country, *who* called his own servants, and delivered unto them his goods.

15 And unto one he gave five talents, to another two, and to another one; to every man according to his several ability; and straightway took his journey.

16 Then he that had received the five talents went and traded with the same, and made *them* other five talents.

17 And likewise he that *had received* two, he also gained other two.

18 But he that had received one went and digged in the earth, and hid his lord's money.

19 After a long time the lord of those servants cometh, and reckoneth with them.

20 And so he that had received five talents came and brought other five talents, saying, Lord, thou deliveredst unto me five talents: behold, I have gained beside them five talents more.

21 His lord said unto him, Well done, *thou* good and faithful servant: thou hast been faithful over a few things, I will make thee ruler over many things: enter thou into the joy of thy lord.

22 He also that had received two talents came and said, Lord, thou deliveredst unto me two talents: behold, I have gained two other talents beside them.

23 His lord said unto him, Well done, good and faithful servant; thou hast been faithful over a few things, I will make thee ruler over many things: enter thou into the joy of thy lord.

24 Then he which had received the one talent came and said, Lord, I knew thee that thou art an hard man, reaping where thou hast not sown, and gathering where thou hast not strawed:

25 And I was afraid, and went and hid thy talent in the earth: lo, *there,* thou hast *that is* thine.

26 His lord answered and said unto him, *Thou* wicked and slothful servant, thou knewest that I reap where I sowed not, and gather where I have not strawed:

27 Thou oughtest therefore to have put my money to the exchangers, and *then* at my coming I should have received mine own with usury.

28 Take therefore the talent from him, and give *it* unto him which hath ten talents.

29 For unto every one that hath shall be given, and he shall have abundance: but from him that hath not shall be taken away even that which he hath.

30 And cast ye the unprofitable servant into outer darkness: there shall be weeping and gnashing of teeth.

*Luke 19:11* And as they heard these things, he added and spake a parable, because he was nigh to Jerusalem, and because **they thought that the kingdom of God should immediately appear**.

12 He said therefore, A certain nobleman went into a far country to receive for himself **a kingdom**, and to return.

13 And he called his **ten servants**, and delivered them **ten pounds**, and said unto them, Occupy till I come.

14 But his citizens hated him, and sent a message after him, saying, We will not have this man to reign over us.

15 And it came to pass, that when he was returned, having received **the kingdom**, then he commanded these servants to be called unto him, to whom he had given the money, that he might know how much every man had gained by trading.

16 Then came the first, saying, Lord, thy pound hath gained ten pounds.

17 And he said unto him, Well, thou good servant: because thou hast been faithful in a very little, have thou authority over ten cities.

18 And the second came, saying, Lord, thy pound hath gained five pounds.

19 And he said likewise to him, Be thou also over five cities.

20 And another came, saying, Lord, behold, here is thy pound, which I have kept laid up in a napkin:

21 For I feared thee, because thou art an austere man: thou takest up that thou layedst not down, and reapest that thou didst not sow.

22 And he saith unto him, Out of thine own mouth will I judge thee, thou wicked servant. Thou knewest that I was an austere man, taking up that I laid not down, and reaping that I did not sow:

23 Wherefore then gavest not thou my money into the bank, that at my coming I might have required mine own with usury?

24 And he said unto them that stood by, Take from him the pound, and give it to him that hath ten pounds.

25 (And they said unto him, Lord, he hath ten pounds.)

26 For I say unto you, That unto every one which hath shall be given; and from him that hath not, even that he hath shall be taken away from him.

27 But those mine enemies, which would not that I should reign over them, bring hither, and slay them before me.

This parable of the Kingdom of God as found in Luke, could have been delivered on the same occasion as the Kingdom of Heaven parable found in Matthew. If so, then we have an indication in Luke 19:11 as to the order of events. Following the discourse recorded in Matthew, Luke begins: **"And as they heard these things, he added and spake a parable, because he was nigh unto Jerusalem** [which tells us that their journey was drawing to an end] **and because they <u>thought</u> the K of G should immediately appear."** Since it says **they thought**…, apparently they had responded to the parable in Matthew in a manner that revealed they misunderstood, so Jesus speaks another parable to clarify the point about the timing of the manifestation of the K of G.

Jesus' parable in Luke clearly defines as erroneous any belief that the K of G — the Church — is a **visible entity** presently instituted upon the earth under human authority. There is no kingdom, either of God or heaven, **appearing** upon the earth until after the Second Coming of Christ. The only visible kingdoms are the kingdoms of men. Any church organization that claims to hold and dispense the authority of any divine or earthly kingdom is competing with God's spiritual kingdom.

In Luke 19:12, concerning the K of G, the **nobleman** is obviously Jesus. He **goes into a far country to receive for himself a kingdom, and to return.** This typifies Jesus ascending into the heavens where he mediates for the Church during the next 2,000 years and brings the invisible K of G to maturity. Notice that he has already **received** the kingdom when he makes his return. Not so with the K of H, which is not set up until **after** his return.

In Luke, the story does not develop with emphasis on the ones who received the money, as it does in Matthew. The focal point of the parable is the citizens who would not allow him to rule over them.

The two accounts represent quite differently those who receive the money. In Luke (K of G), none are thrown into hell at his coming, as is the case with some of the children of the K of H. Another thing unique about the K of G is that the ones who received the money will be granted to rule over cities in the kingdom during the Millennium. In Matthew, which is a discussion of the K of H, the disciples were placed over the twelve tribes, the emphasis being on Israel. Whereas in the K of G, the saints are ruling over cities, not tribes, in Luke, the emphasis is on the Church, which is mostly Gentile. Glorified saints will be appointed, according to their faithfulness, to rule over the cities of the Gentiles during the 1000-year reign of Christ on the earth.

These two parables, though similar in many ways, best epitomize the differences in the two kingdoms. If they were the only testimony we had, they would be sufficient to establish the unique nature of each kingdom. If a man can see this evidence and still think that the kingdoms are the same entity, you could probably sell him one black sock and one white sock and convince him he had a perfect match.

## The Kingdom of God will not come until the Millennium.

| | |
|---|---|
| *Mark 14:24* And he said unto them, This is my blood of the new testament, which is shed for many.<br> 25 Verily I say unto you, I will drink no more of the fruit of the vine, until that day that I drink it new in **the kingdom of God.** | *Luke 22:15* And he said unto them, With desire I have desired to eat this passover with you before I suffer:<br> 16 For I say unto you, I will not any more eat thereof, until it be fulfilled in **the kingdom of God**.<br> 17 And he took the cup, and gave thanks, and said, Take this, and divide it among yourselves:<br> 18 For I say unto you, I will not drink of the fruit of the vine, until the **kingdom of God** shall come. |

This is too obvious to demand a lengthy explanation. Jesus will not drink wine again until the K of G **comes** to the earth. The key word here is **come**. The K of G is present in spiritual reality when God is present in power or indwelling individual believers, but it doesn't **come** in a visible form until the Millennium. We know from Matthew 8:11 and Luke 12:37; 13:28, 29 that at the beginning of the Millennium, the marriage supper of the Lamb will occur and Abraham, Isaac, and Jacob will **sit down** with the disciples and dine. This is the beginning of the Millennium, and it is the beginning of the manifestation and merging of the K of G and the K of H **together** upon the earth.

## The water birth (physical) and the Spirit birth are conditions to entering and seeing the Kingdom of God.

> *John 3:3* Jesus answered and said unto him, Verily, verily, I say unto thee, Except a man be born again, he cannot **see** the **kingdom of God**.
>
> 5 Jesus answered, Verily, verily, I say unto thee, Except a man be born of water and of the Spirit, he cannot **enter into** the **kingdom of God**.

These two verses in John may seem to be redundant, but they are not. They each say something different about the Kingdom of God. As we have already seen, the Bible never speaks of anyone *entering* the Kingdom of Heaven individually, and no one can **see** the K of G at this present time. The key words here are **see** and **enter** — two different experiences. The disciples *saw* the K of G for a brief moment when Jesus was transfigured before them. The K of G will not be *visible* again until Christ's second coming when Jesus will be visible. Thus, Jesus told Nicodemus that only those who are born again will **see** the K of G — see it when it comes at the beginning of the Millennium.

Then, in verse five, Jesus says more about the K of G. Unless a man is born of water (physical birth) and of the Spirit (spiritual birth) he cannot **enter into** the K of G. Only those men of flesh who came into this world by natural means — from the womb of a woman — and who were also born of the Spirit of God, only those can **enter** into the K of G.

Some will question why Jesus would lay down such an obvious condition as being **born of water.** For one thing, it was his response to Nicodemus' puzzled suggestion that being "born again" would entail reentering the womb and emerging again. Jesus is comparing the physical birth, which comes by water, to the spiritual birth, which comes by the Spirit. There is a similarity. During gestation, a child is suspended in a water environment. Natural birth comes by means of water. As the muscles contract, it creates hydraulic pressure on the infant, forcing it through the birth canal and out into the world. In like manner, the Spirit of God surrounds an unregenerate man and places pressure on him (conviction of sin, personal circumstances, etc.), causing him to emerge into a new, spiritual world. Water delivers the first birth; the Spirit delivers the second.

Observe how unique this K of G passage is to the subject. If Jesus had said that a man had to be born again to enter the K of H, this book would never have been written, for it would have completely destroyed the distinction between the two kingdoms.

## Jesus taught only the Kingdom of God after his resurrection.

> *Acts 1:3* To whom also he shewed himself alive after his passion by many infallible proofs, being seen of them forty days, and speaking of the things pertaining to **the kingdom of God:**
>
> 4 And, being assembled together with them, commanded them that they should not depart from Jerusalem, but wait for the promise of the Father, which, saith he, ye have heard of me.
>
> 5 For John truly baptized with water; but ye shall be <u>baptized with the Holy Ghost</u> not many days hence.

After his crucifixion and resurrection, there is no record that either Jesus or his disciples ever mentioned the **kingdom of heaven**, but the disciples immediately preached about the **kingdom of God** and did so constantly.

## Self mutilation to enter the Kingdom of God.
## The Kingdom of God is life in Christ.

| | |
|---|---|
| *Matthew 5:29* And if thy right eye offend thee, pluck it out, and cast it from thee: for it is profitable for thee that one of thy members should perish, and not that thy whole body should be cast into hell.<br><br>30 And if thy right hand offend thee, cut it off, and cast it from thee: for it is profitable for thee that one of thy members should perish, and not that thy whole body should be cast into hell. | *Mark 9:43* And if thy hand offend thee, cut it off: it is better for thee to **enter into life** maimed, than having two hands to go into hell, into the fire that never shall be quenched:<br>44 Where their worm dieth not, and the fire is not quenched.<br>45 And if thy foot offend thee, cut it off: it is better for thee to **enter halt into life,** than having two feet to be cast into hell, into the fire that never shall be quenched:<br>46 Where their worm dieth not, and the fire is not quenched.<br>47 And if thine eye offend thee, pluck it out: it is better for thee to **enter into** the **kingdom of God** with one eye, than having two eyes to be cast into hell fire:<br>48 Where their worm dieth not, and the fire is not quenched. |

Matthew had been discussing the Kingdom of Heaven (5:19-20), so this statement about self-mutilation found in Matthew could easily be in reference to the K of H. There is no problem with applying Matthew's account to either kingdom. But Mark's statements cannot apply to the K of H, since he speaks of **entering into** the Kingdom of God and **into life**. As we have already shown, no one can **enter into** the K of H on an individual basis, for there is no K of H in which to enter until Jesus comes back and establishes his earthly kingdom. But, the K of G is always present in the spiritual realm and is manifest in the Church today. Its door is always open for any who would come and enter into the K of G by faith. They **enter into life** — into the K of G — at the moment they repent and believe in the Lord Jesus Christ.

This passage in Mark has provided us with a very clear and articulate statement about the nature of the K of G. Twice it says, **enter into life**, and the third time it replaces the word **life** with the phrase **kingdom of God.** So, life (eternal life, spiritual life) is said to be synonymous with the K of G. In other words, the life of Christ working in us right now is a living demonstration of the K of G operating in all who believe in Jesus Christ!

If someone is so much in bondage to a certain sin that it prevents him from coming to faith in Christ, then Jesus suggests that he cut off the thing that offends him, so as to remove the obstacle that prevents him from coming to life — into the K of G. This is offensive to modern man, as it must have been to the people in Jesus' day. How many people take their religion seriously enough to resort to such drastic measures? If Christianity is just a religion to soothe the soul, if there is no afterlife, if there is no hell to which most people are going, if God is not greatly offended at sin, if there is no heaven to gain nor a hell to avoid, then Jesus' words were radical and offensive. But if the road **is** narrow, and there **are** many who seek to enter in but will not be able, if many **are** called but few are chosen, if hell **does** last forever, then the removal of **whatever hinders** entrance into the K of G would be a perfectly reasonable act.

## The Kingdom of God is gospel — glad tidings.

| | |
|---|---|
| *Mark 1:14* Now after that John was put in prison, Jesus came into Galilee, preaching the **gospel of the kingdom of God,**<br>15 And saying, The time is fulfilled, and the **kingdom of God** is at hand: repent ye, and believe the **gospel**. | *Luke 4:43* And he said unto them, I must preach the **kingdom of God** to other cities also: for therefore am I sent.<br>*Luke 8:1* ...he went throughout every city and village, preaching and shewing the glad tidings of the **kingdom of God:** |

The Kingdom of God is not a visible institution in this present dispensation. It is life that comes to the sinner who responds to the good news, the glad tidings, a gospel to be believed and received and to be entered into. The Kingdom of Heaven is never referred to in any of these ways.

## The Kingdom of God is righteousness, peace, and joy.

> *Romans 14:17* For **the kingdom of God** is not meat and drink; but righteousness, and peace, and joy in the Holy Ghost.

Here is a verse outside of the Gospels that gets right to the point and clearly defines the Kingdom of God. First it tells us what the K of G is not. It is **not meat and drink**. In other words, looking at the context of this verse, the K of G is not about what you eat or drink. In contrast, the K of H, as mandated under the laws of Moses, had very much to do with what you ate and drank. The K of G is not an institution with laws and customs, with forms and liturgy. It is not tangible. It is righteousness — a gift of righteousness. It is peace (also a gift), and it is joy in the Holy Ghost. These three things are internal, personal, and individual. And, they are immediate.

## The Kingdom of God is power.

> *1 Corinthians 4:20* For the **kingdom of God** is not in word, but in power.

Looking at the context of this passage, we can see that Paul is speaking of those false apostles who came among the believers with divisive words. He spoke of the same issue earlier. "And my speech and my preaching was not with **enticing words of man's wisdom**, but in demonstration of the Spirit and of power" (1 Cor. 2:4). Paul is ready to compare his ministry to theirs, saying that the K of G is not just talk; it is the power of God in our daily lives. No such thing is ever said of the K of H, which is an external kingdom that has **no power** at all in one's personal life.

## The Kingdom of God cannot be moved.

> *Hebrews 12:28* Wherefore we receiving a **kingdom** which cannot be moved, let us have grace, whereby we may serve God acceptably with reverence and godly fear.

We have learned that the Kingdom of Heaven can be **moved** by force (Matt. 11:12), but the Kingdom of God cannot be moved. It is untouchable by either devils or men. It does not ebb and flow with the changeable affairs of men or the rise and fall of earthly kingdoms. It is not confined to the earth, and it exists independent of all that is tangible.

## The Kingdom of God is within you; you cannot see it.

> *Luke 17:20* And when he was demanded of the Pharisees, when the **kingdom of God** should come, he answered them and said, The **kingdom of God** cometh not with observation:
> 21 Neither shall they say, Lo here! or, lo there! for, behold, the **kingdom of God** is within you.

This passage is very definitive. The Pharisees demanded to know when the Kingdom of God would **come.** They did not ask when the Kingdom of Heaven would come. If they had, his answer would have been quite different. No doubt they did not know that there was a difference between the two kingdoms, but then Jesus was not seeking to impart that understanding to them. Remember, he spoke in parables so they would not understand (Matt. 13:11).

Jesus' answer is tremendously revealing. It has thrown more theologians off the trail than *Calvin's Institutes.* **The kingdom of God cometh not with observation.** There is nothing to see at present except the evidence of its behavior-changing power within. You are wasting your time looking for **it.** You can't go to **it** on Sunday or join **it**. **It** will never accept you as a member. **It** has no address. And, **it** does not have any employees or catechisms. You cannot point to a man-made institution anywhere and say, "Look, there **it** is!" **For the kingdom of God is within you,** and **cometh not with observation.**

This is a clincher. How different the K of G is from the K of H!

## The unrighteous will not inherit the Kingdom of God.

> *1 Corinthians 6:9* Know ye not that the unrighteous shall **not inherit the kingdom of God**? Be not deceived: neither fornicators, nor idolaters, nor adulterers, nor effeminate, nor abusers of themselves with mankind,
>   10 Nor thieves, nor covetous, nor drunkards, nor revilers, nor extortioners, shall inherit the **kingdom of God.**
>
> *Galatians 5:21* Envyings, murders, drunkenness, revellings, and such like: of the which I tell you before, as I have also told you in time past, that they which do such things shall **not inherit the kingdom of God.**

The Kingdom of God produces such clearly distinguishable righteousness in believers that it can be said with certainty that those who commit these sins **will not inherit the K of G**. These verses are avoided by fundamentalists even more than they avoid women preachers. The verses speak plainly. The K of G does not contain sinners like those found in these two lists. On the other hand, at the beginning of the Millennium, we find sinners being removed from the K of H. Remember the parable of the tares!

The word **inherit** is key to placing this passage. One **enters** the K of G at the moment he believes, but one does not **inherit** the K of G until he receives his glorified body. See the next passage from 1 Cor. 15:49-53.

## Corruptible flesh cannot inherit the Kingdom of God.

> *1 Corinthians 15:49* And as we have borne the image of the earthy, we shall also bear the image of the heavenly.
>   50 Now this I say, brethren, that **flesh and blood cannot inherit the kingdom of God**; neither doth corruption inherit incorruption.
>   51 Behold, I shew you a mystery; We shall not all sleep, but we shall all be changed,
>   52 In a moment, in the twinkling of an eye, at the last trump: for the trumpet shall sound, and the dead shall be raised incorruptible, and **we shall be changed**.
>   53 For this corruptible must put on incorruption, and this mortal must put on immortality.

We must say it again. To **inherit** the Kingdom of God is not the same as being born again into the K of G. One **enters** the K of G the moment he is saved, but he does not **inherit** the K of G until he gets his glorified body. It is the difference between being **made** an heir and the act or moment in time of **receiving** the inheritance. In this passage, <u>**flesh and blood**</u> **cannot inherit the K of G.** It is not saying that one cannot be saved who is made of flesh and blood. Rather, it declares that all mortal and corruptible flesh must be changed to incorruption and immortality before they inherit the fullness of the K of G.

This is exactly opposite to the K of H. When the children of the K of H are cast into hell, they are still in their flesh and blood mortal bodies.

## The apostolic church was operating in the Kingdom of God.

> *Colossians 4:10* Aristarchus my fellowprisoner. . .
> *11* And Jesus, which is called Justus, who are of the circumcision. These only are my fellowworkers unto the **kingdom of God**, which have been a comfort unto me.

Near the end of his letter to Colossi, Paul refers to several fellowworkers, including Justus, who worked with him **unto the kingdom of God**. So we can conclude that the K of G is a present reality for the Church. We can also conclude that a believing Jew is not in the K of H at this time, but in the K of G only.

## The early Christians were suffering by participating in the Kingdom of God.

> *2 Thessalonians 1:5* Which is a manifest token of the righteous judgment of God, that ye may be counted worthy of the **kingdom of God**, for which ye also suffer:

Since the Christians were suffering for the Kingdom of God, it is logical to conclude that the K of G was a present reality to them, unlike the K of H for which Israel still awaits.

## The Kingdom of God and the Father's kingdom will merge in the Millennium.

| | | |
|---|---|---|
| *Matthew 26:27* And he took the cup, and gave thanks, and gave *it* to them, saying, Drink ye all of it; 28 For this is my blood of the new testament, which is shed for many for the remission of sins. 29 But I say unto you, I will not drink henceforth of this fruit of the vine, until that day when I drink it new with you in **my Father's kingdom**. | *Mark 14:24* And he said unto them, This is my blood of the new testament, which is shed for many. 25 Verily I say unto you, I will drink no more of the fruit of the vine, until that day that I drink it new in **the kingdom of God.** | *Luke 22:15* And he said unto them, With desire I have desired to eat this passover with you before I suffer: 16 For I say unto you, I will not any more eat thereof, until it be fulfilled in **the kingdom of God**. 17 And he took the cup, and gave thanks, and said, Take this, and divide it among yourselves: 18 For I say unto you, I will not drink of the fruit of the vine, until the **kingdom of God** shall come. |

Taking Matthew, Mark, and Luke together, it is clear that the Kingdom of God will be concurrent with the **Father's kingdom** at the beginning of the Millennium. The Jewish K of H and the Church's K of G will come together on the earth at the beginning of the Millennium. When Christ becomes head of both, he will turn them over to the Father, and the merged kingdoms will be called **The Father's Kingdom**. See 2 Timothy 4:1 & John 18:36.

## The Kingdom of God is "his kingdom."

> *2 Timothy 4:1* I charge thee therefore before God, and the Lord Jesus Christ, who shall judge the quick and the dead at **his appearing** and **his kingdom**;

We have already seen that the kingdom of God will merge with the Kingdom of Heaven, and the two will become the **Father's kingdom**. We now see in this verse that **his kingdom** occurs at the Second Coming, as do the other kingdoms. So, at that time, **his kingdom** is equal to the Millennial kingdom.

# Christ's kingdom was not of this world at his crucifixion.

> *John 18:36* Jesus answered, **My kingdom** is not of this world: if **my kingdom** were of this world, then would my servants fight, that I should not be delivered to the Jews: but **now** is **my kingdom** not from hence.

See the two verses discussed above? We know that **my kingdom** is what the Kingdom of God is called after the Second Coming of Christ, when it has merged with the Kingdom of Heaven.

This is beautiful beyond description! The Word of God is perfect in every way. There is no passage in the Bible that could be improved upon. It conceals and reveals truth at the same time. Even during the stress and strain of his trial, Jesus was able to answer Pilate's challenge, speak the truth, say a great deal, and yet he said nothing more than to deny that he was a political revolutionary. What if Jesus had candidly told Pilate that his kingdom was going to smash all kingdoms and grind them into powder (Dan. 2:44-45)? What if he said that he was the King of all kings and the Lord of all lords, that his disciples were going to rule over the cities of Israel, and his Church would rule over all the cities of the world, that he would return on a white horse with a rod of iron to beat in pieces the nations, and feed their carcasses to the buzzards? Instead, he gave a passive-sounding answer that was nonetheless loaded and cocked — **"but <u>now</u> is my kingdom not from hence"**. Notice how Jesus qualified his statements — **but now….** At this present time, my kingdom is not **from hence**. At the time he was speaking, the kingdom he offered to Israel was spiritual, and the kingdom into which so many were **pressing** was **not of this world**. It will never be forced upon anyone. That was all Pilate needed to know, "At present my kingdom is not of this world." Jesus let Pilate know that he was not competing with his pitiful little kingdom out of Rome. He wouldn't be any trouble. Nevertheless, Jesus deceived Pilate regarding his ultimate plans. His words were spoken in a mystery, the mystery hanging on one word — NOW. Let this be a lesson on how Jesus spoke and how the Bible is written. Watch every word. Look for the twist. Discover the mystery. It is God's method.

He says, **"If my kingdom were of this world, then would my servants fight,"** and since his servants didn't fight, it proves that his kingdom is not **now** a kingdom that is interested in ruling the world. Any church that forces laws upon citizens or that uses violence against its own nation or another in the name of the K of G is antichrist and should be scorned as totally unchristian. The Roman Catholic Church especially, and, in a much smaller measure, the Lutheran Church, the Church of England, and the Orthodox Church all have the blood of "heretics" on their "holy" vestments.

If you don't pay attention to what Jesus says, you could end up just as deceived as Jesus intended for his accusers to be.

Think about what Jesus could have said that would have destroyed the distinctions that thus far are so carefully maintained in the gospels. He could have said, "The K of H is not of this world." But the K of H is very much of this world, and no place else. Instead of saying, **but now is my kingdom not from hence**, he could have said, "My kingdom will never be of this world," or he could have just left out the word **now** and repeated **my kingdom is not of this world**, which would have eliminated the Millennium. But he said it perfectly, and from it we have learned even more about the unique characteristics of the two kingdoms.

## The experience of personal tribulation precedes entering the Kingdom of God.

> *Acts 14:22* Confirming the souls of the disciples, and exhorting them to continue in the faith, and that we must **through much tribulation enter into the kingdom of God**.

This passage reveals more than is obvious at first reading. He is speaking of disciples — saved people. They are told to **continue in their faith,** as if future circumstances are going to make this exhortation necessary. Then he explains why they will need to pay special attention to continuing in the faith. The Kingdom of God is associated with **much tribulation**. It is a necessary part of the program.

If it concerns you that he is placing the coming of the K of G at the end of a life of tribulation, remember these facts: one can **receive** the K of G right now, sinners and publicans are getting **into** the K of G right now, the K of G is **within you** right now, but the K of G does not **come** as a visible, earthly power until Jesus returns at the end of the Great Tribulation.

With all that you have learned so far, it is now obvious that this verse could not have been written concerning the K of H. No amount of faith or endurance or tribulation would prepare one to enter into the K of H at the end of his life.

## The kingdom of God is an everlasting kingdom known as the kingdom of Christ.

> *2 Peter 1:11* For so an entrance shall be ministered unto you abundantly into the **everlasting kingdom of our Lord and Saviour Jesus Christ.**

This everlasting kingdom is not called the kingdom of God, though we know from many other passages that the K of G is called Christ kingdom in the Millennium and beyond, whereas the K of H is never identified with Christ's kingdom.

# Matthew switches to the term, "kingdom of God" five times.

Our purpose in this section is to examine more closely the five times that Matthew departs from his dedicated course of writing about the Kingdom of Heaven and speaks of the Kingdom of God instead. We have reviewed these verses already, but we want to look at them again from this singular perspective.

The popular explanation as to why Matthew is the only one to use the term K of H while the rest of the New Testament uses the term K of G is that Matthew preferred one term and the other writers preferred another. If Matthew simply preferred the term K of H, then why did he make these five exceptions? And why are these verses in complete harmony with what the other writers say about the K of G? Furthermore, why did Matthew just happen to change his characterization of the kingdom in these five verses alone, where he speaks of the K of G? Can we really accept that it is just an accident? The believing mind knows that this is an example of the ongoing mystery kept secret from the foundation of the world.

The impact of it all is greatest on the reader when he reads straight through the book of Matthew, preferably in one sitting. He becomes familiar with Matthew's constant reference to the **kingdom of heaven**, and then, as if out of nowhere, he comes across the expression, **kingdom of God**. When you see each of these five verses in their context, they stand out like big question marks. Why did you switch, Matthew? What are you trying to say to us? How are the two kingdoms different?

### Matthew's five Kingdom of God passages

| *Matthew 6:33* | *Matthew 12:28* | *Matthew 19:23* | *Matthew 21:31* | *Matthew 21:43* |
|---|---|---|---|---|
| But seek ye first the **kingdom of God,** and his righteousness; and all these things shall be added unto you. | But if I cast out devils by the Spirit of God, then the **kingdom of God** is come unto you. | Then said Jesus unto his disciples, Verily I say unto you, That a rich man shall hardly enter into the **kingdom of heaven.** 24 And again I say unto you, It is easier for a camel to go through the eye of a needle, than for a rich man to enter into the **kingdom of God.** | Whether of them twain did the will of his father? They say unto him, The first. Jesus saith unto them, Verily I say unto you, That the publicans and the harlots go into the **kingdom of God** before you. | Therefore say I unto you, **The kingdom of God** shall be taken from you, and given to a nation bringing forth the fruits thereof. |

We will now examine each of the five passages in the order they appear in Scripture.

## Seek the kingdom of God.

> *Matthew 6:33* But seek ye first the **kingdom of God,** and his righteousness; and all these things shall be added unto you.

Matthew has mentioned the **kingdom of heaven** six times before this passage in 6:33. The only reason to have switched terms here is that he is quoting exactly what Jesus said, and no such statement was ever made regarding the K of H. Several things Jesus said are unique to the K of G. He said, **seek** the K of G — indicating that it was present and worthy of pursuit. No one could **seek** the K of H. Until heaven sets up its kingdom on earth, there would be nothing to seek. But since the K of G was then present in power and glory in the person of Christ, and it was internal and spiritual, it could be the constant, personal pursuit of believers.

Seeking the K of G involved **righteousness.** Righteousness is personal and individual. It is not a corporate endeavor.

He says that the reward for successfully seeking the K of G is that **all things will be added unto you**, which means that one's pursuit of the K of G could be realized in this life. In other words, the K of G was then present (though it had not *come*) and could be laid hold upon. None of this could be said of the K of H.

## The kingdom of God is come unto you.

> *Matthew 12:28* But if I cast out devils by the Spirit of God, then the **kingdom of God** is **come unto you**.

Matthew speaks of the Kingdom of Heaven five more times between 6:33 and 12:28, and then suddenly switches to the Kingdom of God again. Jesus could not have designated this statement as K of H, for the K of H is never spoken of as coming **unto you**. Furthermore, as we have already discussed, the manifestation of the **Spirit of God** and **power** over devils can only be for the K of G. If Jesus had said, "then the **kingdom of heaven** is come unto you," we would be forced to conclude that the K of H is not just the future reign of heaven over earth, but that it was indeed manifested in power and was a present experience of the disciples at that time. If in this one place Matthew had followed his pattern of speaking of the K of H, he would have destroyed the consistent pattern that compels us to believe that the two kingdoms are not the same kingdom.

## A rich man can hardly enter either kingdom.

> *Matthew 19:23* Then said Jesus unto his disciples, Verily I say unto you, That a rich man shall hardly enter into the **kingdom of heaven**.
> 24 And again I say unto you, It is easier for a camel to go through the eye of a needle, than for a rich man to enter into the **kingdom of God.**

This is a fascinating and revealing passage. Matthew speaks of both kingdoms in the same passage and context. Luke 18:25 says the same thing about the rich man only, and attributes it to the K of G.

Matthew 19:23 and 24 is of great value in our quest of a complete understanding of the difference between the two kingdoms. It explains how two different writers can record seemingly identical sayings and attribute them to different kingdoms. The questions naturally arise, "What did Jesus actually say — **heaven** or **God** or **both**?" This passage reveals the answer. Jesus said it both ways, in the same paragraph. So, contrary to the urging of most Bible scholars, we don't need a *harmony* of the gospels; we don't need to try to determine what Jesus "really said." We only need to understand what the Holy Spirit is saying in these carefully scripted variations.

This is our strongest example of the method Jesus used in teaching. He spoke of both kingdoms in consecutive sentences. His sermons were filled with reference to first one kingdom and then the other. As he spoke, he was drawing distinctions between the two kingdoms, knowing that his audience was not understanding him completely. He was deliberately creating a mystery that would conceal the truth to most people, while revealing it to only a few. It is also unlikely that the gospel writers themselves understood the distinction, even when writing the text. It was the Holy Spirit moving the apostles to produce these carefully balanced texts. The fact that this distinction is so carefully and perfectly maintained through all the writers, and especially through the Authorized Version, is powerful testimony as to the Scriptures being given and preserved by inspiration of God.

If the two kingdoms were actually the same and, as some argue, Matthew just preferred one term above another, then they must not only answer **why** Matthew made these five exceptions, but they must also explain why Jesus would be compelled to use both terms in almost the same sentence. Why would Jesus give the same teaching a second time? If the kingdoms are the same, then Jesus or Matthew was clumsily redundant. But, if they are indeed different, then it is understandable that he would clarify that this truth applied equally to both kingdoms.

## Sinners go into the Kingdom of God.

> *Matthew 21:31* Whether of them twain did the will of his father? They say unto him, The first. Jesus saith unto them, Verily I say unto you, That the publicans and the harlots **go into** the **kingdom of God before** you.

Our fourth Kingdom of God passage found in Matthew is such that, if the Holy Spirit had substituted the word **God** for the word **heaven,** the whole doctrine would be destroyed. But, he said, the harlots **go** (present tense) **into** the **kingdom of God.** No one was *going* into the K of H, not then and not now. To date, no one has ever *gone* into the K of H. It is on an individual basis that one goes into the K of G, whereas the K of H will come to the nation of Israel and then to the entire world.

Furthermore, the harlots <u>were going</u> into the K of G **before** others. This indicates that the **kingdom of God** was open, enterable and available at that time, and that the **kingdom of God** is entered individually, in sequence — one person at a time, some before others. The K of H will come as an institution, and everyone will be in the kingdom at the same time or not at all, and those in the K of H who don't qualify will be removed from the kingdom and cast out into outer darkness.

Only the K of G makes a place for sinners to come and receive forgiveness and be admitted into the kingdom immediately.

## The Kingdom of God will be taken from Israel.

> *Matthew 21:43* Therefore say I unto you, The **kingdom of God** shall be taken from you, and given to a nation bringing forth the fruits thereof.

This is the last of our five Kingdom of God passages found in Matthew, and it is the most revealing. In fact, this is the one place, above all others, that if Matthew had designated this passage as K of H, it would have been completely devastating to Christ's entire kingdom doctrine. If, in this one place, Matthew had changed the word **God** to **heaven,** I could never have even considered writing this book, and over 100 other important Bible doctrines would be affected. There would be no way around it. If Matthew had stuck to his commonly used K of H term, one would look like a fool trying to teach that the Church is not the recipient of the promises to Israel while they are in their temporary state of blindness.

Think what it would mean if Jesus had said to the Jews, "The **kingdom of heaven** shall be taken from you...." <u>It would mean</u> that the Roman Catholic and Reformed Churches could be correct: all the promises God gave to Israel would no longer apply to Israel, but to the Church. <u>It would mean</u> that God is through with the Jews as a special people. <u>It would mean</u> that the book of Revelation would have to be interpreted figuratively, as the Amillennialists do. And, the Lamb on Mt. Zion with the 144,000 (12,000 from every tribe) could **not** be Jesus, and the 144,000 would **not** be 144,000 and they would **not** be from the tribes of Israel. <u>It would mean</u> that all that Jesus said in Matthew 24 and what Paul said in Romans 9-11 could no longer be taken literally. And, <u>It would mean</u> that the many promises God made to Israel in the Old Testament would never be fulfilled. It would mean that the Davidic covenant was a lie. Yes, **if this one word had been changed**, the Bible would be viewed with much more confusion and uncertainty than it already is today among those who think the kingdoms are the same. We would all be Postmillennialists or Amillennialists. If the Church has inherited the role that was formerly given to Israel, the Bible could not be trusted as anything more than a collection of inspiring stories, biographies, history, and allegories. All of this would be embarrassingly correct, if just the one word, *God*, had been exchanged for the word, *heaven*. Thank God that the Holy Spirit was the author of the Holy Scriptures!

Jesus had been offering the nation of Israel both kingdoms. The K of G was a restored relationship to the Father, complete with the Holy Spirit and the power and glory of God upon each one individually. If they had all personally received the K of G, it would have enabled them as a nation to be in a condition to receive the K of H. But the Jews rejected both kingdoms, which is why Jesus announces that he will take the K of G away from them and give it to a nation (the Church -1 Peter 2:9) that would bring forth the corresponding fruits of the Spirit. If you remember, fruit was what John required for the coming of the K of H (Matt. 3:8; Luke 3:8).

Having examined the five times Matthew refers to the K of G, it should be obvious to the unbiased reader that there is something extremely unique about these five verses. They are in sharp contrast to the many K of H passages in Matthew, but are in perfect harmony with the K of G passages in Mark and Luke. Matthew has carefully made a distinction between the natures of the two kingdoms, but he has done it in such a way that it remains a mystery to those who do not want to see.

# Matthew uses "kingdom" 7 times, without identifying which one it is.

As we have seen, Jesus preached about both kingdoms during his ministry, sometimes speaking about one, and at other times of the other. There were also instances when he taught about both kingdoms and compared them, or he would speak about both of them together as being identical in some respect.

Jesus taught openly in parables, but his audience never understood the distinction between the two kingdoms, nor did he mean for them to understand (Mark 4:12). On several occasions he explained to his disciples the mystery of the kingdoms, but even they sometimes failed to grasp his teaching without some private "tutoring."

We have also pointed out that, by inspiration of the Holy Spirit, Matthew wrote from a different point of view than did Mark and Luke. Matthew was directed to write to the Jews from the perspective of the **kingdom promised to David** (1 Kings 9:5). He was moved to select those events and portions of Jesus' sermons that pertained to and described the K of H. And, as we have seen, except for five occasions, he avoided writing about the K of G. In his gospel account, Matthew used the phrase **kingdom of heaven** 32 times, **kingdom of God** five times, and the word **kingdom** seven times. Mark and Luke used the term **kingdom of God** 15 and 31 times, respectively.

Mark and Luke write from a post-Pentecost perspective, even post-Pauline. They are speaking primarily to the Gentiles. By the time they write, the K of H has been postponed, and there is no value in instructing Gentiles in what the Jews had failed to receive.

Thus it is that we have a New Testament with the first book written as a bridge from the old covenant to the new, recounting the historical offer and rejection of the earthly kingdom promised to Israel. Mark and Luke take it from there and record that part of Jesus' teachings that concerns the K of G. That is why the books are in the order we find them in the canon of Scripture.

We are about to examine the seven times where Jesus spoke of a kingdom, but did not designate which one. From the nature of the things he was teaching, we know that all seven occurrences have to do with the K of G, which provokes us to wonder why Jesus would speak about the K of G but not designate it as such. First, it was to maintain the mystery to those who had eyes and ears but couldn't see or hear. Second, for Matthew to make his "bridging" narrative complete, he occasionally gave an account of something said or done that was pertinent to the K of G. Furthermore, the K of G was also relevant to the Jews at the time Jesus was speaking. They, too, were being challenged to enter the K of G individually so they could qualify corporately for the K of H when it was to be instituted. But, like the other writers, Matthew was writing his gospel after it was obvious that the K of H was not going to be set up because of Israel's refusal of its offer by Jesus, its king. Yet, the Holy Spirit moved Matthew to speak to the Jews **and** to the Church and to document God's prophesied attempt to give Israel the kingdom promised to David. While Matthew's primary emphasis was Jesus' teaching about the K of H, to maintain the focus of his readers, he chose not to designate some of the passages that were exclusively aimed at discussing the K of G.

By comparing the content of these verses with K of G passages in Mark and Luke, we can easily identify them as K of G and not K of H.

To suggest that these verses are not intentionally teaching a difference in the two kingdoms, would be to assume a series of coincidences well beyond any reasonable probability. How do you account for Matthew saying things that could only be the K of G, yet never accidentally calling them K of H? Added to the five times he actually designated passages as K of G, he was given seven more opportunities to get it wrong, but he never failed to maintain the distinction. How awesome!

# The gospel of the kingdom.

> *Matthew 4:23* And Jesus went about all Galilee, teaching in their synagogues, and preaching the **gospel of the kingdom**, and healing all manner of sickness and all manner of disease among the people.

> *Matthew 9:35* And Jesus went about all the cities and villages, teaching in their synagogues, and preaching the **gospel of the kingdom**, and healing every sickness and every disease among the people.

Here we have two of the seven times Matthew speaks of the kingdom without designating it. The fact that the same statement is made twice, and both times failing to attribute it to the Kingdom of Heaven, shows a deliberateness with regard to the wording. At that time in his ministry, Jesus was, in fact, preaching both the K of G and the K of H, but the word **gospel** is never applied to the K of H, only to the K of G. The K of G was immediate and present in the person of Christ. As they received the words of Jesus, they received the K of G, and we are told that the K of G came **upon** them and **unto** them and was **within** them, but no such things are ever said of the K of H.

# Thine is the kingdom, and the power, and the glory.

> *Matthew 6:10* **Thy kingdom** come. Thy will be done in earth, as *it is* in heaven.
> 13 And lead us not into temptation, but deliver us from evil: For **thine is the kingdom**, and the power, and the glory, for ever. Amen.

In what is popularly called "The Lord's Prayer," Jesus tells his disciples and the multitudes to address the Father in heaven saying, **thy kingdom come…for thine is the kingdom….** He has defined the kingdom as the **Father's kingdom**, which is spoken of in Matthew 26:29 & 13:43.

Furthermore, we have seen that the K of H is never identified with **power** and **glory**. That is an attribute of the **kingdom of God**, of **Christ's kingdom**, or the **Father's kingdom**. Can you see how absolutely inconsistent it would have been to have said, "For thine is the **kingdom of heaven** and the power and the glory"?

As to the subject of the prayer itself, Jesus tells the disciples to pray that God's kingdom would come to the earth, manifesting power and glory. When the K of G does finally bring about the will of God **on earth as it is in heaven,** it will be the Millennial kingdom, and the **kingdom of heaven** will also be manifested in the Father's kingdom.

# Sit on thy right hand in thy kingdom.

> *Matthew 20:21* And he said unto her, What wilt thou? She saith unto him, Grant that these my two sons may sit, the one on thy right hand, and the other on the left, in **thy kingdom**.

This mother of James and John was ambitious for her two sons, desiring that they might share the throne with Jesus. It is obvious that she was expecting a kingdom like any earthly kingdom. Jesus' answer granted her assumption that the nature of the kingdom would indeed allow for someone to sit on his right and left, but he could not grant her request because it was the Father who would determine the filling of those positions.

At least she got the question right. She did not ask for favors when he sits on the throne of the K of H or the K of G. She spoke of, **thy** kingdom, meaning **his kingdom**. We will review the verses on **thy kingdom** later. It is sufficient now to note that the Scripture has preserved the correct kingdom pattern even in a question asked by an unlearned mother. In the Millennium, the K of H and the K of G will merge into what is called **Christ's kingdom** (thy kingdom) which he will turn over to his Father when it will finally be called, his Father's kingdom.

## Gospel of the kingdom preached to all nations.

> *Matthew 24:14* And this gospel of the **kingdom** shall be preached in all the world for a witness unto all nations; and then shall the end come.

This is the third time Jesus has spoken of the **gospel of the kingdom,** and this gospel will be preached **in all the world… to all nations.** It is important to note the **time** of this preaching of the gospel of the kingdom. It is **during** the Tribulation, just before Christ's return. The gospel of Jesus Christ is no longer preached because the Church, his bride, is complete and has been taken away from the earth. The message at that time will be things **new and old** — the old law of Moses and the new gospel of Messiah. It will be good news of a coming kingdom of Christ upon the earth. It will not be a gospel of regeneration and new birth. The two kingdoms, the K of G and the K of H, will merge at the beginning of the Millennium and exist together during the thousand years under the Kingdom of Christ (his kingdom, thy kingdom).

## A kingdom prepared from the foundation of the world.

> *Matthew 25:34* Then shall the King say unto them on his right hand, Come, ye blessed of my Father, inherit the **kingdom** prepared for you from the foundation of the world:

This event of separating some on the right hand and some on the left will occur after the Tribulation, at the beginning of the Millennium. The kingdoms will have merged into **his kingdom** right after the start of the Millennium, so it would have been incorrect for Matthew to limit Jesus' statement to the K of H. Both kingdoms were prepared from before the foundation of the world. The Church will already be in heaven and will not be part of this judgment of the nations.

## Word of the kingdom (common to both).

> *Matthew 13:19* When any one heareth the **word of the kingdom**, and understandeth it not, then cometh the wicked one, and catcheth away that which was sown in his heart. This is he which received seed by the way side.

This is in the context of the Kingdom of Heaven, but it also applies to the Kingdom of God, so Matthew uses the generic **kingdom** so as to leave it open to either.

# Matthew speaks of His kingdom, the Father's Kingdom, or Thy Kingdom seven times.

All seven of these uses of the word **kingdom** are clearly a reference to the reign of Christ in glory and power, which will commence with the Millennial reign of Christ on the earth. As we have seen in many other passages, at that time the K of G and the K of H will merge into what will then be known as **Christ's kingdom**, which will later become **The Father's kingdom**. It is a mark of the perfection of the inspired Word that in these seven references, the writer withheld assigning any of them to either kingdom.

## Thy kingdom come to the earth.

> *Matthew 6:10*  **Thy kingdom come**. Thy will be done in earth, as *it is* in heaven.

It is during the Millennium, under both kingdoms at the same time, then called Christ's kingdom (thy kingdom), that the will of God will be done on earth as it is in heaven. We can see why the Holy Spirit chose not to designate "thy kingdom" as exclusively either kingdom since both kingdoms will be involved at that time. How beautifully complex, yet simple!

## Thine is the kingdom.

> *Matthew 6:13* And lead us not into temptation, but deliver us from evil: For **thine is the kingdom,** and the power, and the glory, for ever.

Again we see Christ's kingdom, **thy kingdom**, associated with the manifestation of power and glory. It would have been totally inconsistent with the facts to have said, "thine is the **kingdom of heaven**," for such would have been far too limiting to Jesus. His kingdom, while assimilating the temporal **kingdom of heaven**, is much more encompassing.

## His kingdom — kingdom of their Father.

> *Matthew 13:41* The Son of man shall send forth his angels, and they shall gather out of **his kingdom** all things that offend, and them which do iniquity;
> 42 And shall cast them into a furnace of fire: there shall be wailing and gnashing of teeth.
> 43 Then shall the righteous shine forth as the sun in the **kingdom of their Father**. Who hath ears to hear, let him hear.

At that time (the beginning of the Millennium) both kingdoms will have merged into **his Kingdom**, one element of which is the K of H, which contains tares. After the purging, Christ turns **his kingdom** over to the Father where only the righteous shine forth in the **kingdom of their Father**. This passage is a marvelously accurate use of the terms.

## The Son of man coming in his kingdom.

> *Matthew 16:28* Verily I say unto you, There be some standing here, which shall not taste of death, till they see the Son of man coming in **his kingdom**.

Mark 9:1 fixes this experience in the Kingdom of God. **His kingdom** is defined in the next chapter when they see Jesus transformed and speaking with Moses and Elijah. So the **kingdom of God** and **His kingdom** will be the same at that time. **Christ's kingdom** (**His** kingdom/the K of G) is anywhere that Christ rules in power and glory and authority.

It is obvious that any other term used in this passage would have been inconsistent with the rest of Scripture.

## Sit on the right hand and on the left.

> *Matthew 20:21* And he said unto her, What wilt thou? She saith unto him, Grant that these my two sons may sit, the one on thy right hand, and the other on the left, in **thy kingdom**.

The time when someone will **sit down** with Christ in "**thy kingdom**" will obviously be in the Millennium, when the kingdom of heaven is physically ruling the earth in righteousness.

## Drinking wine in the Father's kingdom.

> *Matthew 26:29* But I say unto you, I will not drink henceforth of this fruit of the vine, until that day when I drink it new with you in my **Father's kingdom**.

A kingdom that could contain individuals drinking wine with Jesus must be future, and the Millennium is the earliest possible date. Notice that, by the time the wine is served at the marriage supper of the Lamb, the tares have been purged and **his kingdom** has become **the Father's kingdom**.

You can now see how incorrect it would be to have characterized this passage as referring to the K of H. That would have placed Jesus drinking with sinners (tares). Likewise, if he had called it **his kingdom**, the drinking of wine would have been occurring in a kingdom that had things offensive in it. Only when the kingdom has been purged and has progressed into the **Father's kingdom,** do the festivities with the Church begin.

# Matthew "doesn't" designate it as "kingdom" five times, when Mark or Luke do.

In four of these five passages, had Matthew stipulated them as being Kingdom of Heaven statements, he would have destroyed the otherwise carefully maintained distinction. It is no accident that when speaking on the same subject matter that Mark or Luke record, where they call it the K of G, Matthew chose not to designate it as referring to the kingdom of heaven.

## Left house and family for the K of G.

| | |
|---|---|
| *Matthew 19:29* And every one that hath forsaken houses, or brethren, or sisters, or father, or mother, or wife, or children, or lands, for **my name's sake**, shall receive an hundredfold, and shall inherit everlasting life.<br>  30 But many *that are* first shall be last; and the last *shall be* first. | *Luke 18:29* And he said unto them, Verily I say unto you, There is no man that hath left house, or parents, or brethren, or wife, or children, for the **kingdom of God's sake,**<br>  30 Who shall not receive manifold more in this present time, and in the world to come life everlasting. |

Where Luke calls dedication to Christ and self-sacrifice a characteristic of the **Kingdom of God**, Matthew writes that it is being done **for my name's sake**. From what we have learned of the two kingdoms, there is no way one can **leave** his family and belongings **for** the **kingdom of heaven**. If Matthew had recorded this as speaking of the K of H, he would have been stating that the K of H was then present, so as to permit someone to make sacrifices on behalf of it. Such was true of the K of G, but not the K of H.

Another revelation in these two passages is that, "**my name's sake**" is equated with the **K of G**.

## When you see the trees bud, the K of G is at hand.

| | |
|---|---|
| *Matthew 24:32* Now learn a parable of the fig tree; When his branch is yet tender, and putteth forth leaves, ye know that summer *is* nigh:<br>  33 So likewise ye, when ye shall see all these things, know that **it is near**, *even* at the doors.<br>  34 Verily I say unto you, This generation shall not pass, till all these things be fulfilled.<br>  35 Heaven and earth shall pass away, but my words shall not pass away. | *Luke 21:29* Behold the fig tree, and all the trees; 30 When they now shoot forth, ye see and know of your own selves that summer is now nigh at hand.<br>  31 So likewise ye, when ye see these things come to pass, know ye that the **kingdom of God is nigh at hand**.<br>  32 Verily I say unto you, This generation shall not pass away, till all be fulfilled.<br>  33 Heaven and earth shall pass away: but my words shall not pass away.<br>  (See Mark 13:28.) |

It is plain to be seen that Matthew is recording the same message as Luke, but he leaves out the statement about the signs by which they will know that the **kingdom of God** is nigh at hand. **Nigh at hand** means, near, as to place or position. The disciples had asked the question, **What *shall be* the sign of thy coming, and of the end of the world?** (Matt. 24:3). Jesus gave them the sign of the **fig tree and all the trees**. At the time of the Second Coming and the end of the world, it is the K of G that will be manifested and dominate the scene.

Israel is often represented as a fruit tree or vine, with God as the owner/caretaker. Israel is the fig tree in these passages (Matt. 21:19; Luke 13:6; Rom. 11:17-24), and **all the trees** include the Gentile nations (Ps. 96:12-13; Ezek. 17:23-24; Ezek. 31; Daniel 4:10-26; 7:17-19; 13:32; 21:19; Rom. 11:17-24). Matthew did not mention **all the trees** — Gentile nations — since it was not his subject matter, but Luke adds the concept of additional trees budding (additional nations coming into their own). This is as it should be, since the K of G is predominantly made up of Gentile nations which have little to do with the K of H at that time. If Matthew had designated this parable as a K of H teaching, he would have confused the nature of the K of H, for he was speaking to Jews concerning the reestablishment of their nation in the last days just prior to the rapture of the Church. The fig tree represents Israel. Matthew recorded a very important question and he recorded Jesus' answer, but the answer went beyond the K of H. Rather than to break with his purposes and unnecessarily introduce the subject of the K of G, Matthew just left off the part about the K of G.

## Joseph waited for the K of G.

| | |
|---|---|
| *Matthew 27:57* When the even was come, there came a rich man of Arimathæa, named Joseph, **who also himself was Jesus' disciple**: | *Luke 23:51* (The same had not consented to the counsel and deed of them;) *he was* of Arimathæa, a city of the Jews: who also himself **waited for the kingdom of God**. |

This could have been stated either way and not confused the distinction, but since Matthew did not assign it to the K of H and Luke did not leave it undesignated, Joseph must have been well instructed in the kingdoms and was particular in his anticipation. Clearly, he was anticipating the K of G, but Matthew chose to simply refer to Joseph as one "**who also himself was one of Jesus' disciples**."

Again, by this parallelism we gain a further revelation as to the nature of the K of G: During the ministry of Christ, to wait for the K of G was to be Jesus' disciple.

## Pluck your eye out to enter the Kingdom of God.

| | |
|---|---|
| *Matthew 5:28* But I say unto you, That whosoever looketh on a woman to lust after her hath committed adultery with her already in his heart. <br> 29 And if thy right eye offend thee, pluck it out, and cast *it* from thee: for it is profitable for thee that one of thy members should perish, and not *that* thy whole body should be cast into hell. <br> *Matthew 18:9* And if thine eye offend thee, pluck it out, and cast *it* from thee: it is better for thee to **enter into life** with one eye, rather than having two eyes to be cast into hell fire. | *Mark 9:47* And if thine eye offend thee, pluck it out: it is better for thee to **enter into the kingdom of God** with one eye, than having two eyes to be cast into hell fire: |

Mark says that if there is no other recourse, one should pluck out his eye to remove any hindrance to entering the K of G. Apparently, the accounts of Matthew and Mark represent the same event, for although Mark tells us that Jesus said, "kingdom of God," Matthew says, "enter into life", and we know from previous passages that entering into life and entering into the K of G are synonymous — not so the K of H. Remember, the K of G is the only kingdom that can be personally entered at that time. Matt.18:3 and 19:23 speak of **entering** the K of H, but it is a theoretical offer that is not realized and could not be realized unless the nation meet the conditions for the institution of that physical kingdom,

This was another opportunity for Matthew to interject a phrase that would have completely destroyed the carefully preserved distinction between the two kingdoms, but Matthew chose not to link the statement with any kingdom for the simple reason that Jesus never related this concept as applicable to the K of H.

The issue in both accounts was personal salvation — not the coming of an earthly kingdom. The K of H is never about personal salvation. One could pluck out both eyes and cut off both hands and still not bring about the establishment of the K of H. And as we have pointed out, at that time and at present, no one can **enter** into the K of H under any circumstances. There is no K of H into which you can enter at this time.

These five verses have been powerful in their support of the uniqueness of the two kingdoms.

# Part 3: Kingdom characteristics at a glance

| What the kingdom of heaven and the kingdom of God have in common. |
| --- |
| 17) John the Baptist was not in either Kingdom. |
| 17) Neither K had "come" before or during the time of John. |
| 1) Both kingdoms were at hand. |
| 17) Least in either K is greater than John. |
| 1) Both required repentance. |
| 11) Both are based on righteousness. |
| 3) Jesus preached about both kingdoms. |
| 16) Disciples were sent to preach of both kingdoms. |
| 4) Healing is manifested in both. |
| 35) Must become as little children to enter either. |
| 39) Rich can hardly enter into either. |
| 22) They are both like the seed sown that fell on various ground conditions. |
| 21) Both kingdoms are a mystery, so he speaks in parables. |
| 24) Both grow to be large and all-encompassing. |
| 24) Like a mustard seed, they become great trees with birds (devils) in the branches. |
| 25) False doctrine (leaven) permeates them. |
| 40) The first in chronological time may be last in reward. |
| 9) Both will eventually be manifested on earth. |
| 13) Old Testament saints— Abraham, Isaac, and Jacob — are present and sit down. |
| 13) Sit down in both of them with the prophets. |
| 50, 52) Comes at the Second Coming of Christ. |
| 27) The K of H will become *his K* and then *the K of the Father.* |

## The Kingdom of Heaven is Unique. . .

| |
|---|
| John the Baptist preached the K of H only. |
| The K of H was to be preached to Jews only. |
| The K of H is for the poor in spirit. |
| The K of H was offered as release from persecution. |
| Commandments will be kept in the K of H. |
| Some in the K will be called least or greatest. |
| The K of H was soon to come. |
| Subject to violent overthrow. |
| Enemy sows tares while men sleep — tares are burnt. |
| Treasure to be sought — field to be bought. |
| Like goodly pearls — sell all and buy it. |
| Like a net that contains good and bad fish. |
| Jewish scribes are instructed concerning the K of H. |
| Contains elements both new and old. |
| Keys of the kingdom are imparted to men with power to bind on earth. |
| Disciples argued over who would be the greatest there. |
| Requires one to forgive or lose his own forgiveness. |
| Obtained by works. |
| Men make themselves eunuchs for the K of H. |
| Disciples sit on 12 thrones. |
| Householder hiring laborers for a penny a day. |
| Jews are guests at the wedding of the king's son. |
| Pharisees prevented others from entering it. |
| Gospel of the kingdom preached in all the world…. |
| Ten virgins awaiting it; 5 refused entrance for lack of oil. |
| Children of the K cast into outer darkness. |
| Those who fail to multiply their money are cast into fire. |
| K was prepared from the foundation of the world. |
| One can lose his inheritance in the kingdom. |

| The Kingdom of God is Unique. . . | |
|---|---|
| Power over devils is a manifestation of the presence of the K of G. | The K of H was not present under any circumstances. |
| Sinners [*publicans and harlots*] get **into** the K of G. | No one could get "into" the K of H. |
| Taken from Jews and given to another nation that will bear fruit. | The K of H cannot be taken from the Jews since it is theirs by covenant. |
| "Believe" was preached in connection with the K of G. [*Mark 1:15*] | Belief would have had no effect on the K of H. Repentance was the only requirement. |
| Likened to seed cast — blade, ear, full corn. [*no tares to be burnt*] | The K of H has tares in it. |
| To see the manifestation of Jesus' power and glory was to see the K of G. | Were Christ is manifested the K of G is manifested. The K of H requires the institution of a political system. |
| When healing occurs, the K of G is near. | Not so with the K of H. Healing can occur in connection with the K of H, but it can occur under any dispensation without any reference to or bearing on the dispensation itself. |
| Right condition of heart would put him in the K of G. | No one entered the K of H individually until it was instituted, and then it will be entered corporately. |
| Jesus will not drink wine until he does so in the K of G. | Matt. 26:29 calls it the Father's kingdom, for by the time the wine is served, the K of H that contained tares has become the K of the Father or the K of G. |
| The poor were close to the K of G. | 5) The poor in spirit were in need of the K of H. |
| The K of G was glad tidings. | The K of H is never called "gospel." |
| He who looks back is not fit for the K of G. | Since no one was in the K of H, this would have been an irrelevant statement. |
| To seek the will of God is to seek the K of G. | "Seek" is never used in connection with the K of H. |
| The K of G is sought through righteousness. | See above. |
| Men were pressing into the kingdom, showing it to be a present experience. | The K of H suffered violence and was taken by force. No one could press into something non-existent at the time. |
| The K of G is not visible at that time. | The K of H could not exist in an invisible state. |
| The K of G is within you. | The K of H is visible, not "within you." |
| People had left houses and lands during the life of Christ for the K of G. | Forsaking possessions would have had no bearing on the institution of the K of H. |
| They mistakenly thought it would immediately appear. | The K of H would have appeared if they had received the king. It will appear in the Millennium. |
| The K of G will not come until the Millennium. | No such remark is made regarding K of H. |

| | |
|---|---|
| The K of G is for the regenerated only. | John 3:5. |
| The K of G is entered presently. | Col. 1:13-14. |
| Christ taught K of G after his resurrection. | 16) Kingdom of H preached to Israel only. |
| If necessary, one should pluck out his eye to enter the K of G. | Matthew says nearly the same thing in a discussion of the K of H, but is careful not to call it the K of H. |
| The K message is gospel. | The K of H is never called "gospel." |
| Righteousness, peace, and joy. | No such remark is made regarding K of H. |
| Unrighteous do not inherit it. | No such remark is made regarding K of H. |
| Flesh and blood do not inherit the K of G. Corruption will put on incorruption… | No such remark is made regarding K of H. |
| The K of G is "his kingdom." | No such remark is made regarding K of H. |
| The K of G will become the "Father's K." | The K of H will be absorbed by both. |
| Jesus preached and showed the K of G. | One could not see the K of H. |
| The disciples preached only the K of G. | They never mentioned the K of H. |

| **Matthew, the only gospel writer to use the term "kingdom of Heaven," switches to the term "kingdom of God" 5 times.** | |
|---|---|
| *Matthew 6:33* But seek ye first the **kingdom of God**, and his righteousness; and all these things shall be added unto you. | The K of G can be a living and present reality through obedience and righteousness, whereas the K of H is beyond the reach of any individual until it comes as a visible institution at the Millennium. |
| *Matthew 12:28* But if I cast out devils by the Spirit of God, then the **kingdom of God** is come unto you. | The presence of the power to cast out devils reveals that the K of G is among the believers. |
| *Matthew 19:24* And again I say unto you, It is easier for a camel to go through the eye of a needle, than for a rich man to enter into the **kingdom of God**. | He had just said a similar thing of the K of H, and here repeats it, but switching to the K of G, demonstrating that the kingdoms are different and that Matthew recognized it, intending to make it clear that this applied to both kingdoms. |
| *Matthew 21:31* Whether of them twain did the will of his father? They say unto him, The first. Jesus saith unto them, Verily I say unto you, That the publicans and the harlots go into the **kingdom of God** before you. | Since no one was "getting into the K of H" at that time, it could only be the K of G into which sinners were entering. It is on an individual basis that one enters the K of G, whereas the K of H will come as a political system to the whole nation. |
| *Matthew 21:43* Therefore say I unto you, The **kingdom of God** shall be taken from you, and given to a nation bringing forth the fruits thereof. | The K of H was promised to Jacob's seed and could not be given to anyone or to another nation. However, the K of G is not a covenant right of Israel, and can be given to the Gentiles or to the Jews. |

| | |
|---|---|
| **Matthew uses the word kingdom 7 times without specifying it, but in all cases it is applicable to the K of G only.** | |
| *Matthew 4:23* And Jesus went about all Galilee, teaching in their synagogues, and preaching the **gospel of the kingdom**, and healing all manner of sickness and all manner of disease among the people. | Matthew is addressing his book to the Hebrew people. He does not want to juggle two kingdoms at once. They understand the K of H quite well, but they were not even aware of the nature of the K of G, so in these instances he does not give this any kingdom designation. |
| *Matthew 6:13* And lead us not into temptation, but deliver us from evil: For thine is the **kingdom,** and the <u>power, and the glory</u>, for ever. Amen. | Christ's kingdom is in power and glory. But, at that time it could not be said, "thine is the **kingdom of heaven**—and the power and the glory." There was no K of H, howbeit its imminence. |
| *Matthew 9:35* And Jesus went about all the cities and villages, teaching in their synagogues, and preaching the **gospel of the kingdom**, and healing every sickness and every disease among the people. | This is the second time Matthew speaks of the "gospel" of the kingdom, and again he does not call it K of H, since the K of H is not a message of personal salvation and redemption. |
| *Matthew 13:19* When any one heareth the word of the **kingdom**, and understandeth it not, then cometh the wicked one, and catcheth away that which was sown in his heart. This is he which received seed by the way side. | This is in the context of the K of H, but it also applies to the K of G (Mark 4:14-29; Luke 8:5-18), so Matthew uses the generic "kingdom" in order to leave it open to either. |
| *Matthew 20:21* And he said unto her, What wilt thou? She saith unto him, Grant that these my two sons may sit, the one on thy right hand, and the other on the left, in **thy kingdom**. | Since this speaks of a future event of sitting in his kingdom, it could not be called the K of H, for at that time the K of H has merged with the K of G to become "his kingdom." |
| *Matthew 24:14* And this **gospel of the kingdom** shall be preached in all the world for a witness unto all nations; and then shall the end come. | This is the 3rd time he spoke of the "gospel" of the K. At that time (just before the second coming of Christ), the K of G will be preached as "his kingdom," thus "the gospel of the kingdom." |
| *Matthew 25:34* Then shall the King say unto them on his right hand, Come, ye blessed of my Father, inherit the **kingdom** prepared for you from the foundation of the world: | The kingdoms have merged into "his kingdom" right after the start of the Millennium, so it would have been incorrect for Matthew to label it as the K of H. |

| | |
|---|---|
| **Matthew speaks of His kingdom, the Father's Kingdom, or Thy Kingdom 5 times.** If he had designated any of these as the K of H, he would have destroyed the distinction the Holy Spirit has so carefully maintained. | |
| *Matthew 6:10* Thy **kingdom** come. Thy will be done in earth, as it is in heaven. | "Thy Kingdom" is the Millennium kingdom—the K that will execute the will of God on the "earth." |
| *Matthew 13:41* The Son of man shall send forth his angels, and they shall gather out of **his kingdom** all things that offend, and them which do iniquity;<br>　42 And shall cast them into a furnace of fire: there shall be wailing and gnashing of teeth.<br>　43 Then shall the righteous shine forth as the sun in the **kingdom of their Father**. Who hath ears to hear, let him hear. | At this time – the beginning of the Millennium – both kingdoms will have merged into **His Kingdom**, but there will still be tares in the kingdom of heaven. At end of the Millennium, after the purging, Christ turns his K over to the Father where only the righteous shine forth in the kingdom of their Father. This passage is a marvelously accurate use of the terms. |
| *Matthew 16:28* Verily I say unto you, There be some standing here, which shall not taste of death, till they see the Son of man coming in **his kingdom**. | Mark 9:1 calls this experience the K of G. The fulfillment of it came in the next chapter when three of them saw Jesus transformed and speaking with Moses and Elijah. So the K of God and His K are the same at that time. |
| *Matthew 26:29* But I say unto you, I will not drink henceforth of this fruit of the vine, until that day when I drink it new with you in **my Father's kingdom**. | A kingdom that could contain individuals drinking wine with Jesus must be future, and the Millennium is the earliest possible date. Notice that, by the time the wine is served at The Marriage Supper of the Lamb, the tares have been purged and "his kingdom" has become the "Father's kingdom." |

**Matthew does not designate "which" kingdom five times, while Mark and Luke do.** In four of these five instances, if Matthew had designated it as K of H, he would have destroyed the otherwise carefully maintained distinction.

| | | |
|---|---|---|
| *Matthew 19:29* And every one that hath forsaken houses, or brethren, or sisters, or father, or mother, or wife, or children, or lands, <u>for my name's sake</u>, shall receive an hundredfold, and shall inherit everlasting life.<br><br>30 But many that are first shall be last; and the last shall be first. | If Matthew had specified this as K of H, he would have been stating that the K of H was then present as an institution so as to permit someone to make sacrifices on behalf of it. Such was true of the K of G, but not the K of H. | *Luke 18:29* And he said unto them, Verily I say unto you, There is no man that hath left house, or parents, or brethren, or wife, or children, for the **kingdom of God's** sake,<br><br>30 Who shall not receive manifold more in this present time, and in the world to come life everlasting. |
| *Matthew 24:32* Now learn a parable of the fig tree; When his branch is yet tender, and putteth forth leaves, ye know that summer is nigh:<br><br>33 So likewise ye, when ye shall see all these things, <u>know that it is near, even at the doors</u>.<br><br>34 Verily I say unto you, This generation shall not pass, till all these things be fulfilled.<br><br>35 Heaven and earth shall pass away, but my words shall not pass away. | If Matthew had referred to this as K of H, he would have confused the nature of the K of H, for he is speaking to Jews concerning the reestablishment of their nation in the last days, just prior to the rapture of the Church.<br><br>Luke adds the concept of additional trees budding (additional nations coming into their own). This is as it should be, since the Gentile nations are concerned with the K of G, not the K of H. | *Luke 21:29* Behold the fig tree, and all the trees;<br><br>30 When they now shoot forth, ye see and know of your own selves that summer is now nigh at hand.<br><br>31 So likewise ye, when ye see these things come to pass, know ye that the **kingdom of God** is nigh at hand.<br><br>32 Verily I say unto you, This generation shall not pass away, till all be fulfilled.<br><br>33 Heaven and earth shall pass away: but my words shall not pass away. |
| *Matthew 27:57* When the even was come, there came a rich man of Arimathæa, named Joseph, who also himself <u>was Jesus' disciple</u>: | This could have been stated either way and not confused the distinction, but since Matthew did not call it K of H and Luke did not leave it undesignated, Joseph must have been well instructed in the kingdoms, hence his precise choice of expressing his anticipation. | *Luke 23:51* (The same had not consented to the counsel and deed of them;) he was of Arimathæa, a city of the Jews: who also himself waited for the **kingdom of God**. |

158

*Matthew 5:28* But I say unto you, That whosoever looketh on a woman to lust after her hath committed adultery with her already in his heart.

29 And if thy right eye offend thee, pluck it out, and cast it from thee: for it is profitable for thee that <u>one of thy members should perish,</u> and not that thy whole body should be cast into hell.

*Matthew 18:9* And if thine eye offend thee, pluck it out, and cast it from thee: it is better for thee to <u>enter into life</u> with one eye, rather than having two eyes to be cast into hell fire.

Both times that Matthew addresses this subject, he is careful not to signify it as K of H. The issue is personal worthiness to enter into the K — to enter into life, keep from perishing, and avoid being cast into hell. This would not apply to the K of H, because there, one cannot personally enter into eternal life or sustain a relationship whereby he is guaranteed to not perish. The entrance into life (into the kingdom) could only occur while in this life.

*Mark 9:47* And if thine eye offend thee, pluck it out: it is better for thee to enter into the **kingdom of God** with one eye, than having two eyes to be cast into hell fire:

| | |
|---|---|
| *Mark 9:1*<br>And he said unto them, Verily I say unto you, That there be some of them that stand here, which shall not taste of death, till they have seen the **kingdom of God** come with <u>power</u>. | If the transfiguration that followed had been called the K of H, then the distinctions could not be maintained. |
| *Mark 10:15*<br>15 Verily I say unto you, Whosoever shall not receive the **kingdom of God** as a little child, he shall not enter therein. | If he had spoken of "receiving" the K of H as a child, then it could have been assumed that the K was available on an individual basis by faith. |
| *Mark 12:34*)<br>34 And when Jesus saw that he answered discreetly, he said unto him, Thou art not far from the **kingdom of God**. And no man after that durst ask him any question. | Only **in** the K of G could one have been **nearing** the K of G on the basis of his individual beliefs. |
| *Mark 14:25*<br>25 Verily I say unto you, I will drink no more of the fruit of the vine, until that day that I drink it new in the **kingdom of God**. | We already saw that the wine is not served until the chaff is removed and the K of H has merged into the K of the Father. |
| *Luke 9:27*<br>27 But I tell you of a truth, there be some standing here, which shall not taste of death, till they see the **kingdom of God**. | See Mark 9:1 above. |
| *Luke 11:20*<br>20 But if I with the finger of God cast out devils, no doubt the **kingdom of God** is come upon you. | The K of G was "upon" them at that moment, based on the manifestation of power. This made it a personal event, something that cannot be true of the K of H. |
| *Luke 16:16*<br>16 The law and the prophets were until John: since that time the **kingdom of God** is preached, and every man presseth into it. | It could not be said that men were individually "pressing into" the K of H. |
| *Luke 17:20*<br>20 And when he was demanded of the Pharisees, when the **kingdom of God** should come, he answered them and said, The **kingdom of God** cometh not with observation. | The K of G was not at that time an event that could be observed, whereas the K of H will come as a very visible phenomenon. |
| *Luke 17:21*)<br>21 Neither shall they say, Lo here! or, lo there! for, behold, the **kingdom of God** is within you. | The K of G is defined as an internal experience, not a political event. |
| *Luke 18:29*<br>29 And he said unto them, Verily I say unto you, There is no man that hath left house, or parents, or brethren, or wife, or children, for the **kingdom of God**'s sake…. | If it had told us that they were denying themselves for the K of H, then the K of H would have been a present reality, which it was not. |

| | |
|---|---|
| *John 3:3*<br>3 Jesus answered and said unto him, Verily, verily, I say unto thee, Except a man be born again, he cannot see the **kingdom of God**. | There will be tares in the K of H who will "see" it, but only those who are born again will ever get in a position to actually see Jesus in his glory, i.e., see the K of G. |
| *Acts 8:12*<br>12 But when they believed Philip preaching the things concerning the **kingdom of God**, and the name of Jesus Christ, they were baptized, both men and women. | If he had called the message of the early Church the K of H, it would have contradicted the many distinctions heretofore so carefully maintained. |
| *Romans 14:17*<br>For the **kingdom of God** is not meat and drink; but righteousness, and peace, and joy in the Holy Ghost. | This is a clear definition of the K of G that is in contradiction to all that is said of the K of H. |
| *Colossians 4:11*<br>11 And Jesus, which is called Justus, who are of the circumcision. These only are my fellowworkers unto the **kingdom of God**, which have been a comfort unto me. | The workers in the Church were working in the K of G, not the K of H. |

A Number has been assigned to each passage as they appear chronologically. This number appears through the book as a means to cross reference the passage as it appears in different tables.

| Comment | Matthew | Mark | Luke | Other |
|---|---|---|---|---|
| **Peculiar**<br>John the Baptist preached the K of H only. Jesus preached both. | *Matthew 3:1* In those days came John the Baptist, preaching in the wilderness of Judæa,<br>    2 And saying, Repent ye: for the **kingdom of heaven** is at hand. | *Mark 1:4* John did baptize in the wilderness, and preach the <u>baptism of repentance</u> for the remission of sins. [*Since Mark never mentions the K of H, he did not designate this as did Matthew.*] | | |
| **Secular**<br><br>The world's kingdoms are in competition with God's kingdom. | *Matthew 4:8* Again, the devil taketh him up into an exceeding high mountain, and sheweth him all the **kingdoms** of the world, and the glory of them;<br><br>*Matt. 24:7* For nation shall rise against nation, and **kingdom** against **kingdom**: and there shall be famines, and pestilences, and earthquakes, in divers places.<br>    8 All these *are* the beginning of sorrows. | *Mark 13:8* For nation shall rise against nation, and kingdom against kingdom:<br><br>*Mark 6:23* And he sware unto her, Whatsoever thou shalt ask of me, I will give it thee, unto the half of **my kingdom**.<br><br>*Mark 11:10* Blessed be the **kingdom of our father David,** that cometh in the name of the Lord: | *Luke 1:33* And he shall reign over the house of Jacob for ever; and of his **kingdom** there shall be no end.<br><br>*Luke 11:17* Every **kingdom** divided against itself is brought to desolation;…<br><br>*Luke 21:10* Nation shall rise against nation, and **kingdom against kingdom**:<br><br>*Luke 22:29* And I appoint unto you a **kingdom**, as my Father hath appointed unto me; | *Hebrews 12:28* Wherefore we receiving a **kingdom** which cannot be moved….<br>*James 2:5* Hath not God chosen the poor of this world rich in faith, and heirs of the **kingdom** which he hath promised to them that love him?<br>*Revelation 16:10* And the fifth angel poured out his vial upon the seat of the beast; and **his kingdom** was full of darkness; and they gnawed their tongues for pain,<br>*Revelation 17:12* And the ten horns which thou sawest are ten kings, which have received no **kingdom** as yet; but receive power as <u>kings</u> one hour with the beast.<br>    17 For God hath put in their hearts to fulfil his will, and to agree, and give **their kingdom** unto the beast, until the words of God shall be fulfilled.<br>*Acts 1:6* When they therefore were come together, they asked of him, saying, Lord, wilt thou at this time restore again the **kingdom to Israel?**<br>    7 And he said unto them, It is <u>not for you to know the times or the seasons</u>, which the Father hath put in his own power.<br>*Revelation 11:15* And the seventh angel sounded; and there were great voices in heaven, saying, **The kingdoms of this world are become the kingdoms of our Lord**, and of his Christ; and he shall reign for ever and ever. |

162

| | | | | |
|---|---|---|---|---|
| **Common**<br>After John was put in prison, Jesus began to preach of both kingdoms. "Believe" is never applied to the K of H. – Mark 1:15 Matthew never tells anyone to believe. | *Matthew 4:12* Now <u>when Jesus had heard that John was cast into prison</u>, he departed into Galilee;<br>17 From <u>that time</u> Jesus began to preach, and to say, Repent: for the **kingdom of heaven** is at hand. | *Mark 1:14* Now <u>after that John was put in prison</u>, Jesus came into Galilee, preaching the <u>gospel</u> of the **kingdom of God**,<br>15 And saying, The time is fulfilled, and the **kingdom of God** is at hand: repent ye, and <u>believe</u> the gospel. | *Luke 4:43* And he said unto them, I must preach the **kingdom of God** to other cities also: for therefore am I sent.<br><br>*Luke 8:1* ...he went throughout every city and village, preaching and shewing the glad tidings of the **kingdom of God:** | |
| **Common**<br>Healing is manifested in the preaching of both kingdoms (Matt. 10:7), but Matthew seems to avoid the K of H designation when he links it to "gospel." The K of H message is never called gospel. When Matthew does use the word, gospel, he chooses not to link it to the K of H. | *Matthew 4:23* And Jesus went about all Galilee, teaching in their synagogues, and preaching the **gospel of the kingdom**, and healing all manner of sickness and all manner of disease among the people.<br>24 And his fame went throughout all Syria: and they brought unto him all sick people that were taken with divers diseases and torments, and those which were possessed with devils, and those which were lunatick, and those that had the palsy; and he healed them.<br><br>**Matthew 9:35** And Jesus went about all the cities and villages, teaching in their synagogues, and preaching the **gospel of the kingdom**, and healing every sickness and every disease among the people.<br><br>*Matthew 10:7* And as ye go, preach, saying, The **kingdom of heaven** is at hand.<br>8 <u>Heal</u> the sick, cleanse the lepers, raise the dead, cast out devils: freely ye have received, freely give. | | *Luke 10:9* And heal **the sick that are therein, and say unto them, The kingdom of God is come nigh unto you.**<br>11 Even the very dust of your city, which cleaveth on us, we do wipe off against you: notwithstanding be ye sure of this, that the **kingdom of God** is come nigh unto you.<br><br>*Luke 9:2* And he sent them to preach **the kingdom of God**, and to heal the sick.<br><br>*Luke 9:11* And the people, when they knew it, followed him: and he received them, and spake unto them of the **kingdom of God**, and healed them that had need of healing. | |
| **Peculiar**<br>Matthew speaks of the poor in spirit, whereas Luke speaks of the poor.<br>The poor in spirit is not an appropriate condition for one who is in the K of G.<br>When Matthew speaks of the poor, he does not designate it as K of H. | *Matthew 5:3* Blessed *are* the poor in spirit: for theirs is the **kingdom of heaven**.<br>[*Notice that in this list of the K of H, it is presented as relief from the state of being poor in spirit. Those who mourn will be comforted. Those who hunger will be filled. They inherit so they **won't** be poor in spirit, mourn, or be unfulfilled in righteousness.*]<br><br>*Matthew 11:5* The blind receive their sight, and the lame walk, the lepers are cleansed, and the deaf hear, the dead are raised up, and the **poor have the gospel preached** to them. | | *Luke 6:20* Blessed be ye <u>poor</u>: for yours is the **kingdom of God**.<br><br>*Luke 4:18* The Spirit of the Lord is upon me, because he hath anointed me to <u>preach the gospel to the poor</u>; he hath sent me to heal the brokenhearted, to preach deliverance to the captives, and recovering of sight to the blind, to set at liberty them that are bruised... | **James 2:5** Hath not God chosen the <u>poor</u> of this world rich in faith, and heirs of the **kingdom** which he hath promised to them that love him.<br><br>[*The K of G is personal.*] |
| **Peculiar**<br>The K of H is offered as an answer to those who are already persecuted, | *5:10* Blessed *are* they which are persecuted for righteousness' sake: for theirs is the **kingdom of heaven**. | *Mark 10:29* And Jesus answered and said, Verily I say unto you, There is no man that hath left house, or brethren, or sisters, or father, or mother, or wife, or children, or lands, for <u>my sake, and **the gospel's**</u>,<br>30 But he shall receive an hundredfold | *Luke 6:22* Blessed are ye, when men shall hate you, and when they shall separate you from their company, and shall reproach you, and cast out your name as evil, for the Son of man's sake.<br>23 Rejoice ye in that day, and leap for | |

| | | | |
|---|---|---|---|
| whereas the K of G will **bring** persecution. | | now in this time, houses, and brethren, and sisters, and mothers, and children, and lands, with persecutions; and in the world to come eternal life. | joy: for, behold, your reward is great in heaven: for in the like manner did their fathers unto the prophets. |
| **Peculiar** The commandments will be kept in the K of H. One can be "called" least or great in the K of H. | *Matthew* **5:19** Whosoever therefore shall break one of these least commandments, and shall teach men so, he shall be called the least in the: **kingdom of heaven** but whosoever shall do and teach *them,* the same shall be called great in the **kingdom of heaven.** | | |
| **Common** Both kingdoms demand righteousness. (See 7:21.) | *Matthew* **5:20** For I say unto you, That except your righteousness shall exceed *the righteousness* of the scribes and Pharisees, ye shall in no case enter into the **kingdom of heaven**. | *Luke* **12:31** But rather seek ye the **kingdom of God**; and all these things shall be added unto you. | *Hebrews* **1:8** But unto the Son he saith, Thy throne, O God, is for ever and ever: a sceptre of righteousness is the sceptre of **thy kingdom.**<br><br>*1 Corinthians* **6:9** Know ye not that the unrighteous shall not inherit the **kingdom of God**? Be not deceived: neither fornicators, nor idolaters, nor adulterers, nor effeminate, nor abusers of themselves with mankind,<br> 10 Nor thieves, nor covetous, nor drunkards, nor revilers, nor extortioners, shall inherit the **kingdom of God.**<br><br>*Galatians* **5:21** Envyings, murders, drunkenness, revellings, and such like: of the which I tell you before, as I have also told you in time past, that they which do such things shall not inherit the **kingdom of God.**<br><br>*Ephesians* **5:5** For this ye know, that no whoremonger, nor unclean person, nor covetous man, who is an idolater, hath any inheritance in the **kingdom of Christ and of God.**<br><br>**Matthew 13:43** Then shall the righteous shine forth as the sun in **the kingdom of their Father.** Who hath ears to hear, let him hear. |
| **Common**, in that both Ks will co-exist on the earth. **Peculiar** in that the K of H must "come" as an event to the earth, whereas the K of G can be entered presently. It is undesignated because when the K does come to the earth, it will be both kingdoms having merged into his K. <br><br>The K of H and the K of G and | *Matthew* **6:10** Thy **kingdom** come. Thy will be done in earth, as *it is* in heaven.<br><br>*Matthew* **8:11** And I say unto you, That many shall come from the east and west, and shall sit down with Abraham, and Isaac, and Jacob, in the **kingdom of heaven**<br><br>**20:21** And he said unto her, What wilt thou? She saith unto him, Grant that these my two sons may sit, the one on thy right hand, and the other on the left, in **thy kingdom.** | *Mark* **11:10** Blessed be the **kingdom** of our father David, that cometh in the name of the Lord: Hosanna in the highest. | *Luke* **11:2** And he said unto them, When ye pray, say, Our Father which art in heaven, Hallowed be thy name. **Thy kingdom** come. Thy will be done, as in heaven, so in earth.<br><br>*Luke* **13:28** There shall be weeping and gnashing of teeth, when ye shall see Abraham, and Isaac, and Jacob, and all the prophets, in the **kingdom of God**, and you yourselves thrust out.<br> 29 And they shall come from the east, and from the west, and from the north, and from the south, and shall sit down **in the kingdom of God**.<br><br>*Luke* **19:11** And as they heard these things, he added and spake a parable, because he was nigh to Jerusalem, and because they thought that the **kingdom of God** should immediately appear.<br><br>*Luke* **22:29** And I appoint unto you a **kingdom**, as my Father hath appointed unto me;<br> 30 That ye may eat and drink at my table in **my kingdom**, and sit on thrones judging the twelve tribes of Israel.<br><br>*Luke* **23:42** And he said unto Jesus, Lord, remember me when thou comest into **thy kingdom.** |

| | | | | |
|---|---|---|---|---|
| "thy K" are all the same during the Millennium. | | | | |
| **Peculiar** The kingdom that is Christ's, the kingdom that is power and glory, is the K of G, though the K of G will bring about the K of H upon the earth during the Millennium. | *6:13* And lead us not into temptation, but deliver us from evil: For thine is the **kingdom**, and the power, and the glory, for ever. Amen. *Matthew 16:28* Verily I say unto you, There be some standing here, which shall not taste of death, till they see the Son of man coming in **his kingdom**. | *Mark 9:1* And he said unto them, Verily I say unto you, That there be some of them that stand here, which shall not taste of death, till they have seen the **kingdom of God** come with power. | *Luke 11:20* But if I with the finger of God cast out devils, no doubt the **kingdom of God** is come *upon you.* *Luke 22:29* And I appoint unto you a kingdom, as my Father hath appointed unto me;   30 That ye may eat and drink at my table in my kingdom, and sit on thrones judging the twelve tribes of Israel. | *1 Thessalonians 2:12* That ye would walk worthy of God, who hath called you unto **his kingdom and glory.** *Revelation 12:10* And I heard a loud voice saying in heaven, Now is come salvation, and strength, and **the kingdom of our God**, and the power of his Christ: for the accuser of our brethren is cast down,… |
| **Peculiar** The K of G should be sought as a present reality. | *Matthew 6:33* But seek ye first the **kingdom of God**, and his righteousness; and all these things shall be added unto you. | | *Luke 12:31* But rather seek ye the **kingdom of God**; and all these things shall be added unto you. | |

| | |
|---|---|
| **Peculiar** The K of H is predicated upon obedience, doing the will of God. The K of H is an institution to be entered at a future date in the presence of Jesus. | *Matthew 7:21* Not every one that saith unto me, Lord, Lord, shall enter into the **kingdom of heaven**; but he that doeth the will of my Father which is in heaven.   22 Many will say to me in that day, Lord, Lord, have we not prophesied in thy name? and in thy name have cast out devils? and in thy name done many wonderful works?   23 And then will I profess unto them, I never knew you: depart from me, ye that work iniquity.   24 Therefore whosoever heareth these sayings of mine, and doeth them, I will liken him unto a wise man, which built his house upon a rock: |
| **Common** Both kingdoms merge on earth during the Millennium. At that time, the kingdom will be a place to sit down in. O T saints will also be in the K. | *Matthew 8:11* And I say unto you, That many shall come from the east and west, and shall sit down with Abraham, and Isaac, and Jacob, in the **kingdom of heaven**. [He calls it the K of H here because in the next verse, he wants it to be clear from which kingdom the children of the kingdom will be cast out.]     *Luke 13:28* There shall be weeping and gnashing of teeth, when ye shall see Abraham, and Isaac, and Jacob, and all the prophets, in the **kingdom of God**, and you yourselves thrust out.   29 And they shall come from the east, and from the west, and from the north, and from the south, and shall sit down in **the kingdom of God.** |
| **Peculiar** The children of the K of H will be cast out, while the strangers (Gentiles) will sit down and dine. This could not be said of the K | *Matthew 8:12* But the children of the **kingdom** [*of H, verse 11*] shall be cast out into outer darkness: there shall be weeping and gnashing of teeth.     *Luke 14:15* And when one of them that sat at meat with him heard these things, he said unto him, Blessed is he that shall eat bread in the **kingdom of God.**   16 Then said he unto him, A certain man made a great supper, and bade many:   17 And sent his servant at supper time to say to them that were bidden, Come; for all things are now ready.   18 And they all with one consent began to make excuse. The first said unto him, I have bought a piece of ground, and I must needs go and see it: I pray thee have me excused.   19 And another said, I have bought five yoke of oxen, and I go to prove them: I pray thee have me excused.   20 And another said, I have married a wife, and therefore I cannot come. |

| | | | |
|---|---|---|---|
| of G. This is one of those verses that is absolutely critical to maintaining the distinction. They were invited but were never in the kingdom; i.e., "received him not." | | 21 So that servant came, and shewed his lord these things. Then the master of the house being angry said to his servant, Go out quickly into the streets and lanes of the city, and bring in hither the poor, and the maimed, and the halt, and the blind.<br><br>22 And the servant said, Lord, it is done as thou hast commanded, and yet there is room.<br><br>23 And the lord said unto the servant, Go out into the highways and hedges, and compel them to come in, that my house may be filled.<br><br>24 For I say unto you, That <u>none of those men which were bidden shall taste of my supper.</u> | |
| **See 4:23**<br>Matt. does not designate this as K of H because it is never called gospel, as in a message to believe and presently experience. | *Matthew 9:35* And Jesus went about all the cities and villages, teaching in their synagogues, and preaching the **gospel of the kingdom**, and healing every sickness and every disease among the people. | | |
| **Peculiar**<br>In Matthew, Jesus commands them to not take the K of H message to the Gentiles.<br><br>The commission to the 12 is called K of H in Matthew, but Mark just says "repent", whereas Luke addresses the 70 to preach the K of G. (See 4:23.)<br><br>"Go not to the Gentiles" is linked with preaching the K of H. Luke 9:2 & 10:1-11 do not forbid going to Gentiles.<br><br>The K of H was soon to come. The K of G | *Matthew 10:1* And when he had called unto him his <u>twelve disciples</u>, he gave them power against unclean spirits, to cast them out, and to heal all manner of sickness and all manner of disease.<br><br>**10:5** <u>These twelve</u> Jesus sent forth, and commanded them, saying, <u>Go not into the way of the Gentiles</u>, and into *any* city of the Samaritans enter ye not:<br><br>6 But go rather to <u>the lost sheep of the house of Israel.</u><br><br>7 And as ye go, preach, saying, The **kingdom of heaven** is at hand, | *Mark 6:7* And he called unto him <u>the twelve</u>, and began to send them forth by two and two; and gave them power over unclean spirits;<br><br>8 And commanded them that they should take nothing for their journey, save a staff only; no scrip, no bread, no money in their purse:<br><br>9 But be shod with sandals; and not put on two coats.<br><br>10 And he said unto them, In what place soever ye enter into an house, there abide till ye depart from that place.<br><br>11 And whosoever shall not receive you, nor hear you, when ye depart thence, shake off the dust under your feet for a testimony against them. Verily I say unto you, It shall be more tolerable for Sodom and Gomorrha in the day of judgment, than for that city.<br><br>12 And they went out, and <u>preached that men should repent.</u><br><br>13 And they cast out many devils, and anointed with oil many that were sick, and healed them. | *Luke 10:1* After these things the Lord appointed <u>other seventy also</u>, and sent them two and two before his face into every city and place, whither he himself would come.<br><br>4 Carry neither purse, nor scrip, nor shoes: and salute no man by the way.<br><br>5 And into whatsoever house ye enter, first say, Peace be to this house.<br><br>6 And if the son of peace be there, your peace shall rest upon it: if not, it shall turn to you again.<br><br>7 And in the same house remain, eating and drinking such things as they give: for the labourer is worthy of his hire. Go not from house to house.<br><br>8 And into whatsoever city ye enter, and they receive you, eat such things as are set before you:<br><br>9 And heal the sick that are therein, and say unto them, **The kingdom of God** is <u>come nigh unto you.</u><br><br>10 But into whatsoever city ye enter, and they receive you not, go your ways out into the streets of the same, and say,<br><br>11 Even the very dust of your city, which cleaveth on us, we do wipe off against you: notwithstanding be ye sure of this, that the **kingdom of God** <u>is come nigh unto you.</u> |

| | | | | |
|---|---|---|---|---|
| could come nigh in their immediate experience. | | | | |
| **Common** John the Baptist was at the threshold of the K of H and K of G. Neither had yet come. Both are greater than the O. T. era. | *Matthew 11:11* Verily I say unto you, Among them that are born of women there hath not risen a greater than John the Baptist: notwithstanding he that is least in the **kingdom of heaven** is greater than he. | | *Luke 7:28* For I say unto you, Among those that are born of women there is not a greater prophet than John the Baptist: but he that is least in **the kingdom of God** is greater than he. | |
| **Peculiar** The K of H is of such a nature that it is subject to violent overthrow. | *Matthew 11:12* And from the days of John the Baptist until now the **kingdom of heaven** suffereth violence, and the violent take it by force. | | *Luke 16:16* The law and the prophets were until John: since that time the **kingdom of God** is preached, and every man presseth into it. | |
| **Common** Satan's kingdom. | *Matthew 12:25* And Jesus knew their thoughts, and said unto them, Every **kingdom** divided against itself is brought to desolation; and every city or house divided against itself shall not stand: 26 And if Satan cast out Satan, he is divided against himself; how shall then his **kingdom** stand? 27 And if I by Beelzebub cast out devils, by whom do your children cast *them* out? therefore they shall be your judges. | | *Luke 4:5* And the devil, taking him up into an high mountain, shewed unto him all **the kingdoms of the world** in a moment of time. 6 And the devil said unto him, All this power will I give thee, and the glory of them: for that is delivered unto me; and to whomsoever I will I give it. | *John 12:31* Now is the judgment of this world: now shall **the prince of this world** be cast out. *2 Corinthians 4:3* But if our gospel be hid, it is hid to them that are lost: 4 In whom the **god of this world** hath blinded the minds of them which believe not, lest the light of the glorious gospel of Christ, who is the image of God, should shine unto them. |
| **Peculiar** Power over devils manifests the immediate presence of the K of G. This is one of the five places that Matthew elects to designate it as K of G, and for good reason. It would totally confuse the natures of the two to have done otherwise. | *Matthew 12:28* But if I cast out devils by the Spirit of God, then the **kingdom of God** is come unto you. | | *Luke 11:20* But if I with the finger of God cast out devils, no doubt the **kingdom of God** is come upon you. | *1 Corinthians 4:20* For the **kingdom of God** is not in word, but in power. *Revelation 12:10* And I heard a loud voice saying in heaven, Now is come salvation, and strength, and **the kingdom of our God**, and the power of his Christ: <u>for the accuser of our brethren is cast down,</u> which accused them before our God day and night. |

| | | | | |
|---|---|---|---|---|
| **Common**<br><br>Both kingdoms are a mystery. And to most Bible students, the difference in the two kingdoms remains a mystery. 1 Cor. 4:1 speaks in the plural concerning mysteries. | *Matthew 13:10* And the disciples came, and said unto him, Why speakest thou unto them in parables?<br><br>11 He answered and said unto them, Because it is given unto you to know the mysteries of the **kingdom of heaven**, but to them it is not given. | *Mark 4:11* And he said unto them, Unto you it is given to know the mystery of the **kingdom of God**: but unto them that are without, all these things are done in parables: | *Luke 8:10* And he said, Unto you it is given to know the mysteries of **the kingdom of God**: but to others in parables; that seeing they might not see, and hearing they might not understand. | *1 Corinthians 4:1* Let a man so account of us, as of the ministers of Christ, and stewards of the mysteries of God. |
| **Common**<br><br>The K of H is under discussion here as seen by verse 11.Matthew just calls it "kingdom" without designating it in verse 19, because it is applicable to either kingdom. The two kingdoms are alike in the manner in which the message is received. | *Matthew 13:18* Hear ye therefore the parable of the sower.<br><br>19 When any one heareth the word of the **kingdom**, [of heaven, verse 11] and understandeth *it* not, then cometh the wicked *one* and catcheth away that which was sown in his heart. This is he which received seed by the way side.<br><br>20 But he that received the seed into stony places, the same is he that heareth the word, and anon with joy receiveth it;<br><br>21 Yet hath he not root in himself, but dureth for a while: for when tribulation or persecution ariseth because of the word, by and by he is offended.<br><br>22 He also that received seed among the thorns is he that heareth the word; and the care of this world, and the deceitfulness of riches, choke the word, and *he* becometh unfruitful.<br><br>23 But he that received seed into the good ground is he that heareth the word, and understandeth it; which also beareth fruit, and bringeth forth, some an hundredfold, some sixty, some thirty. | *Mark 4:14* The sower soweth the word.<br><br>15 And these are they by the way side, where the word is sown; but when they have heard, Satan cometh immediately, and taketh away the word that was sown in their hearts.<br><br>16 And these are they likewise which are sown on stony ground; who, when they have heard the word, immediately receive it with gladness;<br><br>17 And have no root in themselves, and so endure but for a time: afterward, when affliction or persecution ariseth for the word's sake, immediately they are offended.<br><br>18 And these are they which are sown among thorns; such as hear the word,<br><br>19 And the cares of this world, and the deceitfulness of riches, and the lusts of other things entering in, choke the word, and it becometh unfruitful.<br><br>20 And these are they which are sown on good ground; such as hear the word, and receive it, and bring forth fruit, some thirtyfold, some sixty, and some an hundred. | *Luke 8:11* . . .The seed is the word of God.<br><br>12 Those by the way side are they that hear; then cometh the devil, and taketh away the word out of their hearts, lest they should believe and be saved.<br><br>13 They on the rock are they, which, when they hear, receive the word with joy; and these have no root, which for a while believe, and in time of temptation fall away.<br><br>14 And that which fell among thorns are they, which, when they have heard, go forth, and are choked with cares and riches and pleasures of this life, and bring no fruit to perfection.<br><br>15 But that on the good ground are they, which in an honest and good heart, having heard the word, keep it, and bring forth fruit with patience. | |
| **Peculiar**<br>The tares are actually in the K of H and are not separated from it until the time of the harvest, which is the day of judgment. Since the K of H is a political event, all who live on the earth will be "in" the K at that time, | *Matthew 13:24* Another parable put he forth unto them, saying, The **kingdom of heaven** is likened unto a man which sowed good seed in his field:<br><br>25 But while men slept, his enemy came and sowed tares among the wheat, and went his way.<br><br>26 But when the blade was sprung up, and brought forth fruit, then appeared the tares also.<br><br>27 So the servants of the householder came and said | *Mark 4:26* And he said, So is the **kingdom of God**, as if a man should cast seed into the ground;<br><br>27 And should sleep, and rise night and day, and the seed should spring and grow up, he knoweth not how.<br><br>28 For the earth bringeth forth fruit of herself; first the blade, then the ear, after that the full corn in the ear.<br><br>29 But when the fruit is brought forth, | | *2 Corinthians 11:13* For such are false apostles, deceitful workers, transforming themselves into the apostles of Christ.<br><br>14 And no marvel; for Satan himself is transformed into an angel of light.<br><br>15 Therefore it is no great thing if his ministers also be transformed as the ministers of righteousness; whose end shall be according to their works. |

| | | | | |
|---|---|---|---|---|
| whether they are a part of the K of G or not.<br><br>It is remarkable that Mark relates a similar event, of sowing seeds and of reaping the harvest, and designates it as the K of G, but he is careful not to include the part about its containing tares which are then burnt. If he had included burning of tares, we would have to conclude that some who are now in the Church—the K of G—will suffer everlasting fire in the day of judgment. | unto him, Sir, didst not thou sow good seed in thy field? from whence then hath it tares?<br><br>28 He said unto them, An enemy hath done this. The servants said unto him, Wilt thou then that we go and gather them up?<br><br>29 But he said, Nay; lest while ye gather up the tares, ye root up also the wheat with them.<br><br>30 Let <u>both grow together until the harvest</u>: and in the time of harvest I will say to the reapers, Gather ye together <u>first the tares</u>, and bind them in bundles to burn them: but gather the wheat into my barn. | immediately he putteth in the sickle, because the harvest is come. | | *1 Peter 1:23* Being born again, not of corruptible seed, but of incorruptible, by the word of God, which liveth and abideth for ever. |
| **Common**<br>The K of G and H are like grains of mustard seeds that become great trees with devils in them. The birds/devils are not false believers; they are spirit beings—devils. | *Matthew 13:31* Another parable put he forth unto them, saying, The **kingdom of heaven** is like to a grain of mustard seed, which a man took, and sowed in his field:<br><br>32 Which indeed is the least of all seeds: but when it is grown, it is the greatest among herbs, and becometh a tree, so that the birds of the air come and lodge in the branches thereof. | *Mark 4:30* And he said, Whereunto shall we liken **the kingdom of God?** or with what comparison shall we compare it?<br><br>31 It is like a grain of mustard seed, which, when it is sown in the earth, is less than all the seeds that be in the earth:<br><br>32 But when it is sown, it groweth up, and becometh greater than all herbs, and shooteth out great branches; so that the fowls of the air may lodge under the shadow of it. | | *Luke 13:18* Then said he, Unto what is the **kingdom of God** like? and whereunto shall I resemble it?<br><br>19 It is like a grain of mustard seed, which a man took, and cast into his garden; and it grew, and waxed a great tree; and the fowls of the air lodged in the branches of it. |
| **Common**<br>Both Kingdoms are corrupted from within by false doctrine.<br><br>Leaven is always viewed negatively. Matt. 16:6, 11, 12<br>Galatians 5:9 | *Matthew 13:33* Another parable spake he unto them; The **kingdom of heaven** is like unto leaven, which a woman took, and hid in three measures of meal, till the whole was leavened. | *Mark 8:15* And he charged them, saying, Take heed, beware of the leaven of the Pharisees, and of the leaven of Herod. | *Luke 13:20* And again he said, Whereunto shall I liken **the kingdom of God?**<br><br>21 It is like leaven, which a woman took and hid in three measures of meal, till the whole was leavened.<br><br>*Luke 12:1* Beware ye of the leaven of the Pharisees, which is hypocrisy. | *1 Corinthians 5:6* Your glorying is not good. Know ye not that a little leaven leaveneth the whole lump?<br><br>7 Purge out therefore the old leaven, that ye may be a new lump, as ye are unleavened. For even Christ our passover is sacrificed for us:<br><br>8 Therefore let us keep the feast, not with old leaven, neither with the leaven of malice and wickedness; but with the unleavened bread of sincerity and truth. |

| | | |
|---|---|---|
| **Peculiar**<br><br>This is dated as the end of the world when the angels reap the fields of the world of people. | *Matthew 13:36* Then Jesus sent the multitude away, and went into the house: and his disciples came unto him, saying, <u>Declare unto us the parable of the tares</u> of the field.<br> 37 He answered and said unto them, He that soweth the good seed is the Son of man;<br> 38 The field is the world; the good seed are the **children of the kingdom**; [of heaven 13:24] but the tares are the children of the wicked *one;*<br> 39 The enemy that sowed them is the devil; the harvest is the end of the world; and the reapers are the angels.<br> 40 As therefore the tares are gathered and burned in the fire; so shall it be in the <u>end of this world</u>. | *John 8:44* Ye are of your father the devil, and the lusts of your father ye will do. He was a murderer from the beginning, and abode not in the truth, because there is no truth in him. When he speaketh a lie, he speaketh of his own: for he is a liar, and the father of it.<br><br>*Philippians 3:18* (For many walk, of whom I have told you often, and now tell you even weeping, that they are the <u>enemies</u> of the cross of Christ:. . . .who mind earthly things.) |
| **Peculiar**<br>The K of H will merge with the K of G and become "the kingdom of their father" at the beginning of the Millennium. There is a switch of Kingdoms from "his" to the Father's. (See 5:20.) | *Matthew 13:41* The Son of man shall send forth his angels, and they shall gather <u>out of his</u> **kingdom** all things that offend, and them which do iniquity;<br>42 And shall cast them into a furnace of fire: there shall be wailing and gnashing of teeth.<br>43 Then shall the righteous shine forth as the sun in the **kingdom** of their Father. Who hath ears to hear, let him hear. | *2 Timothy 4:1* I charge thee therefore before God, and the Lord Jesus Christ, who shall judge the quick and the dead at his appearing and his **kingdom**;<br><br>*Revelation 12:10* And I heard a loud voice saying in heaven, Now is come salvation, and strength, and **the kingdom of our God**, and the <u>power of his Christ</u>: for the accuser of our brethren is cast down, which accused them before our God day and night. |

| | |
|---|---|
| **Peculiar**<br>The K of H is purchased as a field. | *Matthew 13:44* Again, the **kingdom of heaven** is like unto treasure hid in a field; the which when a man hath found, he hideth, and for joy thereof goeth and selleth all that he hath, and buyeth that field. |
| **Peculiar**<br>The K of H is purchased by Christ. | *Matthew 13:45* Again, the **kingdom of heaven** is like unto a merchant man, seeking goodly pearls:<br> 46 Who, when he had found one pearl of great price, went and sold all that he had, and bought it. |

| | | |
|---|---|---|
| **Peculiar**<br>Contains good and bad, and the bad will be severed first. This could be the end of the Millennium. | *Matthew 13:47* Again, the **kingdom of heaven** is like unto a net, that was cast into the sea, and gathered of every kind:<br> 48 Which, when it was full, they drew to shore, and sat down, and gathered the good into vessels, but cast the bad away.<br> 49 So shall it be at the end of the world: the angels shall come forth, and <u>sever the wicked</u> from among the just,<br> 50 And shall cast them into the furnace of fire: there shall be wailing and gnashing of teeth. | *Matthew13:30* Let <u>both grow together until the harvest</u>: and in the time of harvest I will say to the reapers, Gather ye together <u>first the tares,</u> and bind them in bundles to burn them: but gather the wheat into my barn. |

| | |
|---|---|
| **Peculiar**<br>A properly instructed scribe will hold truth that is both old and new. | *Matthew 13:51* Jesus saith unto them, Have ye understood all these things? They say unto him, Yea, Lord.<br> 52 Then said he unto them, Therefore every scribe *which is* instructed unto the **kingdom of heaven** is like unto a man *that is* an householder, which bringeth forth out of his treasure *things* new and old.<br> 53 And it came to pass, *that* when Jesus had finished these parables, he departed thence. |

| | | | | |
|---|---|---|---|---|
| **Peculiar**<br>The K of H is composed of both Old Testament and New Testament truth. This K of H teaching is associated with Jewish scribes. | *Matthew 16:19* And I will give unto thee the keys of the **kingdom of heaven**: and whatsoever thou shalt bind on earth shall be bound in heaven: and whatsoever thou shalt loose on earth shall be loosed in heaven. | | | *John 20:23* Whosesoever sins ye remit, they are remitted unto them; and whosesoever sins ye retain, they are retained. |
| **Peculiar** to the K of G.<br>Matthew does not call this manifestation the K of H.<br>The K of G and "his kingdom" are the same. (See 10.) | *Matthew 16:28* Verily I say unto you, There be some standing here, which shall not taste of death, till they see the Son of man coming in **his kingdom**. | *Mark 9:1* And he said unto them, Verily I say unto you, That there be some of them that stand here, which shall not taste of death, till they have seen the **kingdom of God** come with power. | *Luke 9:27* But I tell you of a truth, there be some standing here, which shall not taste of death, till they see the **kingdom of God.** | |
| **Peculiar**<br>Only in the earthly Millennial kingdom will some be greater and some lesser.<br>(See Matt. 18:4; 19:14.) | *Matthew 18:1* At the same time came the disciples unto Jesus, saying, Who is the greatest in the **kingdom of heaven**? | *Mark 9:33* And he came to Capernaum: and being in the house he asked them, What was it that ye disputed among yourselves by the way?<br>34 But they held their peace: for by the way they had disputed among themselves, <u>who should be the greatest.</u> | *Luke 9:46* Then there arose a reasoning among them, which of them should be greatest.<br>47 And Jesus, perceiving the thought of their heart, took a child, and set him by him,<br>48 And said unto them, Whosoever shall receive this child in my name receiveth me: and whosoever shall receive me receiveth him that sent me: for he that is least among you all, the same shall be great. | |
| **Common**<br>Child-like faith is essential in both kingdoms. Notice the difference in the wording. One must become as a little child to enter the K of H, whereas in Mark and Luke one must *receive* the K of G as a child. The K of H is not *received*, and the K of G does not have a character precondition. Matthew never speaks of receiving the K of H. (See Mark 10:15.) | *Matthew 18:2* And Jesus called a little child unto him, and set him in the midst of them,<br>3 And said, Verily I say unto you, Except ye be <u>converted, and become as little children</u>, ye shall not enter into the **kingdom of heaven**.<br>4 Whosoever therefore shall humble himself as this little child, the same is greatest in the **kingdom of heaven**.<br>**19:13** Then were there brought unto him little children, that he should put *his* hands on them, and pray: and the disciples rebuked them.<br>14 But Jesus said, Suffer little children, and forbid them not, to come unto me: for of such is the **kingdom of heaven**. | *Mark 10:14* But when Jesus saw it, he was much displeased, and said unto them, Suffer the little children to come unto me, and forbid them not: for of such is the **kingdom of God**.<br>15 Verily I say unto you, Whosoever shall not receive **the kingdom of God** as a little child, he shall not enter therein. | *Luke 9:46* Then there arose a reasoning among them, which of them <u>should be greatest.</u><br><br>*Luke 18:16* But Jesus called them unto him, and said, Suffer little children to come unto me, and forbid them not: for of such is the **kingdom of God**.<br>17 Verily I say unto you, Whosoever shall not receive **the kingdom of God** as a little child shall in no wise enter therein. | |
| **Peculiar** of the K of H. | *Matthew 18:4* Whosoever therefore shall humble himself as this little | *Mark 9:35* And he sat down, and called the twelve, and | *Luke 9:47* And Jesus, perceiving the thought of their heart, took a child, | |

| | | | |
|---|---|---|---|
| Only in the K of H is one greater or lesser. When speaking in the same vein, Mark and Luke are careful not to associate the idea of being greater with the K of G. | child, the same is greatest in the **kingdom of heaven**. 5 And whoso shall receive one such little child in my name receiveth me. 6 But whoso shall offend one of these little ones which believe in me, it were better for him that a millstone were hanged about his neck, and *that* he were drowned in the depth of the sea. | saith unto them, If any man desire to be first, the same shall be last of all, and servant of all. | and set him by him, 48 And said unto them, Whosoever shall receive this child in my name receiveth me: and whosoever shall receive me receiveth him that sent me: for he that is least among you all, the same shall be great. |
| **Peculiar** of the K of H. Parable of the king forgiving his stewards<br><br>One can be rejected after being forgiven if he fails to forgive his brother. | *Matthew 18:21* Then came Peter to him, and said, Lord, how oft shall my brother sin against me, and I forgive him? till seven times? 22 Jesus saith unto him, I say not unto thee, Until seven times: but, Until seventy times seven. 23 Therefore is the **kingdom of heaven** likened unto a certain king, which would take account of his servants. 24 And when he had begun to reckon, one was brought unto him, which owed him <u>ten thousand talents</u>. | *Mark 11:25* And when ye stand praying, forgive, if ye have ought against any: that your Father also which is in heaven may forgive you your trespasses. 26 But if ye do not forgive, neither will your Father which is in heaven forgive your trespasses. | *Luke 17:3* Take heed to yourselves: If thy brother trespass against thee, rebuke him; and if he repent, forgive him. 4 And if he trespass against thee seven times in a day, and seven times in a day turn again to thee, saying, I repent; thou shalt forgive him.<br><br>*Luke 6:37* Judge not, and ye shall not be judged: condemn not, and ye shall not be condemned: forgive, and ye shall be forgiven. |
| | | | *James 2:13* For he shall have judgment without mercy, that hath shewed no mercy; and mercy rejoiceth against judgment. |

25 But forasmuch as he had not to pay, his lord commanded him to be sold, and his wife, and children, and all that he had, and payment to be made.

26 The servant therefore fell down, and worshipped him, saying, Lord, have patience with me, and I will pay thee all.

27 Then the lord of that servant was moved with compassion, and loosed him, and forgave him the debt.

28 But the same servant went out, and found one of his fellowservants, which owed him an hundred pence: and he laid hands on him, and took *him* by the throat, saying, Pay me that thou owest.

29 And his fellowservant fell down at his feet, and besought him, saying, Have patience with me, and I will pay thee all.

30 And he would not: but went and cast him into prison, till he should pay the debt.

31 So when his fellowservants saw what was done, they were very sorry, and came and told unto their lord all that was done.

32 Then his lord, after that he had called him, said unto him, O thou wicked servant, I forgave thee all that debt, because thou desiredst me:

33 Shouldest not thou also have had compassion on thy fellowservant, even as I had pity on thee?

34 And his lord was wroth, and delivered him to the tormentors, till he should pay all that was due unto him.

35 So likewise shall my heavenly Father do also unto you, if ye from your hearts forgive not every one his brother their trespasses.

| | |
|---|---|
| **Peculiar** Some made themselves eunuchs. | *Matthew 19:12* For there are some eunuchs, which were so born from *their* mother's womb: and there are some eunuchs, which were made eunuchs of men: and there be eunuchs, which have made themselves eunuchs for the **kingdom of heaven's** sake. He that is able to receive *it*, let him receive *it*. |

| | | | |
|---|---|---|---|
| **Common** Rich hardly enter into either K. <u>Matthew speaks</u> | *Matthew 19:23* Then said Jesus unto his disciples, Verily I say unto you, That a rich man shall hardly enter into the | *Mark 10:23* And Jesus looked round about, and saith unto his disciples, How hardly shall they that have riches enter into | *Luke 18:24* And when Jesus saw that he was very sorrowful, he said, How hardly shall they that have riches enter into | *1 Timothy 6:17* Charge them that are <u>rich</u> in this world, that they be not highminded, nor trust in uncertain <u>riches</u>, but in |

| | | | | |
|---|---|---|---|---|
| of both kingdoms on this point. Notice the different phrasing. Mark and Luke say the same thing the same way. Although Matthew speaks of the same subject, it was said on a different occasion and so is different. | **kingdom of heaven**.<br>24 And again I say unto you, It is easier for a camel to go through the eye of a needle, than for a rich man to enter into the **kingdom of God**. | **the kingdom of God!**<br>24 And the disciples were astonished at his words. But Jesus answereth again, and saith unto them, Children, how hard is it for them that trust in riches to enter into the **kingdom of God**!<br>25 It is easier for a camel to go through the eye of a needle, than for a rich man to enter into the **kingdom of God**. | the **kingdom of God!**<br>25 For it is easier for a camel to go through a needle's eye, than for a rich man to enter into the **kingdom of God**. | the living God, who giveth us richly all things to enjoy;<br>18 That they do good, that they be rich in good works, ready to distribute, willing to communicate;<br><br>*James 5:1* Go to now, ye rich men, weep and howl for your miseries that shall come upon you. |
| **Peculiar**<br><br>According to Matt. 20:1, this is regarding the K of H.<br><br>Only those living during the life of Christ as his disciples are included as those who sit on 12 thrones.<br><br>The first will be last. | *Matthew 19:27* Then answered Peter and said unto him, Behold, we have forsaken all, and followed thee; what shall we have therefore?<br>28 And Jesus said unto them, Verily I say unto you, That ye which have followed me, **in the regeneration when the Son of man shall sit in the throne of his glory**, ye also shall sit upon twelve thrones, judging the twelve tribes of Israel.<br>29 And every one that hath forsaken houses, or brethren, or sisters, or father, or mother, or wife, or children, or lands, for my name's sake, shall receive an hundredfold, and shall inherit everlasting life.<br>30 But many that are first shall be last; and the last shall be first. | *Mark 10:28* Then Peter began to say unto him, Lo, we have left all, and have followed thee.<br>29 And Jesus answered and said, Verily I say unto you, There is no man that hath left house, or brethren, or sisters, or father, or mother, or wife, or children, or lands, for my sake, and the gospel's,<br>30 But he shall receive an hundredfold now in this time, houses, and brethren, and sisters, and mothers, and children, and lands, with persecutions; and in the world to come eternal life.<br>31 But many that are first shall be last; and the last first. | *Luke 18:29* And he said unto them, Verily I say unto you, There is no man that hath left house, or parents, or brethren, or wife, or children, for **the kingdom of God**'s sake,<br>30 Who shall not receive manifold more in this present time, and in the world to come life everlasting.<br><br>*Luke 14:26* If any man come to me, and hate not his father, and mother, and wife, and children, and brethren, and sisters, yea, and his own life also, he cannot be my disciple.<br>27 And whosoever doth not bear his cross, and come after me, cannot be my disciple. | *Matthew 10:37* He that loveth father or mother more than me is not worthy of me: and he that loveth son or daughter more than me is not worthy of me.<br>38 And he that taketh not his cross, and followeth after me, is not worthy of me.<br>39 He that findeth his life shall lose it: and he that loseth his life for my sake shall find it. |
| **Peculiar** to the K of H.<br>This parable expands on the statement of verse 30 – "the first shall be last and the last shall be first."<br>It is a continuation of the answer to | *Matthew 20:1* For the **kingdom of heaven** is like unto a man *that is* an householder, which went out early in the morning to hire labourers into his vineyard.<br>2 And when he had agreed with the labourers for a penny a day, he sent them into his vineyard.<br>3 And he went out about the third hour, and saw others standing idle in the marketplace,<br>4 And said unto them; Go ye also into the vineyard, and whatsoever is right I will give you. And they went their way.<br>5 Again he went out about the sixth and ninth hour, and did likewise.<br>6 And about the eleventh hour he went out, and found others standing idle, and saith unto them, Why stand ye here all the day idle?<br>7 They say unto him, Because no man hath hired us. He saith unto them, Go ye also into the vineyard; and whatsoever is right, *that* shall ye receive.<br>8 So when even was come, the lord of the vineyard saith unto his steward, Call the labourers, and give them *their* hire, beginning from the last unto the first. | | | |

| 19:27 as to who will be the greatest in the coming kingdom. Jesus tells his disciples that those who came later will receive the same blessings as those first engaged. In other words, it is God's business how each person who labors in his vineyard is rewarded. Just labor as you are told. The disciples were first to follow Christ. Many would come later. They may inherit the same as those who bore the heat of the day. | 9 And when they came that *were hired* about the eleventh hour, they received every man a penny.<br>10 But when the first came, they supposed that they should have received more; and they likewise received every man a penny.<br>11 And when they had received *it,* they murmured against the goodman of the house,<br>12 Saying, These last have wrought *but* one hour, and thou hast made them equal unto us, which have borne the burden and heat of the day.<br>13 But he answered one of them, and said, Friend, I do thee no wrong: didst not thou agree with me for a penny?<br>14 Take *that* thine *is,* and go thy way: I will give unto this last, even as unto thee.<br>15 Is it not lawful for me to do what I will with mine own? Is thine eye evil, because I am good?<br>16 <u>So the last shall be first, and the first last:</u> for many be called, but few chosen. | | |
|---|---|---|---|
| **Peculiar**<br>This is also a continuation of the question in 18:1 and 19:27 as to who would be the greatest. This is not designated as K of H or G. It is called "thy kingdom" and points to the reign of Christ on earth.<br><br>Jesus assents to their basic assumption that the kingdom would be restored to Israel. | *Matthew 20:20* Then came to him the mother of Zebedee's children with her sons, worshipping *him* , and desiring a certain thing of him.<br>21 And he said unto her, What wilt thou? She saith unto him, Grant that these my two sons may sit, the one on thy right hand, and the other on the left, in thy **kingdom**.<br>22 But Jesus answered and said, Ye know not what ye ask. Are ye able to drink of the cup that I shall drink of, and to be baptized with the baptism that I am baptized with? They say unto him, We are able.<br>23 And he saith unto them, Ye shall drink indeed of my cup, and be baptized with the baptism that I am baptized with: but to sit on my right hand, and on my left, is not mine to give, but it <u>shall be given to them for whom it is prepared of my Father.</u> | *Mark 10:37* They said unto him, Grant unto us that we may sit, one on thy right hand, and the other on thy left hand, **in thy glory**.<br>38 But Jesus said unto them, Ye know not what ye ask: can ye drink of the cup that I drink of? and be baptized with the baptism that I am baptized with?<br>39 And they said unto him, We can. And Jesus said unto them, Ye shall indeed drink of the cup that I drink of; and with the baptism that I am baptized withal shall ye be baptized:<br>40 But to sit on my right hand and on my left hand is not mine to give; but it shall be given to them for whom it is prepared.<br>41 And when the ten heard it, they began to be much displeased with James and John. | *Matthew 25:34* Then shall the King say unto them on his right hand, Come, ye blessed of my Father, inherit the **kingdom** prepared for you from the foundation of the world:<br><br>*Matthew 19:28* And Jesus said unto them, Verily I say unto you, That ye which have followed me, in the <u>regeneration</u> when the Son of man shall sit in the <u>throne of his glory</u>, ye also shall sit upon twelve thrones, judging the twelve tribes of Israel.<br><br>*Acts 1:6* When they therefore were come together, they asked of him, saying, Lord, wilt thou at this time restore again the **kingdom to Israel?**<br>7 And he said unto them, <u>It is not for you to know</u> the times or the seasons, which the Father hath put in his own power. |

| | |
|---|---|
| **Peculiar** to the K of G. This is the fourth time Matthew breaks with his trend and switches to the K of G. When he says the publicans and harlots "go" into the K of G before you, he reveals that this was a present reality then. This represents the Jew who said he would obey and didn't, and the Gentile who said he wouldn't and afterward did. The primarily Gentile Church, represented by the son who repented, will not be in the K of H. | *Matthew 21:28* But what think ye? A *certain* man had two sons; and he came to the first, and said, Son, go work to day in my vineyard. <br> 29 He answered and said, I will not: but afterward he repented, and went. <br> 30 And he came to the second, and said likewise. And he answered and said, I *go,* sir: and went not. <br> 31 Whether of them twain did the will of *his* father? They say unto him, The first. Jesus saith unto them, Verily I say unto you, That the publicans and the harlots <u>go</u> into the **kingdom of God** before you. <br> 32 For John came unto you in the way of righteousness, and ye believed him not: but the publicans and the harlots <u>believed him</u>: and ye, when ye had seen *it,* repented not afterward, <u>that ye might believe</u> him. |

| | | |
|---|---|---|
| **Peculiar** to the K of G. This is the fifth and last time Matthew uses the term K of G. The K of G could be (and was) taken from Israel and given to another nation, but the K of H is not something that could be given away permanently. This parable describes things past—the response of the nation to the prophets, and then a prediction as to their | *Matthew 21:33* Hear another parable: There was a certain householder, which planted a vineyard, and hedged it round about, and digged a winepress in it, and built a tower, and let it out to husbandmen, and went into a far country: <br> 34 And when the time of the fruit drew near, he sent his servants to the husbandmen, that they might receive the fruits of it. <br> 35 And the husbandmen took his servants, and beat one, and killed another, and stoned another. <br> 36 Again, he sent other servants more than the first: and they did unto them likewise. <br> 37 But last of all he sent unto them his son, saying, They will reverence my son. <br> 38 But when the husbandmen saw the son, they said among themselves, This is the heir; come, let us kill him, and let us seize on his inheritance. <br> 39 And they caught him, and cast *him* out of the vineyard, and slew *him.* <br> 40 When the lord therefore of the vineyard cometh, what will he do unto those husbandmen? <br> 41 They say unto him, He will miserably destroy those wicked men, and will let out *his* vineyard unto other husbandmen, which shall render him the fruits in their seasons. <br> 42 Jesus saith unto them, Did ye never read in the scriptures, The stone which the builders rejected, the same is become the head of the corner: this is the Lord's doing, and it is marvellous in our eyes? <br> 43 Therefore say I unto you, The **kingdom of God** <u>shall be taken from you, and given to a nation</u> bringing forth the fruits thereof. | |

| | | | |
|---|---|---|---|
| rejection of the Son, with the subsequent response of the Father in removing the nation from the position of blessing regarding the K of G, not the K of H. | | | |
| **Peculiar** to the K of H.<br><br>The Jews are bidden to the wedding of the King's son, but do not come. And one who does is thrown out.<br><br>This is a warning and a prophecy to the Jews that they were the intended guests at a wedding, but since they rejected his offer and slew the prophets, the city of Jerusalem will be destroyed and sinners will take their places. | *Matthew 22:1* And Jesus answered and spake unto them again by parables, and said,<br><br>2 The **kingdom of heaven** is like unto a certain king, which made a marriage for his son,<br><br>3 And sent forth his servants to call them that were bidden to the wedding: and they would not come.<br><br>4 Again, he sent forth other servants, saying, Tell them which are bidden, Behold, I have prepared my dinner: my oxen and *my* fatlings *are* killed, and all things *are* ready: come unto the marriage.<br><br>5 But they made light of *it*, and went their ways, one to his farm, another to his merchandise:<br><br>6 And the remnant took his servants, and entreated *them* spitefully, and slew *them*.<br><br>7 But when the king heard *thereof*, he was wroth: and he sent forth his armies, and destroyed those murderers, and burned up their city.<br><br>8 Then saith he to his servants, The wedding is ready, but they which were bidden were not worthy.<br><br>9 Go ye therefore into the highways, and as many as ye shall find, bid to the marriage.<br><br>10 So those servants went out into the highways, and gathered together all as many as they found, both bad and good: and the wedding was furnished with guests.<br><br>11 And when the king came in to see the guests, he saw there a man which had not on a wedding garment:<br><br>12 And he saith unto him, Friend, how camest thou in hither not having a wedding garment? And he was speechless.<br><br>13 Then said the king to the servants, Bind him hand and foot, and take him away, and cast *him* into outer darkness; there shall be weeping and gnashing of teeth.<br><br>14 For many are called, but few *are* chosen. | *Luke 14:16* Then said he unto him, A certain man made a great supper, and bade many:<br><br>17 And sent his servant at supper time to say to them that were bidden, Come; for all things are now ready.<br><br>18 And they all with one consent began to make excuse. The first said unto him, I have bought a piece of ground, and I must needs go and see it: I pray thee have me excused.<br><br>19 And another said, I have bought five yoke of oxen, and I go to prove them: I pray thee have me excused.<br><br>20 And another said, I have married a wife, and therefore I cannot come.<br><br>21 So that servant came, and shewed his lord these things. Then the master of the house being angry said to his servant, Go out quickly into the streets and lanes of the city, and bring in hither the poor, and the maimed, and the halt, and the blind.<br><br>22 And the servant said, Lord, it is done as thou hast commanded, and yet there is room.<br><br>23 And the lord said unto the servant, Go out into the highways and hedges, and compel them to come in, that my house may be filled.<br><br>24 For I say unto you, That none of those men which were bidden shall taste of my supper. | *John 3:29* He that hath the bride is the bridegroom: but the friend of the bridegroom, which standeth and heareth him, rejoiceth greatly because of the bridegroom's voice: this my joy therefore is fulfilled. |
| **Peculiar** to the K of H.<br>The K of H is of such a nature that a few men in authority could prevent it from occurring. No one can shut up the K of G against another. | *Matthew 23:13* But woe unto you scribes and Pharisees hypocrites! for ye shut up the **kingdom of heaven** against men: for ye neither go in *yourselves* neither suffer ye them that are entering to go in. | *Luke 11:51* From the blood of Abel unto the blood of Zacharias, which perished between the altar and the temple: verily I say unto you, It shall be required of this generation.<br><br>52 Woe unto you, lawyers! for ye have taken away the key of knowledge: ye entered not in yourselves, and them that were entering in ye hindered. | |

| See Matt. 4:8 | 24:7 …**kingdom** against **kingdom**… | | |
|---|---|---|---|
| **Peculiar**<br><br>Not designated, though verse 25 would imply the K of H.<br><br>The gospel of the K will be preached to all the world before the end. | 24:9 Then shall they deliver you up to be afflicted, and shall kill you: and ye shall be hated of all nations for my name's sake.<br> 10 And then shall many be offended, and shall betray one another, and shall hate one another.<br> 11 And many false prophets shall rise, and shall deceive many.<br> 12 And because iniquity shall abound, the love of many shall wax cold.<br> 13 But he that shall endure unto the end, the same shall be saved.<br> 14 And this **gospel of the kingdom** shall be preached in all the world for a witness unto all nations; and then shall the end come.<br> 15 When ye therefore shall see the abomination of desolation, spoken of by Daniel the prophet, stand in the holy place, (whoso readeth, let him understand:) | *Luke 21:29* And he spake to them a parable; Behold the fig tree, and all the trees;<br> 30 When they now shoot forth, ye see and know of your own selves that summer is now nigh at hand.<br> 31 So likewise ye, when ye see these things come to pass, know ye that **the kingdom of God** is nigh at hand.<br> 32 Verily I say unto you, This generation shall not pass away, till all be fulfilled. | *Matthew 4:23* And Jesus went about all Galilee, teaching in their synagogues, and preaching the **gospel of the kingdom**, and healing all manner of sickness and all manner of disease among the people. |
| **Peculiar**<br><br>"Then," at that time. The ten virgins are Jews attending the wedding in the Millennium. They are not being admitted into the K when Jesus returns. If the virgins represented the Church, you would have ten brides of Christ and half of them would lose their salvation. | *Matthew 25:1* Then shall the **kingdom of heaven** be likened unto ten virgins, which took their lamps, and went forth to meet the bridegroom.<br> 2 And five of them were wise, and five *were* foolish.<br> 3 They that *were* foolish took their lamps, and took no oil with them:<br> 4 But the wise took oil in their vessels with their lamps.<br> 5 While the bridegroom tarried, they all slumbered and slept.<br> 6 And at midnight there was a cry made, Behold, the bridegroom cometh; go ye out to meet him.<br> 7 Then all those virgins arose, and trimmed their lamps.<br> 8 And the foolish said unto the wise, Give us of your oil; for our lamps are gone out.<br> 9 But the wise answered, saying, *not so*; lest there be not enough for us and you: but go ye rather to them that sell, and buy for yourselves.<br> 10 And while they went to buy, the bridegroom came; and they that were ready went in with him to the marriage: and the door was shut.<br> 11 Afterward came also the other virgins, saying, Lord, Lord, open to us.<br> 12 But he answered and said, Verily I say unto you, I know you not.<br> 13 Watch therefore, for ye know neither the day nor the hour wherein the Son of man cometh. | *Luke 12:36* And ye yourselves like unto men that wait for their lord, when he will return from the wedding; that when he cometh and knocketh, they may open unto him immediately.<br> 37 Blessed are those servants, whom the lord when he cometh [*after his wedding*] shall find watching: verily I say unto you, that he shall gird himself, and make them to sit down to meat, and will come forth and serve them.<br> 38 And if he shall come in the second watch, or come in the third watch, and find them so, blessed are those servants.<br> 39 And this know, that if the goodman of the house had known what hour the thief would come, he would have watched, and not have suffered his house to be broken through.<br> 40 Be ye therefore ready also: for the Son of man cometh at an hour when ye think not. | |
| **Peculiar** to the K of H, in that the ones who failed to multiply their money were cast into the fire.<br>Further, it is a picture of Jesus going away and coming back to take an accounting. | *Matthew 25:14* For *the kingdom of heaven is* as a man travelling into a far country, *who* called his own servants, and delivered unto them his goods.<br> 15 And unto one he gave five talents, to another two, and to another one; to every man according to his several ability; and straightway took his journey.<br> 16 Then he that had received the five talents went and traded with the same, and made *them* other five talents.<br> 17 And likewise he that *had received* two, he also gained other two.<br> 18 But he that had received one went and digged in the earth, and hid his lord's money.<br> 19 After a long time the lord of those servants cometh, | *Luke 19:11* And as they heard these things, he added and spake a parable, because he was nigh to Jerusalem, and because they thought that the **kingdom of God** should immediately appear.<br> 12 He said therefore, A certain nobleman went into a far country to receive for himself **a kingdom**, and to return.<br> 13 And he called his ten servants, and delivered them ten pounds, and said unto them, Occupy till I come.<br> 14 But his citizens hated him, and sent a message after him, saying, We will not have this man to reign over us. | |

<table>
<tr>
<td>

Luke is not talking about the K of G. He is clarifying their misconception that the K of G would immediately appear, and he tells them how the K of G will appear.

The difference in these two parables expresses one of the differences in the two kingdoms.

</td>
<td>

and reckoneth with them.

20 And so he that had received five talents came and brought other five talents, saying, Lord, thou deliveredst unto me five talents: behold, I have gained beside them five talents more.

21 His lord said unto him, Well done, *thou* good and faithful servant: thou hast been faithful over a few things, I will make thee ruler over many things: enter thou into the joy of thy lord.

22 He also that had received two talents came and said, Lord, thou deliveredst unto me two talents: behold, I have gained two other talents beside them.

23 His lord said unto him, Well done, good and faithful servant; thou hast been faithful over a few things, I will make thee ruler over many things: enter thou into the joy of thy lord.

24 Then he which had received the one talent came and said, Lord, I knew thee that thou art an hard man, reaping where thou hast not sown, and gathering where thou hast not strawed:

25 And I was afraid, and went and hid thy talent in the earth: lo, *there* thou hast *that is* thine.

26 His lord answered and said unto him, *Thou* wicked and slothful servant, thou knewest that I reap where I sowed not, and gather where I have not strawed:

27 Thou oughtest therefore to have put my money to the exchangers, and *then* at my coming I should have received mine own with usury.

28 Take therefore the talent from him, and give *it* unto him which hath ten talents.

29 For unto every one that hath shall be given, and he shall have abundance: but from him that hath not shall be taken away even that which he hath.

30 And cast ye the unprofitable servant into outer darkness: there shall be weeping and gnashing of teeth. [*This could not be true in the K of G.*]

31 When the Son of man shall come in his glory, and all the holy angels with him, then shall he sit upon the throne of his glory: [*This is a continuation of his answer in chapter 24 as to when these things will be.*]

32 And before him shall be gathered all nations: and he shall separate them one from another, as a shepherd divideth his sheep from the goats:

33 And he shall set the sheep on his right hand, but the goats on the left.

</td>
<td>

15 And it came to pass, that when he was returned, having received **the kingdom**, then he commanded these servants to be called unto him, to whom he had given the money, that he might know how much every man had gained by trading.

16 Then came the first, saying, Lord, thy pound hath gained ten pounds.

17 And he said unto him, Well, thou good servant: because thou hast been faithful in a very little, <u>have thou authority over ten cities</u>.

18 And the second came, saying, Lord, thy pound hath gained five pounds.

19 And he said likewise to him, Be thou also over five cities.

20 And another came, saying, Lord, behold, here is thy pound, which I have kept laid up in a napkin:

21 For I feared thee, because thou art an austere man: thou takest up that thou layedst not down, and reapest that thou didst not sow.

22 And he saith unto him, Out of thine own mouth will I judge thee, thou wicked servant. Thou knewest that I was an austere man, taking up that I laid not down, and reaping that I did not sow:

23 Wherefore then gavest not thou my money into the bank, that at my coming I might have required mine own with usury?

24 And he said unto them that stood by, Take from him the pound, and give it to him that hath ten pounds.

25 (And they said unto him, Lord, he hath ten pounds.)

26 For I say unto you, That unto every one which hath shall be given; and from him that hath not, even that he hath shall be taken away from him.

27 But those mine enemies, which would not that I should reign over them, bring hither, and slay them before me. [*He does not slay the man who did not develop his talents. The enemies were not the one who failed to develop his talent.*]

</td>
</tr>
<tr>
<td>

**Peculiar**
The K was prepared from the foundation of the world.

Verse 35 shows how this kingdom is obtained by works.

</td>
<td colspan="1">

*Matthew 25:34* Then shall the King say unto them on his right hand, Come, ye blessed of my Father, inherit the **kingdom** prepared for you from the foundation of the world:

35 For I was an hungred, and ye gave me meat: I was thirsty, and ye gave me drink: I was a stranger, and ye took me in:

36 Naked, and ye clothed me: I was sick, and ye visited me: I was in prison, and ye came unto me.

37 Then shall the righteous answer him, saying, Lord, when saw we thee an hungred, and fed *thee*? or thirsty, and gave *thee* drink?

38 When saw we thee a stranger, and took *thee* in? or naked, and clothed *thee*?

39 Or when saw we thee sick, or in prison, and came unto thee?

40 And the King shall answer and say unto them, Verily I say unto you, Inasmuch as ye have done *it* unto one of the least of these my brethren, ye have done *it* unto me.

41 Then shall he say also unto them on the left hand, Depart from me, ye cursed, into everlasting fire, prepared for the devil and his angels:

42 For I was an hungred, and ye gave me no meat: I was thirsty, and ye gave me no drink:

</td>
<td>

*Luke 12:31* But rather seek ye the **kingdom of God**; and all these things shall be added unto you.

32 Fear not, little flock; for it is your Father's good pleasure to give you the **kingdom.**

*Luke 23:42* And he said unto Jesus,

</td>
</tr>
</table>

| | | | | Lord, remember me when thou comest into **thy kingdom**. |
|---|---|---|---|---|---|

43 I was a stranger, and ye took me not in: naked, and ye clothed me not: sick, and in prison, and ye visited me not.

44 Then shall they also answer him, saying, Lord, when saw we thee an hungred, or athirst, or a stranger, or naked, or sick, or in prison, and did not minister unto thee?

45 Then shall he answer them, saying, Verily I say unto you, Inasmuch as ye did *it* not to one of the least of these, ye did *it* not to me.

46 And these shall go away into everlasting punishment: but the righteous into life eternal.

| **Peculiar** to the K of G.<br><br>Matthew reverses his trend. The Father's kingdom and the K of G are the same after the second coming. | *Matthew 26:27* And he took the cup, and gave thanks, and gave *it* to them, saying, Drink ye all of it;<br>28 For this is my blood of the new testament, which is shed for many for the remission of sins.<br>29 But I say unto you, I will not drink henceforth of this fruit of the vine, until that day when I drink it new with you in **my Father's kingdom**. | *Mark 14:24* And he said unto them, This is my blood of the new testament, which is shed for many.<br>25 Verily I say unto you, I will drink no more of the fruit of the vine, until that day that I drink it new in **the kingdom of God.** | *Luke 22:15* And he said unto them, With desire I have desired to eat this passover with you before I suffer:<br>16 For I say unto you, I will not any more eat thereof, until it be fulfilled in **the kingdom of God**.<br>17 And he took the cup, and gave thanks, and said, Take this, and divide it among yourselves:<br>18 For I say unto you, I will not drink of the fruit of the vine, until the **kingdom of God** shall come. |
|---|---|---|---|

# Kingdoms Table, with all passages included

This is the table were the numbers are assigned to each usage of the word kingdom. The numbers are in chronological order as the references appear, beginning in the book of Matthew. Similar or contrasting passages found elsewhere in the Bible are included under the number, though that passage, if it includes the word *kingdom*, will have its own number as well. For example in the second row you will see the number one. That is the number assigned to Matthew 3:2 since it is the first mention of the word kingdom in the New Testament. But the similar passage in Mark 1:15 has the number 61 assigned to it in due course. The numbers in each row are linked to the leading passage, which description is found on the same line with the assigned number. The X is placed beside the passages which conform to the description given on that line. In the first line you see an X beside Mt. 3:2 indicating that "John the Baptist preached about the K of H." There is no X beside Mk. 1:4 because John did not preach the K of G. Matt. 3:1 is included as a cross reference to "the land of Judaea" to demonstrate that the two events are the same.

| Characteristics of the kingdoms | Kingdom of God | | Kingdom of Heaven | |
|---|---|---|---|---|
| John the Baptist preached about the K of H only. | Mt. 3:1, Mk. 1:4 | | X | Mt. 3:2 |
| Repent for the K is at hand. | Mk. 1:15 | X | X | Mt. 3:2: 4:17 |
| Jesus began preaching both Ks after John was imprisoned. Believe is never applied to the K of H. Matthew never tells anyone to believe. | Mt. 4:23; 9:35; 24:14; Mk. 1:14, 15; Lk. 16:16; Lk. 4:43; Lk. 9:11 | X | X | Mt. 4:12, 17; 5:3,10 |
| Healing indicates the closeness of the kingdom of G. | Lk. 9:2, 11; 10:9, 11; | X | | |
| Healing is manifested in both kingdoms. | Lk. 9:2, 11 | X | X | Mt. 4:23, 10:7-8 |
| The K of G was glad tidings. The K of H is never gospel. | Lk. 8:1 | X | | Mt. 4:23 See 15. |
| The K of H is for the poor in spirit. | Lk. 6:20 (poor) | | X | Mt. 5:3 |
| K of H will be a release for those persecuted. | Mk. 10:30 | | X | Mt. 5:10 |
| K of G will bring persecution. | Mk. 10:30; Lk. 6:22-23 | X | | Mt. 5:10 |
| Commandments will be kept in the K of H. | | | X | Mt. 5:19 |
| One can be "called" least or greatest in the K of H. | | | X | Mt. 5:19 |
| Righteousness is demanded in both kingdoms. | Mt. 5:20; 6:33, Lk. 9:62; 12:31; Heb.1:8; 1Cor. 6:9,10; Gal. 5:21 | X | X | Mt. 6:33; 5:20; 13:43 |
| Does not name the K (in Matt.) because it is during the Millennium. | Lk. 13:28-29 | | | Mt. 6:10; 20:21 |
| The K of H comes as an institution. | | | X | Mt. 6:10 |
| K of G (Christ's kingdom) is a manifestation of Jesus' glory and power. | Mk. 9:1; 1Thess. 2:12; Rev. 2:10; 1 Cor. 4:20 | X | | Mt. 6:13; 16:28 |
| To pursue the K of G is to accomplish the will of God.. | Lk. 12:31 | X | | Mt. 6:33 K of G |
| The K of G is a present reality. | Lk. 12:31 | X | | Mt. 6:33; 2Th. 1:5 |
| K of H is conditioned upon obedience. | | | X | Mt. 7:21 |

| | | | | |
|---|---|---|---|---|
| Both Ks will occur on earth during the Millennium. | Lk. 13:28-29 | X | X | Mt. 8:11 |
| Sit down in kingdom with the prophets. | Lk .13:28-30 | X | X | Mt. 8:11 |
| Old Testament saints in both Ks. | Lk. 13:28-30 | X | X | Mt. 8:11 |
| Abraham, Isaac, and Jacob are present and sit down. | Lk.13:28-29 | X | X | Matt. 8:11 |
| Children of the K will be cast out into outer darkness. | Lk. 14:15-24 | | X | Mt. 8:12; 25:29-30 |
| Invited are thrown out and strangers received. 10 virgins. | | | X | Mt. 8:12; 13:41; 25:8-13 |
| Kingdom of H preached to Israel only. | Mk. 6:7-13 | | X | Mt.10:1-10 |
| The K of H was a coming event—not near, not present. | | | X | Mt. 10:7 |
| Disciples sent to preach both—though at different times. | Lk. 9:2;Lk.10:1 | X | X | Mt. 10:5-7; |
| Neither K had come before John. | Lk. 7:28 | X | X | Mt. 11:11 |
| Least in either K is greater than John. | Lk. 7:28 | X | X | Mt. 11:11 |
| John the Baptist was not in either K. | Lk. 7:28 | X | X | Mt. 11:11 |
| K of H is subject to violent overthrow. | Luke 16:16 | | X | Mt. 11:12 |
| Men were pressing into the K of G. It was and is a present experience. | Lk. 16:16; Col. 1:13; Rev.1:9 | X | | Mt. 11:12 suffereth violence |
| Power over devils is a manifestation of the presence of the K of G. | Mt. 12:28, Lk. 11:20, 1 Cor. 4:20, Rev. 12:10 | X | | |
| Mystery, so he speaks in parables. | Mk. 4:11; Lk. 8:10 | X | X | Mt. 13:11-15 |
| The message of the K is like a sower – various forms of ground. | Mk. 4:17 | X | X | Mt. 13:18-23 |
| Enemy sows tares while men sleep – tares are burned. | Mk. 4:26 | | X | Mt. 13:24-38 |
| Mustard seed becomes a great tree with birds—devils. | Mk. 4:30, Lk. 13:18 | X | X | Mt. 13:31 |
| Kingdom grows to be large. | Lk. 13:18; Mk. 4:30 | X | X | Mt. 13:31-32 |
| False doctrine (leaven) permeates both kingdoms. | Lk. 13:20-21 | X | X | Mt. 13:33 |
| Children of the K of H include tares to be burned. | | | X | Mt. 13:38 |
| The K of H and of G will become "his" K, and then "the K of their Father." | 2 Tim. 4:1; Rev. 12:10 | X | X | Mt. 13:41, 43 |
| Treasure to be sought – purchased as a field. | | | X | Mt. 13:43-44 |
| Like goodly pearls — sell all and buy. | | | X | Mt. 13:45-46 |
| Like a net that contains good and bad fish. | | | X | Mt. 13:47 |
| Scribes (Jewish) are instructed concerning the K of H. | | | X | Mt. 13:52-53 |
| Contains elements both new and old. | | | X | Mt. 13:52-53 |
| Keys imparted to men with power to bind. | John 20:23 | | X | Mt. 16:19 |

| Description | Reference | | | Reference |
|---|---|---|---|---|
| The K of G and His K are the same. | Mk. 9:1, Lk. 9:27 | X | | Mt. 16:28 |
| The K is associated with the manifestation of power. | Mk. 9:1; Lk. 9:27 | X | | Mt. 16:28 |
| Disciples argued over who would be the greatest. | Mk. 9:34 (no K) | | X | Mt. 18:1 |
| Like little children, all must become as little child. | Mk. 10:14-15; Lk. 18:16-17 | X | X | Mt. 18:3-4; 19:14 |
| Some will be greater than others. | | | X | Mt. 18:4 |
| Requires one to forgive or lose his forgiveness. | | | X | Mt. 18:23-35 |
| Men make themselves eunuchs for the K of H. | | | X | Mt. 19:12 |
| Rich men hardly enter into the K. | Mt. 19:24; Mk. 10:23-25; Lk.18:24-25 | X | X | Mt. 19:23-24 says K of H & G |
| Disciples sit on 12 thrones judging the 12 tribes. | Lk .18:29, Lk. 14:26-27 | | X | Mt. 19:28 |
| Left houses and lands for the K of G. | Lk. 18:29-30; Mk. 10:29 | X | | Mt. 19:28-20:1 |
| The first will be last. | Lk. 13:28-30 | X | X | Mt. 19:28-30, 20:1,16 |
| Those engaged last will receive the same as the first followers of Christ. | | | X | Mt. 20:1 |
| The Kingdom of God was also a coming event. (waited for) | Mk. 15:43; Lk. 22:16-18, 23:42, 51; 22:16-18; 2 Tim. 4:1; John 18:36; Rev. 12:10 | X | | Mt. 20:21; 25:34 |
| The coming K is called "thy" kingdom. | Mk. 10:37, Mt. 25:34 | | | Mt. 20:20 |
| Sinners, publicans and harlots, get into the K of G. | Mt. 21:31 | X | | |
| Taken from Jews and given to another nation. | Mt. 21:43 | X | | |
| Jews who are bidden to the wedding of the king's son do not come, and the one who does is thrown out. | John 3:29 | | X | Mt. 22:2-7; 25:1 |
| Pharisees shut up the K of H and prevented others from entering. | Lk. 11:51 | | X | Mt. 23:13 |
| Gospel of the kingdom preached in all the world during the tribulation when the faith of Christ will be part of the message. | | | X | Mt. 24:14 |
| 10 virgins, 5 refused entrance for lack of oil. | | | X | Mt. 25:1 |
| Talents to be multiplied (alike and different). | Lk. 19:11-15 Servant not cast out | X | X ? | Mt. 25:14, 28-31 Servant cast out |
| Those who fail to multiply their money are cast into fire. | Lk. 19:11-27 | | X | Mt. 25:14 |
| Comes at the second coming of Christ. | Lk. 22:16,18; Rev. 12:10 | X | X | Mt. 25:31-33; 2 Tim. 4:1 |
| Prepared from before the foundation of the world. | | | X | Mt. 25:34 |
| Obtained by works. | | | X | Mt. 25:34-46 |

| The K of G is the same as the Father's K. | Mk. 14:25 | X | | Mk. 14:24-25 Lk. 22:15-18 |
|---|---|---|---|---|
| Will drink in the Father's kingdom. | Mt. 26:29; Mk. 14:24-25; Luke 22:15-18 | X | | |
| Jesus will not drink until the K is come. | Mk. 14:25, Lk. 22:16-30 | X | | Mt. 26:29 Father's kingdom |
| Believe is in connection with the message called gospel. | Mk. 1:14-15 | X | | |
| Likened to seed cast—the blade, ear, full corn [no tares]. | Mk. 4:26 | X | | |
| The K of G is visible when Jesus is seen in glory & power. | Mk. 9:1 | X | | |
| Pluck out an eye to enter either K. | Mk. 9:47 | X | X | Mt. 5:29; 18:8 (life) |
| Right condition of heart would put him in the K of G. | Mk. 12:34 | X | | |
| The poor (financially) were closer to the K of G. | Lk. 6:20 | X | | Mt. 5:3 in spirit Mt. 11:5 gospel is preached |
| The K of G was "seen" by three disciples. | Lk. 9:27 | X | | Mt. 16:28 his kingdom |
| He who looks back is not fit for the K. | Lk. 9:62 | X | | |
| Eat Bread in the K of G; Jesus corrects this statement. | Lk. 14:15 | X | | |
| The K of G is a different dispensation from the O. T. | Lk. 14:15 | X | | |
| The K of G is not visible. | Lk. 17:20; Jn. 3:3-5, 18:36 | X | | |
| The K of G is within. | Lk. 17:21 | X | | |
| They mistakenly thought it would immediately appear. | Lk. 19:11; 21:31 | X | | |
| Comes after the Tribulation (K of G). | Lk 21:26-31; Rev. 12:10 | X | | |
| The K of G will come as an institution in the Millennium. | Lk. 22:18 | X | | |
| The K of G is for the regenerated only. | John 3:3, 5 | X | | |
| The K of G is entered into. | John 3:5 | X | | |
| Christ taught the K of G after the resurrection. | Acts 1:3; 8:12; 14:22; 19:8; 20:25; 28:23, 31; Col. 4:11; 2 Th. 1:5 | X | | |
| Personal tribulation precedes the K. | Acts 14:22 | X | | |
| Not tangible, but spiritual, not meat and drink. | Rom. 14:17 | X | | |
| K is righteousness, peace, and joy in the Holy Ghost. | Rom. 14:17 | X | | |
| Is the exercise of God's power. | 1 Cor. 4:20 | X | | |
| Unrighteous do not inherit the Ks. | 1 Cor. 6:9,10; 1 Cor. 5:50; Gal. 5:21; Eph. 5:5 | X | | |
| The Kingdom of Christ is the same as the K of G. | Eph. 5:5 | X | | |

| | | | | |
|---|---|---|---|---|
| Christians are in the K of His dear Son right now. | Col. 1:13-14, | X | | |
| Christians are in the K of G right now. | Col. 4:11, 2 Thess. 1:5 | X | | |
| The coming K is a heavenly K. | 2 Tim. 4:18 | X | | |
| The K cannot be moved. | Heb. 12:28 | X | | |
| Flesh and blood cannot inherit the K. | 1 Cor. 15:50 | X | | |
| The K is part of the gospel message. The K of H is never called "gospel." | Mt. 4:23; Acts 8:12; 19:8; 20:25; 28:23, 31; Col. 4:11; 2 Thess. 1:5; Mk. 1:14-15; Lk. 8:1 | X | | |
| The K becomes visible during the Millennium. | Rev. 12:19 | X | X | Mt. 8:11 |

# APPENDIX

## Heaven or Heavenly?

Confusion has resulted as tradition has evolved a religious connotation for the word **heaven**. In a doctrinal context, most people imagine **heaven** and **God** to be closely related. It is commonly reasoned: "The **kingdom of heaven** would have to be God's spiritual kingdom, wouldn't it?" It is not a *heavenly kingdom*, as one might speak of a *heavenly marriage* or a *heavenly day*. The heavens are physical, created by God. The K of H is as physical as the heavens are physical. In contrast, the K of G is as spiritual as God is spiritual.

The word *heaven* is used 739 times in the Bible. Less than 10 of those references would come close to fitting the common definition of *heaven* — a celestial city with golden streets, full of angels and beautiful mansions. The other 729 references clearly speak of the physical universe created by God — a place that will be destroyed by God and then replaced. Here is a representative sampling from hundreds of similar verses:

### The Heavens are Created.

*Genesis 1:1* In the beginning God created the **heaven** and the earth.
*Exodus 20:11* For in six days the LORD made **heaven** and earth, the sea, and all that in them is….
*Psalm 96:5* …the LORD made the **heavens**.
*Isaiah 42:5* Thus saith God the LORD, he that created the **heavens,** and stretched them out; he that spread forth the earth….

The significance of the heavens being created is that the kingdom of heaven must be a <u>kingdom of the created</u> — the physical, the temporal.

### Three Heavens.

The Bible clearly speaks of three heavens — all of them physical and temporal. Paul was caught up **TO** the third heaven and **INTO** paradise, where he experienced the presence of God and received special revelation.

*2 Corinthians 12:2-4* I knew a man in Christ above fourteen years ago, (whether in the body, I cannot tell; or whether out of the body, I cannot tell: God knoweth;) such an one **caught up <u>to</u> the third heaven**. 3 And I knew such a man, (whether in the body, or out of the body, I cannot tell: God knoweth;) 4 How that he was **caught up <u>into</u> paradise**, and heard unspeakable words, which it is not lawful for a man to utter.

Notice carefully the two words: **TO** and **INTO**. It is as one might go **to** Washington and **into** the White House. The Greek language bears out this distinction that is so accurately translated in the King James Bible. Careless, commercial translations like the NIV fail to properly represent the original languages, and are therefore worse than useless for serious study.

The **third heaven** was that part of the universe which contained God's temple and throne. As a bird exists in the **first heavens**, and planets and stars exist in the **second heavens**, so God's throne is a place in the much vaster and most distant **third heaven**.

Note in the following verses how the heavens are spoken of in the plural.

*Genesis 2:1* Thus the **heavens** [*plural*] and the earth were finished, and all the host of them.
*Psalm 115:16* The **heaven**, even the **heavens**, are the LORD'S: but the earth hath he given to the children of men.
*Ephesians 4:10* He that descended is the same also that ascended up far above all **heavens,** that he might fill all things.)

Several verses speak of **the heaven and the heaven of heavens**. God's dwelling place is associated with this **heaven of heavens**. That would be the third heaven of which Paul speaks.

*Deuteronomy 10:14* Behold, the **heaven** and the **heaven of heavens** is the LORD'S thy God, the earth also, with all that therein is.

*1 Kings 8:27-36* But will God indeed dwell on the earth? behold, the **heaven and heaven of heavens** cannot contain thee; how much less this house that I have builded?

*Psalm 148:4* Praise him, ye **heavens of heavens,** and ye waters that be above the **heavens**.

## The First Heaven.

Birds fly in the first heaven.

*Genesis 1:20* … fowl that may fly above the earth in the open firmament of **heaven**….

*Genesis 7:23* …and the fowl of the **heaven**….

*Revelation 19:17* …fowls that fly in the midst of **heaven…**.

Tall structures reached into the first heaven.

*Genesis 11:4* And they said, Go to, let us build us a city and a tower, whose top may reach unto **heaven**….

*Deuteronomy 1:28* …the cities are great and walled up to **heaven**….

Rain, dew, frost, and thunder come from the first heaven.

*Genesis 27:28* Therefore God give thee of the dew of **heaven**….

*Deuteronomy 11:17* …and he shut up the **heaven**, that there be no rain….

*Deuteronomy 28:12* …the **heaven** to give the rain unto thy land in his season….

*1 Samuel 2:10* …out of **heaven** shall he thunder upon them….

*1 Kings 18:45* …the **heaven** was black with clouds and wind…

*Job 38:29* …the hoary frost of **heaven**….

*Isaiah 55:10* For as the rain cometh down, and the snow from **heaven**….

## The Second Heaven.

Stars are in the second heaven, possibly the third as well.

*Genesis 1:15* And let them be for lights in the firmament of the **heaven** to give light upon the earth: and it was so.

*Genesis 22:17* …as the stars of the **heaven**….

## The Third Heaven.

God's abode is located in the third heaven.

God's throne is located on a firmament supported by four cherubim. It was mobile during the vision Ezekiel saw (Ezekiel 1 and 2), and is located in the vast third heaven. From the description in Ezekiel, we recognize the four cherubim as in the same class as the four living creatures before the throne of God mentioned in Rev. 4 and 5. The name of God's abode is not **heaven**. The term "Heaven" when denoting God's abode refers more than anything else to a direction (up from off the earth) than to an actual place. At the end of the Millennium God's throne will come down out of the heavens, having been converted into the New Jerusalem, to sit on the earth as its capitol city. (Revelation 21:2).

*1 Kings 8:30* And hearken thou to the supplication of thy servant, and of thy people Israel, when they shall pray toward this place: and hear thou in **heaven thy dwelling place**: and when thou hearest, forgive.

Heaven is mentioned twice in the following passage. The first time, it is clearly a reference to the first heaven, and the second time, it is the place from which God hears prayers. The Bible usually fails to differentiate between the three heavens, because from a human perspective, everything that is up and beyond is heaven.

*1 Kings 8:35* When **heaven is shut up,** and there is no rain, because they have sinned against thee; if they pray toward this place, and confess thy name, and turn from their sin, when thou afflictest them:
36 Then hear thou in **heaven**, and forgive the sin of thy servants, and of thy people Israel, that thou teach them the good way wherein they should walk, and give rain upon thy land, which thou hast given to thy people for an inheritance.

Again, two heavens are spoken of in the same passage — the place where God dwells and the heaven above one's head. Both alike are heaven, in that they are the created space beyond the earth.

> *1 Kings 8:49* Then hear thou their prayer and their supplication **in heaven thy dwelling place**, and maintain their cause, 54 And it was so, that when Solomon had made an end of praying all this prayer and supplication unto the LORD, he arose from before the altar of the LORD, from kneeling on his knees with his **hands spread up to heaven**.

Note that the throne of God is not heaven itself, but is **set** — located — in heaven.

> *Revelation 4:2* And immediately I was in the spirit: and, behold, a throne was **set in heaven**, and one sat on the throne.

God is said to **walk** in the circuit of heaven with a covering of clouds, which means that the throne of his presence can move (and did in Ezekiel's vision) about in that outer star region.

> *Job 22:12-14* Is not God in the height of **heaven**? and behold the height of the **stars**, how high they are! 13 And thou sayest, How doth God know? can he judge through the dark cloud? 14 Thick clouds are a covering to him, that he seeth not; and he walketh in the **circuit of heaven**.

Note in the following verse that God sits in the heavens (plural), which must be the second and third heaven.

> *Psalm 2:4* He that sitteth in the **heavens** shall laugh: the Lord shall have them in derision.

God's **throne** — **his holy temple** — is located in that region called heaven—the third heaven, no doubt.

> *Psalm 11:4* The LORD is in his holy temple, the LORD'S throne is in **heaven**: his eyes behold, his eyelids try, the children of men.

## The Heavens Contain Enemy Forces.

The heavens contain spirit beings called, **principalities, powers, the rulers of the darkness of this world, and spiritual wickedness in high places.** They all exercise power, but some bear evil influence throughout all three heavens.

> *Ephesians 6:10-12* Finally, my brethren, be strong in the Lord, and in the power of his might. 11 Put on the whole armour of God, that ye may be able to stand against the wiles of the **devil**. 12 For we wrestle not against flesh and blood, but against **principalities, against powers, against the rulers of the darkness of this world, against spiritual wickedness in high places.**

The place called paradise, where Jesus sits on the right hand of God, is located in **places** (plural) called **heavenly places**. In the Bible it means nothing more than the THREE heavens in the physical universe. The Bible never speaks of **a** heavenly PLACE (singular). It is always heavenly PLACES (plural). The reason God is in heavenly PLACES, that Christians are exalted to sit in heavenly PLACES, and that Satan is in heavenly PLACES is because *beings not bound by the physical world are not confined to just one heaven.* The throne of God moves throughout all three heavens, as do the evil spirits.

> *Ephesians 1:20* Which he wrought in Christ, when he raised him from the dead, and set him at his own right hand in the **heavenly places**….

Believers are positionally **seated** together with Christ in those heavenly **places**. It is a *place,* not a condition, as seen by the fact that other created personalities also dwell in heavenly places (Eph. 3:10-13).

> *Ephesians 2:6* And hath raised us up together, and made us **sit** together in heavenly **places** in Christ Jesus:

The family of God is made up of both the living and the dead. The dead have passed into the heavens, while the living remain on earth.

> *Ephesians 3:15* For this cause I bow my knees unto the Father of our Lord Jesus Christ, of whom the **whole family in heaven** and earth is named,

The Church manifests the wisdom of God to the onlooking spirit beings that dwell in the **heavenly places** — the three heavens.

> *Ephesians 3:10-13* To the intent that now unto the principalities and powers in heavenly places might be known by the church the manifold wisdom of God.

## Evil Spirits, Called *gods*, Dwell in the Heavens and in the Earth.

Satan is called the **god of this world,** and other fallen spirits share that distinction with him, dwelling in the heavens, as the next two verses confirm.

> *2 Corinthians 4:3-4* But if our gospel be hid, it is hid to them that are lost: 4 In whom the **god of this world** [*Satan*] hath blinded the minds of them which believe not, lest the light of the glorious gospel of Christ, who is the image of God, should shine unto them.
>
> *1 Corinthians 8:5* For though there be that are called gods, whether in **heaven** or in earth, (as there be gods many, and lords many,)

## Satan has Access to Heaven.

> *Revelation 9:1* And the fifth angel sounded, and I saw a star fall from **heaven** unto the earth: and to him was given the key of the bottomless pit.

We find him coming into an assembly of the righteous angels and reporting that he had been traveling throughout the earth.

> *Job 1:6-7* Now there was a day when the sons of God came to present themselves before the LORD, and Satan came also among them. 7 And the LORD said unto Satan, Whence comest thou? Then Satan answered the LORD, and said, From going to and fro in the earth, and from walking up and down in it.

The following verse is interesting in that it speaks of the second heaven, where the stars are found, and then tells us that the **powers** (devils dwelling in the heavens) of the **heavens** (more than one heaven) shall be **shaken** (the evil power structure will be undermined by the coming kingdom).

> *Matthew 24:29* Immediately after the tribulation of those days shall the sun be darkened, and the moon shall not give her light, and the stars shall fall from **heaven**, and the powers of the **heavens** shall be shaken:

Satan dwells in the heavens (which is not to say that he dwells in the home of God), so we see that he must be ejected from the universe by force and confined to the earth — the center of which is Hell. When the heavens are purged of Satan's powers, the **kingdom of God** will be manifested visibly on the earth. After the heavens are delivered from Satanic influence, the heavens and all who dwell in them are told to rejoice.

> *Revelation 12:7-12* And there was war in **heaven**: Michael and his angels fought against the dragon; and the dragon fought and his angels, 8 And prevailed not; **neither was their place found any more in heaven**. 9 And the great dragon was **cast out,** that old serpent, called the Devil, and Satan, which deceiveth the whole world: he was cast out into the earth, and his angels were cast out with him. 10 And I heard a loud voice saying in heaven, Now is come salvation, and strength, and the **kingdom of our God**, and the power of his Christ: for the accuser of our brethren is cast down, which accused them before our God day and night. 11 And they overcame him by the blood of the Lamb, and by the word of their testimony; and they loved not their lives unto the death. 12 Therefore rejoice, ye **heavens**, and **ye that dwell in them** [plural heavens]. Woe to the inhabiters of the earth and of the sea! for the devil is come down unto you, having great wrath, because he knoweth that he hath but a short time.

When the Jews offered sacrifices to their female goddess, God told them that they were worshiping the **queen of heaven.** Their goddess commanded heaven above. She was reigning as a queen in the heavens.

> *Jeremiah 7:18-19* The children gather wood, and the fathers kindle the fire, and the women knead their dough, to make cakes to the **queen of heaven,** and to pour out drink offerings unto other gods, that they may provoke me to anger. 19 Do they provoke me to anger? saith the LORD: do they not provoke themselves to the confusion of their own faces?

As in the verse above, when the Jews burned incense to their idols, God said they were worshiping gods who lived in the heavens. Thus, a **kingdom of heaven** would necessarily involve the heavens where the evil spirits—called **gods** and **queens**—reign.

> *Jeremiah 19:13* …they have burned incense unto all the **host of heaven**, and have poured out drink offerings unto **other gods**.

The kingdom of Antichrist will extend its power and authority all the way into the heavens where he will cast down some of the angels of God.

> *Daniel 8:10* And it waxed great, even to the **host of heaven**; and it cast down some of the host and of the stars to the ground, and stamped upon them.

Paul was not speaking hyperbole when he warned the Galatians against false doctrine propagated by angels from heaven.

> *Galatians 1:8* But though we, or an **angel from heaven**, preach any other gospel unto you than that which we have preached unto you, let him be accursed.

## The Heavens are Corrupted by Sin and Must be Destroyed.

The presence of Satan and his fallen host in the three heavens has corrupted the entire universe.

> *Job 15:15* …the **heavens** are not clean in his sight.
> *Job 25:5* …yea, **the stars are not pure in his sight**.

## The Heavens Will Perish.

The heavens, which are now the dwelling place of God, righteous angels, fallen angels, Satan, departed saints, and paradise, will be destroyed and replaced with perfect heavens worthy of the coming kingdom.

> *Isaiah 51:6* Lift up your eyes to the heavens, and look upon the earth beneath: for the **heavens shall vanish** away like smoke, and the earth shall wax old like a garment, and they that dwell therein shall die in like manner: but my salvation shall be for ever, and my righteousness shall not be abolished.
> *2 Peter 3:7-13* But the **heavens** and the earth, which are…**reserved unto fire** against the day of judgment and perdition of ungodly men. 10 But the day of the Lord will come as a thief in the night; in the which the **heavens shall pass away** with a great noise, and the elements shall melt with fervent heat, the **earth also and the works that are therein shall be burned up.** 12 Looking for and hasting unto the coming of the day of God, wherein the **heavens being on fire** shall be dissolved, and the elements shall melt with fervent heat?
> *Revelation 20:3* And I saw a great white throne, and him that sat on it, from whose face the earth and the **heaven** fled away; and there was found no place for them.
> *Revelation 21:1* …for the **first heaven and the first earth were passed away**; and there was no more sea. [The word *first* (**first heaven**) is not differentiating between the first, second, or third heaven. It is first as in *former*.]

## New Heavens Will be Created.

Note in the following passages that God will create a new heavens (plural). If *heaven* were synonymous with God's throne, then we would have to conclude that God's dwelling place is unclean and will be destroyed. But other passages make it clear that it is the universe that will be destroyed and then recreated.

> *Isaiah 66:22* For as the **new heavens** and the new earth, which I will make, shall remain before me, saith the LORD, so shall your seed and your name remain.
> *Isaiah 65:17* For, behold, I create **new heavens** [*plural*] and a new earth: and the former shall not be remembered, nor come into mind.
> *2 Peter 3:13* Nevertheless we, according to his promise, look for **new heavens and a new earth, wherein dwelleth righteousness**.
> *Revelation 21:1* And I saw a **new heaven and a new earth**: for the **first heaven and the first earth were passed away**; and there was no more sea.

## Jesus is Exalted Above and Beyond All Three Heavens.

Since the heavens are created and will perish, we would not expect God to be limited to the dimensions of the three heavens. Man cannot think beyond the physical bounds of the universe, but the following three verses reveal that God is above and beyond the heavens.

*Psalm 8:1* O LORD our Lord, how excellent is thy name in all the earth! who hast set thy glory **above the heavens**.

*Psalm 113:4* The LORD is high above all nations, and his glory **above the heavens**.

*Ephesians 4:10* He that descended is the same also that ascended up **far above all heavens**, that he might fill all things.)

## The Heavens Rule.

Men think they are in control of the destiny of this planet, but the atmosphere and universe around us is filled with two factions locked in a physical and moral struggle — both contending for the rule of this celestial body. God told king Nebuchadnezzar that he must come to understand that **the heavens do rule** — over the earth and the kingdoms of men. This will later translate into the **kingdom of heaven**.

*Daniel 4:26* And whereas they commanded to leave the stump of the tree roots; thy **kingdom** shall be sure unto thee, after that thou shalt have known that the **heavens do rule**.

Cyrus, king of Persia, recognized that the kingdom of men which he ruled was controlled from the heavens, and that God gave it to whom he would. Cyprus was a puppet ruler of an earthly kingdom usurping the position of the K of H.

*Ezra 1:2* Thus saith Cyrus king of Persia, The LORD God of **heaven** hath given me all the **kingdoms of the earth**; and he hath charged me to build him an house at Jerusalem, which is in Judah.

The righteous angels are called an **army of heaven**, reflecting their struggle for the kingdom. When Nebuchadnezzar speaks of the **King of heaven**, he is not referring to God's role in ruling paradise, but of his role in ruling the heavens, of which the earth is the main focus.

*Daniel 4:35-37* And all the inhabitants of the earth are reputed as nothing: and he doeth according to his will in the **army of heaven**, and among the **inhabitants of the earth**: and none can stay his hand, or say unto him, What doest thou? **36** At the same time my reason returned unto me; and for the **glory of my kingdom**, mine honour and brightness returned unto me; and my counsellors and my lords sought unto me; and I was **established in my kingdom**, and excellent majesty was added unto me. **37** Now I Nebuchadnezzar praise and extol and honour the **King of heaven**, all whose works are truth, and his ways judgment: and those that walk in pride he is able to abase.

The angel tells Daniel that the saints will eventually possess the kingdom that Antichrist takes by violence. The kingdom **under the whole heaven**, which he calls an **everlasting kingdom**, is the one that **saints will possess**. It is the Millennium kingdom followed by the kingdom in the new heavens and the new earth.

*Daniel 7:27* And the kingdom and dominion, and the greatness of the kingdom **under the whole heaven**, shall be given to the people of the saints of the most High, whose **kingdom is an everlasting kingdom**, and all dominions shall serve and obey him.

*The eventual goal is one kingdom made up of elements of both heaven and earth.* The following four verses express the fact that The Kingdom of God encompasses a dimension much broader than this planet.

*Ephesians 1:10* That in the dispensation of the fulness of times he might gather together in one all things in Christ, both which are in **heaven**, and which are on earth; even in him:

*Ephesians 3:10,15* To the intent that now unto the principalities and powers in **heavenly** places might be known by the church the manifold wisdom of God, **15** Of whom the whole family in **heaven** and earth is named,

*Colossians 1:16,20* For by him were all things created, that are in **heaven**, and that are in earth, visible and invisible, whether they be thrones, or dominions, or principalities, or powers: all things were created by him, and for him: 20 And, having made peace through the blood of his cross, by him to reconcile all things unto himself; by him, I say, whether they be things in earth, or things in **heaven**.

*Philippians 2:10* That at the name of Jesus every knee should bow, of things in **heaven**, and things in earth, and things under the earth;

### The Kingdom of Heaven is "Established."

God's kingdom is tangible and is a rival to earth's kingdoms, as seen by the fact that it is set up, it is constituted and organized so as to replace all the other kingdoms of the world.

*Daniel 2:44* And in the days of these kings shall the God of heaven **set up a kingdom**, which shall never be destroyed: and the kingdom shall not be left to other people, *but* it shall break in pieces and **consume all these kingdoms**, and it shall stand for ever.

### The coming kingdom will be a place in which to sit down and eat and drink with the Lord Jesus Christ.

*Matthew 26:29* But I say unto you, I will not drink henceforth of this fruit of the vine, until that day when **I drink it new with you in my Father's kingdom**.

*Revelation 7:17* For the Lamb which is in the midst of the throne **shall feed them**, and shall lead them unto living **fountains of waters**: and God shall wipe away all tears from their eyes.

### The Kingdom Will be a Place of Great Pleasures.

*Psalm 36:8* They shall be abundantly satisfied with the fatness of thy house; and thou shalt make them drink of the river of thy pleasures.

*Psalm 16:11* …in thy presence is fulness of joy; at thy right hand there are **pleasures for evermore.**

### Our eternal abode with God will be an environmentalist's paradise. Rivers and fruit trees, herbs that heal, no curse, and the holy presence of God; who could want more?

*Revelation 22:1-3* And he shewed me a pure river of water of life, clear as crystal, proceeding out of the throne of God and of the Lamb. **2** In the midst of the street of it, and on **either side of the river, was there the tree of life**, which bare twelve manner of fruits, and **yielded her fruit every month:** and the leaves of the tree were for the healing of the nations. **3** And there shall be no more curse: but the throne of God and of the Lamb shall be in it; and his servants shall serve him:

### Jesus Will Reign Over a Kingdom That Will Never End.

*Luke 1:33* And he shall reign over the house of Jacob for ever; and of his kingdom there **shall be no end**.

### Not only will we be members of a perfect society, but his kingdom will continue to increase forever.

*Isaiah 9:6-7* For unto us a child is born, unto us a son is given: and the **government** shall be upon his shoulder: and his name shall be called Wonderful, Counsellor, The mighty God, The everlasting Father, The Prince of Peace. **7** Of the **increase of his government** and peace there **shall be no end**, **upon the throne** of David, and upon **his kingdom**, to order it, and to establish it with judgment and with justice from henceforth **even for ever**. The zeal of the LORD of hosts will perform this.

## Mistaken about Heaven?

How could anyone confuse the word *God* with the word *heaven*? God is uncreated, eternal, and nonmaterial. The heavens are created by God and are of decaying matter.

The Holy Spirit has perfect command of all languages. He has chosen to compose the Scripture with words that best express the point God desires to make. It must be noted that God has chosen to speak of **kingdoms**, meaning: the domain of a king.

Most people think that Adam's life in the garden was a temporary state on the road to something more — perhaps more religious or spiritual — certainly more Divine. Hardly anyone entertains the concept that his simple life — loving his wife, raising children, tending the garden, and fellowshipping with God — was actually God's perfect and long-range plan for the human race.

After reaping the wages of sin and suffering the pains of body and soul, man dreams of "going to heaven," to a place where there is no more pain or carnality. Our songs and sermons, our imaginations, take us far away from that earthy garden of touch, taste, smell, and feel into a far-away golden city with walls to protect us and gates to confine. We think of heaven as a sort of retirement home for the righteous, a dead-end rest, a safe place, the goal of our very existence, the focal point to which all things move. What need we more?

If this could be true, then planet earth and the Garden of Eden were indeed just teases, temporary wayside stops, God never intending for man to live there with the flowers and animals in harmony of body and soul. Good riddance, then, to the sensual experience and to earth with its fragile environment. Let us flee from this failed experiment in free-will and self-determination. May God start over and do it right the next time!

But these mistaken ideas were fostered upon us when we were suffering, when loved ones were dying, when war and disease came near, when sin wearied us to the point of despair and we turned our attention to selected portions of the Bible that comforted. We wanted out — far away. When our bodies get old and tired, and when we can no longer sleep, and when sleep no longer brings rest, songs and sermons of an eternal rest in a far-away city appeal to our sin-weary souls.

God did not place Adam and Even in a temporary environment. The Garden of Eden was not a stepping stone, a preparatory school that anticipated the real thing. It **was** Paradise itself — the ultimate human abode.

After creation was finished and Adam and Eve were installed as King and Queen over the earth, **God saw every thing that he had made, and, behold, it was very good (Genesis 1:31).** Not just good, but **very good.** It could not have been better — not then; not ever. God was there every day, walking and talking with them. There was no death, no pain, and no conflict.

God's original intention was and still is his ultimate intention. He will return to where he started, and, notwithstanding the fall of man and the wicked dominion of Satan, it will not cause God to change course or adopt a more secure, better plan. He will not "finish up here" and then retreat into "heaven," abandoning the earth to eternal ruin. He will not give his enemy the satisfaction of having thwarted his designs for the earth and its inhabitants. That which was **very good** so long ago is still very good. Man will populate the earth and rule the universe as planned. He will eat of the fruit that grows on either side of the river. He will lie down in green pastures. He will drink from the fruit of the vine, and the streets of the cities will be full of boys and girls playing. The lion and the lamb will lie down together. Mortal flesh will put on immortality, and the corruptible will put on incorruption, and death will be swallowed up in victory. There will be singing and dancing, and the earth will be full of his praise. Sing hallelujah!

Even now there is a holy city **prepared for those who love him,** but it will **come down** to the **new earth** and sit as the capital city, bearing the name, NEW JERUSALEM, having replaced the old. It will be the home of the saints, but they **will go in and out** of that city. The new earth will be fresh with infinite possibilities for the glorified saints. **The LORD of hosts shall reign in mount Zion, and in Jerusalem, and before his ancients gloriously.** David will rule with him over the whole earth, **for ever — world without end.**

Any theology that relegates the earth to eternal ashes and places man in some celestial city far away, riding atop the clouds and playing an all-too-small harp, is based on fable and folly and will burn up with the same fire that cleanses the old heavens and earth. God started out to build a kingdom on this earth with Adam and his descendents, and he will bring it to pass. He told us to pray, **"Thy kingdom come, thy will be done on earth as it is in heaven."** We pray it, but far too few of us understand much of what it is that we are to be praying for.

# Table of Contents

# Index of all Kingdom Scripture

| | |
|---|---|
| Matthew 25:1 | 75, 115, 116, 117, 178, 183, |
| Matthew 25:14 | 73, 75, 82, 118, 120, 130, 131, 179, 183, |
| Matthew 25:34 | 19, 20, 95, 111, 146, 157, 175, 179, 183, |
| Matthew 26:29 | 145, 148, 154, 158, 184, 192, |
| Mark 1:14 | 84, 86, 127, 134, 164, 181, 184, 185, |
| Mark 1:15 | 85, 124, 154, 164, 181, |
| Mark 3:24 | |
| Mark 4:11 | 52, 55, 56, 90, 91, 169, 182, 184, |
| Mark 4:26 | 79, 102, 124, 169, 182, 184, |
| Mark 4:30 | 81, 92, 170, 182, |
| Mark 6:23 | 163, |
| Mark 9:1 | 148, 158, 161, 166, 172, 181, 183, 184, |
| Mark 9:47 | 150, 160, 184, |
| Mark 10:14 | 93, 172, 183, 187, |
| Mark 10:15 | 161,173, |
| Mark 10:23 | 94, 174, 183, |
| Mark 10:24 | 94, 174 |
| Mark 10:25 | 94, 174 |
| Mark 11:10 | 7, 53, 87, 163, 165, |
| Mark 12:34 | 126, 161, |
| Mark 13:8 | 163, |
| Mark 14:25 | 126, 161, 184, |
| Mark 15:43 | 183, |
| Luke 1:33 | 163, 192, |
| Luke 4:5 | 22, 168, |
| Luke 4:43 | 66, 86, 134, 164, 181, |
| Luke 6:20 | 96, 126, 164, 181, 184, |
| Luke 7:28 | 90, 168, 182, |
| Luke 8:1 | 77, 86, 87, 91, 134, 164, 181, 185 |
| Luke 8:10 | 55, 56, 90, 169, 182, |
| Luke 9:2 | 86, 164, 181, 182, |
| Luke 9:11 | 164, 181, |
| Luke 9:27 | 161, 172, 183, 184, |
| Luke 9:60 | |
| Luke 9:62 | 181, 184, |
| Luke 10:9 | 84, 86, 164, 181, |
| Luke 10:11 | 111, |
| Luke 11:2 | 87, 165, |
| Luke 11:17 | 163, |
| Luke 11:18 | 22, |
| Luke 11:20 | 84, 85, 122, 125, 161, 166, 168, 182, 185, |
| Luke 12:31 | 128, 165, 166, 179, 181, 182, |
| Luke 12:32 | 20, 24, 47, |
| Luke 13:18 | 65, 81, 92, 170, 182, |
| Luke 13:20 | 81, 92, 170, 182, |
| Luke 13:28 | 87, 88, 132, 165, 166, 181, 182, 183, |
| Luke 13:29 | 87, 88, 132, 154, 166, 181, 182, 183, |
| Luke 14:15 | 99, 112, 167, 182, 184, |
| Luke 16:16 | 90, 101, 128, 161, 168, 181, 182, |
| Luke 17:20 | 135, 161, 184, |
| Luke 17:21 | 129, 161, 184, |
| Luke 18:16 | 93, 172, 183, |

| | |
|---|---|
| Luke 18:17 | 93, 172, 183 |
| Luke 18:24 | 94, 174, 183 |
| Luke 18:25 | 94, 141, 174, 183 |
| Luke 18:29 | 94, 149, 159, 161, 174, 183 |
| Luke 19:11 | 82, 87, 118, 130, 131, 165, 179, 183, 184, |
| Luke 19:12 | 82, 118, 130, 131, 132, 173, 179, 183, |
| Luke 19:15 | 82, 118, 130, 131, 179, 183, |
| Luke 21:10 | 163 |
| Luke 21:31 | 184, |
| Luke 22:16 | 183, 184, |
| Luke 22:18 | 184, |
| Luke 22:29 | 87, 163, 166, |
| Luke 22:30 | 46, 47, 166, |
| Luke 23:42 | 166, 180, 183, |
| Luke 23:51 | 150, 159, |
| John 3:3 | 133, 162, 184, |
| John 3:5 | 155, 184, |
| John 18:36 | 46, 137, 138, 183, 184, |
| Acts 1:3 | 42, 133, |
| Acts 1:6 | 13, 111, 163, 175, |
| Acts 8:12 | 162, 184, 185, |
| Acts 14:22 | 139, 184 |
| Acts 19:8 | 184, 185, |
| Acts 20:25 | 184, 185, |
| Acts 28:23 | 184, 185, |
| Acts 28:31 | 184, 185 |
| Romans 14:17 | 29, 135, 162, 184, |
| 1 Corinthians 4:20 | 122, 135, 168, 181, 182, 184 |
| 1 Corinthians 6:9 | 136, 165, 181, 184, |
| 1 Corinthians 6:10 | 136, 165, 184, |
| 1 Corinthians 15:24 | 21, 47, |
| 1 Corinthians 15:50 | 185, |
| Galatians 5:21 | 136, 165, 181, 184, |
| Ephesians 5:5 | 165, 184, 185 |
| Colossians 1:13 | 155, 182, 185, |
| Colossians 4:11 | 162, 184, 185, |
| 1 Thessalonians 2:12 | 125, 166, 181, |
| 2 Thessalonians 1:5 | 137, 182, 184, 185, |
| 2 Timothy 4:1 | 137, 171, 182, 183, |
| 2 Timothy 4:18 | 185, |
| Hebrews 1:8 | 29, 117, 165, 181, |
| Hebrews 11:33 | |
| Hebrews 12:28 | 135, 163, 185, |
| James 2:5 | 96, 126, 163, 164, |
| 2 Peter 1:11 | |
| Revelation 1:9 | 182, |
| Revelation 11:15 | 21, 22, 36, 47, 61, 164, |
| Revelation 12:10 | 122, 125, 166, 171, 182, 183, 184, |
| Revelation 16:10 | 163 |
| Revelation 17:12 | 163 |
| Revelation 17:17 | 163 |

## To Train Up a Child
### ~ 500,000 In Print! ~

From successful parents, learn how to train up your children rather than discipline them up. With humor and real-life examples, this book shows you how to train your children before the need to discipline arises. Be done with corrective discipline; make them allies rather than adversaries. The stress will be gone and your obedient children will praise you.

*122pg Book*

## Created to be His Help Meet

Somewhere over the passing years and changing culture, women have lost their way. This book is written to lead them back home. Regardless of how you began your marriage or how dark and lonely the path that has brought you to where you are now, I want you to know that it is possible today to have a marriage so good and so fulfilling that it can only be explained as a miracle.

What God is doing through this book is incredible! We constantly receive testimonies from women who's marriages have been renewed or restored from reading this book.

*Available in: single volumes, cases of 24 (40% discount) and MP3 audio reading*

## Romans Commentary chapters 1-8

Michael has been studying and teaching the book of Romans for 40 years. this 222 page, verse-by-verse commentary is not devotional in tone. It addresses all the hard theological issues that have been the foundation of the Christian faith down throught the centuries. It is original in many ways, not a restatement of other writers. Though controversial interpretations are supported by analyses of the Greek language, it is written for the layman from the unique perspective of a student that believes the Bible rather than a scholar that critques it.

*222pg Book*

## By Divine Design

If you are philosophically minded, this book will appeal to you. Michael discusses difficult questions that trouble many: How can I believe and trust a "sovereign God" who allows so much evil? Why did God even make us capable of sinning? Why would the Creator let souls live forever in Hell and not just destroy them so they would not have to continue to suffer?

*85pg Book*

## Romans – audio teaching

Verse by verse, word by word, this is a commentary on the book of Romans. We continually receive testimonies of lives changed and souls saved through listening to this greatest of all New Testament books. Until you know the book of Romans you don't know the Bible. If you have never listened to any Bible teaching by Michael Pearl, this is the place to start.

*Available in: 20 CD set, 17 Cassette set or 1 MP3 CD*

## Sin No More

The big question is: "So how do I stop sinning?" You have confessed your sins, received the baptism of the Holy Ghost with evidence of everything but ceasing to sin; yet you are still a Romans 7 defeated Christian. I assure you, God not only saves his children from the penalty of sin but he saves them from its power as well.

You can stop sinning.

*Available in 7 Cassette set or 9 CD set*

## Righteousness

This set contains four messages on salvation and righteousness: The Man Christ Jesus, Saving Righteousness, Imputed Righteousness and The Blood. The messages explore intriguing topics such as the humanity of Christ and why he refered to himself as "The Son of Man", why man's blood is required when he spills the blood of another man, God's clearly defined method of making a person righteous enough to get to heaven and how the blood of Jesus washes away our sins.

*Available in a 3 Cassette set or a 4 CD set*

## Free Magazine Subscription

No Greater Joy Ministries Inc. publishes a bimonthly magazine with answers to questions received in the mail. The 24-page magazine covers topics such as child training, family relationships, homeschooling and Bible teaching.

Send your name and mailing address to NGJ, 1000 Pearl Road, Pleasantville TN 37033, and we will put you on our mailing list. Your information is confidential and will not be shared with anyone. If you are on our mailing list, you will also receive notification of when the Pearls are speaking in your area.

You can also read additional material on our website www.nogreaterjoy.org or you can sign up on our website to receive *No Greater Joy*.

## Free Online Resources

There is a wealth of free resources and materials on our website, www.nogreaterjoy.org. The entire teaching of Romans is available for free download as well as the Am I Saved? series and a new weekly Bible teaching every Saturday. Read or listen to excerpts of many of our products or browse our topical archive of over 240 past NGJ magazine articles on subjects from child training to homemade herbal tinctures.

The store also offers several free products for ministry use, just tell us how many you want and we'll send it to you.

*www.NoGreaterJoy.org*